A
TUSCAN-AMERICAN
KITCHEN

A
TUSCAN-AMERICAN
KITCHEN

Cassandra Vivian *and* Vivian Pelini Sansone

PELICAN PUBLISHING COMPANY
GRETNA 2011

ISBN: 9781589809062

Illustrations by Elhamy Naguib and Louise Hammond

Front-cover photograph: From the Parigi family archives, this photograph is of a picnic held on a Pennsylvania farm in the 1920s. On far left is Carolina Paggini Parigi turning the roasting chickens. On the far right, Nazzareno Parigi. Third person from the right is Elizabeth Parigi Vivian (with the tie and short hair).

Back-cover photograph: St. Joseph's Table at Rizzo's Malabar Inn in Crabtree, Pennsylvania. Each March, in honor of St. Joseph, the restaurant has a weeklong celebration offering special foods in honor of the saint. Photograph by Cassandra Vivian.

Printed in the United States of America
Published by Pelican Publishing Company, Inc.
1000 Burmaster Street, Gretna, Louisiana 70053

Dedicated to the immigrants:
Nazzareno Parigi and Carolina Santa Paggini Parigi
and Egino "Gino" Pelini and Alessandra "Sandrina" Pitti Pelini

Contents
Indice

Preface
Prefazione

The first publication of this book was called *Immigrant's Kitchen: Italian*. It was published in 1993 and brought a great deal of joy to many people. Over the years, we have received requests from people all over America asking for copies to give to their children or their grandchildren. This new publication answers those requests.

There are changes. The American pantry has changed in the past two decades. We have updated the ingredients and the methods to adapt to those changes. The most significant alteration is the expansion of the essays and the comments within the recipes. A sharp distinction has been made between Tuscan cooking and the cooking of the remaining regions of Italy. The title also reflects that change.

Acknowledgments
Ringrazziamenti

A note of gratitude goes to the men who shared the secrets of wine and cured meats. Without their help, those special chapters could not have been written: William "Bob" Pelini, who carried on his father's wine-making traditions; Beppe Parigi, our cousin in Italy, who still makes *vin santo;* Pamerino Ciotti, who specializes in *porchetta;* and especially Joseph Stromei, his wife, Ida, and daughter, Lydia. Joe is a fourth-generation professional butcher and makes a delicious *prosciutto.* On our visit to his home, he cut a fresh one and let us drink his homemade wine. Taste buds that had been dead for years sprang to life and memories of other times came rushing back. We will be forever grateful.

A very, very special thank-you to Norma J. Iervoline, who tested dozens of recipes with gusto and enthusiasm, and to her family who tasted and commented. To Joseph D'Andrea, vice consul of Italy; the Reverend Monsignor P. Lino Ramellini; and Janice Guiducci Vairo, who graciously corrected our Italian, more thanks. Janice is the granddaughter of my grandmother's lifelong friend Amabile Sodi and daughter of Giuliano Aurelio and Rena Sodi Guiducci, with whom we have reestablished contact thanks to this book.

Additional thanks to Nigel Ryan, Charlotte "Chuckie" Amico Pelini, Maria Albertini, Helen Shepler, Mary Bitonti, Rita Mele, Carol Kaufmann, and Lena Poletini Falbo, who all helped in various ways.

Introduction
Introduzione

There were many ethnic pockets in our community. Almost every block of our small town in southwestern Pennsylvania had a different language and culture and exotic and wonderful smells wafted from the neighborhood kitchens. There were nearly a dozen Catholic churches, each designated not by its name, but by the origin of its ethnic congregation: the Italian church, the Slavic church, the Irish church. There were Greeks, Finns, African-Americans, Ukrainians, Poles, Serbs, Slavs, Croatians, Carpatho-Rusyns, Syrians, Belgians, French, Mexican, and even a few Chinese families in our town. In summer, church picnics were held each Sunday afternoon at one of the local parks and each weekend in winter the women prepared meals in the different halls throughout the town: the Sons of Italy, the Italian Hall, St. John's Russian Orthodox Church, the Slovak Home, and the Polish and Sokol's clubs. Oh, the wonderful dishes we ate. In addition to our diverse Italian-American regional foods, including the *Piedmonti, Fruili, Veneto, Tuscana, Abruzzo, Calabria,* and *Sicilia,* we had Greek grape leaves, *moussaka, pastitsio,* and *baklava;* Syrian *kibbeh, kofta,* and *shish kebab;* Finnish *nisua, hetelma soppaa,* and *sill salla;* African-American ribs, chops, and sweet-potato pie; and Slavic *halupki, halushki, paska,* and that incredibly delicious *pagach* (why *pagach* shops, like pizza shops, are not found around the world is beyond me).

But amid all this diversity, growing up Italian-American was special and growing up Tuscan-American was extraordinary. The sounds, tastes, and smells of childhood still surround me as I think back to those wonderful times: of Nonna listening to the Italian radio program on Saturday morning; of Nonno reading the Italian newspaper through his gold-rimmed spectacles; of evenings around the kitchen table playing Italian card games like *tre sette, scopa,* and *briscola,* winking at partners to indicate aces, twitching the mouth to indicate threes, touching the ring finger to show diamonds, and always getting caught amid a roar of laughter.

The Italian community was divided into regional groups that held tightly together. Southern Italians, from *Abruzzo* to Sicily, with names ending in *o*'s and *a*'s lived in one section. Northern Italians, from Tuscany to the Piedmont, with *i*'s at the end of their names, lived in another area. Each group had its own style of cooking, its own section of the street, its own grocers who specialized in its regional foods, and its own men's club and women's auxiliary. Southerners wanted a *salami* like meat they called *soprassata*. Northerners thought *soprassata* was headcheese. Southerners planted fig trees. Northerners had sage bushes. Southerners had the feast of the seven fishes. Northerners never heard of it.

One thing they did have in common was Italian pride. They were not satisfied with any old meeting place for their clubs; they built huge buildings that were the civic centers of the community, where women would gather to celebrate saints' days and Mother's Day, and men would gather to play *bocce* and *morra*.

I am a grandchild of the immigrant wave that came to America at the turn of the twentieth century. These daring men and women were mainly farmers and tradesmen, people who worked with their hands, were close to the land, and kept the traditions of their homeland alive. Regardless of their province in Italy, they were escaping from the dreaded *padrone* system where their families had been serfs, *contadini*, on the land for centuries. They came to America to be free. They were the fabric that built America during the Industrial Age. Their labor made the coal come out of the ground, the steel brew in blast furnaces, the bridges rise over the waterways, the rails stretch west to California, and the roadways circle America. Their resolve created a true middle class, which after centuries of oppression won for them the respectability of a good wage, a decent home, and education for their children. If we are looking for the greatest generation, regardless of its ethnic origin, the one that gave us the middle class gets my vote.

The nonnos and nonnas who raised our families came from the village of *Quarata*, a small farming community in the glorious Tuscan hills northwest of *Arezzo*. Nonno and Nonna never let an opportunity pass to tell us we were special, we were Italian and Tuscan, and should be proud of our heritage. Just out of their teens, these adventurers crossed the ocean in steerage to a new life in a new land. What courage they had. As they approached Ellis Island fearful that they would be turned back, not understanding a word of English, hopeful to find a job, a new world opened for them. Those that had gone before led the way to small towns throughout America. They were the people who were to man the meat-packing plants of Chicago, the steel mills of Pennsylvania and Ohio, the fishing boats of San Francisco and New Orleans, and the new auto factories of Detroit.

What it must have been like in that village in Italy as family after family lost children to America. The Bindi, the Poletini, the Ghinassi families, who live beside my uncles and aunts in *Quarata*, have relatives living down the street from me in America. It made us all responsible to each other, and kept the feeling of family alive. As a member of a family, you were responsible to it for your actions. As a member of the village of *Quarata*, you were responsible to the other villagers for its reputation, and as an Italian in a town of many ethnic groups, you were responsible for the reputation of all Italians.

Fifty years after my grandparents came to America, I visited *Quarata* for the first time. As soon as I entered the beige stucco villa at the edge of the small country town and saw my grandfather's brother, I knew I was home. Before we sat down my uncle presented me with a glass filled with that magical Italian wine, *vin santo*. The glass was crystal and etched into the side was the word *Nazzareno*, the name of my grandfather. With tears in his eyes, my uncle told me that the last time that glass was used was by my grandfather on the day he departed for America. Then, like now, it was for a toast. Then a *buon viaggio*, now a *ben venuto*. My uncle had cherished that glass and carried it into the hills with him when Germans occupied the town during World War II. Who could not cry at such a moment?

Then I sat down at a table in the ancestral home and ate a meal that could have come from my grandmother's or mother's kitchen. It started with a freshly laundered tablecloth. Dressing the table was as important to my Zia Bettina as it was to my grandmother as it is to me. You never, never, never put food down on an old tablecloth, a soiled table, or a barren table. Never! The table honors the food as the food honors the table. I remember once when we were visiting the Pelini watching Vivian iron the folds out of the tablecloth before it was placed on the table. Yes, the folds. We always kept a tablecloth on our kitchen table. Always. Each evening it was removed, and the dinner tablecloth was put on the table. Once the meal was over, the dinner cloth was removed and the kitchen tablecloth was put on again. We were peasants in Italy and millworkers in America, but we ate like lords both in manner and in taste. Everything was where it should be: napkin to the right; cutlery properly laid out to the right and left of the plates; wine and water glasses set in proper place and proper order; dishes stacked atop each other to be used as the meal unfolded.

Likewise, I knew every dish placed on the table that wonderful Tuscan day: *crostini,* followed by *minestra,* followed by *umido,* followed by *arosto,* and ending with a *dolci, formaggio,* and *frutta.* My cousin teased my uncle about his new wine, a conversation I had heard many times back home when the Pelini family would come to visit, or we would visit them. The women were in the kitchen. The men were cutting the homemade *prosciutto* and preparing the wine for the table. It was home. These were my people. In a small town in southwestern Pennsylvania, the traditions of a small town in central Italy had been maintained.

Note to this Edition

Along with Tom and Vivian, my coauthor, I took my mother back to Tuscany in 1999. It had been seventy years since she left our village as a young girl. She was at the very beginning of a descent into Alzheimer's disease. What a wonder it was, that month in Tuscany with our family. My mother was the eldest of all the cousins. All of my nonno and nonna's siblings were dead, but my mother's cousins were thrilled that we were home again. We searched for our history and made our way through mounds and mounds of delicious food, still on clean tablecloths, still in numerous courses, still serving the same recipes from hundreds of years ago. What we did and who we saw and what we learned I put into a book. I take it out and read it again and again and again *(The Overseer's Family: A Memoir of the Tuscan Countryside).*

In 2009 I returned alone. I was the last of the family that came to America and lived the life portrayed in this cookbook. My American family was gone. I went wounded. But I found family again. One cousin resembled my mother. Another had my nonno's nose. A third had his mannerisms. Oh, yes, I had family. Day after day, we ate, we talked, we ate, we visited, we ate, we laughed. I healed and healed and healed. When I returned to America, I returned with a sense that our family was alive and well. Not only were we bound by blood, but by tradition, tradition that led far back into the distant past.

Nazzareno "Gumbone" Parigi and Carolina Santa Paggini

My grandfather, Nazzareno Parigi, was born March 27, 1891,

the first of four boys and three girls. His father was Giuseppe Parigi, the overseer, *fattori,* of the Guillichini lands around *Arezzo.* The Guillichini were a noble family from *Arezzo.* As their overseer, my great-grandfather, *Bisnonno,* was responsible for all the farmers, the *contadini,* on the land. He decided the schedules for planting and harvesting. He determined how to care for the animals, when to harvest them and make all the *salumi* like *prosciutto.* He knew when extra help had to be hired to pick the olives or grapes or grain. He ordered threshers and other machines. Above all, he kept the records for the entire estate, often consisting of thirty or forty farms.

Nonno's mother, Elisa Silvestro Pasquini, was the *fattoressa,* the overseer's wife. In addition to the role of the *reggitrice,* the sharecropper's wife, who cooked, wove, made clothes, and performed other household chores including laundry, she took care of the barnyard animals. She took their milk and made cheese. She took their eggs and sold them at the market where she used the profit to buy oil and salt. Not only did she hold the reigns of her family's comfort, the *fattoressa* also had to fulfill all the needs of the *padrone* and his family. My nonno was the eldest son of this family and destined to take the role of *fattori.* He traveled around the land with his father learning how to be an overseer. However, he never took on that role. He fell in love, left the land, and came to America.

In April of 1913, he left his young bride in Italy and arrived in the United States on May 5, aboard the steamship *Tormegnia.* He came to the boomtown of Monessen along the banks of the Monongahela River, twenty-five miles south of Pittsburgh. Why Monessen? Like so many immigrants, the choice was made for him—Domenico (Menco) and Laura (Nonno's cousin) Bindi from *Quarata* were already there. Mr. Bindi was a straw boss at Pittsburgh Steel and Nonno got a job as a laborer in Bindi's Italian labor gang. Nonno worked supervising the horses that were used to haul steel. When the horses were replaced by motorized vehicles, he chose not to continue working in that department and instead began to erect fences. He traveled all over western Pennsylvania putting up chain-link fences, content to be a laborer, out-of-doors, and refused to be a supervisor or move to another job.

This was when unions were organizing. Working conditions were deplorable. There was no job security. Nonno worked a twelve-hour day, seven days a week. There were no vacations, no retirement programs, no health insurance, no compensation for injuries, no safety regulations, and immigrants were paid less money for the same jobs as nationals.

The Great Steel Strike of 1919, the same year Prohibition was legislated, was yet another attempt by workers to unionize. They were fighting for an eight-hour day, higher wages, and the dismemberment of company unions. The companies broke the strike with propaganda, strikebreakers, spies, and state and local police. The strike ended on January 9, 1920, simply because the families were starving and losing their homes.

Life must have been impossible. Dominico "Menco" Bindi was a company man and had to go to work. Nonno's loyalty was to him, for Bindi was from *Quarata*. This must have been a scenario reenacted throughout Monessen among all the ethnic groups. So some of the Italian labor gang crossed the picket lines each day and went into the mill. Nonno was given a gun for protection, but he brought it home and hid it. I found it more than forty years later after he had died and Nonna was coming to live with us. That is when I first heard this story.

In June of 1921, disillusioned with the violence in America, Nonno packed up his family and went back to Italy. But things had changed. Nonna was no longer happy living in an extended family; she wanted her own home and kitchen. Thus, two years later they returned to America. Because my mother was born in the United States and a U.S. citizen, the family was able to return to America without difficulty. They sailed first-class on the maiden voyage of the SS *Giulio Cesare* on July 1, 1923. Nonno talked about the elegant journey all his life.

One thing he did bring to America was the expertise his father taught him. Nonno made the best wine in his family, and, we thought, the best in Monessen. He also made delicious sausage and *prosciutto*. He had learned the lessons well. His wine cellar was a child's dream, and I spent many a Saturday morning there with my grandfather. My nonno was a red-headed *buongustaio*, a man who liked good food, and he spent his life laboring over the making of excellent *prosciuttos*, sausages, and wine. I always sat next to him at the table (my nonna said to protect the guests from his ample distribution of wine), and I think he passed his palate on to me. My eyes twinkle like his when I sit down to a hearty feast. He had gout in his waning days, and, despite its pain, he smiled because he considered it a badge of honor for years of good eating.

Carolina Santa Paggini was born in *Capolona*, a small village north of *Quarata,* on April 23, 1891. Her father was Paolo Paggini and her mother, Elisabetta Lesi. They were *contadini* on the Guillichini land, under the supervision of my *bisnonno* Giuseppi. Nonna had four sisters and five brothers. She married my grandfather in August of 1911.

Carolina was a woman of substance. She taught herself to read and write, paraded for women's suffrage, campaigned for politicians, helped bring the first Italian Catholic church to Monessen, and, until she died at the age of ninety-four, never spent a day when her hands were not busy. I can still hear the clicking of her steel knitting needles. She was so proficient that she would sit on the couch with my head on her lap, and as we watched television, the needles would click away. By evening's end, a baby's jacket, trimmed with white angora, would be completed. Along with Sophia Poletini, her lifelong friend, and Anselmo Bonchi, another resident of *Quarata,* who ultimately resided in Aliquippa, Pennsylvania, my grandmother came to the United States in October 1913. They passed through Ellis Island; Nonna was eight months pregnant with what was to be her only child and terrified they would send her back because she was pregnant. They did not.

Nonno became an American citizen shortly thereafter. It was many years before Nonna applied for citizenship in the United States. On January 5, 1939, the day she was to appear before the judge, a terrible snowstorm gripped the northeast. But Nonna insisted she had to go to the courthouse in Pittsburgh. My father drove her, and it took them almost four hours to travel the twenty-five miles. When she entered the courtroom, they were closing because of the bad weather. The judge asked her what she wanted, and when she told him, he smiled, "You must want it pretty bad to travel in this weather. Who is the president of the United States?" She answered. "Citizenship granted," he said. "Now go home."

Nonno died young. He finished working in the mill at age sixty-five. After forty-three years of service, he received a pension of $40.00 a month. He had earned a total of $28,000 in forty-three years. In 2010, as an annual salary, that sum is just above poverty level. After Nonno's death, Nonna came to live with us. She always took a *passeggiata* after dinner, and our dog would go with her. They were great friends. Nonna loved fresh fruit and always enjoyed an apple or orange on a winter evening, or peaches, watermelon, or cantaloupe in the summer. She always shared a bit with our dog. Until she died, whenever a piece of fruit was taken from the refrigerator, Kimba would come running. I often wondered if she was thinking of Nonna.

Nonna lived long enough to enjoy five generations in our family. When her great-great-grandchildren, Patty Ann and Mikey, would come to visit, I would sit beside Nonna on the couch and play the old Italian game *bicci-coo-coo*. As I rubbed my hands over their backs and sang the chant, Nonna would come out of her dream world, lift her head, laugh, and join in the fun. It was the only time she responded. I guess the sounds of her own childhood awakened the ancient memories.

My mother, Elizabeth, an only child, was born November 27, 1913, just a month after Nonna entered the United States. Elizabeth married Alfred "Freddie" Vivian, who, despite the name, was pure Italian. They had two children, Alfred and me. My brother, whom we called Bebe, married Margaret Ann Angele, and they had four children: Kathleen, Thomas, Michael, and Kristin. All married. My father died in 1965, my grandfather in 1966, my grandmother in 1984 (at the age of ninety-four), my brother in 1989, my sister-in-law in 2004, and my mother in 2006 (at the age of ninety-three). I am now the oldest of the family. My mother and father had nine great-grandchildren: Patricia Ann and Michael Karbowsky, Jr.; twins Michael Jr. and Joseph Vivian; Roger and Jessica Strautmann; and Thomas, Alan, and Lyndsie Vivian. There are also two great-great-grandchildren, Paul and John Spinneweber, the children of Patricia.

It has fallen to my brother's son Michael to take over the family cooking. Thanks to the first printing of this book in 1993, he now prepares the holiday meals for the entire family. From *cappeletti* to *lasagna, the gran fritto misto to fiocchi*, he is in charge.

Egino "Gino" Pelini and Alessandra "Sandrina" Pitti Pelini
By Vivian Pelini Sansone

My father Egino "Gino" Pelini was born in the little hill town of *Fillignini*, Province of *Arezzo*, Italy, in the year 1896. Times were tough and the main source of nourishment for the family came from an abundance of heaven-sent chestnuts, which were stored on the bedroom floor and meted out as needed. The hardships were many, so at the tender age of eight, Gino; his brother Luigi; and his father, Isaia, journeyed to France to work as foresters, for my grandfather was a lumberjack. By being very frugal, they saved money and returned home to the family bosom, which consisted of four boys, two girls, and my grandmother, Diomira.

My grandparents had three boys before my father's birth and named each Giovanni Battista, but all died within the first year of birth. When my grandmother was pregnant with my father, they decided not to name this child Giovanni Battista, but Egino, and broke the chain of tragedy (eventually they did have a son named Giovanni Battista and, praise the Lord, he lived to a ripe old age).

When Gino was nineteen, the futility of their life and future convinced him and his brother Luigi, who was twenty-three at the time, to come to America. Since their close *amici* (friends) Gesue (Natalino) and Annetta Chiapparri were already in the mountain state of West Virginia, the Pelini boys followed them. After some time the Chiapparri family moved to New Castle, Pennsylvania, and the boys went with them. They got jobs at the Shenango Pottery Company in New Castle (you can imagine how surprised we were one day when the china set on our breakfast table in *Quarata* was from Shenango Pottery).

The yearning for home and family kept tugging at them, and after saving enough money, they decided to return to Italy to buy their parents a home and to open a *bottega* (bar and store) in the charming town of *Quarata*. The home still stands, and on our visits to Italy, we sleep in Gino's original bedroom. But success was not that easy. Luigi proclaimed that he, being the eldest, was entitled to remain in *Quarata* and run the family business while Gino, the younger, would have to leave and fend for himself. Since my father had invested all his savings, all that is but the fare back to America (the ever-cautious Gino), he prepared to return to the United States. However, he could not return. Immigration was closed. Fate then played its cards.

Alessandra "Sandrina" Parigi Pitti was born in New York City in 1903 to Pietro Pitti and Maria Parigi Pitti. Her father became ill, and on his doctor's advice, the Pitti family returned to Italy in 1907 when Sandrina was four years old. Gino and Sandrina met, fell in love, and were married on January 11, 1923. In March they went to Naples where they sailed to America as newlyweds on the *President Wilson*.

Upon reaching New York on March 14, they had to go through Ellis Island as Gino was not a U.S. citizen (he became one on November 27, 1928). In those days the men were separated from the women, and Sandrina, being a very young and sheltered twenty-year-old, was frightened to death. By some miracle, her prayers were answered, and she was befriended by a woman named Mafalda from the south of Italy who helped her. They never saw each other again, but Mafalda became a part of our family lore.

Finally, they arrived in New Castle. They moved in with the Chiapparri family, and my father got a job at a cement plant. My mother was pregnant and homesick. My brother Pietro, named after my grandfather Pitti, was born prematurely and died when he was forty days old, on the exact day he was due to be born. So once again, the Pelini *malocchio* (evil eye) convinced my father that none of his children would be named after a deceased person, and so neither I nor my two siblings received family names.

In 1926, after staying with a family named Zazzerino, my father and mother built a home on Beckford Street and moved in with their new baby Arnold, who was named after a character in a book my father was reading at the time. When my mother was pregnant with her second son, she would often attend the prizefights held each week at the end of their street. She decided to name her new son Bobby, after her favorite prizefighter. But a more knowledgeable friend told her that the proper name for Bobby was William, so my brother William, to this day, is called Bobby. The next generation rectified the long-standing goof by Arnold naming his firstborn son Robert.

Confusion over names was to haunt the young immigrants. When Sandrina went shopping with her friend Dolores "Georgia" Calderini Guiducci, they saw the sign SALE on lawns, in department stores, and everywhere they turned. They were amazed. *Sale* in Italian meant salt, and they could not imagine why so many people in America sold salt.

They did not know the American names for so many of the things they had to buy. So my mother would act out what she wanted and Georgia would vocalize. When buying diapers in the dry goods store, my mother took a piece of cloth and folded it like a diaper while Georgia cried like a baby.

When the Depression hit, we would have lost our dream house if it had not been for my father's star boarders, namely his younger brother Oliver and a good friend, Carlo "Cirli" Albertini, who came to his aid.

In 1970, the entire family went to Italy to visit. One day in August all the relatives in Italy were gathered and a large family dinner was held at a mountain-top restaurant, *Vallombrossa*. It was a wonderful experience as all the brothers and sisters of my father and mother were present with their mates and children.

My mother was a professional seamstress in Italy, and her mother and grandmother did all the cooking. She never liked to cook. When she came to America, she leaned heavily on friends until she became the great cook she was. She instilled in me a love of cooking, and I enjoy perfecting new recipes and old standbys, much to the joy of my family, especially my husband, Tom.

Gino and Sandrina had four children. The first born, Pietro, died after forty days. The other three were Arnold, William "Bobby," and Vivian. Arnold married and had two sons, Robert who married Jane Musiek and Richard who married Kim Atwood. Richard had three children, Gregory, Joshua and Rebecca. William married and had two children, Gina and William. Gina married and had three children, Audrey, Donna and David. Gina has nine grandchildren.

I still enjoy having family over for dinner and making all the old standbys, which they enjoy. We reminiscence of all the dinners we had at my parents' home and the many funny stories of all their encounters. I lost my husband, Tom, but still continue to cook. He loved to eat, and it was such a pleasure to cook for him.

Tuscan Country Cooking
La Cucina della Campagna Toscana

Italians do not need much reason to have a *festa;* if one does not exist, they invent it to honor a city, a saint, or a food. There are polenta festivals, mushroom festivals, cheese, wine, fish, and even a pine nut festival. The first fruit of each harvest is an opportunity to celebrate. Food is so important to Italians that official government boards have been established to supervise the production of cheese, wine, vinegar, and other products to guarantee their quality.

These festivals take place all over the peninsula. At each celebration, the foods reflect the district, its terrain, and its history. As mentioned, an Italian is not an Italian is not an Italian. He or she is a *Siciliano,* a *Fruliani,* or a *Tuscano.* Those regions do not determine the holiday, which is national, but they absolutely determine the types of foods that are placed on the table for the holiday. In Sicily the Christmas Eve meal begins with a pasta, but in Tuscany it begins with a hearty bean soup. In Bologna they put cream in their meat sauce. In Tuscany they do not. There are hundreds, if not thousands, of these differences.

The traditional foods were determined by two things: physical environment and regional history. The things that separated the regions—the climate, the geography, and the soil—determined the types of foods eaten in the region. Goats rambled the hills of the south. Cows grazed the plains of the north. This meant as one moved north from the tip of Italy the hot, mountainous regions of the south gave way to rolling plains and cooler weather of central Italy, and eventually ended in high, snow-covered mountains and cold, cold temperatures in the north. That meant the growing seasons were different, and the types of things grown and raised were different too.

Historically, the south of Italy was dominated by the Greeks, the Arabs, and the French and the north by the French and the Austro-Hungarian Empire. In terms of food and foodways, it meant that Sicilians not only grew and grow different products than the *Frulani* or *Tuscani,* they also combine different ingredients and cook them in different ways. The south enjoys rice and pine nuts straight from the Arab world; the north eats *polenta* and strudel with an Austro-Hungarian twist. Thus, the foods are not the same. These facts are not exclusive to Italians, but to any ethnic group that immigrated.

As for the foods of Tuscany, they reach far back into antiquity. In ancient times Tuscany was the center of the Etruscan civilization, a culture to which ancient Rome is heavily indebted. From the eighth to the fourth centuries b.c., twelve city-states, including *Arezzo,* created a high culture of seafarers, merchants, and artists, speaking a language it has taken scholars twenty centuries to transcribe. The Etruscans created the grills of the modern Tuscan pantry. They ate pork roast with rosemary, pig liver with bay leaf, and pork stews: all foods we enjoyed in Italy and America centuries later and whose recipes are found in this book.

In the Renaissance, Tuscan foods continue to be exemplary. Catherine de Medici, a member of the ruling Florentine Renaissance family, was a driving force in the Renaissance development of Tuscan gastronomy. It was she who introduced the Florentine fork to France, from where it moved to England, and ultimately to the world. When she married Henry II of France, as part of her dowry, she brought her chefs to Paris and delighted the French court with Tuscan dishes of game, sweets, and vegetables. From those early exports, Italian, or should I say Tuscan, cooking has become an international gastronomy enjoyed by more people than any other ethnic cuisine.

Today Catherine's pride in her Tuscan heritage is felt in almost every kitchen in Tuscany from the noble houses to the peasant's hovel. Almost every village has its own recipes, and although they were all made with the same ingredients, they taste different from house to house. It is the pride of the family that good cooks live among them.

Throughout Italy, Tuscans are known as *Tuscani mangiafagioli,* Tuscan bean eaters. They are considered tight-fisted (although you would never know it in my family). They carry the heritage of the Renaissance with pride. They are arrogant because they are descendents of Michaelangelo, DiVinci, and a host of Renaissance artists who revolutionized the world. The pride in their heritage runs deep and includes their foods. Tuscan food is wholesome and hearty, too. Heavy bean soups, bread without salt, fried bread, flat-bread (the forerunner of pizza), and heaped platters of rabbit, pheasant, duck, and capon are the hallmarks of the cuisine. The *panforte* of *Siena* is a national sweet of Italy. The wines of *Chianti* are known worldwide. The grilled steaks of Florence are considered the best in Italy. Although Tuscans use spices abundantly, these wonderful steaks, grilled to perfection over an open and living fire, are never eaten with spices.

As for the spices, true to all Italian cooking, the region determines the spice. The basic spices of *Quarata* are rosemary, sage, thyme, and fennel: spices that grow naturally in southeastern Tuscany. These spices, as terrific as they are, are not necessarily the spices of all of Tuscany. Confusing? Well, each Tuscan town has its own traditions. *Quarata* and *Arezzo* use wild fennel a lot: in duck, in *porchetta,* even in *salami.* The rest of Tuscany eliminates the fennel and puts rosemary in *porchetta. Siennese* cooks frequently use tarragon as a spice. It is so prevalent that it is called *'erba di Siena,* the *Siennese* herb. Red hot pepper is rubbed on *prosciutto* in the Tuscan town of *Pratovecchio* in *Il Casentino.* So as the region of Italy determines the food and its seasonings, so the district within the region does the same.

Despite the reputation that Tuscan cooking can be simplistic, Tuscan cooking can also be complicated. Take the recipe called *Cotta Tre Volte.* It has three stages of cooking, each requiring a different pot or pan, each a different process. The bean soups have an amazing number of steps too, including mashing the beans into a puree (in the past without a blender). If there is a surprise in Tuscan cooking it is that many of its dishes are low in calorie. An even bigger surprise is that the Tuscan table has many, many delicious vegetarian dishes. From soups to salads to grills and even appetizers, the dishes are healthy, just like the Mediterranean diet's reputation.

Tuscan cooking would be incomplete if we did not mention the man's contribution. Nonno's culinary prowess is also represented in this book. Traditionally, Italian men were very much involved in producing food. From cultivating, picking, and preparing the grape for the wine process to growing, feeding, and harvesting the pig for *salami* and *prosciutto*, the man was as important to the food of the family as was the woman. Their gardens and wine cellars brought the food to the kitchen and the women took it from the kitchen to the table.

The foods of our village of *Quarata* make good eating and more than a touch of the peasant origins remains intact in America. That is a little this side of a miracle. Food items available back home in Tuscany were not necessarily available in Pennsylvania, or Oregon, or Texas. That was true of all the Italian immigrants no matter where they settled. This is one more factor in defining the differences between Italians and Italian-Americans. Where an Italian came from in Italy and where they settled in America combine to create their individual heritage. That in turn influenced their table. Compromise was in order. *Abruzzo* immigrants to Pittsburgh lamented they did not have their beloved fig tree. That did not stop them from planting one. Each winter they bend it down and cover it up to protect it from the cold and give it a rebirth every spring. Tuscans are known for their love of eating wild boar, those untamed beasts that eat truffles and race out of the forest to raid crops in peasant fields. Truffle-fed boar were not found in the hills and mountains of Pennsylvania. So no wild boar appeared on our table, but the recipes were adapted to the regional hogs. The move to America created problems for all the immigrants from every country in the world. Where there was no *ricotta*, some substituted cottage cheese. Where no saffron existed, they eliminated it. Even when these ingredients did become available in America, some families did not revert to the original recipe.

If regionalism in Italy and location in America were not problems enough, today we have further complications in sustaining the Italian table. Food habits in America have changed. Fast foods and meals under a half-hour have replaced "slow foods." (Thank God a slow food movement is circling the globe.) Modern butchers in big supermarkets have replaced the corner butcher so it is harder to get exactly what you need. They have cut the fat and eliminated the bone and a host of other dubious things that make us take a second look or a new adaptation on old recipes. You need fat and bone for flavor and basting. You want tender: you need fat. You want flavor: you need bone. In addition, companies have adapted to newer emigrants from other countries in the world. For example, canned tomatoes are not the same as they were twenty or thirty years ago. For our cooking they contain too much puree. The puree is too thick and dominates the flavor too much. To prepare any recipe in this book that required tomatoes we had to find an alternative method to eliminate the puree. There are plenty of reminders here that solve the problems of modernization.

In this cookbook authentic Tuscan cooking has sometimes taken a strange twist, but all was done with Italian hands and stem from a tradition that was born in the hills of Tuscany and matured and developed in the valleys of western Pennsylvania.

The Immigrant Year
L'Anno dell'immigrante

As we have seen, people close to the land live by the land and are governed by its moods. On the rich soil of the Tuscan hills, the farmer's whole existence is ruled by his farm: spring planting, summer bounty, and fall harvest. The kitchen aromas follow the seasons: the pork and beans of winter, baby lambs of spring, fresh fruits and vegetables of summer, fermenting grapes of the autumn wine, and wild game of the fall hunt.

In Italy, food is still ritual. It is impossible to divorce the myths, legends, and superstitions of the Italian people from the foods they eat, for they are one: the lamb of Easter is the Christ, the lentils of the new year, coins of prosperity. The symbolism is a bond between the farmer and the sacrificial animal, which is often honored with a festival in gratitude for sustenance.

In America, most immigrants were no longer farmers, but part of the industrial revolution, devoid of ritual. They filled the ranks of steel mills, meat-packing plants, and auto factories: places of technology alienated from both the land and its traditions. Italians in America created their own ritual. They clung to the ancient customs and traditions. They froze their parents and grandparents habits and traditions in time and brought them forward through the generations. Where the immigrant families created a garden, kept a rabbit hutch or a chicken coop for sustenance, the following generations kept them, or a semblance of them, for tradition. Nonna's spaghetti sauce became holy, not to be changed. Nonno's wine barrels are still stacked in the basement, although they will never be used again. They are too important to throw away: given to a museum, yes; thrown away, no. From the immigrant kitchen came special foods to feed the need for things from back home and form a symbolic link to the past. It was unthinkable to be without pork on Shrove Tuesday, or not to have the ingredients for special dishes for Christmas or Easter. These items had to be provided at all costs, or devastation would follow.

The gift of these ancient beliefs, both in Italy and America, was the united family. Families stayed together in the garden, in the wine cellar, in the kitchen, and in the dining room. Because the holiday meals were complicated, more than one set of hands was needed to prepare the various dishes, and the women shared the chores and the time together. Thus not only did the traditions survive, but so did the family.

However, change had to happen. While America's Italians clung to traditions, their relatives in the homeland moved forward, modernized, changing habits and customs. Dialects flourished in America while they disappeared in Italy. Eventually the Italians went to the store to buy pasta; their cousins in America brought out the old pasta machine and spent hours making it by hand, "just like Nonna." Yet, when the Italian-Americans bought electric stoves and gave up charcoal for propane, the Italians knew the open fire with fruit woods added flavor and would not be given up for modernization. They might give up making pasta, but not the ancient custom of grilling meat over an aromatic fire.

Today, the immigrant families that came to America at the dawn of the Industrial Age are in their fifth and sixth generations. Things have changed even more. The modern age with its hustle and bustle has cut into the time needed for tradition. Young children "don't like" many of the old family foods. Women cannot spend an entire week preparing for a holiday, for they have left the hearth for the workplace. Extended families, often separated by distance, can no longer celebrate holidays together. Ethnic loyalty in marriage and in neighborhoods is not as strong as it once was. So maintaining all the traditions is getting harder and harder to do. Today, if one dish remains on the holiday table to celebrate the past most families are satisfied.

But Italian food has moved out of the immigrant kitchen and into the restaurant. There are more Italian-style restaurants in the United States than any other ethnic group. Those restaurants are identifying themselves by their region and province. Therefore, people are no longer just eating Italian. They are eating Tuscan, or Sicilian, or Roman, or, the style that for generations most people thought was the only Italian food, Neapolitan (*Campagna*). What America has discovered, as the essay below illustrates, is that Italian food is not just *spaghetti* and pizza.

January
(Gennaio)
January, the coldest and least productive month of the year,

begins the rituals in an Italian home. On New Year's Day (*Capo d'Anno*) dark and light grapes are eaten for good luck, as are lentils, symbols of wealth. The coins of the Roman god Janus, who looked backward and forward, have become small circular foods of prosperity. Chicken is never served, for it is believed if one eats chicken on the new year, one scratches backward. Pork is the meat for New Year's Day, and in a Tuscan and Tuscan-American home like ours, *cotechino* sausage with lentils is the food that fulfills all the promise for the days to come. In other parts of Italy, the tradition is the same, but the food is different. The modern *Bolognese* and their *Bolognese*-American cousins eat their circles as lentils with *zampone*, a stuffed pig's foot. The *Abruzzeze* choose the tiny orange lentil for their hopes of prosperity. *Umbrians* prefer the deep brown lentil and a pastry called *chiacchiere* (small talk), sweetened dough balls that look like lentils that are drizzled with honey. They also eat *torciglione* (spiral), a coiled cake of almonds, sugar, and egg whites. Not only is that a circle, but coiled like a snake, it symbolizes renewal because a snake sheds its skin. In the Piedmont where rich sauces, stews, white truffles, and rice dominate the cuisine, the air is filled with the aroma of a white *risotto*, making rice their symbol of prosperity (the reason we throw rice at newlyweds). The entire year will follow the same pattern: a saint's day uniting all of Italy; the saint's foods and proverbs, divide the country by its regions.

The first celebration after the new year is Epiphany (*Befana*), January 6, when the three wise men visited the Christ child. Epiphany, the twelfth day of Christmas, marks the end of the winter holiday. It is traditionally the day of the *Befana,* an old woman who is considered the mother of Santa Claus. Legend states that the *Befana* was invited to join the wise men on their quest for the Christ child, but she refused. Regretting her decision, she set out alone, got lost, and has been searching ever since. Stockings are still hung in Italian homes for her visit. But the *Befana* is the accountant of bad deeds, and some children fear she will put ashes in their stockings. Arnold Pelini was so afraid of her that each year he was sure to have a stocking full of coal (followed by a gift of course).

Although the celebration is national, many regions have their own poem or song connected with the *Befana,* whose roots seem to be planted in ancient Roman lore. Of course the treats associated with *Befana* varied too. Our Tuscan family made a hard-as-nails *cavallucci* cookie and filled the children's stockings with an orange, a fig, a *cavallucci* cookie, and sometimes a *salsiccia secca*, a dried sausage. Our American family followed the tradition of oranges, nuts, and cookies (I never remember getting a *cavallucci* or a sausage!), but we hung our stockings on Christmas Eve and not on Epiphany, so we changed the rules a bit (which many families did). In some regions of Italy they make lemon-flavored cookies called *Bufanini*. In Sicily, where the variety and intensity of sweets is famous, they still make a cake with a lucky almond and whoever finds it is king of the celebration. This sounds much like the king cake of Mardi Gras in New Orleans, where many Sicilian-Americans live. The king cake is credited to the French inhabitants of the city, but the French and Italians have many similar traditions, and the king cake belongs to both of them (after all, the Bourbon King was in Sicily at one time and, of course, Catherine D'Medici took her kitchen to France when she married a king).

In western Pennsylvania, January weather is unpredictable, so life for the immigrants was routine. Monday was wash day, and the clothes were boiled in copper boilers *(caldaie)*, run through a hand ringer, loaded into baskets, and hung in the cellar, or carried outdoors. Bushel after bushel, the wet clothes were hoisted to blow dry in the breeze. Tuesday those same bushels were piled in the kitchen for ironing. Every Thursday was bread day, and the house was filled with the wonderful aroma of baking bread. By noon, if one was lucky, there was enough dough left over for frying. We called this simply, *pasta fritta,* or fried dough, but today, sold at fairs and carnivals throughout America, this simple but absolutely delicious snack carries various names including "elephant ears," "beaver tails," and "tiger ears." Saturday morning the soup pot came out and the broth simmered for hours.

Every Sunday was a holiday in an Italian household. We ate our four-course meal after twelve o'clock Mass at 1:00 P.M. Although homemade soup began each meal during the week, the first course on Sunday was pasta, and the pots were on the stove as early as 5:30 or 6:00 A.M. so the sauce would be simmering in time to go to eight o'clock Mass. The aroma of the sauce clung to the coats of the women and the church was filled with the fragrance. When Mass was over, the kitchen was a' bustle as the rest of the meal was prepared: a stew of beef or lamb served with a vegetable in tomato sauce, then a roast of chicken, veal, beef, or pork, and finally a dessert. The last thing to be done was to cut fresh homemade bread and bring the wine up from the cellar. I can still see Nonna as she tucked the bread into the crook of her arm, cutting up toward the shoulder, in what I have discovered is the traditional way to cut Tuscan country bread. It was a full, four-course dinner. Every Sunday! Every week! Every month! Every year!

There are few special days in January, but the seventeeth is the Feast of St. Anthony the Abbot *(Sant'Antonio Abate)*, patron saint of animals. On this day in the hill towns and farms of Italy, animals were brought to the church for blessings. *Quarata* was no exception. Once again it was time for a feast. Once again the food varied. In Milan in *Emilia-Romagna cassoeula*, an ancient Celtic-influenced dish of pork spare ribs, sausage, and savoy cabbage is still eaten to honor the saint. In *Cremona* in the Lombard, they make a *torta dura*, a corn cake with mint flavoring. Near Rome in Tuscania, a *Sangra delle Frittelle* is held where they have a choice of a sweet or a salted *frittelle al cavolfiore* (battered and fried cauliflower). In Naples, a bonfire is part of the celebration, while street vendors sell *sofritto*, or *zuppa forte*, made of scraps from the pig cooked in red sauce and served over grilled bread. More bonfires are ablaze in Sardinia where *su pupasinu*, sweet breads, are served.

For most of Italy the celebration of the saint inaugurated the harvest of the pig. All over Italy, pigs were killed and *prosciutto*, sausage, *salami*, and other Italian delicacies were prepared. We did not bring animals to the church, but we did dress a pig. Our family spent many hours in the cellar and many months enjoying the foods made from the fresh and cured pork, but we did this in November. Then, as the rest of Italy did in January, pork, fixed in a variety of delicious ways, was on the menu for weeks and weeks and weeks.

February
(Febbraio)
Linking the year with a series of religious observations, the church played a very important role in immigrant lives. Every month had dozens of saints' days. Saints were linked with animals, grains, fruits, or vegetables and joined to the land, what it produced, or what it fed. Thus, the church formed another link to Italian roots. Often superimposed on ancient pagan holidays, the saints' days were the great educators of the peasants. Each saint had a proverbs, which told the farmer when to plant, when to harvest, and often how to live. The proverbs, like the foods, varied from region to region because the planting seasons changed

with the climate. For example, *Per San Luca chi non ha seminato si speluca.* "For Saint Luca he who has not sown is fleeced," told the Tuscan farmer when to plant and the repercussions if he did not plant by that date. That date would not work in Sicily where the climate was hotter, or in *Aosta* where the climate was colder. They had their own set of proverbs.

In addition to the proverbs, the saint had a special food that was eaten in his or her honor. That food was linked to what was growing or being harvested at the time. In the middle of July in Tuscany, the fresh beans called *Fagioli di Sant' Anna* in honor of Saint Anne are harvested around her special day (July 26). That bean, called a black-eyed bean, was not truly finished growing until the fall, but in July it needed to be thinned out, thus the proverb and the myriad dishes that grew from it.

The result of the proverbs was the education of an entire culture that otherwise had no formal education. When I asked our cousin Natalina, who lives in *Pratovecchio* in *Il Casentino*, Tuscany about the proverbs, she said them to me in the chant of her childhood. That is how she learned them, repeating the phrase again and again, probably under someone's supervision, until she knew the rhyme and its message by heart, never to be forgotten.

The February feast days begin with Candlemas Day *(Candelora)*, celebrating Christ's entry into the temple of Jerusalem, which falls on the same day and carries the same ancient tradition as Groundhog Day in America. In Tuscany, they say, *"Se per la candelora cola, dall'inverno siamo fuora"* ("If on Candlemas Day it is dripping, from winter we've escaped"). February 3 is the day of Saint Blaise *(San Biagio)*, and it was traditionally a time to eat one last piece of the Christmas *panettone,* which was tucked away for this day and believed to protect from sore throats. Nonno loved it. Vivian remembers going to the church for the blessing of the throat and then bringing home candles to replace the old ones each Catholic family kept for use when they had to call a priest to the house.

Predominate among the foods of Saint Blaise both in Italy and other Catholic countries is *Pan Bendito,* Saint Blaise Sticks, what we often call bread sticks. They symbolize the candles used in the blessing of the throat. In the *Campania,* the fishermen who specialize in shellfish honor the saint because Saint Blaise died a cruel death: he was scraped to death using oyster shells. In Sicily, a variety of small breads and cookies are made in honor of the saint:

panuzzi, an oval cake or cookie topped with toasted hazelnuts, and *miliddi (militti),* an ancient honey biscuit, are among them. In one Sicilian town, *Trapani,* they actually shape their *panuzzi* into little grasshoppers and call them *cavadduzzi.* The inhabitants believe that when the grasshopper invaded the town back in the sixteenth century the saint intervened. In the town of *Taranta Peligna* in *Abruzzo,* they make a sourdough bread called *panicelle,* in the shape of a hand with four fingers, which is distributed at the entrance to the church. This tradition is in honor of another aspect of the saint, for he was the patron of shepherds, too.

February 5 brings Saint Agatha: *Sant'Agata, conduce la festa a casa. Perché siamo sulla fine del carnevale.* "For Saint Agatha, hold your feast at home because we are near the end of carnival," is the proverb. It is an obvious reminder to keep the Lenten fast on the saint's day and avoid temptation by staying home. The main food to honor Saint Agatha is a pastry called *minni di virgini* or Virgin's Breasts, for the saint's breasts were cut off as part of her martyrdom. The cookie is white, round, and filled with almond, lemon peel, chocolate chip, and candied cherries, with a cherry in the center.

March
(Marzo)

The winds of March brought expectation to Italian immigrant households, signaling preparations for carnival, Lent, and Easter. During this time came one of the biggest saints' days of the year: St. Joseph's Day. March 19 is St. Joseph's Day *(Festa di San Giuseppe)* in honor of the earthly father of Jesus Christ, patron of the family. In our household, no festivities were connected with St. Joseph's Day, but superstitions and special foods were. It is believed that if you cut your hair on St. Joseph's Day it will grow faster and fuller. In the kitchen, Nonna made a rice fritter called Fritter of St. Joseph *(Frittelle di San Giuseppe).* My mouth waters every time I think of it.

In Italy, St. Joseph's Day is a much bigger affair, for he is also the patron saint of pastry chefs, and region by region, the Italians outdo themselves in his honor. In Sicily, there is a Table of St. Joseph *(Tavola di San Giuseppe),* an altar of flowers and varieties of breads and an abundance of food. In Molise, the people eat a lunch of thirteen courses, which includes *pasta con la mollica (reginella),* a thick pasta with bread crumbs, which symbolize the saint's beard); pasta with anchovies; rice cooked in milk; *baccalá* baked with bay leaves; fried *baccalá;* fried fish; boiled vegetables; a sweet and sour vegetable dish; and *calzoni* (puff pastry cakes filled with chickpeas and flavored with spices). Not to be outdone, *San Marzano, Monteparano,* and *Lizzano* (still in *Apulia*) make thirteen peppery dishes and very sweet desserts.

It is the fritter, however, that is the most popular dish to honor Saint Joseph: fritters made with fish, apples, lemons, or rice. Village after village has a variation. In *La Spezia* in *Liguria,* the citizens hold a *Festa di San Giuseppe* and eat *friscieu,* croquettes made of apples, currants, and sultana raisins. In the *Trionfale* district of Rome, street vendors make both deep-fried *bigné* and *zeppoli.* (*Bigné* are fried and filled with cream. *Zeppoli* are fried and eaten without a filling.) Interestingly *zeppoli* can be found as far afield as *Umbria* and Sicily, where they are made with rice, or *Sardinia* and *Campania,* where flour replaces the rice. In Naples, they make their *zeppoli* topped with sugar and cinnamon.

March also brings carnival, a time of festival, and Lent (*Quaresima*), a time of fasting and repentance. Many tales are told of the naughty goings on of persons safely hidden behind masks and costumes during the carnivals of the Middle Ages and Renaissance. Along with elaborate and costly costumes, balls, street parades, and buffoonery, food was served on a scale that surpassed almost every other holiday of the year. Everything from *minestra* to *gnocchi* is served throughout the peninsula, but the sweets, like St. Joseph, are famous—and fabulous.

In *Emilia-Romagna,* they make *castagnoli con la crema*, fritters filled with cream and shaped to resemble chestnuts. In *Umbria,* the fried dough is joined by candied fruit, almonds, honey, and pine nuts in the form of a cake called *Cicerchiata.* Ada Boni, who borrowed the early cookbook writer Pellegrino Artusi's recipe for this delicious pastry, uses the more poetic name "Lover's Knots" to describe them.

By the time I came around, carnival was no longer a wonderful tradition in our home or community, but my mother remembered the balls held in Italian clubs in our valley. Nonno did not like to go to the dances, so Nonna and my mother went: once as George and Martha Washington, again as a *contessa* and her lady-in-waiting, winning first prize both times.

Carnival culminates during the week before Lent (*La Settimana Grassa),* from Maud Thursday *(Giovedi Santo)* to Ash Wednesday

(Le Cenere), the first day of Lent. On Shrove Tuesday *(Martedi Grasso)*, the day before Lent, pork must be eaten at all costs. Nonna's meal began with pasta with meat sauce, followed by pork chops on a spit, and a salad of endive and celery. This was right in keeping with the traditions of our family in Italy, where the chops were roasted over an open fire in our ancestral home. In 1985, *Zia Beppina* still used the ancient fireplace in the kitchen of the Parigi home for most of her cooking. (Her son Beppe still used it in 2009.) Beside it she had a wood-burning stove, which she said was only good for boiling water and roasting with aromatic woods, and a gas stove, which she did not use at all (ditto for Beppe). For dessert, in her home and ours, we enjoyed rich, flavorful *fiocchi*, a fried cookie topped with confectioners' sugar.

There are six weeks in Lent, and in the middle, at *Mezza Quaresima*, a rag doll representing an old woman *(La Vecchia)* appears. In Florence (in Tuscany, of course), she is hung in one of the squares and, amid great ceremony, cut open, allowing delicacies to cascade on the waiting children below. My mother remembered attending such parties at the NIPA, the Northern Italian club near our home, but they did not last long as the ceilings were too high and the children could not reach the caches of candy.

April
(Aprile)
Busy March is followed by joyous April, a month filled with the rites of spring. April 23, St. George's Day *(San Giorgio*, the patron of dairymen, who ate a rustic bread of corn flour, *pan e mei*, in his honor) was Nonna's birthday. April 25, the Feast of St. Mark *(San Marco*, patron saint of Venice) was celebrated with *risi e bisi*, a soupy *risotto* of rice and peas that originated in Venice.

But April is dominated by Holy Week *(Settimana Santa)* and Easter *(Pasqua)*. Palm Sunday *(Domenica delle Palme)* marks the day Jesus Christ entered Jerusalem amid olive branches and palm fronds. The church was draped in purple and each person attending Mass receives a sprig of palm to take home. Holy Thursday *(Giovedi Santo*, the day of the Last Supper) must have been the busiest day of the year in an Italian immigrant home. The young lamb had to be slaughtered and dressed, and Easter bread had to be made (Nonna always said the bread would not rise on Good Friday). While Nonna was in the kitchen, Nonno was tilling the land for the spring garden, traditionally begun on Holy Thursday.

Onions, parsley, and leaf lettuce were ready for picking within a month; fresh garden vegetables would join the daily menu.

No work was done in an immigrant home between noon and 3:00 P.M. on Good Friday (*Venerdi Santo*), the time of Christ's crucifixion. Women were at church.

Holy Saturday (*Sabato Santo*) began as a fast day, but at noon, the fast was broken with a meal of blessed Easter bread, blessed eggs (eggs, symbols of renewal, were originally prohibited during Lent), and *salami*. It was also the day of the *gran fritto misto*, a medley of fried foods that took hours to prepare and an equal number of hours to eat. Chicken, veal, fish, pork, and lamb sliced into serving pieces and dipped in bread crumbs or flour, then soaked in beaten egg were fried a golden brown. The five varieties of meat were joined by artichokes, beans, cauliflower, mushrooms, and *zucchini*, also dipped in eggs and flour or coated with a batter. I can still see Nonna at the stove cooking this meal hour after hour with the big black iron skillets sizzling away, filling the house with tempting aromas.

The *gran fritto misto* was arranged on an extra-large platter with each item having a corner of its own. Nonna always laid a flat plate upside-down in the middle of the platter so the meats would drain and pile high. The vegetables were usually around the edges. The entire masterpiece was trimmed with fresh lemon wedges, their juices dashed over the fried foods to enhance the taste. The melt-in-your-mouth *gran fritto misto* was served with a simple leaf lettuce and onion salad, dressed with oil and vinegar.

On Easter Sunday, the table was set with the best china and cutlery (except for Nonno's fork, which he had filed down until each prong was as thin and sharp as a needle). Fresh flowers dressed the buffet, and we all sat around the huge dining room table in my grandparents' home. As the platters of sliced *salami*, blessed eggs, and Easter bread came to the table, a large dish of canapés made of milt and chicken livers topped with thin slices of *prosciutto* joined them. These succulent *crostini* were washed down with white wine. When they were cleared from the table the bowls of *cappelletti* swimming in golden broth arrived. Topped with grated Parmesan cheese, the soup was a meal in itself.

Then the lamb dishes began. Stewed lamb accompanied by spinach cooked in a garlic and rosemary sauce sprinkled with white flecks of grated Parmesan cheese was followed by spiced roast lamb with oven potatoes and a simple salad of garden leaf lettuce and onions in oil and vinegar. Of course the wine was red, and each course had fresh bread as an accompaniment. And amid the dyed Easter eggs and chocolate rabbits were a golden sponge cake *(pane di Spagna)* and rice pudding served with strong Italian coffee and *vin santo,* the best of Italian wines. When it was all over, we were stuffed with good food and filled with good conversation.

For the Pelini family, the entire ritual was repeated a week later on White Sunday *(I Bianchi),* when converts were traditionally taken into the church. The Bonchi's, our Italian cousins from Aliquippa, Pennsylvania, joined them that day for another gigantic feast. Easter was great.

Of course other parts of Italy have their own variations on this theme. In the south, the lamb is replaced by kid and the spices change from rosemary to *oregano.* The Easter meal in *Abruzzo* begins with soup and its main course is lamb roasted over a spit. The Easter soup of *Umbria* is a little less complicated. It is made with mutton and flavored by marjoram *(maggiorana).*

Easter is a time of rebirth and rejoicing and these foods add much to the celebration. In homes all over America variations of these dishes can be found in Italian American homes. In some families, like ours, the entire tradition is maintained. In other families, as long as one dish remains from the original immigrant meal, they are satisfied that they are maintaining their link to the past. In other families they have blended the traditions of parents and grandparents who came from different provinces taking a few dishes from each family. In all, the Italian-American Easter is a memorable event.

May
(Maggio)

Nonno's second spring planting was in late May and green beans, beets, chard, carrots, and celery were planted. At the end of the month the final planting included cucumbers, peppers, tomatoes, and *zucchini.*

May 1 is *Calendimaggio,* the Ides of May. I don't remember any special foods for us in America or in *Quarata* and *Arezzo,* but nearby Florence, rival to *Arezzo* for centuries, hosts the prestigious three-day *Maggio Musicale Fiorentino* festival, with music in all its forms from operas to dramas. Both it and nearby *Assisi* in *Umbria,* where they hold a medieval parade and games, celebrate with that succulent, terrific, fabulous dish *porchetta*. If you have never tasted *porchetta*, you have missed one of the most outstanding dishes in the Italian pantheon. Let your mouth water. *Porchetta* is mostly a northern dish. In *Arezzo*, they say, *"Non e festa se non e la porchetta."* "It is not a feast if there is no *porchetta*." Here, too, there are variations. Where most of Tuscany flavors the pork with rosemary, in *Quarata* and *Arezzo* fennel is used.

As mentioned, my grandfather went to an Italian club. It was called the North Italian Political Association, the NIPA (Niii paa). In towns across America, clubs like these joined the Italian community as much as they divided it. In Monessen, the northerners segregated themselves from the southerners. The southerners built their own club. Although Nonno went to the club *(sala)* all year long, in the spring the gaming area *(pallaio)* came alive with the game of *bocce*. On the first warm days, the playing surface was prepared: weeds cut, ground rolled flat, new sand laid down and rolled again, spectator benches repaired and freshly painted. Finally, as the buds of May graced the trees, the first tournament was held. The different clubs in the community and in our valley competed against each other in a well-organized league that lasted from spring to fall. What an event.

The air was filled with shouts as the two teams took turns throwing a small iron ball *(pallino)* down the sand-covered lane. It was the linchpin, and the two teams took turns trying to place larger balls near it. There were "oohs" and "ahhs" as one ball would gently kiss the *pallino*, coming to rest as close as possible, placing a team at the advantage. The opponents would bring out their ace player, who with lightning precision would swack the offensive ball away with the swift exactness of a surgeon, leaving the *pallino* untouched. The game went on all afternoon, and eventually lights were installed in the gaming area so the fun could continue into the evening. No one complained that there was too much noise in the neighborhood.

Nonno went to the *sala* each evening after dinner, and many times, I would charge in looking for him to beg for a quarter. There he would be, pipe in mouth, freshly drawn glass of beer in front of him, sitting in the same place year after year. His face would light up when he saw me and sometimes I would sit long enough to have a soft drink. I can still recall the beery smell that hung in the air and see the dimly lit hall with the wonderful long wooden and brass bar running its entire length.

Today the club stands empty. Weeds grow in the *pallaio*. The windows are broken. The upstairs hall, where so many Italians had their wedding receptions and older women were crowned with flowers on Mother's Day, gathers dust. These clubs, be they Italian or German or Slovak, have outlived their purpose. In addition to gathering similar people together, they served them as interpreters with the English language and assistants in filling out forms, finding jobs, understanding general concerns, and numerous other issues that immigrant's faced. Oh, how sad, to leave it all behind. To replace it with fast food and television. To not have a place for the gathering of the clan. To not hear the lyrical Italian language echo on a Sunday afternoon.

June
(Giugno)
Four saints have major festivals throughout Italy in June: Saint Paulinus, Saint John the Baptist, and Saints Peter and Paul. The most colorful and popular festival in June and maybe throughout the entire year is June 22, Saint Paulinus' Day, patron of the town of Nola near Naples. We did not do anything special on this day, but it serves as one of the best examples of how traditions were adopted in America. On Saint Paulinus' Day, the modern *Nolani* still celebrate a feast called *I Gigli di Nola*, the Lilies of Nola, in the saint's honor. The lilies are eight large towers that are carried by men called *paranze* who represent the different guilds of the town. They arrive in the *piazza* when the men perform acrobats. The astounding thing is not only the decoration of the *papier-mâché* towers, which are decorated with angels, flowers, and birds, but that a complete brass band rides atop the *Gigli* platforms. In a most astounding feat, the *paranze* have been carrying the entire orchestra too.

The *Gigli di Nola* has been transplanted to America. Brooklyn has a large *Nolani* population, and each year on the saint's day, they, too, reenact the carrying of the *Gigli*. They only have one—sixty-five-foot-tall tower, but it weighs two tons. The ritual began in the early decades of the twentieth century and continues to this day. Around 1950, the *Gigli* was changed in Brooklyn to include the feast of Our Lady of Mount Carmel (July 16) so now the festival lasts for two and a half weeks. The foods in America are not the same as those in *Nola*, Italy. Instead, they are the typical Italian-American mix of pastas, sausages, and desserts.

June 24, Midsummer Night's Eve, the birthday of Saint John the Baptist (*San Giovanni Battista*), is the time to announce engagements and sprinkle salt at the door to keep away evil spirits. Nonna always made chamomile tea on St. John's Day, and she would have a dickens of a time getting us to drink it (now I buy chamomile in tea bags and wonder why I did not learn to enjoy it earlier). She also made *pannini de San Giovanni*, small breads in honor of the saint. They make them in *Grillo* in *Umbria* as well, but there they stamped the image of the saint on top. I don't remember any stamp. John the Baptist is the patron of Florence, and the Florentines hold a cricket *festa* and medieval games in his honor. Another interesting festival in honor of the saint is enacted in nearby *Emilia-Romagna*. The people take to the orchards in groups of twenty-one (seven sacraments times three) on the eve of the holiday to pick the walnuts for a walnut liqueur called *nocino*. It is aged forty days for the wandering in the desert.

Through most of Italy, fish and snails honor the saint. In *Genoa*, the boats of various confraternities are decorated and set sail around the harbor. At Lake Como, small snail shells filled with oil are lit and then set down to float on the lake. They are joined by a fleet of boats carrying relics of the saint to the church. A whole district of Rome is called *San Giovanni*, and on the saint's day, they have a grand *festa* with snails and *porchetta*. They eat their snails on Saint John's Eve and cook them with garlic, hot pepper, mint, and tomatoes.

But June was the time for immigrant weddings. In Italy, couples were married on Monday, and that tradition was transported to America. My mother and father were married on Monday, June 18, 1934. In Italy, the veil of the bride was an heirloom. All the women in our family wore it for communion, confirmation, and marriage: the rites of passage. Nonna's heirloom was in Italy with her family, so my mother had to buy a veil. Sandrina did pass her wedding gown on to her daughter Vivian but not as a wedding dress. In 1938, Vivian was in a Christmas play at her school. Her parents could not afford a proper dress so Sandrina cut up her wedding gown and made a pleated skirt and long-sleeved top trimmed with a red velvet ribbon.

By the time I came along, Saturday had become the traditional day for weddings. Each weekend the hall at the NIPA was festooned with crepe paper, and the kitchen was filled with dozens of hands preparing a feast for the guests. Of course there was pasta. But the pastries were special, with mounds of *brigidini* (called *pizzelles* in other regions), *biscotti,* and anise cookies topped with pastel icing. There was always an Italian band, and the highlight of the evening was not the bride dancing with the groom, but a woman dancing with a broom, an Italian square dance called the *quadrella,* and the most famous of all Italian dances, the *tarantella.* The *tarantella* is a story set to dance. Originally, it was the story of a young boy and his mother. Bitten by a tarantula, he was told to dance faster and faster to rid his body of the poison. Over the years, it became a dance of seduction, danced by a man and woman. Ironically, the Northern Italians would not allow a Southerner to join their club, but they let this Southern dance come to visit.

All of the rites of passage for Italians were ritualized. Baptisms occurred, of course, year-round, but communion and confirmation ceremonies, both accompanied by processions, were performed in the spring. When my mother was born, the midwives thought she was going to die so the two women who assisted at her birth wrapped her in a blanket and walked to St. Leonard's Church to baptize her. But the Irish priest (there was no Italian church in Monessen at that time) refused to name her Darna, the name my grandmother had selected. The women were afraid to walk back to my grandparent's house and then back to the church for fear my mother would die, so they named her *Liza Betta,* after her two grandmothers. Her American birth certificate reads Elizabeth, and that is what she is called.

The final major saint's day in June is the twenty-ninth, which is dedicated to Saints Peter and Paul. In *Molise* at *Iserina,* the feast to the two saints began in 1254. There they celebrate with the onion, for which the region is renowned throughout Italy. At *Palermo,* Sicily, the fishermen decorate their boats and tour the harbor. In *Palazzolo Acreide, cudduri,* small breads shaped like wreaths or snakes are carried to the church by carts to the tunes of the local bands. At the church, they are blessed and sold by auction to the highest bidder.

This festival has come to America too. It is mostly celebrated along the seashores by fishermen who hold fishing festivals in the saints' honor. In Gloucester, Massachusetts, the Church of Saint Peter honors both the saint and their Sicilian heritage on Saint Peter's Day. They hold ship parades, enjoy Sicilian food, and have games. This celebration first began in 1931.

July
(Luglio)

July begins with the Tuscan proverb, *Quando canta l'assiolo, con tadini semina il fagiolo.* "When the horned owl sings, the farmers plant the beans." Nonno didn't plant beans, but Gino did. His garden was always bigger than Nonnos. July was the month to plant the winter crops and a number of proverbs told the Tuscan farmer when to plant. *Per Santa Croce e San Cipriano semina in costa e semina in piano.* "For Santa Croce and San Cipriano plant in the seashore and plant in the plain." *Per Santa Cristina (July 24), la sementa della saggina.* "For Saint Christina, sow sorghum." Our planting was in the garden, not in the fields, so we did not plant wheat, sorghum, or such huge crops.

Family picnics are a summer favorite, and as early as 1925, when few city or county parks existed in our area, the farms of friends became sites of festivities each Sunday. These were our festivals, newly created, with no proverbs or saint in view. The women would begin preparations on Wednesday or Thursday, making bushels of *biscotti* or *fiocchi* and gallons of sauce for home-made pasta. By Friday and Saturday, they had moved on to prepare the fresh spring chickens for the spit.

No store-bought chickens here: the chickens were bought live and carted home in crates. The women would gather in the basement of one of the homes and would begin by wringing the necks of the chickens and hanging them from the rafters to settle the blood. Then, in assembly-line fashion, they would continue to clean the chickens. One by one, they would dip them into scalding water to remove the feathers. When the chickens were cleaned, each would be passed to a second group of women who would slit the abdomen below the breast to remove the innards, and then they would remove the head and neck. The final group of women would wash the springers inside and out, drain them, and place them in a bushel basket. They were now ready for the spit.

The spit was made to order in the foundry of the local steel company (this was called a "government job" and the company knew nothing about it). It was a square rod 1½ inches thick and fifty inches long, and held twenty chickens. Pointed on one end for the skewering, it had a flat, round six-inch disk at the other end to hold the chickens firm. Beside the disk was a grooved wooden wheel to which a sixty-foot rope was attached. This created the pulley. Once the fire was laid and the chickens were in place, it was the job of the children to take turns working the pulley and rotating the chickens. The spit was supported by two iron pegs, twenty to twenty-four inches long, which were pounded into the ground. One peg had an eye to thread the spit, while the other had a cradle to hold it in place. Four thin sticks, the length of the spit (usually made from the wood of a twenty-pound spaghetti box), were placed on either side of the chickens to keep them in place. Thin wire was wrapped around the sticks.

The fire, built six to eight inches upwind from the spit, was made from dry fruitwood, preferably cherry wood, usually found on the farm. While the women were putting the chickens on the spit, the men would prepare the fire. Once the chickens were ready, the spit would be hung in a tree until it was time to place it on the fire. The picnic meal was served outdoors on white tablecloths with china dishes and proper glasses.

It was Prohibition, but the wine from the various wine cellars was also bottled, packed, and transported. Nothing stopped these celebrations: rain, mist, or fog. A favorite story is of Nonna walking in front of the car down a country lane because the fog was so dense it was impossible to see.

There is one July feast day worth mentioning even though it is not Tuscan. If one looked at the ratio of Tuscans who came to America as compared to other regions, one would find fewer Tuscans and, therefore, fewer public festivities devoted to Tuscans. Sicilians, on the other hand, form a much larger family in America. They celebrate a plethora of public celebrations. One of the biggest feasts of the calendar year is the Feast of Saint Rosalie, the patron saint of *Palermo.* She reputedly saved the city from the Black Plague. The city celebrated the festival by building a cart in the shape of a ship and serving seeds and nuts from its shelves. The first cart was built around 1701, a second in 1741. These carts were huge, as high as the houses and equally as long. The church stopped their construction in the 1860s, but the celebration and its traditions have been revived today. The foods of the festival include seeds and nuts: broad beans *(fava)*, chickpeas *(ceci)*, carob *(carruba)*, lupin *(lupine)*, pumpkin seeds *(semi di zucca)*, hazelnuts *(nocciole)*, peanuts *(arachidi)*, barley *(orzo)*, and dried chestnuts *(castagne).* Pastry shops make small sugar carts displayed in their windows. More substantial foods include *babaluci,* a garlic- and parsley-flavored dish of snails, and *caponata,* a medley of vegetables under vinegar.

This festival has been transposed to Bensonhurst, Brooklyn, where the people celebrate a ten-day festival by closing down an entire street. Among the foods are *zeppole,* sausage sandwiches, baked clams, *linguine* with mussels, and *collari,* a deep-fried bread stuffed with *prosciutto,* provolone, and Calabrese olives. It's got to be delicious. The celebration is decades old. Today, however, with the neighborhoods changing, many Italians have moved away and the various stands reflect those changes. In the midst of Italian food stands, one is now likely to find *arepa* from South America, *empanada* from Portugal, and fried Oreo cookies directly from the United States. The times they are a-changin'.

August
(Agosto)
August brought hot, humid, lazy days in Pennsylvania: a time for eating fresh garden tomatoes, delicate *zucchini* flowers, and green peppers; and time for planting the winter garden of endive, escarole, and Savoy cabbage. The winters were too harsh in Pennsylvania so this was another tradition that was lost. But someone was planting them somewhere because all of these wonderful plants graced our table.

August 7 is the day of *San Donato,* the patron saint of *Arezzo.* Although *Arezzo* is less than five miles from our village of *Quarata,* we never celebrated this holiday. (In America there is a *San Donato Festa* in Waterbury, Connecticut, and in Blue Island, Illinois.) I am sure my aunts and uncles walked to *Arezzo* to join the festivities, but in their homes and ours, there was no celebration at all. Since 1580 in *Arezzo,* there has been a procession, a *reinfresco,* and a horse race. The food, of course, was *porchetta.* The horse race, in modern times, has become a second Joust of the Saracen (see September below for details). It takes place on the last Saturday in June and is called the *San Donato* Joust.

Soon after *San Donato* comes August 10 and the Feast of *San Lorenzo,* Saint Lawrence. *San Lorenzo* was slowly "roasted" to death, so traditionally only cold foods are served on this day. It is obvious that he would be the patron of burns, and it is not a stretch to see how he is the patron of bakers and cooks, but he is also the patron of librarians. That is because he kept the books for the church. A cold meal is not such a bad thing when it is prepared the way the various Italian provinces do. In Florence, they eat pork and sheep cold cuts and *porrea,* a leek tart, in honor of *San Lorenzo.* Nearby *Marradi* enjoys watermelon. In *Imperia,* a salad of tomatoes, cucumbers, sweet peppers, olives, and anchovies is served. That is not such a hard dish to put together for the hot days of summer. Almost every Sunday we ate cold foods for dinner. After our main four-course meal in the middle of the day, the cook closed the kitchen. In the evening we cut the *prosciutto, salami,* cheese, and homemade bread; made a salad; and washed it all down with good homemade wine. There is nothing better!

August 15 is the celebration of the Feast of the Assumption of the Virgin Mary *(Ferragosto).* All of Italy goes on holiday, and travelers stay out of Italy because everything is closed during the *Ferragosto.* During the Renaissance, the Romans also celebrated this day. They flooded *Piazza Navorna* in Rome and filled it with fake fish. People would then throw coins into the artificial lake and young boys dove to retrieve them. More recently in *Calabria,* feast baskets of grain were prepared to celebrate the good harvest. In *Sassari,* men carried a *Candelieri* through streets much like the Lilies of Nola.

Throughout the United States there are dozens of street fairs for the *Ferragosto.* One such fair began in 1895 in Cleveland, Ohio's Little Italy. In Atlantic City, New Jersey, from the turn of the century to World War II (and revived recently), a Wedding of the Sea Festival was held on the Feast of the Assumption. The procession ran along Mississippi Avenue where the Virgin was paraded to the sea. The actual festival took place on the grounds of St Michael's Church. Around the same time in August, Boston's North End still holds a Fisherman's Feast in honor of the *Madonna del Soccorso.* It began in 1911 in Boston but was really started in *Sciacca,* Sicily, the hometown of many of the Boston participants. The Madonna protected the town. A statue of the Madonna was created in Palermo in 1503, but was too heavy to transport to *Sciacca,* so the fishermen sent their boats to collect it. The festival honors the parade of boats carrying the statue.

Each celebration is bound to have an Italian band for an immigrant summer was not complete without bands, so popular throughout western Pennsylvania. An Italian band from Monessen was the Order of the Sons of Italy Band organized in the early 1900s by John Janotta. It later became the Monessen Fireman's Band, then the Monessen Civic Center Band, and by midcentury revived as the MARS Community Concert Band for the Mon Valley

Association of Retired Steelworkers, who helped the band stay to-gether. The MARS band performed regularly at cultural heritage festivals and summer park concerts. Today the bands from all the small towns in our valley have merged into one and they play a variety of music. The Red Coat Band *(La Banda Vestita di Rosso)* of New Castle (Mahoningtown) was organized in 1898 by Feliciano DeSantis who taught music. It was also known as the Duke of Abruzzi Italian Band and later divided into two bands, the Red Coat Band and the Blue Coat Band. (These unusual names were given because of the color of the uniforms. The official name of the Blue Coat Band, for example, was *La Banda Vestita d'Azzurro di Santa Margherita,* Mahoningtown, "The Band Dressed in Blue of St. Margaret Mahoningtown.)

Whatever the names, the bands of western Pennsylvania pro-vided hours of entertainment and they were formed along ethnic lines. In addition to the Italian bands, there were bands from al-most all ethnic groups and it was important to all of them that they had glorious uniforms to accompany their distinct, ethnic music. Each had to outdo the other for ethnic pride. The July 4, 1919, parade in Monessen had eight divisions that included ten local bands: Louhi Finnish Band (renown throughout the world), Pittsburgh Steel Product Band, New Eagle Band, McKeesport Drum Corps, Italian Citizens Band, Charleroi Slovak Band, Mon-essen Slovak Band, Monessen Polish Band, Monessen Drum Corps, and Monessen Hungarian Band. The Italian Band led the fourth division, which consisted of the Italian Benevolent Society, the Italian Civic Society, and the Franco-Belgium Society (the four Italian clubs did not attend). Not to be outdone, the Slovaks had twelve units in their division. Ten thousand people stood on the sidewalks to watch this extravaganza. Today this is but a memo-ry. There are no bands. There is no music. What happened to all the bands? What has happened to all the musicians? Does no one play music anymore?

The Feast of *San Rocco* (Saint Roch) is August 16, the day of his death. He is remembered as the patron of wool carders and cooks and the protector against plague and contagious diseases. There are many traditions that reflect his legend. In *Calabria,* in order to petition the saint for help, *panpepati,* small spicy cook-ies (as opposed to the dark chocolaty fruit cake *panpepato*), are designed in the shape of the part of the body petitioning the saint to protect or cure. In the *Villa Santo Stefano* in *Abruzzo,* they make a rosemary-flavored *ceci* (chickpea) soup called *la panarda;* it is part of the huge feast by the same name where dozens of dishes are prepared and eaten. It is made in huge copper caldrons. To accompany the soup they make a bread called *la pagnotta di San Rocco,* the loaf of San Rocco. In Florence, *San Rocco* is honored by a flower festival accompanied by medieval costumes and races.

In the United States, the *San Rocco* celebration has been transplanted to many places including New Castle, the home of the Pelini, where it has been celebrated since 1914. The rituals there are similar to nearby Aliquippa, Pennsylvania, which has many transplants from the village of *Patrica,* near Rome. *San Rocco* is *Patrica's* patron saint. They hold a festival and parade each year (since 1925) sponsored by the Musical and Political Italian Club on the weekend nearest August 16 in a replica of the parade in Italy. The parade is more than two miles long, and the statue is carried by eight men. During the parade, people pin money to a large banner of *San Rocco* while children carry a flag by its corners so people can toss more money into it. As the parade progresses through the community, it stops at various locations for drinks and tastes of *ciambelle,* a sweet bread made into a ring and topped with various sweet toppings like grape syrup, orange syrup, or caramelized chestnuts. The penitents, hoping for favors from the saint, walk barefooted. The feast includes sausage, a *morra* tournament, music, and games. The most unusual event is the evening doll dance. To the tune of the *tarantella,* a man dances with a life-sized doll that has been covered with fireworks. One after another, the fireworks ignite as the dance continues.

Wherever a cluster of immigrants from the same village or region in Italy have settled, you can be sure a festival with rituals and foods from "back home" can be found. This festival is a good example.

September
(Settembre)
September is a month of dividends and returns for all the hard work of summer. The first Sunday in September is the Joust of the Saracen *(Giostra del Saracino)* in *Arezzo.* It is a jousting tournament rooted in the city's medieval tradition. *Arezzo* is the hub of a number of small hamlets in south-central Tuscany including our small village of *Quarata,* which is only a few miles to the northwest along an ancient roadway. The game originated during the

Crusades and was revived in 1931, too late for Nonno and Nonna to enjoy it.

The *Giostra* is held twice a year, and on one of my visits to Italy, I was lucky enough to see it. Teams made up of people from the different gates of the walled city, dressed in traditional medieval costumes, compete with each other to attack the Saracen (Arab). The Saracen in this case is a stationary figure with a shield in his left hand and a whip tipped with lead balls in his right. A horseman, complete with a long jousting stick, attacks the Saracen. As he hits the statue, he must get away without receiving a hit from the lead balls, which whip around as the Saracen turns from the force of the blow.

The game was wonderful as were all the beautiful costumes and festivities. But *Arezzo* and its tournament were too far away for us to enjoy back in Pennsylvania. One Saturday in September, we would head for the Salotti farm. It was time to pick the fresh fruit waiting for us in the hilly Pennsylvania orchards. Eventually it was a chore for Nonna and me. Off we would go, our baskets piled high and empty in the backseat of the car. What a day we had climbing the trees and picking the fresh fruit. The farm boys would be there to help, but Nonna liked to do it herself, climbing the ladder in her black, wide-heeled shoes and cotton dress. Eventually they would leave us to it, and grandmother and grandchild roamed the hillside looking for trees heavy with ripe fruit.

Nonna would spot a tree and up she would go, her skirt flapping in the wind (I never saw her in pants). I always wanted to shake the tree and let the apples fall to the ground, but that was sacrilege, not to be done. We picked a variety of apples, and then we hit the pear trees. By the end of the day, we were exhausted, but there was always time to visit the owner in her rambling farmhouse filled with hidden stairways and mysterious rooms. It was so Victorian and spooky that I would tingle with excitement as I crossed the threshold. On the way home, we barely had room to sit. I can remember going apple picking from the time I was seven years old.

In later years, when Nonna was too old to climb trees, we still went out to the farms each October, but now we selected from the bushels of fruits already picked by the farmers. The Salotti farm was sold, Nonna's friend gone, and few farmers permitted people to pick their own fruit. But Nonna was just as fussy and, much to the annoyance of the farmer, spent hours poking into each basket until she made her choice. She wasn't beyond taking a few good apples from one basket and putting them into the one she wanted to take home. Of course, she replaced them—but with inferior apples.

As for the proverbs and saints' days for September, probably the most famous for Americans is *San Gennaro,* September 19. *San Gennaro* is the patron saint of Naples, and the Neapolitans have built a weeklong festival with special foods. They eat *maccheroni* with eggplant and peppers and *coniglio in umido,* rabbit in red sauce. In New York, where the most famous *San Gennaro* festival is held in the United States, the foods are more "generic" Italian: pizza, sausage, and *cannoli. Cannoli,* as we know, is a Sicilian sweet, not a Neapolitan one. The New York festival, held on Mulberry Street in Little Italy, was begun in 1925 by Neapolitan immigrants. Today, even though many Italians have moved away from the area, the event continues with a procession of the statue, a parade of floats, and food, food, food.

We ate *fegatelli,* liver wrapped in its own veil, for saints Cosmos and Damian *(Il Medici)* honored on September 27. They do the same in *Bari* in the region of *Puglia* at the heel of Italy and add *torrone,* the wonderful candy. The feast is a big event in Cambridge, Massachusetts, too. The foods are sausage and a host of Italian cookies. Streetlights and flags decorate a number of streets, which are sandwiched between a chapel at one end and a carnival at the other. The highlight of the celebration is a parade. As the statues exit the church, they are greeted with fireworks and a shower of confetti. Through a candlelight procession, they are taken to the temporary chapel at one end of the street. The next day a second procession is held with bands, marchers in purple satin capes, and floats. The statues are carried through the streets and pause at various homes, which hold an open house. This goes on for most of the day.

September 29 belongs to *San Michele,* better known as Michael the Archangel, the general of the heavenly army that threw the devil out of heaven. The English call the day *Michaelmas,* eat goose, and repeat the proverb, "Whoever eats goose on Michaelmas Day shall never lack for money for his debts to pay." The Italians eat fruits, meats, and stews and say, *Per San Michele il caldo va in cielo,* "For San Michele heat goes into the heavens," and *Per San Michele ogni straccio sa di miele,* "For San Michele all the last fruits of the year are honeyed and ripe."

In Tuscany, in *Impruneta* the *Festa dell'Uva* is held with floats with grape themes. There they eat a beef stew called *il peposo*, which is seasoned with garlic and filled with tomatoes and peppers. Once it was eaten during the wheat harvest where it is cooked for six or seven hours (while the pickers were working in the fields). In *Carbonara* in *Apulia*, they eat mutton chops seasoned with thyme. The mutton is specially raised and grilled over a fire of hazelnut shells and seasoned with branches of thyme. By now it is obvious that the regions have their own foods connected to special days, but it is more obvious that we will never totally comprehend the countless foods prepared in Italy. It has such unending depth.

October
(Ottobre)

As spring was busy with sowing, fall was busy with reaping, and in most years, the bounty was plentiful. There were fruits to be picked, festivals to enjoy, and wine to be made. And we did them all. But first we celebrated the feast closest to our heart. The first Sunday in October is the *Festa di Quarata,* the festival of the village in Italy where most of our family still lives. The festival celebrates the Battle of Lepanto of 1571. That is how long that same festival has been honored by my ancestors. We are talking nearly five hundred years. It does not really hit home until you realize you are talking about your own, great-great-great-grandparent. Then the fact that it has been taking place for five centuries is overwhelming. The village holds a procession carrying the Madonna through the streets. We had a procession too. We were driving to New Castle or they were driving to us. Now, with most of the family gone, we call each other on the phone and give greetings.

It is not the procession, but the foods that keep this tradition alive in our home. Duck from the marshes around *Arezzo* is the main food of the *Festa di Quarata*. It is prepared three different ways: in *sugo,* in *umido,* and in *porchetta*. The *prima piatta* of the *Festa di Quarata, pappardelle con sugo di anitra,* is an Aretine specialty. The second plate of the *Festa,* between the *maccheroni* and the roast, is *anitra in umido con sedano,* duck in red sauce with celery, a *cotta tre volte* dish. The roast, or main course, of the *Festa di Quarata* is *porchetta*. Giovanni Righi Parenti in *La cucina degli etruschi,* tells us that *"porchetta* of Arezzo is an institution. There is no festival where *porchetta* is not served." Ours was not pig in *porchetta* for this *festa*, but duck. Yes, duck in *porchetta*. We did not raise ducks in America, we bought them from a farmer. Nonno always said that if you raised ducks, you had to have a pond or running water so they could swim or the flesh would taste of mud. What wisdom they had. What knowledge of how to survive.

Above all, October was the month to make the most important product of the year, the new wine. If Nonno had settled in California instead of Pennsylvania, we could have been a dynasty of wine makers. His wine was known far and wide, including back home in Italy, as delicate, clear, and powerful. During Prohibition, more than one person came to Nonno to ask him to start a bootleg wine business. But Nonno always refused.

In Italy, the grapes were harvested in September and early October, and Tuscany, home of *Chianti*, was the center of great wine making. It was a grand affair with grape festivals and gigantic meals served to the pickers in the fields.

To me, this time of year always has a faint smell of new wine and memories of Nonno's wine cellar. What a special place: drying sausages hung from the rafters beside curing *prosciuttos* and hundreds of green or brown wine bottles filled the shelves along the walls. At least three oak casks were set on their sides filled with wine—two for red, one for white—and for a little while each fall, another for half wine *(mezzo vino)*.

How many hours I spent in the wine cellar with my grandfather I'll never be able to count. He would sit in his black, overstuffed rocking chair, pipe in mouth, and I would crawl up on his lap and beg him to tell me stories. My favorite was always a trip to Italy. The closer we got, the bigger the fish in the sea and the bigger the smile on my nonno's face. I can still see in my mind the images I conjured up during those stories. We went by train and boat. As the train approached *Arezzo,* we ate a picnic lunch of *prosciutto* and drank good red wine. The first time I visited my family in Italy I went by train from Rome and relived those hours with my grandfather in his wine cellar.

My brother, seven years older than me, preceded me in the wine cellar. He would beg for a sip of wine and Nonno would eventually give it to him. As he tasted it, he would smack his lips, and Nonna, ever vigilant from her kitchen, would yell down, "Nazzareno, don't give that boy any wine." My brother would look up at Nonno with his big blue eyes and say, "How did she know, Nonno?"

I cannot leave October without recalling one Halloween. I was
in kindergarten and was dressed as Robin Hood. We had a grand
parade around the grounds and the teacher awarded prizes. I did
not win, but at the end of the day, Nonna was waiting for me with
a wonderful leather pencil box with several drawers and a dozen
multicolored pencils.

November
(Novembre)

November 1 brings All Saints' Day *(I Santi)*. On that day, it is
traditional to eat roasted chestnuts and drink wine, which we do
with gusto. Chestnuts are a staple of the Tuscan countryside. This
very adaptable fruit, yes a fruit, can be roasted, baked, made into
cakes and sweets, and ground into flour. Throughout Italy, fairs
in honor of the chestnut are held and *castagnaccio,* a cake of raisins, pine nuts, and rosemary, sometimes called the *panforte* of the
poor, is served. It is a flat, strange cake that is an acquired taste. It
can be used in dozens of ways. At other festivals, we find chestnuts sweetened with sugar and *grappa (Cal d'Aosta)* and chestnuts
and sweet potatoes *(Verona).*

In addition to chestnuts, it is traditional for us to eat pork chops
and chicken wings seasoned with sage, salt, and pepper and roasted slowly on a spit. Delicious! We also make and enjoy a small
bread called *Panini di Santi,* with saffron and raisins. The farm la-
borers make enough bread on All Saints' Day to last all winter.

All Souls' Day *(I Morti)*, November 2, is a day set aside to
remember the dead. In Italy, it is believed that on the night of
November 1, the dead return to the world and walk the streets
searching for gifts for children (like our Halloween). Thus, it is
another day of gift-giving. A spoonful of *ceci* and vegetable
minestrone is left outside the window in *Asti* on November 1 so
ancestors may eat as they run through the town. On All Souls'
Day, families go to the cemetery to visit their ancestors laden with
baskets of food and chrysanthemums, which are the Italian flower of the dead. This custom is a very ancient one.

Combined the two days are second only to Saint Joseph's Day
in traditions and foods. In Milan on All Souls' Day, people eat *ceci
con la tempia,* a stew of chick peas, loin of pork, and pig's temple.
In Piedmont, they make *cisra,* a soup of *ceci* and pork. In *Apulia,*
a *calzone* of anchovies, almonds, pine nuts, and raisins is eaten
as well as *U Grane Cuotte (aka Colva),* a sweet of flour, chopped

almonds, walnuts, chocolate, citron, cinnamon, and pomegranate seeds. *A pan dei morti*, bread of the dead, of *polenta* called *tressian* is part of the tradition in the *Veneto*.

Among the sweets to grace the table and tempt the palate on the scary night between the two days is a cookie called *ossi di morti*, bones of the dead, shaped like a human bone. In *Perugia* in *Umbria stinchetti*, a tibia-shaped cookie is eaten. In Venice, *fave dei morti*, red, white, or brown almond-paste cookies shaped like *fave* beans, are given to girls by their lovers. In Sicily, they enjoy *frutta dei morti*, fruit of the dead, which is shaped into seeds, beans, and nuts, from *pasta reale* (marzipan). While the real seeds, beans, and nuts are also on the menu.

Among the presents given out on these days are *pupi di cena*, sugar dolls made with molds: knights like Roland or Tancred for the boys and ballerinas, brides, and clowns for the girls. This practice is of Arab influence. The Arabs make their sugary knights for the *Mulid el Nebi*, the Prophet's Birthday.

November 11 is St. Martin's Day *(San Martino)*, an important day for winemakers (see the wine section for details). The saying goes: *Per San Martino si chuide la botte e apre il vino*, "For St. Martin's Day one closes the barrel and opens the wine." It is also the time to harvest and press the olives.

The first Sunday in November, Gino, Cirli (Carlo Albertini), and Pino (Giuseppe Guiducci) would take to the forests and fields of Pennsylvania in search of rabbit, pheasant, and quail. The second Sunday in November, they headed to Monessen, game well cooled, to celebrate the autumn hunt.

A trip between New Castle and Monessen was quite an event in those days. There were no interstates and no turnpikes. My grandfather never learned to drive. In fact, we had a hard time getting him into a car at all. He only agreed when it was absolutely necessary, like going to Pittsburgh for grapes to make wine and going to New Castle. (Nonno did not like the telephone either and seldom used it.) Gino had a Jewett car and would crank it up at 4:00 A.M. to arrive in Monessen at 11:30. In 1937, he bought a used 1936 Plymouth, which he bargained down from $250 to $190; he kept the car until 1947 when he finally sprang for a new Plymouth.

The road was always an adventure filled with flat tires, wrong turns, and picnic lunches. One time the Pelini family, along with our friend Annetta Chiapparri, headed for Monessen in Annetta's Grand Paige. After a flat tire and a lot of tension, they ended up in Donora. Our journey north was also an adventure. My mother, riding in a two-car caravan with Tom and Elvira Cherubini Celli and my grandparents in one car and Arturo Moncini driving Alfredo and Amabile Sodi and their daughter Rena in his Ford coupe (yes, four people in a one-seat car), ended up near Washington, Pennsylvania, after having taken a wrong turn onto the newly constructed Route 19. It took them eight hours to get to New Castle. Today we make the journey in less than two hours, but we do not make it as often.

One can imagine how many times during those journeys the favorite Italian sayings of *"per bacco," "mannaggia cane," "accidenti," "porca miseria,"* and *"figure"* were used. These sayings' original meanings are lost in time, but they are the same as the American expressions "you're kidding," "gosh darn," "damn," "can you figure it," etc.

We were Americanized into Thanksgiving, but November also saw the beginning of Christmas preparations in our home. The first item to be made was the fruitcake. This required a trip to Pittsburgh to buy candied fruit at Donahue's on Fifth Avenue. The Friday after Thanksgiving, we walked down to the bus station and took the early bus. We shopped all day, saw a movie that evening, and took the last bus home. We would come home weary from shopping and carrying pounds of candied cherries, pineapples, mixed fruit, and the finest unshelled nuts money could buy. How many nights we spent cutting the fruit and chopping the nuts I do not remember, but the warm kitchen table filled with shells and chopped nuts, is etched into my memory.

December
(Dicembre)
We had plenty of birthdays in December and these were augmented by night after night of Christmas baking. Nonna had a handmade *brigidini* iron with her initials pressed into the center. It was long-handled so one did not have to stand too close to the open flame, and as each spoon of batter was placed on the hot iron, it would sizzle. You had to judge the cooking time just right, turning the iron so both sides browned evenly. Soon mounds of delicious anise-flavored wafers topped the kitchen table: soft at first, they hardened as each day passed, tasting more delicious with age. They were good in coffee, dipped in red wine, or, a favorite of the children, in milk.

Although we shopped at the Italian food store year-round, the Christmas trip was special. The very smells that offended other nationalities still fill me with joy. Barrels of olives fermenting in tangy juices lined one wall: green olives, wrinkled black olives, and shiny, plump black olives. Our shopping list included cod (*baccalà*), *panforte, amaretti,* sweet tobacco for Nonno's pipe, and tightly wrapped *DiNobile* cigars that looked like little twigs and smelled of strong tobacco. (Recently, as I was checking out at an Italian store, I picked one up and could not put it down. I paid for it and took it home.)

As long as Nonno was alive, we did not have to buy *prosciutto.* A fresh one was taken from its peg in the wine cellar and cut for Christmas. The same was true of sausage and wine. Our wine cellar was bursting with bottles, some from the first batch of wine Nonno made in America. In fact, I never really learned to buy good wine until I was an adult and Nonno was gone.

Although December is dominated by Christmas, there are other days of celebration as the four weeks before Christmas are part of Advent. Where Lent is a time of fasting and penitence, Advent is a period of renewal. It marks the beginning of the ecclesiastical year.

But joyous and glorious Christmas *(Natale),* the festive day in midwinter, is the focal point of December. Christmas Eve *(La Vigilia)* has its own special foods.

Our Tuscan meal began with chickpea soup and wide egg noodles, followed by boiled cod in oil and chickpeas, and cod and onions in tomato sauce or cod with garlic and sage in tomato sauce. The salad was always lettuce and celery. How excited I would get when the cod was put to soak in the cellar. The anticipation would last all week.

In our Tuscan and Tuscan-American homes we never followed any set number of dishes for Christmas Eve: not seven for the seven deadly sins (among others), not nine for the trinity said three times, not thirteen for Jesus Christ and his apostles. Those traditions were more Southern Italian than they were northern. We definitely had pasta. Ours, be it here in America or in *Quarata* and *Arezzo,* was *pappadelle,* the wide pasta specific to the *Arezzo* area. And we ate it in a hearty *ceci* soup. Yes, a soup. In *Palermo,* it is sardines, *pasta con le sarde,* pasta with sardines. Many regions throughout Italy began their pasta with a base of the Roman-inspired *aglio e olio,* pastas with oil and garlic. The ingredients added to the *aglio e olio* set it apart. In Rome, it was anchovies, *alle alici*. In *Molise*, it was bread crumbs, walnuts, and raisins called *pasta con la mollic*, pasta. In nearby *Abruzzo* it is tomatoes, anchovies, pine nuts, and raisins, definitely of Arab influence. While an Austro-Hungarian influence is felt in the *Veneto* where *lasagne da fornel* is garnished with melted butter, crushed walnuts, poppy seeds, raisins, grated apple, bits of fig, and sugar. The Piedmont has a similar *lasagne della Vigilia* flavored with butter, anchovies, garlic, Parmesan, and black pepper. There are hundreds more.

That is just the pasta course or courses. Then the fish: eel cooked in a dozen ways; smelts, mostly fried, and on most tables regardless of the region; *calamari* stuffed, or ringed and fried. Then the king of fishes: *baccalá*. There are as many ways to prepare *baccalá* as there are provinces and towns in Italy. The Neapolitan *baccalá* stew is filled with potatoes, celery, onions, garlic, and chunks of *baccalá* swimming in a tomato broth. In *La Spezia* in *Liguria* they make a *baccalá fritter* that includes cabbage, from their Austro-Hungarian heritage. In *Abruzzo*, Christmas *baccalá* is cooked with celery, pine nuts, golden raisins, black olives, and tomatoes, a dish screaming of Arab influence. Ours is smothered in onions or spiced with sage, both in tomato sauce. If there is one meal where the region can be identified by the food on the table, Christmas Eve dinner is that meal.

The next day was a feast to lay low even the heartiest of appetites: liver canapés covered with *prosciutto, cappelletti* in broth, *macaroni* in meat sauce, beef in red sauce with celery, roast capon with oven potatoes, and a leafy green salad. We ate for hours, then paused before dessert and coffee. The desserts would tempt the gods themselves. Nonna's wonderful dark fruitcake, over which we had labored since Thanksgiving, was joined by *panforte* from *Siena, torrone* from *Cremona,* and *amaretti,* a bittersweet almond cookie that some think was created in the seventeenth century. We had white wine to begin the meal, red wine with the *macaroni,* white wine with the capon, and in the end *vin santo,* holy wine, with the sweets. When it appeared as if the meal was over out would come a medley of fresh fruit, nuts and cheeses accompanied by more *vin santo, espresso,* and *sambuca*. Both Nonno and Gino always said, "If the serving trays were empty at the end of the meal, the cook did not prepare enough food."

My mother never received gifts at Christmas, but at Epiphany, twelve days later. Instead, at Christmas it was traditional to kick the Yule log for the candy and fruit inside in hopes of good gifts on Epiphany.

Epilogue
(Epilogo)

Thus the time passed—year after year of growing up in an Italian family. Today so many of these wonderful traditions are gone. Nonno and Nonna are dead. So are my father and brother. When they were alive, my mind did not question, but there are so many things I want to ask them now. My mother died in 2006. During the last years of her life, as she was slowly succumbing to Alzheimer's, I took care of her. It was a long and difficult struggle. We were all that remained of Nonno and Nonna's family. When holidays would come, I did not prepare the huge meals my nonna served. At least I did not prepare them in a single day. I spread them out over the holiday week. We had the four or five Christmas Eve meals over four or five days. Each time she tasted a dish, my mother's eyes would brighten in recognition. It was worth the effort. Now I am alone. I am the last. I was beginning to let the foods of Tuscany fall from my hands.

Because of the first edition of this cookbook, my nephew Michael has taken on the mantle. As noted before, he makes the broth. He makes the *cappelletti*. He makes our signature sauce. He fries up the *gran fritto misto*. He fries up the *fiocci*. Yet as wonderful as that is, he and his siblings do not enjoy much of what we ate and loved. No *fegatelli*. No lamb at Easter. No *acciugata*. No *fritelli* for St. Joseph's Day.

In 2009, I returned alone to *Quarata*. I was back in the bosom of my traditional family. Each day I watched as meal after meal of familiar dishes appeared on my cousin's table. If I mentioned it, the next day it was on the table: *fegatelli, cotta tre volte, gnocchi, crostini neri*, oh, the joy of it all. For a month, I was reenergized, and on returning to America, I began to cook our Tuscan foods again.

Cassandra Vivian, Monessen, Pennsylvania, 1993,
and Mount Pleasant, Pennsylvania, 2010

Shopping *all'Italiana*
Far la Spesa all'Italiana

It was not easy for immigrants to find the foods and equipment needed to maintain their traditions. A few immigrants carried precious seeds or prized kitchen implements to help with their gardening and cooking as they traveled across the Atlantic, for to try to find items on the American market that suited an Italian household was next to impossible in the early part of the twentieth century. As the skills of the Italian communities grew, Italian carpenters came to the rescue. They made pastry boards, rolling pins, wooden spoons, and molds. Metal workers forged cookie irons and spits. Even Italian crockery became available in America. Eventually some Italian men became peddlers, visiting neighborhoods by horse-drawn cart loaded down with Italian goods. They sold twenty-pound boxes of spaghetti, Italian tuna, *toma* cheese *(Aosta)*, anchovies in salt, and cookie and cake items at Christmas. It was just like home.

These merchants did a lot to homogenize Italian cooking. Neapolitan *mozzarella* was sold beside Veneto *Asiago* (when they could find it). As time passed, the traveling merchants became stationary and established stores in Italian neighborhoods. The neighborhood determined the products on the shelves and in the coolers. In southern Italian neighborhoods, they sold olive oils and mozzarellas. In the Northern Italian neighborhoods, it was butter, chestnuts, and a type of Parmesan cheese. In our hometown of Monessen, Auselivi's, Coccari's, and Dreucci's catered to northerners, while Imbrogno's and Severino's sold items for southerners. There was also DeSua's, Moio's, and DeNunzio's. Eventually one store moved downtown to the main street and attempted to cater to everyone: the Italian Food Store run by our friends, the Colangelo's. In New Castle, it was Graziani's, Frediani's, Saccomani's (in Mahoningtown), and Troggio's.

When our families became more adventuresome they journeyed to the Strip District in Pittsburgh to do some of their shopping. In the Strip, there were stores that maintained they could provide any Italian product, and they did.

In the 1990s, neighborhood Italian food stores were almost a thing of the past, but the demand for Italian specialties in western Pennsylvania was so strong that it was not hard to find the special ingredients needed for the recipes in this book. In addition, ethnic foods have become the province of the gourmet, so many of the items can be found in gourmet shops. Over the years, the quest for unusual ingredients had become a joke in our family. Where once butchers threw away meat organs and good soup bones, and would gladly give them to us for nothing just to get rid of them, today these same items are considered delicacies and command high prices in food stores.

The biggest boon to Italian shopping is the Internet. Once I heard the complaint, "I live in Mississippi and cannot find good Italian bread, let alone *prosciutto*." That lament is over. No matter where you live in America, you can order items from stores in New York, Chicago, and almost every town in Italy. But you have to be ready to pay high prices for your treasures.

We have also found that products have changed since 1993. Some canned tomatoes now contain peels, catering to other ethnic cooks. Purees have begun to dominate canned tomatoes. **Purees are too strong for the recipes in this book.** (This warning will be repeated *ad nauseum* in the pages that follow.) In other cans, tomatoes are prepared with herbs and spices. No tomatoes with basil and garlic please. If we want garlic, we add fresh. So we no longer buy the brands we once did. That alters everything. We have left notes in the text to guide you along the way.

Anchovies

The anchovy, *acciuga,* when under oil or salt, or *alici,* when fresh, is a small silver fish used in breads, pizzas, canapés and even some pasta sauces. Anchovies are available filleted in oil in two-ounce tins or salt packed. I have seldom seen fresh anchovies in the U.S. The salt packed is the best buy, for the anchovy is whole and retains its taste.

To use a salt-packed anchovy, soak it in a bath of 4 parts water to 1 part vinegar for a few minutes. Wash under running water, place on a cutting board, split lengthwise, and remove the spine.

To store, wrap entire opened tin in plastic and keep in a cool, dark place (cellar, refrigerator). Do not disturb the individual salt-packed anchovies until you are ready to use them. If anchovies are not whole when can is first opened, return the tin for the salt has consumed them.

Bread Crumbs

Never buy bread crumbs when they are so easy to make yourself, especially if you have a grinder or food processor. Keep them unseasoned to use in different dishes. If you insist on buying bread crumbs, buy them unseasoned (I must admit I sometimes buy them).

Capers

The caper, *cappero,* found in ancient Roman recipe books but originating in the Arab world, grows wild in Italy. In America, capers are readily available packed in brine in 3.5-ounce jars found in most supermarkets.

Although a caper, which is really a seed, must retain the tangy taste of the brine, wash it generously under running water and squeeze gently before using. In Nonna's day, one could buy capers under salt, but, until recently, we had not seen them on the market for a long time (we recently found them online and ordered some).

Cheese

Formaggio, the Italian word for cheese, comes from the word *forma,* referring to the wicker baskets in which ancient cheeses were stored to dry. Cheese is so valued in Italy that in addition to festivals celebrating the cheeses, laws exist to ensure the quality of at least thirteen specific types of cheese, including *Asiago (Veneto), Fontina (Aosta), Gorgonzola* (Lombardy), *Parmigiano Reggiano (Emilia-Romagna),* and *pecorino* (Most regions of Italy have their own *pecorino.* Each one has a distinct taste).

The process of making cheese is an Italian institution dating back to the Etruscan era, before ancient Rome. There are more than five hundred varieties of cheese in Italy, and most small villages have their own specialty, made from the milk of carefully tended goats, sheep, cows, and even buffalos. The cheese from each herd has its own distinct taste, depending on the food eaten by the animal that produces the milk.

Cheeses should be stored in a cool place, or in the refrigerator. Never store different types of cheeses in the same container, but always cover each cheese separately in foil or plastic. We eat cheeses from all over Italy. Here are the ones we use most often.

Asiago

Produced at the foot of the Alps in the *Veneto* in the village of the same name, *Asiago* is a straw-yellow cows' milk cheese, which comes in several varieties. The *mezza-nello*, or *Asiago di taglio*, has a short aging period, remains sweet, and is good eating, especially for dessert. The *Asiago vecchio*, aged twelve months, is for eating too, but has a tangy taste. The *Asiago stravecchio*, aged eighteen months, is used as a grating cheese.

Fontina

An eating cheese favored in fondue, *Fontina* dates to ancient Rome and is produced in the *Val d'Aosta* from purebred *Valdostana* cows. It is made in summer when the cows are grazing high on the mountain. Aged four months to a straw-yellow color, the longer it ages, the sharper the taste.

Gorgonzola

Gorgonzola, or *stracchino Gorgonzola*, is a cows' milk cheese made since the Middle Ages in the town of *Gorgonzola*, Lombardy. It is soft, creamy, and flecked with specks of green or blue mold, called *dolce*, when sweet and young, and *piccante*, when sharp and aged.

Gorgonzola con Mascarpone

This delicate and delicious layered torte of *Gorgonzola* and *mascarpone* cheeses is a true masterpiece. Unfortunately, it spoils quickly and must be eaten the day you buy it to achieve the ultimate taste. We never refrigerate it. It is hard to find in the U.S. and mail order brands have never measured up for us.

Mascarpone

A very rich triple cream cheese made in twenty-four-hours, which must be consumed in a relatively equal time or it will go bad, *mascarpone* is used in place of whipping cream in Italy and is an ingredient in many tortes. It originates near *Lodi* in Lombardy.

Mozzarella

Originally a water buffalo cheese from southern Italy, today, with demand all over the world, it is made from cows' milk. The rare *mozzarella di bufala,* made from buffalo milk is a pungent, tangy delicacy never wasted on a pizza but served as an appetizer. *Ricotta* from *mozzarella di bufala* is another delicacy.

Parmigiano

Boccaccio wrote that paradise was a mound of grated Parmesan cheese surmounted by pasta makers. Today Parmesan, the king of cheeses in Italy, maintains its high appeal and is recognized worldwide for its delicate color and flavor. Parmesan was originally made during winter (November 15 to April 15) in only five villages around *Parma,* Italy, in the *Emilia-Romagna.* Stamped with the name *Parmigiano Reggiano,* it is so valued that it has been stored in bank vaults and traded like gold.

Made mostly by individual farmers, six hundred quarts of milk are needed to produce one seventy-five-pound wheel of *Reggiano.* The milk is left out overnight and the cream is skimmed and stored. The skimmed milk begins the process. Blended with whole milk, the two are heated and allowed to coagulate. The curd is stored in cheesecloth and the whey (watery part of milk) given to animals that in turn produce milk for cheese. When the whey is drained, the fresh cheese is lowered into *fascera,* wooden forms, that press it into shape. Once formed, the cheese is submerged in brine for twenty-five days, then bathed in the rays of the sun and stored for two to three years.

Parmesan is married to Italian sauces; however, eaten as is, it is a delicacy in its own right. Never buy Parmesan (or any cheese) already grated, unless you watch the cheeseman grate it; take it home and use it within the next day or two. You can get good Parmesan, imported or domestic, at Italian food stores and gourmet shops. To us, if it is not *Regganio* it is not on our table.

Pecorino Romano, Pecorino Tuscano, or Caciotta

A specialty of Tuscany, probably dating to their illustrious ancestors, the Etruscans, *pecorino* is the oldest known cheese in Italy. As its name implies, it is made from sheep's milk. Made in forty-pound wheels for commercial purposes or in six-inch wheels by local farmers, it can be eaten fresh but is most often aged for grating. The most famous *pecorino* in America is *Pecorino Romano,* directly from Rome. As noted, every region has its own *pecorino* and each has its own taste. Once a year, on the first Sunday of September in the Renaissance village of *Pienza,* near *Siena* in Tuscany, there is a fair devoted to *pecorino.*

Provolone

Provolone is a cheese that has migrated. Originally from southern Italy, the most famous brands are now made in the Po Valley in the Lombard and *Veneto*. It is dipped alternately in boiling water, then cold water, and left to age for two to five months. There are three varieties: *provolone dolce,* sweet, aged three months; *provolone piccante,* sharp, aged longer; and *provolone affumicato,* smoked, aged two months. It is an eating cheese. Great for grilling, frying, or melted in sandwiches, omelets, and pizzas.

Ricotta

Ricotta is not cottage cheese and the latter should never be used as a substitute. Rather, it is a delicate, highly perishable, creamy white cheese made from the whey of the second curd when making other cheeses like *Parmesan*. It is sold fresh on the market and not permitted to age; therefore, it does not store well. The earliest known *ricotta* comes from Sicily and may have an Arab origin.

There are hundreds of other delicious cheeses in Italy. These are the ones used most often in this book.

Chestnuts

Chestnuts, *castagne*, ripen in the fall. When Gino Pelini was in Italy, they were the staple of the family diet. In addition to the traditionally roasted chestnut, necessity created a host of uses, including finely ground flour used in cakes, *polentas*, pastas, and puddings.

Chestnut flour is available on a hit-or-miss basis in gourmet shops and Italian food stores and is definitely available online.

Cured Meats

The wonderful cured meats of Italy are not only sold, but also produced in more countries of the world than any other type of cured meat. The best buy is always the original, for the animal's environment cannot be reproduced. The water and feed an animal ingests and the air it breathes are also ingredients that create the ultimate flavor.

Most ethnic food stores have a variety of cured meats, both imported and domestic, and making a selection is not easy. Since Italy is undergoing a health awareness, we can expect a "lite" (less fat, fewer calories) variety of cured meats to reach the market. Some cooks say you should cut the fat from the *prosciutto* and other cured meats. DON'T DO IT. Cut the fat in your diet in other ways. Stay away from fast foods. Good food needs fat. It should have fat on the outside, like *prosciutto* and roasts, and on the inside for marbling like a good steak.

Importing some cured meats from Italy into the United States is forbidden as of 2011, so don't try to pack any away in your suitcase.

Bresaola

Originating in the Lombardy district of Italy, this is a salted, air-dried beef, which is served like *prosciutto*.

Mortadella

A specialty of *Bologna (Emilia), mortadella* is a big, fat sausage that has been ground; mixed with pieces of fat, pistachios, or olives; stuffed into a bladder; and boiled. The imported brands can be as large as sixteen to eighteen inches in circumference, enough to feed the appetite of a king. *Mortadella* should be sliced as thin as possible and never stored in a refrigerator where it loses its delicate taste. Nonno stored our *mortadella* in the wine cellar. It was wrapped in cloth and hung on a hook from the rafters. Today I buy only what I will use at a sitting even though I have to drive twenty miles to get good imported *mortadella*. *Mortadella* is the father of American bologna (baloney).

Pancetta

Pancetta is a cured meat like *prosciutto,* but where the *prosciutto* is the hindquarter of the pig, the *pancetta* is the belly, or the bacon.

Once *pancetta* was difficult to find, but it is now prepared like a small slab of bacon, neatly packaged, and laid beside the bacon in most supermarkets (in Italian stores *pancetta* is rolled, complete with rind). *Pancetta* lasts a long time and only a small quantity is needed for cooking, so it is best to buy it in small pieces of a half-pound or less. It is easily stored in the refrigerator wrapped in foil or plastic. In a pinch, you can use fat back or fat belly. I have never heard of anyone slicing it like *prosciutto* and eating it that way. It has too much fat. It is mostly used in cooking, cut into chunks.

Prosciutto

The king of Italian cured meats, *prosciutto* is the salted and aged hindquarter of a pig under two years old. It is not smoked; however, one variety called *speck* is a cured, smoked ham. The most famous *prosciutto* in Italy is *prosciutto di Parma,* originating in the same area as *Parmesan* cheese. The pigs are fattened on the whey of the famous cheese and produce a sweeter meat. It is this *prosciutto* that is best served as an appetizer with melons or figs.

Prosciutto di Parma is one of three brands of *prosciutto* that have been given the prized DOC rating in Italy. The other two are *prosciutto San Daniele* and *prosciutto Veneto*. But almost every village in Italy has its own variety of homemade *prosciutto*, and they are all delicious.

Today you can buy *prosciutto* deboned (it helps with the aging but affects the taste) and by the pound. First, it should be sliced paper thin but not chipped. Second, *prosciutto* slices should never be stacked, but laid one beside the other and covered with tissue paper before placing the next layer. Third, if possible, it should not be stored in a refrigerator, but in a cool place. Never wrap in plastic.

As a child, I remember Nonno hanging his homemade *prosciuttos* from the rafters in the wine cellar. Once cut, it was wrapped in cloth and hung beside the uncut *prosciuttos*.

Salami

The true name of this excellent cold cut is *insaccato*, meaning "things put in a sack," and the varieties are endless. The thickness or thinness of the grind, the amount of salt, the type of pork, and the individual spices vary from village to village and region to region.

Probably the most famous *salame* in America is Genoa *salame*, but to the Italian connoisseur, *salame Fabriano* is the best from central Italy, and *salame Felino,* from the same area as *prosciutto di Parma*, is considered the best, period.

There are excellent *salami* found in small mountain villages where the inhabitants have never tried to enter the commercial market. A Tuscan variety, which my family has made for centuries, is called *finocchino* and is flavored with fennel.

Almost any food store in the United States sells some type of *salami*, but to find an interesting selection, one must go to an Italian food store. There the array is overwhelming: imported or domestic, hard or soft, lean, cooked, or aged. You can buy *salami* freshly sliced, in a piece or whole.

Flour

American white flour is of a better quality than Italian flour.

When baking breads, use all-purpose flour. Always sift flour for pastry but never for bread.

Corn flour, *farina di grano turco* (Indian corn), is ground finer than cornmeal but is even better when stone-ground, thus rough. Cornmeal, again stone-ground, is grittier. Buy regular, not degerminated.

Garlic

Garlic, a member of the lily family, is synonymous with Italian food. It is also good for you, helpful for a bevy of ills. In some cultures people wear a piece of garlic on their person, not only for its curative powers, but to keep away evil spirits.

Although always popular in ethnic America, the soldiers returning from Europe after World War II helped make garlic an acceptable ingredient in American foods.

If you grow your own garlic, store it in a brown paper bag in a cool room. If you buy garlic, look for small, firm bulbs and buy small quantities. Although it is picturesque to see garlic bunches hanging in kitchens, for a longer life and fresher flavor, store the garlic in the refrigerator.

In our kitchen, we peel cloves of garlic to chop or fry, but do not peel garlic when it is pounded or crushed. Garlic salt or powder will not do when making good Italian dishes.

Herbs and Spices

Trade routes that linked Asia and Africa to Europe via the Middle East were a lifeline of exotic treasures during the Middle Ages. Spices, important to that trade, dominated the economy of the medieval world. And the Venetian merchants who brought the spices into Europe, dominated the European market. Once culinary experts defined herbs (mint, basil, parsley, sage, rosemary, thyme) and spices (cinnamon, cloves, ginger, fennel, pepper) differently, but today all aromatic plants and seeds used to add flavor to a dish are called spices.

When spices arrived in Italy, the Italian chefs were quick to incorporate them into recipes. One can usually tell a recipe that originated at that time, like *panforte,* for the ingredients include a number of different spices.

In addition to salt and pepper, the four main spices in Tuscan cooking are basil, parsley, rosemary, and sage. Secondary are nutmeg, thyme, and fennel.

The modern cook is lucky for not only do supermarkets offer spices and herbs in neat little boxes and jars, but fresh spices are available in the produce departments of most super markets. For the recipes in this book, use fresh spices whenever possible.

Spices lose their fragrance so it is best to buy small quantities and once a year clean out your spice cupboard.

Anise Seeds

Blooming in July and August, the licorice-flavored anise seed *(semi di anice)* is not only flavorful in cooking, but is good for digestion. In Tuscan cooking, it is used to flavor sweets eaten at the end of the meal.

Basil

There are a variety of basil *(basilico)* plants on the market: lemon-scented, tall, with purple leaves, full-leafed, and the most common, sweet basil. Served in a salad with fresh homegrown tomatoes steeped in oil, basil is ambrosia. It is also good for you. Basil clears congestion and cures headaches.

Fennel

Fennel *(finocchio)* has a licorice taste and comes into season in the fall. Florentine fennel, a vegetable that looks like celery, is sold fresh on the stalk. The seeds of common fennel, another variety of the plant, are dried and used as a seasoning. Fennel is the signature spice of the Arezzo region of Tuscany.

In our kitchen, we eat Florentine fennel raw or cooked in a stew and use common fennel as a flavoring for chicken, duck, and pork.

Oregano

Until pizza took over the world, oregano was seldom used in an American kitchen, or in ours. Oregano is a southern Italian spice. In addition to pizza, it is also good on roast chicken.

Parsley

Always use the flat-leafed Italian parsley *(prezzemolo)* for the recipes in this book. Save the curly parsley to decorate the dinner plate as a garnish. Never, never, never use dried parsley—you might as well add a piece of paper to your recipe.

Rosemary

Called dew of the sea, rosemary *(rosmarino)* is recommended for failing eyesight and headaches. It is also delicious.

Dried rosemary loses its fragrance after a year and must be thrown away. There is nothing as good as fresh rosemary, but it is difficult to grow. We tend to our plants carefully but have lost them repeatedly. We use rosemary to flavor beef, lamb, and pork and our Christmas Eve soup.

Saffron
Saffron *(zafferano)* is the stigma of the crocus flower and is mostly imported from the Middle East. It is extremely expensive and difficult to find and substitutes are often used. You can buy saffron in small quantities in pharmacies and gourmet shops.

Sage
The Italian word *salvia* (sage) means to heal. True to its name, sage is good for everything from bad breath to bruises.

Fresh sage is best for Italian cooking. Sage thrives well in a garden, and we have always had a plant growing in the backyard. Whenever we want to make a dish with sage, we pick it fresh from the plant. We use it in sauces and to flavor poultry.

Thyme
Thyme *(timo)* is often used in the bath to give courage. It is excellent to flavor meats and the best thyme recipe in this book is the stew of veal and peas (see index).

Mushrooms
The most flavorful mushrooms in Italy are the *porcini,* named after the pig *(porco)*, and found growing wild in the autumn fields. They have a musty taste and are very expensive in the United States. A few *porcini* added to the readily available white mushrooms of Pennsylvania will add good flavor to a dish at one-fourth of the cost. Once only available in gourmet shops and Italian food stores, *porcini* are now available in most supermarkets.

Oil
We use two types of oil in our kitchen: corn and olive, the first for most cooked dishes, the latter for salads and specialties.

The best Italian olive oil in Italy is the rich, fruity Tuscany oil. The variety of olive oils available on the American market is growing. Our old staple tends to be less pungent and is an accustomed ingredient in foods. Extra-virgin olive oil is from the first pressing of the olive (which normally goes through three pressings) and is usually darker in color and has a strong flavor. The type of oil you use has to be determined by your palate.

Growing up we did not have access to extra-virgin olive oil, so the recipes in this book do not use it. If you use it for these dishes, it will alter the taste considerably. We never fry in olive oil. We use a vegetable oil.

Pasta

Although most European cultures have some type of pasta, the word and the food are synonymous with Italian cooking. There seems to be an infinite number of pastas, with new cuts being added to the American food scene yearly.

Traditional cuts and shapes of pasta have a distinct purpose and we have arranged them on the following pages according to their use. If a pasta ends in *loni* or *elle,* it denotes a large size, *ette* or *etti* denotes a small size. The basic cuts of homemade Tuscan pasta are: *pappardelle, cappelletti, ravioli,* and *gnocchi.*

Pastas for Soup
Pastina

Acini di pepe
"peppercorns"

Chioccioline
"small shells"

Anellini
"little rings," with or
without grooves

Ditallini
"little thimbles,"
small and tubular

Orzo
"barley," shaped like
barley or rice

Quadrucci
"little squares"

Stelline
"stars"

Tripolini or farfalline
"small bows," egg bows

Long Pasta
Spaghetti is "a length of cord or
string," and the various names
for the pasta are determined
primarily by the thickness.

Bucantini (Roman)
Perciatelli (Neopolitan)
long, thin tubular pasta with a
hole, "buco," in the middle

Linguine (small tongues) or
Bavette, flattened spaghetti
¼-inch wide

Fusilli
"twists," twisted spaghetti

Gemelli
"twins," two strands
twisted together

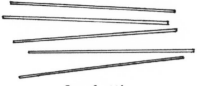

Spaghetti
"cords," thin, round,
long pasta

Spaghettini
"little cords,"
a thinner *spaghetti*

Tagliolini
ultrathin, long, flat noodles
sometimes used in broth

Vermicelli
"little worms," thin, round,
long pasta

Long Flat Pasta

Fettuccine, Tagliatelle
"small ribbons,"
⅛-inch wide

Mafaldi, Pappardelle
1-inch wide and fluted
on the edge

Lasagna
"pots," a broad, thin noodle
usually 2 to 3 inches wide

Short Pasta

Cavatelli
dumplings made of semolina
and flour from Naples
and the Abruzzo

Conchigliette
"tiny shells"

Gnocchi
potato, *ricotta*,
or semolina dumpling

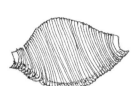

Conchiglie or *chiocciole*
"shells"

Penne
"quills," cut on the
slant and ridged

Diti
"fingers," short, fat,
tubular pasta

Pennette
"small quills"

Farafalle
"bows" or "butterflies"

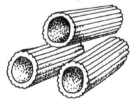

Rigatoni
thick tubular pasta
2 inches long

Tontiglioni
"springs," a large
twisted pasta

Rotelle
"wheels," a circular
pasta wheel

Ziti
similar to *penne*
but cut straight

Stuffed Pasta

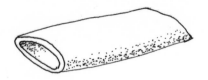

Cannelloni
"large reeds" or "canes"
same as *Manicotti*, "small
muffs," 3- to 4-inch long
tubular pasta for stuffing

Capelletti (Tortellini)
"small hats," or "belly
buttons" like a *ravioli*

Ravioli
2-inch squares of dough
filling with stuffing

Pine Nuts

I am adding pine nuts to this list because I must give you a
warning. Some pine nuts imported from China leave a bitter taste
in your mouth. It lasts for as long as ten days. Every time you eat
during those days, you end up with that same bitter taste. Therefore, it is best to avoid buying pine nuts from China.

Rice

Never, never, never prepare the dishes in this book with minute rice. We have always used American long-grained rice. I have
been unsuccessful with imported *arborio*, a flat, fat rice. *Arborio*
rice is found in Italian food stores and specialty shops. Read the
instructions for cooking *arborio* rice carefully, for it can become a
glutinous mass if cooked improperly.

Salt

Many ingredients in Italian cooking are already salty, so use salt sparingly, and not at all when using anchovies, salted cod, and cured meats like *prosciutto* and *salami*.

Most of our stews and sauces call for *soffritto,* which contains enough flavor to carry the sauce, so salt need not be added. The best way to decide if you want to add salt is to taste before adding. In our home, we have a heavy hand and measurements in this book reflect our preference. If anyone picks up a saltshaker at our dinner table, the cook has failed to prepare the dish properly.

Sausage

The varieties of sausage from central and southern Europe are amazing. They come in all shapes and flavors. From blood sausage made with, of course, blood, to *cotechino,* often made with pork rinds, sausage is a staple of Italy and has become an American institution. There is sweet sausage, garlic sausage, hot sausage, dried sausage, and even turkey and chicken sausage, where a lighter meat replaces the traditional pork.

We have always made our own sausage, and we prefer garlic sausage. In addition to eating it fresh, we enjoy tasty dried sausage, which we cut and eat like *salami*.

For more information on sausage, consult the chapter on pork.

Tomato

The tomato is the most noble of Italian vegetables and is amply represented throughout this book, especially in the preparation of sauces. Take heed! No tomato sauce in this book should look bright red—it should be deep red, leaning toward brown. If red, the sauce has not simmered long enough. A sauce with tomatoes must simmer until the oil separates from the tomato and rises to the top. Then the sauce is done.

When buying fresh tomatoes leave the hothouse varieties for someone else. Until scientists solve the problem of tasteless winter tomatoes, in the winter use good canned tomatoes.

In summer, when in season, select firm tomatoes with deep color for salads and fresh tomato recipes, but for stews and sauces look for soft, very ripe tomatoes. Never select a tomato with broken skin. To age tomatoes place them on a windowsill for several days.

We plant a garden and use every tomato the garden gives us. All summer long, in addition to eating fresh tomatoes, we are freezing them for the winter. When the last green tomatoes are on the vine and a frost is coming, we pick all of them, wrap each one in newspaper and store them in the cellar. They will slowly ripen and we have fresh tomatoes as late as November.

We plant extra tomato vines expressly to freeze them for winter. We use tomatoes in soups, stews, and sauces. To freeze a tomato is easy. Wash each tomato carefully and allow it to dry. Place on a cookie sheet and freeze. When frozen, remove from cookie sheet and place in a plastic bag. Store in freezer.

When ready to use, remove from freezer. If you want to remove the skin, place the frozen tomato under the water faucet and the skin will peel off easily.

This bears repeating: There have been quite a few changes in food products since we wrote this book! One of the most important to the recipes here is canned tomatoes. Too many have heavy puree. The recipes in this book work better without heavy puree. Buy crushed tomatoes without puree. If need be, buy whole tomatoes and run them through a food processor.

Vinegar

Ordinary wine vinegar will do for the recipes in this book, but we also use balsamic vinegar for a delicate, mellow taste. *Aceto balsamico,* traceable to medieval times, is made from fresh grape juice boiled into a concentrate in a copper kettle and aged in casks of various woods for twelve years. As the liquid evaporates, the vinegar is transferred to various casks of chestnut, cherry, or juniper wood. Each cask is smaller and the smallest contains the best vinegar.

Balsamic vinegar is considered one of the treasures of Italy, and, like wine, its production is controlled by the government to ensure its high quality. It was once only available on the American market in Italian food stores and gourmet shops, but you can now find it just about anywhere.

Shopping Online

Italian specialty stores were problematic in certain areas of the country where Italians did not settle. That is no longer a problem. You can shop online for food items from all parts of the United States and Italy as well. Everything is available from *cannoli* and *prosciutto* to special cheeses, *ravioli* with a variety of stuffings, and more. Simply place the name of the item in your browser's search engine and hit return for a world of good eating.

Our Italian Kitchen
La Nostra Cucina Italiana

One hundred years of good cooking in our family kitchens has taught us that there are four basic recipes that must be mastered to have a good Tuscan kitchen: a good *soffritto (battuto)*, a tasty bread stuffing, a basic soup stock, and a rich, deep red *umido*. They form the base of 80 percent of Tuscan main courses.

Although we give these warnings at the beginning of each recipe, the points are so important to the outcome of the dish that we want to stress them here. We cannot repeat enough the proper way to prepare these basic recipes. If they are right, the dish is right. If they are not, to our way of thinking, the dish is a disaster.

Battuto means something that is chopped into pieces. When it is fried in oil, it is called *soffritto*. Both are used universally as a base for soups, stuffings, and sauces. They are a combination of onion, celery, parsley, carrots, salt, pepper, garlic (sometimes), and *pancetta* (see index for basic recipe). In soup stock, then called *battuto*, the mixture is boiled with the meat. Once the broth is properly simmered, the mixture is passed through a sieve and added to the finished broth. It provides flavor, color, and texture.

As a base for stuffings and stews, *soffritto* is ground in a meat grinder and fried in oil. There are two important points here. If ground in a meat grinder, the juices add richness and moisture to the final dish. When fried, *soffritto* must simmer until it is well blended, the ingredients turning dark, and it has reduced to half its size. That is when *soffritto* is at its best. It is so flavorful no additional salt or flavoring need be added to the final recipe.

The basic bread stuffing begins with a good *soffritto*. We use it as a stuffing for meats, poultry, and vegetables. It must be moist. If dry to the hand, it will be dry to the palate. It can be made with bread crumbs or bread cubes, and some additional spices may be added. But a good basic stuffing needs no help. It is delicious with just the *soffritto*, bread, eggs, and soup stock (see index for stuffing recipe).

There are also a few basic "must dos" for soup: fresh ingredients, adequate simmering, and the proper use of water. Soup must simmer for three to four hours until the meat falls from the bone. Never, never add additional water once the soup begins to boil and always cover the pot with a lid to stop the liquid from turning into steam. Finally, as mentioned previously, pass the vegetables through a sieve into the broth.

Of all the sauces in Italian cooking, tomato sauce dominates the cuisine. When making a stew of meat or vegetables, a pizza topping, or a pasta sauce, the main point to remember about Tuscan sauces is that the sauce must simmer until the tomatoes turn a rich red-brown and separate from the oil. If they are the same color as when they first hit the skillet, the sauce has not simmered long enough and the dish will have a heavy tomato taste. When tomato sauce is properly cooked, the oil should float on top of a thick brown-red sauce where it can easily be skimmed.

The most difficult part of assembling these recipes was not the organization or the testing; it was the perplexing question of how to turn each recipe into an entity unto itself. In Nonna's kitchen, everything was integrated. If it was bread day, she used a bit of the dough to make a pizza, a *schiacciata,* or fried dough. If it was soup day, she added a potato and made potato salad and used the meat from the soup for several different dishes of the *bolitto misto.* When making pasta dough, she made a large quantity of *cappelletti*, a smaller quantity of *ravioli*, and cut extra pasta into noodles for sauce or for soup.

Quantity also became an issue. "*Cappelletti* for four?" We never heard of it. Nonna made *cappelletti* by the hundreds and used them immediately. My mother also made hundreds, but she froze them. In Nonna's day, the amount of each ingredient in a dish was usually a little of this, a handful of that. Not so when preparing a cookbook.

Authenticity, too, reared its ugly head. Some of the recipes in this book, sin of sins, are not Tuscan. Where and how Nonna and Sandrina first made them, we do not always know. But it is obvious that the melting pot of America had its hand in the stew, so to speak. With so many Italian families from so many different Italian provinces living together in the same small town, a little recipe sharing was bound to go on. However, recipes that were sacred, part of provincial pride and heritage, were never altered.

The most gratifying part of creating this book was that our kitchen became a Tuscan kitchen once again. And it is going to stay that way.

Kitchen Aids

Cheese grater. Any variety of cheese grater will do as long as one remembers to grate the cheese fresh each time you use it. Pregrated cheese dries out and loses its flavor. When large quantities are needed, you can buy the whole cheese in an Italian store and watch as they grate it. Take it home and use it immediately. If you absolutely must use it the next day, store it in a dry, cool place. That goes for whole cheese too. Some cheeses can be placed in the freezer.

Colander. No kitchen should be without a colander and especially a kitchen where pasta is made. For soups and sauces, you need a fine mesh colander, for pasta a thick mesh.

Garlic press. Found in the kitchen section of most department stores, this handy gadget is used exclusively for crushing garlic to obtain the juice. If a recipe calls for crushing garlic in a press there is a reason, trust us.

Meat grinder. Recipes that call for minced foods suggest a meat grinder. This is the old-fashioned type of grinder with a hand-operated handle and a variety of templates of different sizes. They are available in Italian food stores and gourmet shops. Although we have said you can use a food processor, the consistency will not be the same. The grinder grinds the food into fine pieces and releases the juices to keep the mixture moist. My niece once ate stuffing at a friend's house. She told my mother, "She puts celery in her stuffing; I saw big chunks of it," and wrinkled her nose. My mother laughed. We put celery in our stuffing, too, but it is so finely ground, it blends with the bread.

Pots and pans. In most recipes requiring a pan, you will note that the recipe calls for a black iron skillet. We have used these skillets in a variety of sizes as far back as I can remember. They are still the best for making traditional recipes. Why? They hold the heat evenly, they last forever, they move from stovetop to oven to open fire, and you can cook anything in them including cakes. I still use my mother's pans, which were probably bought about eighty years ago. Every once in a while, we have to reseason them. You should not soak cast iron in soapy water. You should not let them set to dry. In both instances, they can begin to accumulate rust. Yes, rust. I have a 14", 12", 10", 8", and 6". There are larger pans, but I have never seen a smaller one. We do not have a pot.

You may use other types of pans to prepare these recipes, and the food will taste delicious because the ingredients are of fine quality, but Elizabeth will taste the difference and Nonna will turn over in her grave.

Today cast iron, both in pots and pans, is becoming popular again. Many are lined with porcelain or enamel. If you have old iron skillets from your grandmother, do not throw them away. They are worth their weight (and they are heavy) in gold.

Pasta machine. A crank pasta machine is the best one for the recipes in this book, but we also have a pasta machine that mixes the dough and makes various cuts of noodles, and we find it satisfactory when in a hurry. They are available in most gourmet shops and department stores.

Pastry board *(spianatoia)*. This item is almost mandatory if you are going to make pasta. When in need of a large workspace, we recommend a hardwood, preferable cherry wood, bread or pastry board.

Ours is wooden and we have been using it, like our pans, for eight decades. Needless to say, it was so worn that we had to have the wood turned about twenty years ago.

Modern nutritionists do not recommend wooden boards for they maintain that food remains in the wood and can cause poisoning. We have never been poisoned. No one has ever been sick after a meal in our home. If you are concerned, use a plastic bread or pastry board. Sorry, Nonna. The marble and granite counter tops popular today can also be used.

Rolling pin *(matterello)*. Our family's *matterello* was made by a friend who made all the wooden utensils for the Tuscan cooks in our area. It is now an heirloom handed down through three generations and still going strong. Made of hardwood, it is 32 inches long and 1¼ inches thick.

Stoves. Nonna cooked on a gas stove. My mother preferred an electric stove. During the process of creating this cookbook, we had to buy a new one. Our wonderful porcelain-finish, thirty-year-old oven just could not be mended anymore. When our new oven arrived, we were appalled to discover that times, especially in roasting and baking, varied. Take heed! There is no replacement for the cook. The final decision as to when a dish is finished remains with the person preparing the meal, not with the times listed in recipes.

Times. After we wrote all the recipes, we tested them following our own written instructions. Well, we had to alter quite a few recipes to achieve the taste that was equal to our traditional foods. That is when we added many of the times listed in the recipes that follow. The times only serve if the heat is the same. If your idea of simmer is faster than our idea of simmer, then the times will vary for stews and sauces. If you make a cookie larger or smaller than we do, the time will not be the same. If your oven heats hotter than ours, that is also a problem. We used an oven thermometer in both our old and new ovens, but the new oven bakes and roasts faster than our old oven.

Our outside testers working in their own kitchens found our times accurate, but our advice is as follows: use our carefully calculated times as a gauge, an approximation, and use your eyes and taste as the final judge.

We wish you good cooking and hours and hours of good eating, wonderful conversation, and genuine friendship enjoying the special foods in this book.

Buon Appetito!

Appetizers
Antipasti

The flavor that begins a meal (*anti pasti,* "in front of the meal") must blend with the dishes that follow. It is the true beginning of an Italian meal, and in Tuscany it is always eaten at table, never served with cocktails but with good wine. The only exception to this rule in the recipes that follow is *bagna calda,* a salty dish often served at stag parties accompanied by gallons of homemade Italian wine.

Nonna's favorite *antipasto* was a milt with chicken liver canapé, which was served so often we simply called it *crostini,* the Tuscan name for all canapés. In Tuscany, this *crostini* is called *crostini neri,* "black" canapés because of its color, a dark brown. Today milt is next to impossible to find, and several butchers have told me it is illegal to sell milt in the United States. In Nonna's day, we went to the slaughterhouse to get it, and, because they threw it away, it was free. Today, when we are lucky, we make the chicken liver canapé with milt; when we are not lucky, we make it without. Both recipes appear in this chapter.

Most Italian appetizers tend to be salty, offering an invitation to eat and drink abundantly, and the ones listed in this chapter are no exception. Throughout this book are additional recipes that can be turned into appetizers by adjusting the size or the cut: stuffed escarole, Italian meatballs, sweet *farina,* fried anchovy puffs, anchovies with onions and parsley salad, anchovy and butter sandwich, *polpette,* headcheese, stuffed Italian peppers or tomatoes, and any *schiacciata* or fried vegetable (just to name a few).

Today traditional *antipasti* have turned into the meal itself, and are an exciting addition to any buffet. They have also become popular as snacks. Anyway you serve them, they are exciting.

Antipasto

¼ lb. each thinly
sliced *salami, pro-
sciutto, mortadella,
mozzarella, cheese,*
and *provolone*
6 oz. black olives
4-5 celery ribs

Pick your favorite serving tray. Arrange meat and cheese to taste: either in rows or in segments, flat or rolled. Garnish with celery and black olives. Serve with *bagna calda* (see recipe) or fresh Italian bread.

Serves: 12-15.

Hot Bath & Vegetables
Bagna Calda e Vegetali

Delicious *bagna calda* was prepared by Nonna Parigi whenever Nonno's friends came to visit. It was never eaten as a family meal, which is very much in keeping with the origin of this delicious appetizer. Centuries old in Italy, *bagna calda* was traditionally served as part of the workers' meal during the autumn grape harvest. They ate it in the fields, at tables set up for them. When the meal was almost finished, the grape pickers often added an egg to the remaining liquid and scrambled it over low heat. You eat *bagna calda* like fondue: pick a vegetable, dip it into the hot bath, and eat. It is tangy and delicious, a meal in itself. If you find the artichokes too much of a bother, eliminate them. Simply add more of the other ingredients. You can make this dish in a fondue pot or a Crockpot. It is good warm or cold.

2 fresh artichokes
1 tsp. lemon juice
Pinch salt
2 cups water
1 tsp. olive oil
1 bunch cardoons*
3 celery hearts
2 green peppers
2 red peppers
4 carrots
7-8 radishes
¾ cup olive oil
3 tbsp. butter
2 tsp. chopped garlic
8-10 flat anchovy fillets
1 tsp. salt
1 tsp. pepper

Wash all artichokes. Remove outer layer of hard leaves (for illustrations see the chapter on vegetables). To loosen the leaves hit each artichoke on a drain board 3 or 4 times, then hold the artichoke by the head and spread the leaves to expose the center. Remove pointed and hairy parts in center of artichoke with a small knife. Then cut away the tips of the remaining leaves with kitchen shears or scissors. Wash by placing in fresh water to which lemon juice and salt have been added and allow to soak for half an hour. Drain upside-down on drain board. Dry each artichoke. Baby artichokes, when you can find them, do not have the hairy parts in the center and are easier to clean but are not good for this dish.

Stand artichokes upright in a deep saucepan. Cover the bottom of the pan with water and sprinkle a little oil over each artichoke. Cover and steam cook for 1 to 1½ hours. Check water level every 15 minutes and, if necessary, add more hot water. To eat artichokes with *bagna calda* tear off a leaf, dip into the bath, place between the teeth, and pull out of the mouth, eating only the tender heart of the leaf.

Clean the cardoons and celery hearts and chop each rib into 3-inch pieces. Wash peppers and carrots and dice into 3-inch strips. Wash radishes, remove stems and roots; if small, serve whole, if large, cut in half. Allow all vegetables to drain before arranging either in individual dishes or on one large platter.

Heat the olive oil and butter in a 6-inch iron skillet over medium-high heat. When the butter is thoroughly liquefied and begins to foam, add the garlic and sauté briefly. Lower heat. Do not brown the garlic. Chop the anchovy fillets, add to skillet and dissolve them into a paste by mashing with a fork. Add salt and pepper to taste (note that anchovies are already salty, so use salt sparingly). Stir.

Pour the hot liquid into a chafing dish and bring to the table. If possible, place on a warming rack, for *bagna calda* must stay warm. Arrange the vegetables around the chafing dish. To eat, select a piece of vegetable, dip it in the *bagna calda*, and eat.

Serves: 4

Variation: This is *bagna calda* all dressed up with cream and ready for a party. Prepare as in recipe above. When anchovies have completely dissolved, remove from heat. Let stand a few minutes, then blend in 1 cup clotted cream (can use sour cream).

Notes: *Cardoons are not readily available in the United States, and when you do find them in a specialty store, they are often bitter and not as nice as those in Italy. They are also seasonal, appearing in the late fall and winter. You may wish to eliminate the cardoons and double the quantity of celery. Vegetables can be prepared ahead, then placed in a bowl of cold water with the juice of a lemon. Just before serving, drain and allow to dry.

Blue Cheese & Green Olive Spread
Condimento di Gorgonzola e Olive

7 oz. green pimento olives
⅓ lb. blue cheese

With both ingredients at room temperature, blend in a meat chopper or food processor. Remove and mash with a fork until well blended. Form into a ball and serve with crackers. Salty.

Serves: 15-25.

Chicken Liver Canapé
Crostini di Fegatini di Pollo (Crostini Neri)

This recipe is a variation of the milt and chicken liver recipe that follows. It was served often in the Pelini household. Both recipes are typical of Tuscany where they are called *Crostini Neri*, Black Canapé. Another way of making them is to eliminate the capers and anchovies. That is how our family in *Quarata* makes them today. We never made them without capers and anchovies, and I don't know why our recipe is different from theirs.

6 fresh chicken livers
2 slices *prosciutto*
1 small onion
1 tbsp. fresh parsley
3-4 anchovy fillets
1 tbsp. butter
Pepper
¼ cup dry white wine
10-12 slices day-old bread
½ cup broth
3 oz. capers

Be sure livers are fresh. Wash and remove all large veins. Chop fine. Remove fat from *prosciutto*. Chop lean portion into tiny pieces. Wash and dice onion and parsley. Drain anchovies and chop fine.

Place small-sized iron skillet on medium-high heat. Melt butter. Add onion. Sauté until transparent. Add livers, *prosciutto*, parsley and cook, stirring often. When mixture is almost cooked, add anchovies and a little pepper

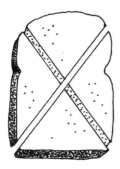

(the anchovies should produce enough salt, but you may wish to add a little). Finally, add wine and let mixture come to a boil. Boil for 3 minutes or until most of wine is absorbed. Let cool.

Slice 10 to 12 thin slices of day-old bread. Cut into wedges. Place on a tray and dry in a 250-degree oven until golden on both sides, about 15 minutes. Place broth in small wide-mouthed bowl. Dip one side of bread lightly in broth. If the bread turns soggy you have used too much broth. Spread liver mixture on dampened toast wedges. Top with a few capers. Place on garnished flat dish and serve immediately.

Yield: 40-48 pieces.

Note: *Crostini di fegatini di pollo* are also good topped with thin slices of *prosciutto* and can be served on thin slices of French *baguette*.

Milt and Chicken Liver Canapé
Crostini di Milza e Fagatini di Pollo (Crostini Neri)

Crostini with anchovies and capers always began a holiday meal in the Parigi household. We used *milza* (milt, or beef spleen) in addition to the chicken livers and had to purchase it from the slaughterhouse. Now it is almost impossible to find on the market so we make this dish without it. In modern Tuscany, you can buy the mixture already prepared in a grocery store and only need to spread it on good bread to have a delicious treat. The store bought mixture does not have capers and anchovies.

1 small beef spleen
(milt)
1 small onion
2-3 sprigs fresh
parsley
3-4 celery leaves
2 tender celery ribs*
¼-inch-thick slice
pancetta
4 fresh chicken livers
1½ tbsp. butter
2 tbsp. broth
Peel of ½ lemon
1 tsp. tomato paste
2 oz. anchovies
3½ oz. capers
10-12 slices day-old
bread
6 oz. dry white wine
12 thin slices *pro-
sciutto*

Wash milt in warm water. Place on board, cut in half (see A). Using back blade of a butcher knife, scrape milt to loosen pulp inside (see B). Hold milt at top. Scrape away from you until all pulp comes out the cut end. Discard outer membrane. Set pulp aside. Repeat with second half.

Place onion, parsley, celery leaves, ribs, and *pancetta* in meat grinder or food processor and grind fine. Place chicken livers in same. Chop until fine. Set both aside.

Place small-sized iron skillet on medium-high heat. Heat to warm. Add butter. Melt. Add onion mixture, sauté until transparent (about 15 minutes). Do not brown. Add chicken livers. If dry, add 1 tbsp. broth. Once all is brown (about 7 minutes), add milt and cook for 10 minutes. Slice lemon peel into ¼-inch strips and add. Cook 5 minutes. Add 1 tbsp. broth to tomato paste to soften. Add tomato paste. Cook 30 to 35 minutes. Remove and cool.

Drain anchovies and capers. Place on bread board. Chop with knife into fine pulp. Blend into cooled milt mixture (can refrigerate up to 2 days).

To serve: Remove from refrigerator. Bring to room temperature. Cut thin slices of bread into wedges (see Chicken Liver Canapé). Toast in broiler until golden on both sides. Place wine

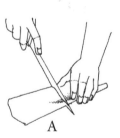

A

B

in wide-mouthed bowl. Dip one side of toast lightly in wine (if soggy you have added too much wine). Spread mixture on dampened toast. Top with ½ slice of *prosciutto.* Place on flat dish and serve. Do not stack.

Yield: 40-48 pieces.

Note: *Celery ribs should be from center of plant and less than 2 inches long.

Hard-Boiled Eggs with Anchovy & Caper Sauce
Uova Sode con Acciugata

Traditionally served with *bollito misto* (boiled mix), eggs with anchovies are good anytime. We eat them on days when broth is made, spooning the sauce generously over the boiled chicken from the soup. Try it on a steak! Added to a buffet, this recipe presents a colorful, tasty dish.

1 cup *acciugata* (see index)
6 eggs

Prepare anchovy and caper sauce *(acciugata).* Boil eggs. Cut lengthwise, arrange on dish, and cover with sauce. Serve with Italian bread.

Yield: 12 pieces.

Stuffed Mushrooms
Funghi Ripieni

This recipe, a favorite of the Pelini family, is always a sensation when presented to guests. It was brought back from Italy on a visit in the 1970s.

20 large fresh mushrooms
8 oz. Italian sausage
½ clove garlic
1 tbsp. fresh parsley
Salt and pepper
⅓ cup bread crumbs
¼ cup freshly grated *Romano* cheese

Take 1 mushroom at a time, cut off the stem and remove blemishes on crown. Rinse and brush clean. Dice stems into small pieces. Peel and mince garlic. Mince parsley.

Place a small-sized iron skillet over medium-high heat. Do not add oil. Add sausage meat, breaking it up with a fork. When sausage has been frying for 5 minutes, add chopped mushroom stems, garlic, and parsley. When completely cooked, add salt and pepper (the cheese has enough salt to our taste). Remove from heat and add bread crumbs and cheese. Stir well.

Lay a mushroom cap on a flat surface. Fill mushroom with mixture. Repeat. Place stuffed mushrooms on an oiled baking pan. Add a little water to the pan and bake in a 350-degree oven for 25 minutes (do not add water until ready to bake or mushrooms will absorb it).

Yield: 20 pieces.

Marinated Green Beans, Artichokes, & Mushrooms
Fagiolini Freschi, Carciofi, e Funghi alla Marinati

I have made this dish for hundreds of buffets and covered-dish dinners. It has always been the hit of the day, especially when I added pasta to it. I have used a number of salad dressings, but the one listed here is the best.

6 oz. tuna (Italian style)
2-3 cups cooked fresh green beans
6½ oz. artichoke hearts in brine
2 oz. anchovies
2-3 tbsp. capers
1 can button mushrooms (can use fresh)
2 tbsp. grated onion

dressing:
1 package Good Seasons Italian

Drain tuna and break into chunks. Cut cooked beans into 1½-inch pieces. Cut artichoke hearts in half. Drain anchovies and cut in half, or quarters. Rinse capers under faucet, squeezing out excess moisture. Combine ingredients in large mixing bowl, add mushrooms and onion, and toss.

In a 10- to 12-oz. lidded jar, combine oil, vinegar, water, and seasonings. Mix and pour over mixture. Toss and refrigerate for a few hours to marinate. Serve with fresh Italian bread.

Serves: 8-10.

Variations: Add 2 cups cooked short pasta and you have an excellent pasta salad.

Note: May be stored for 3 to 4 days in refrigerator. The longer it marinates, the better it tastes.

Oil, Salt, and Pepper Dip
Pinzimonio

We have individual crystal bowls approximately 1 inch in diameter for *pinzimonio*. They sit to the right of the dinner plate at each place setting. *Pinzimonio* is a cold Tuscan variation of *bagna calda* (see index).

1 cup cauliflower
1 cup *broccoli*
1 heart of celery
5 radishes
5 green onions
½ tsp. salt
½ tsp. pepper
3-4 tbsp. olive oil

Use ¼ of a cauliflower or buy pieces at a deli. Wash cauliflower and *broccoli* and break into florets.

Clean celery heart and chop into 3-inch pieces. Wash and trim radishes. If large, cut in half. Clean and peel green onions. Drain vegetables and arrange on platter.

In a small bowl, mix salt, pepper, and oil. Place on table near vegetables, or in individual bowls. Select a vegetable, dip in *pinzimonio*, stir, and eat.

Serves: 8-12.

Prosciutto with Cantaloupe or Figs
Prosciutto con Melone o Fichi

This excellent appetizer, now a favorite in Italian restaurants all over the world, attests to the fact that salty ham is not only good in savory items, but can also garnish sweets. The best *prosciutto* to use for this dish is the sweeter *prosciutto di Parma*.

1 wedge of canta-
    loupe, or 1 fig
2 slices *prosciutto*
Parsley to garnish

Slice a wedge of melon, remove rind, and chill. Lay a slice of freshly cut *prosciutto* on top of the melon, garnish with a sprig of parsley and serve on an elegant plate. For figs, slice a fig in half and top with *prosciutto*.

Serves: 1.

Tomato Canapé
Crostini di Pomodori

6 very ripe fresh tomatoes, or 12 oz. canned, no puree
2 tbsp. capers
3 anchovy fillets
½ clove garlic
¼ tsp. black peppercorns
1 tbsp. olive oil
Salt (optional)
6-8 slices day-old bread cut into wedges

Lay tomatoes on a pastry board. Peel and remove as many seeds as possible. Rinse capers under cold water and squeeze out excess moisture. Chop capers and anchovies very fine. Peel garlic and chop into fine pieces or press through garlic press.

Place a medium-sized iron skillet over medium-high heat. Add tomatoes, bring to a boil, lower heat, cover. Simmer, crushing with a fork to reduce pulp, until most of the liquid is gone. It should reduce to a puree. Add anchovies and capers to the tomato mixture. Allow to simmer 5 to 10 minutes. Add garlic, peppercorns, olive oil, and salt (if needed) and continue to simmer until thick and spreadable.

Cut 4 or 5 thin slices of day-old bread (or a *baguette*) into wedges. Place on a tray and dry in a 250-degree oven until hard, about 15 minutes. Spread tomato mixture on toast. Top with a few capers (or parsley). Place on garnished flat dish and serve immediately.

Yield: 1 cup or 25-30 canapés.

White Canapé
Crostini Bianchi

The first time Vivian Sansone tasted these luscious *crostini* was on a trip to Italy in the '70s. While being entertained in a relative's home, a variety of *crostini* was served, including several represented in this chapter.

4 oz. butter
3½ oz. tuna in olive oil
Juice of 1 lemon
Salt (optional)
5-6 slices day-old bread
10 marinated artichoke hearts

Make sure butter is at room temperature. Place in a medium-sized bowl and cream. Drain tuna and add to butter. Mix by hand until smooth and creamy. Add lemon juice and a little salt if necessary.

Slice 5 to 6 thin slices of day-old bread (or use a French *baguette*). Cut into wedges. Place

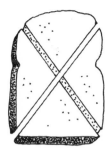

on a tray and dry in a 250-degree oven until hard, about 15 minutes.

Spread tuna mixture on bread wedges. Cut artichoke hearts into halves. Top each canapé with a slice of marinated artichoke heart.

Place on garnished flat dish and serve immediately.

Yield: 20-25 pieces.

Notes: Tuna mix can be frozen. Bring to room temperature and mix before serving. French *baguettes* may be substituted for day-old bread.

Beverages
Bevande

Italian beverages are as famous as Italian foods. It would be difficult to find a person in Western culture who has not heard of *espresso* or *cappuccino*, the strong Italian coffees. In the past decades, Americans have been introduced to dozens of flavorful coffee-shop coffees that have their origin in Italian cuisine but are strictly an American invention. So are the prices. Teas too are enjoying a renaissance in America. Until recently, few knew of the medicinal teas concocted by thousands of peasant women in the hills and valleys of Italian provinces, but those too are making their way into American supermarkets and restaurants. However, most of the world concedes that wine is Italy's most famous and greatest gastronomic treasure. Like the food, the region creates the special taste. The soil, the sun, and the plant all work together to produce a unique flavor. In fact in the hills of Tuscany one field may be worthy of being harvested by *Chianti* for its famous wines while a field only a few meters away is not.

Traditionally the choice of wine for a meal was just as important as the cut of meat or the blend of spices, and in our home that choice traditionally belonged to Nonno. Red meats and pastas with red sauces require dry red wine. White meats and pastas with white sauces, including pork, poultry, and fish, dry white wine. When a meal is as abundant as a proper Tuscan holiday meal, a different wine is served with each course. Wine often accompanies the *antipasto* but is removed from the table for the soup course, reappearing thereafter.

A few specialty wines were made in Nonno's wine cellar. Their lives were short, but their arrival at the table was anticipated each year. They included *mezzo vino*, a half wine and half water byproduct of the new wine, and *puntello*, a sweet wine using water and sugar. Holy Wine, *vin santo*, a sweet wine made from raisins, was the wine of wines as far as we were concerned.

Italians also have excellent liqueurs. *Anisetta* is a licorice-flavored drink that can be added to coffee, or sipped slowly for the full bouquet of its heavy taste. *Amaretto* is an almond-flavored liqueur. The most famous commercial brand of *amaretto* is *Amaretto di Saronno* first created in the sixteenth century in the Lombard region of Italy. *Sambuca* comes from the elder tree and is most often served with a coffee bean and called *sambuca con la mosca,* "sambuca with a fly." It is Middle Eastern in origin and belongs to the *Civitavecchia* district near Rome. *Grappa* is distilled from crushed grapes after wine has been made, aged for two years in an oak cask, and usually served in morning coffee. It comes from the ancient Romans. *Limoncello,* a fairly new liqueur to our table, came originally from the isle of Capri. *Marsala,* originally made in Sicily, is named after the town in which it was first produced and is mainly a cooking wine. *Galliano,* easily recognized by its tall slim bottle and yellow color, is another licorice drink. It is Tuscan in origin. We made none of these in America, but my cousins in Italy still brew interesting variations in their homes including a concoction called *Centi Erbe,* 100 herbs, which is so strong it will knock your socks off.

Coffees
Caffè

Coffee was introduced to the world from the Yemen on the Arabian Peninsula during the Middle Ages. Thanks to the Venetian traders who almost monopolized Eastern trade at the time, it soon (between 1585 and 1615) reached Italian shores.

Espresso

Strong, rich *espresso* is traditionally served after a large meal in an Italian home. In Italy, they say it aids in digestion. One way to make *espresso* is to use an *espresso* machine that forces steam through the coffee. *Espresso* machines, used in a *bottega* (coffee shop) in Italy and in upbeat restaurants and coffee shops in America, are also available for the home.

In an Italian *bottega,* one has choices: *un caffè* or *un espresso* is a standard, demitasse cup; *caffè doppio* or *caffè alto* is a double portion; *caffè macchiato* is coffee with a dash of milk; and *caffè corretto* is *espresso* with *grappa* or brandy.

But you do not need to go to a coffee shop

or buy an *espresso* machine to make a good cup of *espresso* coffee. An Italian coffeepot produces the same results. There are two types of coffeepots: the *Napoletana* (A), a drip coffeepot, and the *Moka* (B). The latter is named after Mocha, the seaport in Yemen where coffee was first exported. It is the type we have used on both sides of the Atlantic.

Espresso coffee is finely ground, almost a powder. It can be purchased packaged in Italian food stores or in various blends at gourmet shops where any flavor, including decaffeinated brands, can be ground for *espresso*. It is served in demitasse cups.

1 tbsp. *espresso* grounds ¼ cup water Sugar to taste	Prepare coffee as per instructions on your coffee machine. Usually 1 tbsp. of *espresso* needs ¼ cup water.

Serves: 1.

Variation: Run a piece of lemon over the lip of the cup and dip the rim in sugar. Add coffee and sip through the sugar.

Cappuccino

Once, after a meal in *Lago di Garda* in the *Veneto,* I asked for a *cappuccino.* The restaurant owner refused to make me one. He said *cappuccino* is good in the morning, or as an afternoon pick me up, but after lunch or dinner only *espresso* would be served.

Varieties of *cappuccino* were once quite simple and included the standard half steamed milk and half coffee; *cappuccino senza spuma,* coffee with hot milk that has not been steamed; and *caffè con panna,* coffee topped with sweetened whipped cream. Today the varieties are endless.

If you have trouble making foam for a *cappuccino,* use skim milk. Heavier milks and creams sometimes refuse to foam.

½ cup skim milk 1 tbsp. *espresso* grounds ½ cup water Sugar to taste Cinnamon, chocolate, cloves, or flavor of choice as garnish	Place the milk in a steel cup and set it in the freezer while you prepare the coffee. The metal helps to chill the milk. Prepare *espresso* according to instructions on your machine. If you have an espresso machine, when the brewed *espresso* reaches the steam level, remove

the skim milk from the freezer, place it under the steam nozzle with the nozzle barely below the surface of the milk. It will begin to foam immediately. Allow to foam for 30 seconds to 1 minute. Be sure to use a potholder to hold the metal container or it will become too hot to handle.

Pour the *espresso* in a cup. Add sugar and stir. Spoon steamed milk over the *espresso*. Garnish with a dash of cinnamon, chocolate, cloves, or any flavor of choice.

Serves: 1.

Teas
Te

Nonna, like so many immigrant mothers, was a storehouse of medicinal knowledge. When I had my first two-wheel bike, one day I flew over the handlebars and landed on my right knee. I could not walk. Nonna made a poultice of melted soap and rags, which hardened into a protective cast. I wish she were here today as that old wound is now arthritic. Sandrina also had her remedies—she boiled wine to drink for coughs and sore throats.

Whenever a woman in our town was pregnant, our local doctor would say, "When it's time, call Mrs. Parigi to assist me." Children were born at home at that time and my nonna was there when my brother was born, and seven years later when I came along. But she also helped with operations. During the Depression, one of the men in our neighborhood injured the heel of his foot and it was badly infected. The doctor operated at home and Nonna assisted. Well, the man began to wake up before the operation was over and Nonna had to run out into the street to get men to hold him down while the doctor finished.

Nonna was the seventh child of the seventh child. Whether you believe in the superstition that that child has psychic powers or not, I know my nonna was uncanny in her warnings. She always knew when something was wrong, or about to go wrong. One evening she came running to our house and asked where my brother was. My mother said he was at his friend's house. Nonna said, "Call and tell him to come home." At that moment, the phone rang, our dog howled, and my mother was told that the car my brother was working on had fallen on him. It was a terrible time in our family.

We never believed in psychic powers and Nonna never tried to develop her abilities, but I believe that she possessed them. Psychic or not, she always had a remedy whenever anyone was not up to par, and the remedy was often a tea. I wish I remembered all the recipes for her teas.

Chamomile Tea
Te di Camomilla

Once a year, Nonna brewed up a pot of chamomile. Chamomile is a daisylike flower that blooms in June and Nonna used it for its calming properties. Today one can buy chamomile tea all nicely packaged, but if you want to do it Nonna's way, here's how:

Be sure you have the proper flower. Gather bunches from the field. Rinse and pat dry. Lay them flat in a cool, dry place and allow to dry. Do not stack too high or they will rot. Once the flowers are dry, store them in an airtight sack but never in plastic wrap.

1-2 flowers, stems and all 1 cup boiling water	Combine flowers and water. Steep to taste. The longer you steep, the stronger the taste. Chamomile tastes good with sugar, lemon, or honey.

Yield: 1 cup.

Wine
Vino

In Italy, the Etruscans nurtured the grape and made wine in the Tuscan hills 4,000 years ago. Ancient Italy had a reputation among its neighbors for its wine, and the Greeks called their Italian colony *Oenotria*, the land of wine. Although French wines appear to dominate the market in modern times, Italian vintners have regained the title of the best of the winemakers and Italy exports more wine than any other country. Wine is so important to the Italian economy that the government supervises its production, and each vintner must conform to strict regulations. (These restrictions are also on a number of cheeses, *prosciuttos,* and other *salumes.*) Supervised by the *denominazione di origine controllata* (DOC), in 1993, 220 wine-growing areas producing eight hundred types of wine were approved by the Italian government with six wines distinguished as *denominazione di origine controllata garantita* (DOCG) or guaranteed authenticity. These were *Barbaresco, Barolo, Brunello di Montalcino, Chianti, Vino Nobile di Montepulciano,* and *Albana di Romagna.* Today there are thirty-nine DOCG wines. In 1993, Tuscany was the home of three of the DOCG wines: *Brunello di Montalcino, Chianti,* and *Vino Nobile di Montepulciano.* Today *Morellino di Scansano* from *Grosseto, Aleatico dell'Elba* from the Island of Elba, *Vernaccia di San Gimignano* from *San Gimignano, Carmignano* from *Prato* and Florence, and a few additional *Chianti* wines have been added. The most popular is *Chianti;* the most prestigious is *Brunello di Montalcino* produced south of Siena.

I grew up on wine. Not the wine of *Brunello di Montalcino* or *Chianti*—although an occasional bottle would make its way to our table—but the wonderful reds and whites of my nonno's cellar. We had wine for dinner every day, and on Sundays and holidays, we would enjoy a different type of wine for each course. Two things are always placed on an Italian table: bread and wine, symbolically, the body and blood of Jesus Christ.

Wine can be stored indefinitely and we believe it continues to age in the bottle. In fact, Nonno Parigi always saved a few bottles of a special year, and when my brother got married, we drank the wine from the year he was born. We still have a bottle of wine from 1933, the year my mother graduated from high school. That wine is nearly seventy years old. It, like all the bottle-aged wine that came before, stands on the shelf, as opposed to lying on its side. When Nonno opened one of these aging bottles, he was very careful not to disturb it too much. Once he delicately uncorked the bottle, he very cautiously inserted a special stick *(tromba)* and tilted the bottle, pouring out the contents in one continuous, slow-pouring flow. The sediment remained in the bottle. Then he rebottled the wonderful wine and brought it to table.

Wine should be kept out of bright sunlight and in a cool room between 50 to 60 degrees in temperature. If the storage area is too warm the wine will not be good.

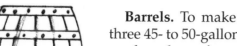

Equipment

A

Barrels. To make wine you need at least three 45- to 50-gallon wooden barrels: two for mash and one for storage. The mash barrels are open on one end, while the storage barrel must be closed at both ends to allow aging and have at least one, if not two, openings, both plugged by a bung *(spina della botte)*, a wooden cork. All barrels must be leak-proof. To assure that the barrels are leak-proof, with the tap bung in place, swell the wood by filling the barrels with water. Allow barrels to set overnight.

B

Half barrel. Catches the wine (see B).

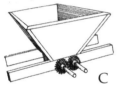

C

Grinder. A grape grinder *(mostatoio* or *pigiatrice,* see C) replaces the ancient method of stomping the grapes and mashes them to begin the fermentation process.

D

Plunger. A plunger *(pistone,* see D) is used to push the mash down each day during fermentation.

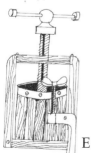

E

Press. After the wine has been removed from the barrels, the residue of mash is passed through the press *(strettoio* or *torchio,* see E) to extract the juices for half wine or other specialties.

Grapes. When trains no longer delivered grapes to our town, Nonno went to the Strip District in Pittsburgh and picked his grapes trackside as the trains arrived from California. Then he would wait patiently—maybe not so patiently—for the grapes to be delivered to his house in Monessen, twenty-five miles away. Our neighborhood would be filled with anticipation, as day after day trucks would arrive with grapes for the anxious men. Some experts maintain shipped grapes are too old and do not produce good wine. They should have tasted Nonno's wine, or talked to the men in our town. Nonno insisted on California grapes from the Kookamunga region.

Our wines have no additives, no sugar (except *Puntello*), no chemicals, no yeast. They are pure, uncontaminated, and delicious.

Table Wine
Vino da Tavola

Gino's Red Wine
22 cases *zinfandel*

Nazzareno's Red Wine
20 cases *zinfandel*
4 cases *muscat*

Gino's Mixed Wine
14 cases *alicante*
8 cases *muscat*

Nazzareno's White Wine
12 cases *muscat*

you will need:
1 50-gallon mash barrel with lid
1 50-gallon storage barrel with 2 holes and 2 bungs
1 grinder (or a pair of boots)
1 plunger
1 large funnel
½ barrel
1 wooden spigot
2 vats (if stomping)

Preparing the Workspace

Traditionally the process of making wine should commence on October 15. Create ample workspace when making wine. Twenty-two cases of grapes at 36 pounds each take a lot of space. Stack crates no more than 6 high near the mash barrels within easy reach.

Grapes must be clean and cool when you begin. Remove only the excess heavy stems and any leaves. The remainder goes in the mash.

Preparing the Equipment

All equipment must be free of contamination. Wash each wooden tool 3 times in lukewarm water combined with 1 cup baking soda, rinse 5 to 6 times in boiling, clear water, and check barrels for leaks. Set aside to dry for several days. Some winemakers buy new barrels every year, but Nonno and Gino used the same barrels year after year and their wine never turned to vinegar.

Mashing

To mash grapes, you can use any non-porous material (including your feet). Nonno always used a grape grinder (*mustatoio*, see B); however, many home brewers, even today, feel that using the feet is the best way to get a good crush, and Gino followed this method. Eleven cases of mashed grapes should fit into one barrel (approximately 50 gallons).

F

To grind the mash: Place grinder on open end of first barrel (see F). Pass 11 cases of grapes through grinder, crushing them and allowing juice to fall into barrel. Crush remaining grapes in second barrel.

To stomp the mash: Remember grapes are very susceptible to bacteria and everything that touches them must be absolutely clean. Gino had a pair of rubber hip boots he used exclusively for stomping and he cleaned them in hot sudsy water, then rinsed them 5 or 6 times in boiling, clear water and hung them to drip dry (wiping would contaminate). They must never touch the ground, so it is not easy.

Place 1 case of grapes into each vat. Enter vat and lift feet up and down until grapes are well crushed (about 5 minutes for each vat). Remove grapes to mash barrel (mind your boots), step into second vat, add fresh grapes, and continue until all are crushed and both barrels are full.

The grapes have now become a *mosto*, or must (or mash), and they should be covered to protect the must from fruit flies and other bacteria that will spoil wine. Cover with barrel lid; a clean, heavy cloth; or even a newspaper.

Fermentation

After grapes have been mashed and barrels are full and covered, allow to stand for 4 to 8 days. If weather is warm it will probably

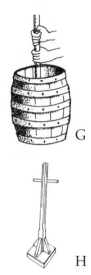

G

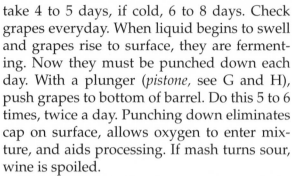

H

take 4 to 5 days, if cold, 6 to 8 days. Check grapes everyday. When liquid begins to swell and grapes rise to surface, they are fermenting. Now they must be punched down each day. With a plunger (*pistone*, see G and H), push grapes to bottom of barrel. Do this 5 to 6 times, twice a day. Punching down eliminates cap on surface, allows oxygen to enter mixture, and aids processing. If mash turns sour, wine is spoiled.

Fermentation ends when must stops bubbling and rising to top, or rises very slowly. Do not plunge or push mash down after bubbles subside or it will become cloudy and cloud finished wine. Allow wine to set for 24 hours to clear the wine. In addition to taste, clarity is a requirement for good wine.

Removing the Wine

Now it is time to remove the wine from the fermentation barrels and transfer it to the storage barrels. If the storage barrels are new, or have not been used yearly, in addition to washing and rinsing in boiling water, they must be sweetened (any new barrel must be sweetened). To sweeten, mix 6 quarts of must with 3 to 5 gallons of boiling water in a plastic pail or wooden tub. Strain and pour juice into storage barrel. Roll all around the storage barrel, empty, and rinse with warm water. Place upside-down to drain for several hours.

All storage barrels should have a permanent tap on the side, which has been plugged up during fermentation (see notes that follow).

Place a wooden tub or ½ barrel under the opening of the mash barrel to catch wine (see I). Let juice flow until it stops. At this point, wine is not clear because of the fermentation process.

If you are not making *mezzo vino* or *puntello* remove mash from barrel, place in press (see

I

J

J), and press mash. Add to wine. If you are making additional wine, eliminate this step.

Storing the Wine

Place storage barrel on its side, in permanent location. It must be absolutely level. Transfer wine using a funnel. After transfer, wine is still foaming. Do not seal opening. Filled to top and as wine foams impurities will spill over sides. Top barrel with wine every day. Allowing the wine to breath and foam is the most important step in making good wine.

On November 11, Saint Martin's Day (if begun on October 15), seal barrel by hammering a bung into opening. Dampness from barrel will swell and seal it. Wine must be in airtight barrel (Nonno and Gino placed fresh cement over the bung to ensure no air would enter and ruin the wine).

Store for 6 months or more in a cool, dry place to continue fermentation. Sediment will settle to bottom and juice will become a clear wine.

Tapping the Wine

K

After 6 months (around Easter), during dark of moon (from full moon to new moon), tap new wine. Boil spigot (see K) in clear water, and with hammer or wooden mallet pound it into bung on front side of barrel. Move quickly and accurately. Bung is soft and spigot will swell to seal opening.

You may place wine in prepared clean 5-gallon, 1-gallon, or quart containers, or leave it in the barrel. You may cover the wine with a little oil and seal with a press cap (like Gino) or cork the wine and cover the cork with melted wax seal (like Nonno).

A Few Warnings

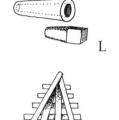

If fermentation does not start, the must could be too cold or too hot. If fermentation does not stop, let it continue, the longer it processes the more sugar will be converted into wine. It makes it stronger. If the final wine is vinegary, it has been contaminated and must be discarded or used as vinegar.

Notes: Buy a spigot or, as Gino did, make your own. The spigot is made of wood (usually from a grape box or broom handle). Drill hole through the center of wood and make plug to fit into hole (see L). The plug must be tapered. It is placed into hole to stop flow of wine and removed to allow liquid to flow.

Gino also placed a handmade wooden sieve (see M) inside the barrel above the spigot opening. This prevented grape seeds, skins, and stems from coming through the spigot with the grape juice.

Twelve cases of grapes produce 25 to 30 gallons wine, or 2½ gallons juice from 1 case grapes.

Half Wine
Mezzo Vino

Mezzo Vino is a special type of wine enjoyed after the new wine is set to age. It is a combination of water and the used mash from the new wine. In addition to good drinking, it indicates the success or failure of the new wine now aging in barrels. It shows the clarity and previews the bouquet.

Old mash
2 cases new grapes
10 gallons water
15-gallon barrel with
    spigot
1 mash barrel
1 grinder
1 press
1 plunger
½ barrel
1 large funnel

Prepare equipment and be sure it is clean. Pour boiling water and 1 cup of baking soda into the 15-gallon barrel and rinse with hot clear water. Repeat 3 times. Do not wash mash barrels.

Make wine as described in the previous section. After all wine has been drained from the mash, add 10 gallons of water to

1 mash barrel. Grind 2 new cases of grapes into barrel, remove mash from second barrel and add.

Ferment for 2 days, punching down with plunger if mash rises to the top or begins to bubble. Drain as described in previous section. Place in a 15-gallon barrel and seal.

If this is last wine, press mash and add to barrel before fermenting. If not, save mash for Prop Wine.

Yield: 15 gallons.

Prop Wine (Raisin Jack)
Puntello

Used mash
3 gallons water
5 lb. raisins or 1 lb. sugar
15-gallon barrel with 1 press
½ barrel
1 large funnel

Be sure all equipment is sterile and all liquid is drained from the mash. Make wine and half wine as described in previous section. After half wine has been drained from the mash, grind raisins over mash, add water and stir. Add sugar if desired.

Cover and allow to ferment 1 day. Tap and pour into freshly cleaned and boiled barrel or clean glass gallon jugs. After all wine has been drained from mash, remove mash from barrel. Place press (see J) over barrel, and press mash so juices flow into barrel. Remove juices and add to *puntello.*

At this point, the *puntello* will be cloudy. Allow to rest for a day to clear. It is ready to drink.

Yield: 6-8 gallons.

Holy Wine
Vin Santo

Vin Santo was the wine of wines in our home. My mother maintains Nonno never made it in America. I insisted he did. None of us recalls grapes hanging in the cellar to age, but we all remember drinking *vin santo.* I finally had to concede that his white muscat wine, made with the same grapes (not allowed to age to raisins) and served only on special occasions is what I remember.

Vin santo is a specialty of Tuscany. It is a wine of ritual. The wine is given to anyone who is ill and served to the new bride as a symbol of welcome by the father of her husband as she enters her new home for the first time. In the month of June during the wheat harvest, called *la battuta del grano, vin santo* is served before the huge breakfast given to the people who would go out into the fields.

On my second visit to Italy in 1967, *Chianti* had just begun to make a commercial *vin santo*. My cousin Lydia's husband, Narciso, brought a bottle to my Uncle Geno's table. What a hullabaloo. And it was not a momentary thing. The discussion and the tasting went on all day with men from other homes coming to taste. It endeared my uncle to me, as it was the same back home when men came to visit my nonno. Wine, *prosciutto,* and *salami:* these were the topics. No sports. No cars. Food was the topic. Each man priding himself on his ability and many kept the ingredients or the recipe a secret.

The following method for making *vin santo* comes from our cousin, Beppe Parigi, Uncle Geno's son. Beppe grows his own grapes for this wine. When they are ready for harvest, he hand-picks them and carefully sews the clusters together to hang in rows on the rafters of our ancestral home. He refuses to add central heating to the house, which is heated by fireplaces, because he feels central heat will harm the *vin santo.* In fact, when the grapes are drying, he keeps the house shuttered against the fumes of modern-day automobiles.

When I took my mother home to Tuscany in 1999, Beppe greeted us with his *vin santo.* It was very good. When I went back, alone, in 2009, Beppe greeted me with his *vin santo.* It was better than in 1999. In fact, it was the best I had ever tasted.

3 cases white muscat

you will need:
1 15-gallon mash barrel with lid
1½-gallon barrel
1 5-gallon storage barrel with spigot
1 grinder (or a pair of boots)
1 press
1 large funnel
1 vat (if stomping)

Pick 1 bunch of grapes at a time, remove excess leaves, and hang grapes on a nail. Allow to age in a cool, dry place for 6 to 8 weeks until they become raisins. The wine-making process usually begins around Christmas.

Read all instructions for making table wine. Prepare all equipment as described. You will need smaller barrels for this wine.

Once all grapes have aged and all equipment is sterilized, remove excess leaves and stems from the grapes and crush grapes in a grinder or by stomping.

Place the grinder on the open end of the first barrel (see F). Pass the raisins through the grinder, crushing them and allowing the juice to fall into the barrel.

Cover the must to protect it from fruit flies and other bacteria that will spoil the wine.

Let stand for 4 to 5 days, if cold, 6 to 8 days. Check grapes daily, and when they begin to rise to the surface, fermentation is under way.

Plunge mash down with plunger (*pistone*, see G and H), pushing the grapes to the bottom of the barrel. Do this 5 to 6 times, twice a day. Punching down eliminates the cap on the surface, allows oxygen to enter the mixture, and aids processing.

Fermentation is over when must stops bubbling and rising to top, or rises very slowly. Do not plunge or push mash down after bubbles subside or it will become cloudy and cloud the finished wine.

After fermentation is over allow, the wine to set for 24 hours to clear it. In addition to taste, clarity is a requirement for good wine.

Remove from barrel, transfer, and seal.

After sealing, *vin santo* is stored in a cool place for a minimum of 2 years and preferably 4 to 5 years. It is not tapped until the wine has reduced to half its original size. The keg is tapped around Christmas. It is put into dark glass bottles, sealed, and opened as needed.

Yield: 6-8 small bottles.

Breads, *Schiacciate,* and Pizzas
Pane, Schiacciate, e Pizza

Senza il pane tutto diventa orfano, "without bread, everything is an orphan," goes an Italian saying. Bread is the staple of the Italian kitchen, and hundreds of varieties of it are produced in Italy, where restaurants have begun to serve a different bread with each course of the meal. Attempts have been made to officially classify and control the production of bakery bread, like wine, to ensure the quality and accuracy of its many forms and tastes.

Today, Italian bakeries, *panetteria,* make long loafs, flat loafs, brown bread, white bread, stuffed bread, sweet bread, breads of rice, corn, or potato flour, and even saltless bread, a specialty of Tuscany. Bread is called by dozens of different names: *corona,* the crown; *mattone,* the brick; *pagnotta,* round; *panino,* rolled; *schiacciata,* flattened; *sfilatino,* long and thin; and *treccia,* braided. The flat bread of Sicily is called *carta di musica,* sheet-music bread, and there is even *pane dei morte,* bread of the dead. There are breads for special days: All Souls' bread, Saint Anthony's bread, the sourdough bread of Saint Blaise *(panicelle di San Biagio),* and Easter bread *(panina di Pasqua).*

Bread is used for everything from sandwiches to an ingredient in salads. It is taken to the church for blessing and given by the church in the name of a saint, and it is a sin to throw it away. In medieval times it was used in place of the fork and spoon, served as a napkin to wipe the mouth or clean the knife, and, when aged into a thick slice, was used as a dish or serving tray.

When Nonna was a girl the brick bread ovens of the village were fired up daily, but each family had access only once a week. By the end of the week the bread had turned quite hard and a host of recipes were devised to use it: bread in soup, bread in salad, bread as stuffing, and bread as crumbs.

The most famous bread of Tuscany, *pane Toscano o pane sciocco,* is a saltless bread. Tradition has it that Tuscans, ever mindful of their purses, refused to pay the salt tax in the Middle Ages and had to cook without salt. When my grandmother told her father that she was going to America with her husband he said, "You'll learn the price of salt." The implication went over her head and she wrote back to him from America, "Salt is only five cents."

Today, Italian-American bakeries are producing many of the wonderful varieties of bread found in Italy, and American palates have been educated about the incredible Italian breads.

Homemade Bread
Casareccio

Every Thursday was bread day in Nonna's kitchen. Out came the *spianatoia* (bread board), on went the apron, and the kitchen would be tied up for hours. The aroma promised a treat to please the most critical gourmet.

Almost everything affects the final outcome of a loaf of bread: the type of water, the kind of day (damp days are the worst), the altitude, and probably the temperament of the baker. Patience is the name of the game when making true Italian bread, patience and a lot of time. Nonna used the whole day and baked copious amounts; my mother only baked a few loaves at a time; I don't bake bread at all. It is now left to Vivian, who makes it occasionally.

This recipe is a fourth of what Nonna prepared. And unlike the typical Tuscan bread, our recipe contains salt. We do not know if Nonna, having been warned of the value of salt, added it once she came to America, but we never made saltless bread.

10 cups white flour
3 cups water, divided
1 oz. dry yeast
¼ lb. (1 stick) marga-
    rine or butter
¼ cup granulated
    sugar
2 tsp. salt
¼ cup white flour for
    kneading, or as
    needed
4 bread pans

Put flour into a large mixing bowl. Heat 1 cup water to 90 degrees. Add dry yeast, dissolve, and set aside (be sure yeast water is not over 90 degrees or it will cook the yeast and the bread will not rise).

To 2 cups of water, add margarine, sugar, and salt and heat until dissolved (be sure this water is warmer than yeast water, from 115 to 120 degrees).

Make a well in the center of the flour (see A) and slowly add the lukewarm yeast water. Mix with a fork. When yeast water has been absorbed into the flour, slowly begin to add the warmer sugar water. Keep mixing until all the liquid is absorbed.

A

Prepare a large workspace (2 by 3 feet), preferably a large pastry board, and dust it

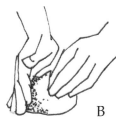

B

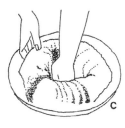

C

with flour. Use flour sparingly as it is only a bonding agent. If dough is already firm, limit the extra flour. Turn dough onto board, and begin to knead (see B).

Kneading is a long process and one must work the dough for half an hour, adding flour as needed to keep the mixture from sticking.

Once the dough has been kneaded, place it in a large mixing bowl (Nonna always blessed the bread 3 times with the sign of the cross at this point), cover with at least 1 clean cloth and 2 to 3 blankets (bread must be kept warm and we always used blankets), and let rise about 1½ hours until double in size.

Uncover the dough and punch down 10 to 12 times. To punch down (see C), form a fist and beat the bread like a punching bag (get out frustrations). Flip dough over, cover, and allow to rise for 1 hour.

When dough is almost ready, prepare 4 baking pans greased with a little shortening so the bread will not stick. Begin to pan the loaves immediately, filling each baking pan to little more than half full. Then cover with cloth and blankets and allow to rise for 1 hour. Ten minutes before uncovering, heat oven to 350 degrees.

Bake the loaves for 50 to 60 minutes or until golden (see note). Remove from oven, place on a wire rack to cool, and cover with a thin cloth.

Yield: 4 loaves.

For sandwich buns: Prepare bread as above. When ready to pan, take enough dough to make 1 roll the size of a hamburger bun (at this point dough is half of the final size and the size of the sandwich roll is up to the chef). Roll the dough between your hands into a ball and place on a greased cookie sheet. Six bread balls should fit on a sheet. Continue until all dough is rolled. Cover bread and allow to rise for 1 hour. Bake in 350-degree oven for 45 to 50 minutes.

Yield: 24 buns.

Note: To check bread, remove from pan and tap the bottom with your fist. If it sounds hollow, the center of the bread is well done.

To make less than 4 loaves:

¼ recipe (1 loaf):	**½ recipe (2 loaves):**
2½ cups flour	5 cups flour
¼ cup water	½ cup water
¼ oz. yeast	½ oz. yeast
½ cup water	1 cup water
2 tbsp. margarine	4 tbsp. margarine
2 tbsp. sugar	4 tbsp. sugar
½ tsp. salt	1 tsp. salt
⅛ cup flour	¼ cup flour
1 pan	2 pans
Knead: 15 minutes	Knead: 20 minutes
1st rise: 30 minutes to 1 hour	1st rise: 1 hour
2nd rise: 30 minutes to 1 hour	2nd rise: 1 hour
(must double at each rise)	

Garlic (Grilled) Bread
Fett'unta

Called *bruschetta* in Rome and *fett'unta* in Tuscany, grilled bread is an Italian export made popular in America by returning GIs during World War II. As famous as pizza, grilled bread can be found in any Italian restaurant and it is enjoyed as an accompaniment to pasta and salad, or as a snack.

True Tuscan *fett'unta* is made with olive oil, not butter, and crushed garlic cloves, not garlic salt or powder. The olive oil and fresh garlic produce a stronger taste, but to our palates, the stronger the better. For lunch Nonna would sometimes cut a thick slice of homemade bread and drizzle oil and vinegar over it. This simple fare, topped with salt and pepper to taste, is excellent. Another variation is the *Struffa Struffa* open-face sandwich (see index).

Today in Italy and America, the names *bruschetta* and *fett'unta* refer to toasted bread heaped with tomatoes and other succulent fare. These are also variations on this theme.

4 slices Italian bread
8 tsp. olive oil
4 cloves garlic
Salt and pepper

Place bread slices in a broiler or, preferably, a charcoal grill. Brown 1 side until golden (see note).

Drizzle 1 tsp. oil over untoasted side of each slice. Press garlic in a garlic press and spread juice and pulp generously on each slice (the amount of garlic is a matter of taste, but fresh garlic is stronger than powders or salts).

Add salt and pepper to taste and pour additional tsp. of warmed olive oil on each slice. Return to broiler and brown garnished side until golden.

Serve immediately.

Serves: 2.

Note: Before second broiling, sprinkle freshly grated Parmesan cheese over each slice.

Variations: Toppings for grilled bread are endless. Grill and top with cheese, or freshly chopped tomatoes and basil, or *prosciutto*, or *mascarpone*, or anchovies and capers. You decide.

Bread Stuffing
Ripieno di Pane

Bread stuffing forms the base of dozens of recipes in the Tuscan kitchen and is one of the four most important recipes mentioned in the chapter "Our Tuscan Kitchen." It is good with game, poultry, meat, and vegetables.

It begins with a good *soffritto*. I always make extra *soffritto* and freeze it because I am always in need.

1 onion
¼-inch-thick slice
  pancetta
1 celery rib with
  leaves
1 small carrot
1 tsp. fresh parsley
¼ cup corn oil
1 tsp. pepper
1 tsp. salt
4 cups bread cubes
3 eggs
4 tbsp. freshly grated
  Parmesan cheese
1 cup broth

Peel and wash onion; cut into wedges. Dice *pancetta*. Peel celery and carrot, wash, and cut into 1-inch pieces. Chop parsley fine. Combine all and grind in a meat grinder or food processor (the grinder is better because it releases the juices).

Place a medium-size iron skillet over medium heat. Heat to hot. Add oil. When oil is warm, add chopped ingredients, pepper, and salt, and sauté until onions are transparent, stirring often. The longer you cook this mixture the better the stuffing will be. When it begins to stick to the skillet (15 to 20 minutes), it is done.

Place bread cubes (see note) in a large bowl. Remove onion mixture from heat and add to bread cubes. Then add eggs and cheese. Mix. Add broth and mix again. If cubes are moist, stuffing will be moist, so be generous with broth.

Serves: 4-5.

Notes: You can substitute bread crumbs for cubes. For some dishes, garlic is added. You must use all the oil and might even need more.

Sweet Breads
Pani Dolce

From the mountains in the north to the tip of the boot in the south, there must be hundreds of different sweet breads in Italy. In *Genoa* it is the *Pan Dolce,* in *Verona* it is *Pan d'oro,* and in a number of places including Milan and our region of Tuscany there is *Panettone.* All are slightly different and have different dried or candied fruits and nuts.

Easter Bread
Pane di Pasqua o Panina

Nonna's kitchen was ahummin' on Holy Thursday as Easter bread filled with plump raisins was mixed, panned, and baked. This is a bountiful recipe——a good way to give an Easter present to a friend. In our family, every Holy Thursday promptly at four o'clock Tom Cherubini Celli would appear at Nonna's door to collect his Easter bread. This tradition is still maintained at Vivian's home—but the delicacy is Sandrina's oiled *schiacciata* (see index) and the recipients are her brothers' families.

Our Easter bread is made of eggs, saffron, and raisins. The Pelini family make a traditional *schiacciata di Pasqua* with *pancetta,* orange rind, the juice and rind of a lemon, lemon and vanilla extract, and five eggs. The Easter bread of *Umbria* (east of Tuscany) is called *crescia al formaggio,* a wonderful Parmesan-*Pecorino-Romano*-egg bread, baked in a flowerpot. Farther north, in *Friuli,* the sweet bread is called *gubana* and contains fruit, nuts, and spirits. In Milan the families bake (today mostly buy) the *Colomba Pasquale,* the Easter dove, a sweet bread covered with sugar and almonds and shaped like a dove (of course). Moving south, the modern Romans enjoy a *pizza civitavecchia* of egg, *ricotta,* sweet wine, and anise seed. The Neapolitans of *Campania* make *pastiera,* a cake of flour, *ricotta,* eggs, orange extract, and candied orange peel. In *Abruzzo* they make 2 types of Easter bread: a pizza of dimpled dough covered lightly with oil and sea salt and a braided egg bread. It is similar in *Calabria,* but whole eggs are inserted in the braids.

3 tbsp. Spanish saffron*
½ cup boiling water
1½ lb. raisins
Hot water
3 eggs
3 tbsp. olive oil
1 tsp. salt
2 sticks (8 oz.) margarine or butter
1 cup granulated sugar
1 cup water
1½ oz. rapid-rising dry yeast
5-6 cups flour
3 (8-inch) pie plates
Shortening

A

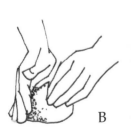

B

Add Spanish saffron to ½ cup boiling water, stir, and set aside to brew and come to room temperature. Beat eggs in mixer; slowly add olive oil and salt.

Place raisins in a bowl. Add hot water to cover and allow to set. This plumps the raisins.

Place a small-size iron skillet over medium-high heat. Cut margarine or butter into 1-inch squares and place in skillet. Do not allow to brown. When butter is partly melted add sugar. Stir slightly, turn off burner, and allow to remain on cooling burner until needed.

Heat 1 cup water to 90 degrees. Dissolve dry yeast in water and set aside. If yeast water is above 90 degrees the bread will not rise.

Put 5 cups white flour on a board or into a large mixing bowl. Make a well in the center (see A). Add 1 to 3 tbsp. flour to the yeast mixture until it begins to hold some shape. Pour yeast mixture into the well and begin to pull flour from the sides of the well until yeast mixture is absorbed.

When yeast water has been absorbed, strain saffron tea that has cooled to room temperature. Be sure this water is no hotter than 115 to 120 degrees or it will cook the yeast and the bread will not rise. Add saffron tea to dough and keep mixing until all is absorbed. Add egg mixture. Drain raisins and add to dough. Continue to pick up flour until all is well blended.

Prepare a large workspace, preferable a large pastry board, and dust it with flour. Turn dough onto board and begin to knead (see B). This is a long process and one must knead the dough for ½ to ¾ hour, adding flour as needed to keep mixture from sticking. Return the dough to a clean mixing bowl, cover with at least 1 clean cloth and 2 blankets, and allow to rise for 2 hours (sweet bread is slower to rise than regular bread).

Remove covers and punch dough down 10 to 12 times. To punch down, form a fist (see C) and beat the bread like a punching bag (get out all your frustrations). Flip dough over. Cover again and allow to rise an additional 1 to 1½ hours.

When dough is almost ready, prepare 3 baking pans. Grease all pans with a little shortening so the baking bread will not stick to the sides. Pan bread immediately, filling each baking pan to little more than half. Cover once more with cloth and blankets and allow to rise for 1 to 1½ hours. Ten minutes before uncovering, heat oven to 350 degrees.

Place bread in oven and bake for 45 to 60 minutes. When done (see note), remove from oven, remove from pan, place on wire rack, cover with a thin, clean cloth, and allow to cool.

Yield: 3 loaves.

Notes: *Spanish saffron can be purchased in pharmacies or gourmet shops.

To check bread, remove from pan and tap the bottom with your fist. If it sounds hollow, the center of the bread is well done.

Snack Idea: Easter bread makes wonderful toast and is especially delicious topped with cream cheese. It is also nice served with *salami* for a sweet and savory snack.

Panettone

In Italy, *panettone,* originally from Milan, is a Christmas bread. There are many stories as to the origin of *panettone,* most about the poor who enjoyed it only once a year as a special treat. One story tells of a poor baker whose beautiful daughter caught the eye of a rich man. He sent the baker, named Tony, oranges, lemons, and other delicacies that Tony baked into his bread. Of course his bread was wonderful, the rich man married his daughter, and the bread of Tony, *pane di Toni,* became famous. Today in Italy *panettone* is tall and cylindrical (see illustration), a form popularized after our immigrants were in America.

Sandrina got this recipe from her mother, and when she came to America and made it for her family, she used certain bowls and pans that were the right size for all the ingredients. Those same bowls are still used by Vivian, who converted all the measurements for this book.

⅔ cup raisins
1 cup hot water
¼ cup butter
1 egg and 2 egg yolks
½ cup granulated
  sugar
2 ½ cups flour
½ cup milk
¼ tsp. salt
1 ½ tsp. cream of
  tartar
1 tsp. baking soda
½ cup candied fruit
½ tsp. lemon zest
1 tbsp. soft butter
1 tbsp. flour
1 tbsp. granulated
  sugar

Place raisins in bowl, add hot water, and allow to plump. In medium-size bowl stir room-temperature butter and eggs until smooth. Slowly add sugar, flour, milk, and salt, alternating and stirring constantly. When smooth, add raisins, cream of tartar, baking soda, candied fruit, and lemon zest. Turn onto floured board. Knead 5 minutes, or until dough is soft and sticky. If too sticky, add a little flour.

Grease round pan or 1-qt. casserole with 1 tbsp. butter. Combine 1 tbsp. each of flour and sugar and dust interior of pan. Distribute evenly, especially up sides, or bread will stick. Place dough in pan. Do not allow to rise. Heat oven to 350 degrees; bake 1 hour or until top is golden. Remove from oven and allow to cool on a rack.

Yield: 1 loaf.

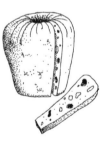

Variation: To make high *panettone* use ½ oz. dry yeast, 5 tbsp. sugar, ¼ cup warm water, 3 cups flour, ¼ cup water, 3 eggs, 2 yolks, ½ tsp. salt, ¾ cup soft butter, 1 tbsp. vanilla, 1 tbsp. grated lemon peel, ⅓ cup citron, and 1 cup raisins. Dissolve yeast in ¼ cup warm water and 1 tbsp. sugar. Let foam and add ½ cup flour. Form ball, slash top, cover, and rise to double. Combine all but butter, citron, and raisins and knead. Add butter and knead 10 minutes. Add citron and raisins. Cover; rise for 1½ hours. Punch down, cover, and refrigerate overnight.

Remove, punch down, place in high pan, and set 4 hours until double in size. Brush with beaten egg. Bake at 400 degrees for 10 minutes and 350 for 40 minutes or more.

Fried Dough with Sugar
Pasta Fritta con Zucchero

While the bread was rising in the pans, Nonna prepared leftover dough as a wonderful sweet snack. This is our answer to the doughnut. We eat fried bread so fast that when the last one is frying it belongs to the cook. The rest are gone. You can find this recipe at fairs across America, often called elephant ears.

½ Homemade Bread recipe*
1 cup corn oil
1 cup granulated sugar

Prepare the dough as described in the Homemade Bread recipe (see index). If making only enough dough for this recipe, divide the recipe in half. After the last rising, knead, and divide dough into 16 to 20 pieces (size is a matter of choice).

Place a medium-size iron skillet over medium-high heat. Heat to hot. Add oil. Stretch each piece of dough to look like a veal cutlet. Drop into hot oil. It will puff up immediately. Brown one side, turn, and brown on second side.

Remove from oil and place on a paper towel. Sprinkle with sugar to taste, and eat. Continue until all the bread is fried.

Eat at once, for fried dough, like every fried food (veal, mushrooms, artichokes, etc.), is best served piping hot.

Yield: 16-20 pieces.

*You can buy fresh bread dough from a bakery or pizza parlor. You can also buy frozen bread dough, but it tends to lack substance.

Stuffed Breads
Pani Imbottiti

Today, throughout America, stuffed breads have been adopted as a quick microwave snack. What these commercial outfits have not discovered are the amazing fillings immigrants from all over the world have always enjoyed in their homes. The commercial versions of Italian fillings all seem to have tomatoes and pepperoni in them. There are no tomatoes here.

Fried Anchovy Bread
Pane Fritto con Acciuga

From the kitchen of Bob Pelini's Sicilian mother-in-law, Mrs. Amico, this recipe was a Christmas Eve specialty in her home, which we all adopted.

3 oz. anchovies
3 cups flour
1 tsp. granulated
    sugar
Pinch salt
¼ oz. dry yeast
1 egg
2 cups water
1 tbsp. olive oil
3 cups corn oil

Drain anchovies and cut each fish into thirds. Set aside. Combine flour, sugar, salt, and yeast in a bowl. Beat egg and combine with water and 1 tbsp. oil. Add egg mixture to flour and mix until blended. Dough should be soft and runny. Place in a bowl, cover, and let rise for 1 to 1½ hours.

When dough is double original size, remove from bowl and set on pastry board. Pinch off 1 tsp., flatten in palm of hand, and place anchovy in center. Seal the anchovy inside the dough and roll.

If dough is too soft to handle, allow it to remain in bowl. Keep a little extra flour on hand. Take a teaspoon, dip into dough, and pull up enough dough to fill the spoon. With flour on fingers, trim off hanging dough. Place anchovy in center of dough and fold dough over it. Do not place on board, but drop directly into hot oil, coaxing dough from spoon with a floured finger. You may want to fill several spoons before dropping into oil to keep the pot full.

Place a 2-qt. pot over medium-high heat.

Heat to hot. Add oil. Allow to heat. Drop anchovy balls into hot oil. They will puff immediately. Allow to brown. Turn. Remove and drain. Eat warm.

Yield: 35-40.

Notes: Anchovy puffs are best eaten immediately, but they can be zapped with the microwave for 30 seconds to warm. They can also be frozen and zapped for 30 seconds.

Variations: You can eliminate the anchovy, fry the dough, and coat it with sugar or honey. If you add corn, you have corn fritters.

Sausage in a Blanket
Involtini di Salsiccia

When the dough is ready to rise, the battle is on: should we have fried dough, anchovy bread, or sausage in a blanket? When Nonna was baking, fried dough usually won, but sausage has always been my favorite.

8 fresh sausage links
¼ of Homemade
    Bread recipe (see
    index)
Vegetable shortening

A

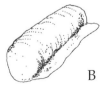

B

Place a medium-size iron skillet over medium-high heat. Do not add oil. Add the sausage links and fry about 10 minutes, turning once. Drain on paper towel.

If panning bread, set the dough for 1 loaf aside. If making dough for this recipe, simply make ¼ recipe. After the second rise, divide dough in eighths and wrap each piece around a cooked sausage (see A and B). Seal well.

Grease cookie sheet with a little shortening. Set each sausage roll on cookie sheet and cover. Allow to rise about 1 hour, or until double in size. Place cookie sheet in oven and bake at 350 degrees for about 25 minutes, or until done.

Serves: 8.

Note: You can buy fresh bread dough from a bakery or pizza parlor. You can also buy frozen bread dough, but it tends to lack substance.

Variations:
Sausage with cheese: The sausage filling can be dressed with a number of ingredients. In the center of each blanket place 1 cooked sausage, 1 slice mozzarella, 1 slice salami, and 1 slice provolone (see C). Fold over the ends of the dough to wrap the filling firmly inside. If not sealed well, cheese will leak. If you wish, you can chop sausage, salami and cheeses together and spoon onto dough.

C

Sausage with escarole: A Pelini family favorite and mine too, this combines ½ lb. sausage, 1 cup cooked chopped escarole, 1 onion, and 2 cloves garlic. Peel and dice garlic and onion. Sauté in corn oil until soft. Wash and boil escarole; cook until done. Break up sausage meat and cook. Combine garlic, onion, oil, escarole, and sausage, and continue as above.

Serves: 4.

Schiacciate

Schiacciata (stiacciata in *Quarata),* also known as *focaccia,* and called pizza in Naples, is a flattened bread made in Tuscany. The size of the *schiacciata* can be anything from a large 18-inch rectangle to a tiny 2-inch pie, and the toppings are just as varied. Probably the fried dough with sugar (see index) that we enjoy so much is a version of *schiacciata.*

You can buy fresh bread dough from a bakery or pizza parlor. You can also buy frozen bread dough, but it tends to lack substance.

Classic *Schiacciata*
Schiacciata Classica

This *schiacciata* is as Tuscan as it gets: good bread, good olive oil, fresh rosemary, and coarse salt. Nonno loved it, and I can still see him sitting under the grape arbor enjoying a *schiacciata classica* for lunch.

¼ Homemade Bread
recipe (see index)
1 tbsp. olive oil
1 tsp. coarse salt
1 tbsp. rosemary

Prepare ¼ of Homemade Bread recipe.

After the last rising, knead, place into an oiled cookie sheet or pizza pan and flatten the dough to cover the bottom of the pan. Brush with olive oil and sprinkle with salt and rosemary.

Bake in 400-degree oven for 15-20 minutes or until brown.

Serves: 6-8.

Variation: Sprinkle with pressed garlic or cheese.

Schiacciata with Grapes
Schiacciata con Uva

Schiacciata with grapes was a specialty of the grape harvest each October. At noon, the owner of the vineyard served up this delicious meal.

¼ Homemade Bread
recipe (see index)
1 lb. red seedless
grapes
¼ cup granulated
sugar
2 cups walnuts
1 tsp. fennel seeds
3 pats butter
1 tbsp. olive oil

Prepare ¼ of Homemade Bread recipe. After last rising, knead, and flatten the dough on oiled cookie sheet or pizza pan. Cut half the grapes in half and combine grapes, sugar, nuts, and fennel. Top dough with mixture. Cut up butter and top. Drizzle olive oil over all. Bake in 400-degree oven for 25-30 minutes or until brown.

Serves: 24 (1½-by-3-inch) pieces.

Sandrina's Oiled *Schiacciata*
Schiacciata Unta alla Sandrina

This recipe is a specialty of Holy Week in the Pelini home. With variations, it is the traditional *schiacciata di Pasqua* to which *vin santo* and anise seeds are sometimes added.

½ oz. fresh (cake) yeast
1 cup warm water
3 cups flour
1 tbsp. vegetable shortening
¼ lb. diced *pancetta**
1¼ cups sugar
1 4-oz. stick butter at room temperature
Rind of 1 orange
Rind of ½ lemon
Juice of ½ lemon
1 tsp. lemon extract
1 tsp. vanilla
1 tsp. salt
5 large eggs at room temperature
1 cup flour, more as needed
¾ to 1 cup lard**
½ to 1 cup granulated sugar

Dissolve yeast in ½ cup warm water. Sift flour into a large pan (approximately 8 qt.). Make a well in the flour and add the dissolved yeast, remainder of warm water, and shortening. Mix into flour to form a dough and knead for 10 to 15 minutes until no longer sticky, adding small amounts of additional flour if needed.

Remove dough from pan. Clean pan and grease with a little shortening. Place dough into the pan. Cover, and let rise 1½ hours. Punch dough down. Add *pancetta*, sugar, butter, orange rind, lemon rind and juice, lemon extract, vanilla, salt, and eggs (at room temperature). Mix well using your hands making dough into ribbonlike. Add 1 cup of flour and continue to mix into a soft dough. Continue adding flour until dough is manageable. Could be an additional cup or more. Remove from pan, clean and grease pan with shortening, then return dough to pan and cover. Allow to rise for 2 hours.

Grease 6 or 7 9-inch cake pans and cut the dough into an equal number of parts. Spread dough like pizza over bottom of each pan. Cover and let rise for 1¼ hours. Uncover and with fingers make indentations in the dough. With a butter knife put a small piece of lard (reason it is called *unta*) in each indentation. Sprinkle entire pie with sugar.

Heat oven to 400 degrees. Place in oven and bake for 20 to 25 minutes or until golden brown. Do not over cook.

Yield: 6-7 loaves.

Notes: *Because we made this *schiacciata* during Holy Week, we omit the *pancetta*. If using *pancetta*, then dice it into small pieces, place in a small-sized skillet over medium-high heat, and cook until well rendered. Drain and add as indicated above.

**Lard is available in supermarkets (use vegetable lard on fasting days).

Pizza

Pizza is Naples' gift to the world. When the tomato arrived from the new world, it was the good citizens of Naples who wed it to flatbread. As an added treat, planting the tomato in the volcanic soils of the region made it one of the best-tasting tomatoes in the world. Today pizza is one of the most popular foods in the United States, but as its twins, *schiacciata* and *focaccia*, it was once the bread of the poor and topped with whatever ingredients were fresh, cheap, and available.

Toppings today have gone far beyond Italian favorites. Hawaiian Pizza, Gyro Pizza, and Taco Pizza are the norm. I've said it before and I will say it again: why no one is making the Slovak *pagach* pizza is beyond me. It is fabulous. *Pierogi* pizza is close, but it is not the same.

Classic Italian-American Pizza
Pizza Classica Italio-Americano

dough:
2½ to 3 cups flour
¼ oz. quick-rising dry
   yeast
1 cup warm water
½ tsp. salt
1 tbsp. granulated
   sugar
¼ cup corn oil
1 tsp. olive oil or
   cornmeal

sauce:
1 clove garlic
1 tbsp. corn oil
¼ tsp. salt
⅛ tsp. pepper
½ tsp. dried oregano
2 cups whole canned
   tomatoes, no
   puree
¼ cup broth

toppings:
16 oz. *mozzarella*
   cheese
4-6 tbsp. freshly
   grated Parmesan
   cheese
1 stick pepperoni

Put flour (reserve 1 cup) into large bowl and set aside. Combine yeast and water and dissolve yeast. Make a well in the flour and add yeast, salt, sugar, and oil. Mix until all is dissolved, turn onto floured pastry board, and knead for 10 minutes. Gradually add reserved flour until dough is no longer sticky. Dough will be soft. Place in a greased bowl, cover, and let rise for 1½ hours. Punch down, cover, and let rise for 45 minutes.

Take a 12-inch circular or rectangular pizza pan or pie plate. Coat the bottom with a little olive oil or cornmeal. Place a ball of dough in the center of the pan and begin to stretch it until the entire pan is covered. If you like thick pizza (Sicilian style), use more dough. If you like thin pizza, stretch paper-thin and cut off remaining dough. Use the tips of your fingers to push the dough toward the edge of the pan.

Let dough rest for 20 minutes.

Sauce

Cut garlic into small pieces. Place a medium-sized iron skillet over medium-high heat. Heat to hot. Add 1 tbsp. corn oil. When oil is warm, add garlic, salt, and pepper, and sauté until garlic is brown. Press with a fork into tiny pieces. Add oregano.

Add tomatoes. Rinse tomato can with broth or water and add to mixture. Reduce heat and simmer for 30 minutes, or until reduced.

While sauce is simmering, grate *mozzarella* into course pieces and Parmesan into fine pieces. Slice pepperoni thin or thick to taste. Set on pastry board in individual piles.

When pizza is rested, spoon on sauce to completely cover the dough. Top with shredded *mozzarella* cheese, sprinkle the Parmesan cheese over the *mozzarella,* and finally add the *pepperoni.*

Bake in 425-degree oven for 15-20 minutes or until done. The thicker the crust the longer it will take to bake.

Yield: 1 (12-inch) pizza.

Topping Combinations
Traditional Pizza. Any combination of sausage, pepperoni, anchovy fillets, chopped green peppers, sliced canned or fresh mushrooms, and sliced black olives (Italian or Greek variety) added to the tomatoes and cheese.

Seafood Pizza. This is a cheeseless pizza. Bake the pizza shell for 10 minutes. Remove from oven. Top with pizza sauce. Select 6 pieces each of crab, shrimp (whole), scallops (whole), squid rings, and cod (cut into small pieces) and marinate for at least half an hour in 1 tsp. olive oil, salt, pepper, and garlic chopped into small pieces. Stir 4 to 5 times. Drain. Arrange around pizza. Top with additional sauce (and cheese, if desired, but cheese and seafood are not a good match). Sprinkle with basil and oregano. Bake an additional 10 minutes or until seafood is done.

Vegetable Pizza. Top with tomato sauce and any combination of raw or cooked *broccoli,* cauliflower, *zucchini,* green peppers, mushrooms, onions, black olives, tomato slices, and marinated eggplant. You may add additional sauce (and cheese).

White Pizza
Pizza Bianca

Long before we made what is known as pizza, we made white pizza and so did most Italians. Our recipe includes cheese, but many variations do not.

dough:
2½ to 3 cups flour
¼ oz. quick-rising dry yeast
1 cup warm water
½ tsp. salt
1 tbsp. granulated sugar
¼ cup corn oil
1 tsp. olive oil or cornmeal

topping:
4 cloves chopped garlic
1½ tbsp. chopped basil
6 oz. shredded *mozzarella* cheese
4 oz. thinly sliced *Fontina* cheese
¼ cup freshly grated Parmesan cheese
½ tsp. pepper
2 tbsp. olive oil
Coarse salt

Sift flour into large bowl, reserving 1 cup, and set aside. Combine yeast and water and dissolve yeast. Make a well in the flour and add yeast, salt, sugar, and oil. Mix until all is dissolved, turn onto floured pastry board and knead for 10 minutes. Gradually add reserved flour until dough is no longer sticky. Dough will be soft. Place in a greased bowl, cover, and let rise for 1½ hours. Punch down, cover, and let rise for 45 minutes.

Take a 12-inch circular or rectangular pizza pan or pie plate. Coat the bottom with a little olive oil or cornmeal. Place ball of dough in the center of the pan and begin to stretch it until the entire pan is covered. If you like thick pizza (Sicilian style) use more dough. If you like thin pizza, stretch paper-thin and cut off remaining dough. Use the tips of your fingers to push the dough toward the edge of the pan. Let dough rest for 20 minutes.

Peel and chop garlic and basil. Shred *mozzarella*. Slice *Fontina*. Grate Parmesan.

Combine basil, pepper, garlic, and olive oil. Spread over stretched dough. Top with *mozzarella, Fontina,* and Parmesan. Sprinkle with coarse salt.

Heat oven to 350 degrees. Bake pizza for 15 to 20 minutes or until cheese is bubbly and crust is brown around the edges.

Yield: 1 (12-inch) pizza.

Note: If you do not want to make pizza dough you can buy dough from bakeries, pizza shops, or in the frozen-foods section of your supermarket.

Variation: Our original white pizza did not have cheese. Spread oil mixture over dough, add coarse salt, and bake. We cannot make up our minds, so we often do half the pizza with cheese and half without.

Another choice is to use only Parmesan.

Desserts
Dolci

When I was in Italy in the 1970s, my *Zia Ada* made me a dessert using *mascarpone,* that wonderful cream-cheese-like dairy wonder. I wanted the recipe, but she said that we did not have *mascarpone* in America. She was right then, but we have it now. All the Italian-American bakers can now undo the changes in their recipes and incorporate *mascarpone* once again. That is, if this generation knows that it was eliminated in the first place.

Tuscan cookies tend to be hard, equally at home dunked in good wine or cold fresh milk. Cakes are rich and chewy, filled with nuts and candied fruit and laced with spices, or light and airy and layered with cream. The hardness of some Tuscan desserts reaches back to Etruscan days when storage was a problem. A hard cookie or cake lasted longer and could accompany a traveler, including an army, on difficult journeys.

Spicy northern Italian desserts had their birth in the Middle Ages when Venetian merchants first brought back spices from Africa, the Middle East, and Asia. As Italian cooks discovered the rich taste of these spices they used them abundantly, often combining half a dozen flavors in one delicious dish. *Cavallucci* and *panforte,* two of our favorites, are representative of this type of dessert.

One of the specialties of Tuscany is the chestnut. It is ground into flour, used in breads and *polentas,* chopped like a nut as a filling for sweets, boiled in milk, candied, dried, or roasted. The chestnut staved off famine in the Middle Ages, when in some Italian villages it was the only food available. Chestnuts did the same for Gino's family. Chestnut flour *(farina dolce)* is not easy to find in the U.S. market and there is no good substitute. Look for it online or in specialty or gourmet shops. Not all people will like *castagnaccio,* the unusual chestnut cake blended with rosemary and pine nuts, but for those who do, it is a delicacy.

Citron is another Tuscan specialty used in desserts. Grown for its rind, which is then candied, it looks like a lemon but is longer in shape. It can be found in candied form in Italian food stores and gourmet shops.

Candy
Caramelle

Almost every province in Italy has a candy-making center like *Perugia,* in *Umbria* where a variety of sweets are made. Our favorite candy is *confetti,* a sugar-coated candy with an almond, licorice, or liquor center, which always appears at important events such as weddings, baptisms, and special holidays. We never made *confetti* but sure do eat and enjoy them. We do make another non-Tuscan treat, *torrone,* a chewy nougat that is a favorite at Christmas and Easter.

Italian Nougat
Torrone

Torrone has been a specialty at Christmas since it was first made in the town of *Cremona* in Lombardy (home of Stradavari violins) to celebrate a royal wedding in 1441. On that occasion it was shaped like the city bell tower. At least that is what the good people of *Cremona* say. There is evidence to suggest that this wonderfully delicious sweet is yet another gift from the Arab world, where a similar candy called *turun* is made. Who brought it to Europe is also debated. Some scholars say the Roman army brought it back from the Middle East. Others say the Sicilians spread it throughout Europe. We may never know the true origin, but we do know that it is delicious.

3 tbsp. pistachio nuts
½ cup hazelnuts
2 cups almonds
2 cups water
⅓ cup honey
1 egg white
⅛ tsp. salt
½ cup granulated sugar
1 tsp. vanilla or orange extract
2 tbsp. water
2 sheets wafer paper (*ostie*)*

Peel and chop nuts into desired thickness. Set aside. Fill bottom of double boiler with water and place over medium heat. When water comes to a boil, place top of boiler over water and add honey. Stir constantly with spoon until honey forms a hard ball (265 to 270 degrees on candy thermometer).** Add salt to egg white, beat until stiff, and fold into honey.

Place small saucepan over medium-high heat. Add sugar, vanilla, and water. Stir constantly until it reaches crack (275 to 280 degrees on candy thermometer). Blend two mixtures into saucepan and continue stirring until thermometer reaches 280 degrees. Remove from heat, add nuts, and stir well.

Line the bottom of a loaf pan or an ice cube tray with a layer of paper thin wafers *(ostie)*. Pour mixture into pan, smooth out top, and cover with additional wafer paper. Press down with palm of hand until firm and smooth. Allow to cool.

Once cool, remove from pan and cut into 1½-inch-by-2½-inch rectangles. Wrap each in foil. Store in a covered jar in a cool place.

Yield: 10-12.

Notes: **Ostie* are wafer-thin sheets of edible paper found in confectioners' stores.

**If you do not have a candy thermometer, test nougat with cold water. Drop a pinch of nougat into cold water. If it forms hard ball, proceed.

Cakes
Torte

Light and airy or hard and spicy, Nonna always had a delicious cake on hand for holidays. They are all favorites, but each belonged to a special season and appeared only at that time. Like most of our foods, the ingredients were not available year-round in Italy and each season dictated what was to appear at our table. We kept to the traditions in America.

Chestnut Cake with Rosemary and Pine Nuts
Castagnaccio

Castagnaccio is a Florentine specialty sold by street vendors in the autumn when chestnuts are in season. Its origin has been lost, but its unusual blending of chestnuts, pine nuts, and rosemary creates a semisweet and tangy taste. The chestnut is sweet enough without adding sugar, but the flavor of this cake is definitely an acquired taste.

2 tbsp. white raisins
¼ cup water
1½ cups chestnut
　　flour
¼ tsp. salt
2 tbsp. corn oil
1 cup water
2 tbsp. pine nuts
1 tsp. rosemary

Place raisins in ¼ cup water and allow to soften for at least half an hour. Drain and set aside.

In a mixing bowl combine flour, salt, corn oil, 1 cup water, and raisins. Mix until smooth and pour into a well-oiled 8-to-9-inch pie pan.

Sprinkle the top with pine nuts and rosemary and bake at 350 degrees for 45 minutes, or until the top begins to crack.

Yield: 1 (9-inch round, 1-inch-high) cake.

Notes: Chestnut flour is semisweet, but for a sweeter cake add 1 tbsp. sugar. Chestnut flour is sometimes available in gourmet and health-food stores.

Remember that pine nuts from China can leave a disagreeable taste in your mouth that lasts a long time and reemerges each time you eat.

Medieval Fruitcake
Panforte

Of all Italian desserts, this rich, chewy cake filled with spices, candied fruit, and nuts is the epitome of things Tuscan. Its origin is obscure: it may have come from the kitchens of *Siennese* monks. But we do know it accompanied medieval knights on crusade. *Panforte* (strong or pungent bread) is a specialty of the Tuscan city of Siena, where each baker has guarded the ingredients, especially the spices, for centuries. It is the best and most famous torte of Italy and is shipped all over the world, especially at Christmas. In our family it was a must at Christmas, served at the end of the meal along with coffee and the fruitcake on the next page.

1 cup hazelnuts
1 cup peeled whole
    almonds
1¼ cups candied fruit
1 tsp. candied lemon
    peel
⅔ cup flour
1 tbsp. cocoa
1 tsp. cinnamon
¼ tsp. coriander
¼ tsp. cloves
¼ tsp. nutmeg
⅛ tsp. white pepper
½ tsp. vanilla
⅓ cup granulated
    sugar
½ cup honey
Confectioners' sugar
1 parchment sheet
    (optional)

Spread hazelnuts and almonds on separate cookie sheets. Toast at 350 degrees for 5 to 6 minutes. Remove; rub hazelnuts in a towel, removing skins. Chop nuts in half (can remain whole). Chop candied fruit and lemon peel into chunky pieces. Combine all in a large bowl and add flour, cocoa, cinnamon, coriander, cloves, nutmeg, pepper, and vanilla. Toss.

Grease bottom of 9-inch springform pan and line with parchment paper (optional). Grease paper.

Place sugar and honey in saucepan and heat to 242 degrees (use a candy thermometer) until it becomes a clear syrup. If it bubbles, remove from heat and stir until bubbles subside. Pour over fruit-nut mixture, stir, and pour into springform pan. Smooth top with a floured spatula.

Heat oven to 300 degrees; bake 35 minutes. Remove sides of pan. Allow to cool 1 hour. Add enough confectioners' sugar to make it pure white. Press down firmly. Allow to cool another hour.

Turn upside-down (will be soft at this point). Remove parchment paper and bottom of springform pan and cover second side with confectioners' sugar (if pan resists, run a dull knife between it and the cake). Allow to set 1 hour. Wrap in plastic. Store 1 month (we cannot wait and eat it the next day).

Serves: 10-12.

Note: Can be stored in freezer. You may wish to make small cakes and hang them from the Christmas tree or simply give them as presents, just as they did in sixteenth-century Tuscany.

Fruit and Nut Cake
Torta di Frutta Candita e Noci

I almost gave up hope when trying to find if Nonna's fruitcake was truly Italian. I could find no equivalent until I presented it as a gift to one of the translators of this cookbook. His eyes lit up in recognition.

Fruitcake took a month to make and added to the anticipation of Christmas. Shelling and chopping nuts was a family affair. After dinner each evening we would sit at the kitchen table and eat more nuts than we chopped. This is a dark, rich, cake with a wonderful flavor. It needs to age a bit before cutting or it will crumble. When I was young and hated candied fruit, I always insisted my mother make me a little cake with just nuts. Today, older and wiser, I like the candied fruit too.

1 lb. almonds
1 lb. Brazil nuts
1 lb. walnuts
1 lb. hazelnuts
1 lb. dates
½ lb. red candied cherries
½ lb. candied pineapple
2 lb. mixed candied fruit
6 tbsp. flour
4 cups flour
1 tsp. salt
1 tsp. cloves
1 tsp. nutmeg
2 tsp. cinnamon
1½ cups butter
2¼ cups brown sugar
6 eggs
2 tsp. vanilla
½ cup molasses
2½ tsp. baking soda
2 shots whisky or rum
1-2 cups strong black coffee

Shell and chop nuts into large chunks. Blanch almonds in hot water, remove skins, cut lengthwise. Cut Brazil nuts, walnuts, and hazelnuts sideways. Set aside. Cut dates in thirds, cherries in half, and pineapple slices in eighths. Add candied fruit and combine all in a large bowl or pot. Add enough flour to coat and keep from sticking together (4 to 6 tbsp.). Set aside (may be stored covered for several days).

Sift flour, salt, cloves, nutmeg, and cinnamon together. Set aside. Cream butter on medium speed, slowly add sugar; cream. When well mixed add eggs, one at a time, then vanilla.

In separate bowl combine molasses with baking soda. Stir. When bubbly alternately add it and sifted ingredients to the butter mixture. Mix. Add whisky or rum. Remove from mixer and add to dry ingredients in a large bowl or pot. Mix with your hands. Use enough strong coffee to wash out the mixing bowl (1 to 1½ cups), and add to the combined batter. The consistency should be very thick.

You will need 4 to 6 baking pans depending on size. Put similar sizes into oven together. Line all pans with wax paper. Fill each to 1 inch from top. Push exposed fruit and nuts into batter. Rinse empty bowl with more coffee and pour onto panned cakes, covering the tops evenly. Trim excess wax paper.

Bake in 300-degree oven for 1½ to 2 hours. When cool, de-pan and remove wax paper. Allow to set for a day. Wrap in foil. Store in cupboard or freezer. If you freeze it, allow to age for a week or so before freezing. Two days before serving, remove, unwrap, and cover with a cloth saturated with rum or whisky.

Yield: 4-6 cakes.

Sponge Cake
Pane di Spagna

Nothing but nothing epitomizes our Tuscan kitchens like the *pane di Spagna* (some spell it *pan di Spagna*). As its name implies, *pane di Spagna* came to Italy from Spain, arriving with the Spanish conquest of Italy in 1412. On holidays the women of *Quarata* would take turns beating an enormous *pane di Spagna* by hand (including the egg whites), quickly passing the bowl so as not to miss a beat.

When Nonna was in her eighties, she played cards once a week with her friends. Along with the ice cream and coffee, a *pane di Spagna* was always served. *Pane di Spagna* was a ritual in the Pelini home, too. Whenever someone was not feeling well, Sandrina would whip up this pleasing cake. This is her recipe.

6 egg yolks
½ cup water
¼ cup corn oil
1½ cups granulated sugar
½ tsp. almond extract
½ tsp. lemon extract
1 tsp. vanilla
½ tsp. salt
1½ cups cake flour
6 egg whites
¾ tsp. cream of tartar
Confectioners' sugar

In a large bowl separate yolks from whites. Beat yolks until they become lemon colored. Slowly add water and oil, and beat until thick and foamy. Add sugar a little at a time. Add all extracts. Combine salt with flour, mix, and slowly add to batter. When well mixed remove from mixer.

Place egg whites in a large bowl and beat slightly with mixer. Add the cream of tartar and continue to beat until stiff. With a large spoon fold beaten egg whites into batter.

Preheat oven to 325 degrees. Pour batter

into ungreased tube pan and bake 1 hour or until golden (see note). Remove from oven and invert. Allow to stand until cool. Remove from pan and dust with confectioners' sugar.

Serves: 6-8.

Sponge Cake 2
Pane di Spagna 2

Every kitchen had a slight variation of the traditional *pane di Spagna*. My Nonna's and ultimately my mother's recipe varied from the Pelini recipe slightly. For example, no vegetable oil was used in my mother's recipe and only one extract, almond or lemon.

6 large eggs
1¼ cups granulated sugar, divided
¼ cup cold water
1 tsp. vanilla
1 tsp. almond or lemon extract
1 cup cake flour
½ tsp. salt
½ tsp. baking powder
½ tsp. cream of tartar
Confectioners' sugar

In a large bowl, separate yolks from whites. Beat yolks in electric mixer for 10 minutes until they become lemon colored. Slowly add ¼ cup sugar. Beat yolks and sugar until creamed. Take your time and let all the sugar dissolve. Add cold water, vanilla, and almond or lemon extract and beat until lemon colored.

Sift flour. Blend with 1 cup sugar. Add salt and baking powder. Stir by hand until well blended. Add to yolk mixture a little at a time. Blend well and remove from mixer.

Place egg whites in a large bowl and beat slightly with mixer. Add the cream of tartar and continue to beat until stiff. Beat until you can turn the bowl upside-down and the egg whites will not fall out. With a large spoon, slowly fold beaten egg whites into batter. Fold; do not stir.

Preheat oven to 325 degrees. Slowly pour batter into ungreased tube pan and bake 1 hour or until golden (see note). Remove from oven and invert. Allow to stand until cool. Remove from pan and dust with confectioners' sugar.

Note: For sixty years we baked this cake for 1 hour. In our new oven, it bakes in 45 minutes.

Sponge Cake with Cream
Zuccotto

Finally, the queen of Tuscan cakes in our home, *zuccotto*. The first time I ate this cake was in my *Zia Ada's* home in Italy, where it was made with *mascarpone* cheese. We did not have *mascarpone*, so we used whipping cream.

Zuccotto, named for the pumpkin squash, or *zucco*, is also said to resemble the orange-colored cupola of *Il Duomo*, the famous Florentine cathedral.

1 *pane di Spagna*
7 oz. semisweet chocolate
2 cups whipping cream or 6 cups *mascarpone* cheese
¾ cup confectioners' sugar
1 cup chopped hazelnuts
1 cup chopped almonds
8-10 maraschino cherries
1 tbsp. cocoa
3 tbsp. confectioners' sugar

Prepare a sponge cake(see index). Divide chocolate in half. Place half in double boiler and melt until smooth, stirring occasionally. Allow to cool. Grate remainder into slivers.

Place whipping cream in a blender and whip. If using *mascarpone* eliminate this step, but allow to come to room temperature and stir. Once cream peaks, slowly add confectioners' sugar and continue to blend. Divide into 2 portions. Into first half fold melted chocolate and hazelnuts. Into second, almonds and chopped chocolate. One half should be dark, the other white.

Select a 7-to-8-inch-deep bowl that is narrow at bottom and wide at top. Line with wax paper.

Cut sponge cake into 10 to 11 oblong pieces (1½ inches wide, 4 to 5 inches long) resembling ladyfingers (you can substitute ladyfingers for the sponge cake if you desire).

Place cherry juice in a wide-mouthed bowl. Dip each cake finger into juice, abundantly wetting one side.

Place each piece of sponge cake into wax-paper-lined bowl vertically (see A), lining entire perimeter, with saturated side facing inside of bowl.

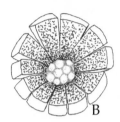

Place 8 to 10 cherries in bottom of the bowl (enough to fill the hole, see B). Top with the almond mixture, then hazelnut mixture. The bowl should be full. Cover with foil and chill for several hours.

Remove from refrigerator, turn upside-down on a serving platter, and remove bowl (slips out easily). Remove wax paper. Place a strip of foil on either side of a finger of sponge cake. Sprinkle cocoa through a sieve on uncovered finger (see C). Skip next finger and repeat, alternating coatings around cake. Once cocoa is completed, repeat with confectioners' sugar.

Serves: 6-8.

Cookies
Biscotti

You cannot "eat just one" of these delicious Tuscan cookies. They are all chewy and dunkable and absolutely delicious. The *cavallucci* are intentionally hard; so are a number of other Tuscan cookies. That is because the recipe is old, perhaps ancient, and the cookie was intended to travel with people over long distances.

Almond Cookies
Ricciarelli

A specialty of *Siena, ricciarelli* are made of almond paste and have a chewy marzipan texture. They were originally a Christmas cookie, but we serve them all year long. You will, too, once you taste the rich flavor and see how easy and quick they are to prepare.

1½ cups almonds
3 cups almond paste
3 egg whites
¾ tsp. baking powder
2 tsp. vanilla
Confectioners' sugar
Flour as needed

Place small pot over medium-high heat and add water. Heat to boiling. Pour over almonds. Cover and allow to set for 20 minutes; peel almonds. Allow almonds to dry and then grind in a meat grinder or food processor until powdery.

Combine almonds with almond paste.

Mix by hand and add egg whites (do not beat whites); mix by hand until soft. Add baking powder and vanilla, and mix by hand. Dough should be firm and a bit sticky.

Sprinkle a little flour on a pastry board. Add dough. Divide dough into 4 to 5 batches. Roll out each batch until 1 inch thick. Cut with a floured knife into 1½-inch rounds. Roll in confectioners' sugar (if dough is too sticky, flour your hands to roll out).

Lay each piece flat and flatten with hand to half the thickness. You can press a whole, peeled almond into the center of each cookie if you wish.

Place on slightly greased cookie sheet and let stand at least 2 hours but preferably overnight.

Heat oven to 300 degrees and bake for 20 to 25 minutes or until beige. Do not allow to brown. Cookie should be chewy, not crunchy.

Yield: 3-4 dozen.

Notes: It is important to cut cookies into 1½-inch pieces or the baking time will be too long and the cookie will be hard instead of chewy. Can be frozen.

Anise Cookies
Biscotti all' Anice

Anise cookies are traditionally served at Italian weddings, where they are arranged on silver trays, their pastel icing of yellow, blue, pink, or green gleaming enticingly. There are two recipes here, ours and the Pelini version. Both are terrific.

cookies:
8 cups flour
2 cups granulated sugar
1 heaping tbsp. baking powder
1½ cups shortening
3 tsp. anise seeds
12 large eggs
3 tbsp. vanilla or lemon extract

icing:
2 egg whites
1 box confectioners' sugar
1 tsp. vanilla or lemon extract
Dash milk (optional)
Red, green, blue, and yellow food colorings

In a medium-size bowl, sift together the flour, sugar, and baking powder. With a pastry cutter *(mezza luna)*, cut in shortening and anise seeds until the consistency of pie dough. (There is no liquid in this cookie, so the texture is dependent on the proper amount of shortening. Be generous.)

In a mixing bowl blend eggs and vanilla or lemon extract. Add egg mixture to the dough. Mix with hands into a tender, but not sticky, dough. Add more flour if necessary.

Remove from bowl and place on pastry board. Dust hands with flour. Pinch off piece of dough and roll into ball. Place balls on ungreased baking sheet that has been dusted with flour. Fill sheet and bake 10 to 15 minutes at 375 degrees or until lightly brown. Repeat until all dough is used. Allow to cool and ice.

Make icing by beating egg whites with confectioners' sugar and vanilla or lemon extract. If too thick, add a little milk to soften. Divide into 3 or 4 bowls. Add scant drop of the different food colorings to individual bowls (too much and icing will be too dark). Mix well. When cookies are cool, place a dab of icing on each cookie and spread with a spatula.

Yield: 10-12 dozen.

Note: This cookie can be frozen.

Anise Cookies 2
Biscotti all' Anice 2

6 eggs
⅔ cup corn oil
1 tbsp. lemon or anise extract
1 cup granulated sugar
2 cups flour
3 tbsp. baking powder
Pinch salt

Beat eggs; add oil and extract. Continue to beat; add sugar gradually, then flour, baking powder, and salt. Dough will be soft. Heat oven to 350 degrees. Drop teaspoonfuls of cookie mixture onto greased sheet. Bake 10 to 12 minutes. Cool and ice.

Yield: 7-8 dozen.

Cooked-Twice Cookies
Biscotti

Biscotti are the most popular Italian cookies. In fact, the name *biscotti* is often used for any type of cookie. *Biscotti* are dipped in coffee for breakfast and in wine at the end of the meal and were served on all holidays. No Italian wedding was complete without a mound of *biscotti* waiting to be served. Children love them dunked in milk. *Biscotti* are cooked twice, *bis cotto,* so they can be stored, almost forever. To Gino a meal was never complete without 2 or 3 *biscotti* and he always reminded Sandrina when the store ran low.

The first time I made *biscotti* Nonna was in her 80s. One day she said, "I think I'll make *biscotti* today." Then she proceeded to say, "Get this; get that. Sift the flour, grate the lemon, etc." By the time we were finished I made the cookies; she sat at the kitchen table giving instructions. I think it was her way of teaching me how to make them.

As with several of our recipes, we have two versions of *biscotti* here. The first is my Nonna's version. It is more cakelike. The second, from the kitchen of the Pelini, is closer to the crisp, dry *biscotti.*

Today *biscotti* are made in an infinite variety: chocolate, coffee, orange, with any number of different nuts, with candied fruit, and on and on and on. Size has changed too. The 3-inch *canducci* are a smaller version of this cookie. We never made them. In fact, we never knew of *canducci* until I brought them back from Italy a decade ago. Boy, are they terrific. To make *canducci,* simply make a smaller roll and, after baking and toasting, let it age until hard—everything else is the same.

biscotti:
4 tsp. baking powder
½ tsp. salt
4 cups flour, sifted
⅔ cup shortening
6 eggs
2 cups granulated
  sugar
Grated rind of 1
  lemon
2 tsp. vanilla
Juice of 1 lemon
2 tsp. lemon extract
⅔ cup pine nuts or
  chopped toasted
  almonds

topping:
3 egg yolks
3 tbsp. granulated
  sugar

In a small bowl, combine baking powder, salt, and sifted flour. Set aside. In another bowl, cream shortening. Add eggs one at a time, alternating with sugar. Allow to blend. Add lemon rind, vanilla, and lemon juice and extract. Blend well. Add nuts and dry ingredients. Blend.

When dough is firm, but soft, turn onto floured board. Knead. If dough is too sticky, add flour, up to ¼ cup, until firm. Knead for 20 minutes. Cut dough into 4 pieces. Form each piece into a 12-inch-by-3-to-4-inch loaf that is higher in the center and tapered at the sides. Length is not important. Place on a greased cookie sheet. Combine yolks and sugar and brush top of each loaf.

Bake at 375 degrees for 20 minutes or until light brown. Remove from oven. Let sit for a few minutes. Cut into 1-inch-thick cookies. Lay each cookie on its side on cookie sheet. Return to oven; toast until light brown on each side.

Yield: 15 cookies per loaf, or 60 cookies.

Variation: The Pelini variation includes 6 tsp. baking powder, 5 cups flour, 1½ sticks margarine (replacing shortening), 1¾ cups granulated sugar, no lemon rind or lemon juice, no pine nuts, but toasted almonds. Bake at 350 degrees for 30 minutes. The remaining ingredients are the same and so is the process.

Bows
Fiocchi

The shape determines the name of this tasty fried cookie made especially for carnival in northern Italy. Called *bugie* (little lies) in Piedmont, *chiacchiere* (gossips) in Lombardy, and *lattughe* (lettuce) in *Emilia-Romagna*, they have three different names in Tuscany: *cenci* (rags), *guanti* (gloves), and *fiocchi* (bows), depending on how you tie them. We serve *fiocchi* on *Martedì Grasso* (Shrove Tuesday), ending a meal of homemade pasta, pork chops on a spit, and endive salad with celery.

4 eggs
6 tbsp. granulated sugar
4 cups sifted flour
1 tsp. baking powder
3 tbsp. corn oil
1 shot whisky
1 tsp. lemon extract
1 tsp. vanilla
1 cup corn oil
4-5 tbsp. confectioners' sugar

Beat eggs and sugar in a large bowl until lemon yellow in color. Gradually add flour (reserve ¼ cup), baking powder, oil, whisky, extract, and vanilla, mixing until blended and manageable (not sticky). Turn onto a floured board and knead into a very soft dough for about 20 minutes, adding remaining flour as needed. Form into a ball, cover with a small bowl, and set to rest for half an hour.

Break dough into 6 pieces and work 1 piece at a time. Roll the piece out gently to the thickness of pie crust (if using a pasta machine roll to #4 thickness—see note). Cut into 1-inch-by-6-inch strips. Place each strip flat on the board. Cut a 2-inch slit (see A). Bring the bottom of the strip up and through the slit (see B). Place on clean piece of cloth. Do not stack.

A

Place a large skillet on high heat and fill with corn oil. Bring to high heat for *fiocchi* must fry quickly. When hot, drop the *fiocchi* into the fat one at a time. Do not crowd (see C). They will puff up immediately and increase slightly in size. Fry to a golden color (about 30 seconds on each side—see note). Turn only once. Remove and lay on paper towel. When slightly cooled, sprinkle with confectioners' sugar.

B

Yield: 7 dozen.

C

Variation: In the Pelini version the procedure is the same, but the ingredients are: 3 cups flour, 4 eggs, 2 tsp. baking powder, 1 tbsp. corn oil, 2 tsp. lemon extract. Cut into strips. Now tie the dough into a bow, just as you would a ribbon. Fry as above.

Notes: If rolled finer than #4, *fiocchi* are fluffier. If they fry too fast, lower heat.

Brigidini

Almost every European ethnic kitchen has some variation of this sweet waffle (see C). Also known as gallets or *pizelles, brigidini* were first made in Italy in the convent of Saint Brigida in *Pistoia.* They are made with a waffle iron. Our original iron was created in the foundry of the local steel mill and we used it for decades. Cooking was a long process as dozens and dozens of *brigidini* were made in a single evening and once the iron was hot, it was nonstop until the last bit of batter was gone. Today, we use an electric iron.

3 eggs
¾ cup granulated
   sugar
¾ cup melted butter
2 tsp. vanilla
1½ cups flour
1 tsp. baking powder
1 dash salt

Beat eggs in a large bowl. Add sugar a little at a time. When eggs and sugar have been blended, add melted butter and vanilla, then flour. Beat by hand until smooth. Add baking powder and a pinch of salt. Mix well. Dough is thick but runny.

Chill dough 2 hours or overnight to enrich flavor. To use, dough must be at room temperature.

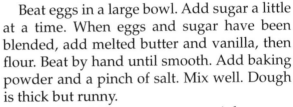

A

Using a hand iron: Clean iron (see A) and grease slightly with butter or corn oil. Heat burner on stove to high. Place 1 tsp. of mixture in center of warm iron. Close lid and secure. If batter spills over side, clean it off. Place iron over heat for 25 to 30 seconds. Turn. Cook other side for additional 25 to 30 seconds. Open iron and remove waffle. It should be golden brown. The amount of time needed to cook each waffle may vary with type of iron.

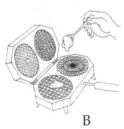

B

Using an electric iron: An electric iron (see B) is easier because it makes 2 or 4 waffles at the same time. Each type of iron varies slightly, but the procedure is the same. Add 1 tsp. of batter to the center of each rosette, close the lid, and allow to cook for about 1 minute. Electric irons do both sides at the same time.

Yield: 3 dozen.

C

Variations: The Pelini version of this cookie substitutes 4 oz. corn oil for butter and uses 1 tsp. lemon and vanilla, 1½ cups flour, and no baking powder.

Anise flavored: Add 1 tbsp. anise seeds.

Chocolate flavored: Omit anise; add ¼ cup cocoa or ½ square melted semisweet chocolate and 1 tsp. vanilla.

Italian Macaroons
Amaretti

A sure bet to be on the table during holiday seasons, *amaretti* are a tangy, crisp, bitter *(amaro)* almond-flavored cookie originally made in *Uboldo* in Lombardy. The original *amaretti* cookie contains bitter almonds, which are illegal in the United States because they contain lethal prussic acid when raw and are considered toxic (the acid disappears once the pit is heated). American recipes substitute peach or apricot pits that have been blanched and toasted in a 250-degree oven for 10 minutes, or until pale gold. Peach and apricot pits also contain prussic acid, which is also destroyed by heating, but they are legal in the United States.

1 cup almonds
3 tbsp. bitter apricot pits or 1 tsp. almond extract
¾ cup confectioners' sugar
1 tsp. flour
2 egg whites
⅓ cup granulated sugar

Place a small pot over medium-high heat and add water. Heat to boiling. Pour over almonds. Allow to set for 20 minutes, then peel almonds. Repeat for apricot pits. Allow both to dry and then grind in a meat grinder or food processor until powdery. Add confectioners' sugar and flour to nuts.

Beat egg whites until soft peaks form and add the sugar a little at a time until stiff. Fold nuts into mixture. If substituting almond extract, add it now.

Spoon into a pastry bag with a plain ½-inch tip. Squeeze 1½-inch mounds onto a greased cookie sheet. If you do not have a pastry bag, shape cookies into patties 1½ inches wide and ¼ inch thick. Sprinkle with granulated sugar and let stand for 2 hours.

Heat oven to 400 degrees. Bake 10 to 15 minutes until light brown.

Turn off oven and allow cookies to dry for additional 20 minutes. Enjoy.

Yield: 30-36 cookies.

Little Horses
Cavallucci

Cavallucci are a special Christmas cookie filled with spices. Known in Italy since medieval times, they are named after *caval-lari*, horse drivers, who ate them in copious quantities at *osterie*, or country inns. The best way to eat these wonderful very hard biscuits is to soak them in coffee or milk or a good glass of *vin santo*.

Cavallucci are served on All Saints' Day and Christmas. For years at Christmas the Pelini family received a holiday package from Italy. Among the precious cargo was a handful of *cavallucci*. Each child got one cookie and sucked on it all day. Their father Gino said, "*Cavallucci* sharpen the teeth."

1 cup water
1¼ cups granulated sugar
½ cup candied orange peel
½ cup walnuts
1 tsp. anise
1 tsp. coriander
½ tsp. baking powder
½ tsp. cinnamon
½ tsp. ground cloves
Dash white pepper
2½ cups flour

Place a medium-size pot over medium-high heat. Add water and sugar and stir. Bring to a boil and remove from stove (sugar should be dissolved). Add all other ingredients except flour in exact order. Water will froth up when baking powder is added. Stir for 30 to 40 seconds. Then add flour.

Allow to cool for at least 15 minutes and turn onto a floured pastry board. Dough should be heavy and sticky.

With floured knife cut dough into quarters. With floured hands roll each piece on pastry board into an inch-thick rope. Cut into 2-inch pieces with a floured knife (if you make the cookie smaller the baking time will be incorrect). Turn each cookie and flatten, leaving a thumb print. Continue until all dough is gone.

Heat oven to 350 degrees. Place cookies on

a greased cookie sheet and bake for 25 minutes. Do not allow to brown. They will come out soft but harden quickly.

Yield: 3 dozen.

Notes: This is a hard cookie. It can be frozen.

Ices and Frozen Desserts
Freddi e Semifreddi

Half Cold
Semifreddo

In 1956 Gigi and Quintina Pitti, Sandrina's brother and his wife, came from Italy to live with the Pelini family. Quintina brought this recipe with her.

Semifreddo is an elegant dessert with an exotic and wonderful taste. It can be made ahead and kept in the freezer. It is much like the popular *tiramisu*, which was invented in *Treviso* in the *Veneto*.

2 eggs
½ lb. butter
1 ⅛ cups granulated sugar
½ cup strong coffee, divided
½ cup *Marsala*, divided
24 ladyfingers
1 oz. grated chocolate
5 oz. slivered almonds

Separate eggs and beat whites until stiff. Set aside. Cream butter and sugar until creamy. Add yolks and continue beating.

Add ¼ cup each of coffee and *Marsala*, a few drops at a time. When well mixed, fold in egg whites.

Place remaining *Marsala* and coffee in shallow bowl. Lightly dip each ladyfinger, dampening the bottom.

Place 12 dampened ladyfingers on a flat oval platter to form a single layer (be sure you can freeze the platter). Cover with half of the egg mixture. Top with half of the grated chocolate and almonds. Top with remaining dampened ladyfingers. Repeat toppings.

Set 10 minutes, cover with plastic wrap, and freeze overnight. Serve frozen.

Serves: 6-8.

Notes: *Marsala* is an Italian cooking wine

found in supermarkets and liquor stores. The latter variety is better for this dish.

Coffee should be at room temperature.

Sponge cake can be substituted for ladyfingers. Cut cake into 5-by-1-by-1-inch pieces.

Pies
Crostate

Foolproof Pie Crust
Crostate per Torte

4 cups flour
1 tbsp. granulated
    sugar
2 tsp. salt
1 egg
1¾ cups shortening
1 tbsp. vinegar
½ cup water

In a medium-size mixing bowl, combine flour, sugar, and salt. Mix with fork until well blended. In separate bowl beat egg, shortening, vinegar, and water. Combine, stirring with a fork until blended.

Divide into 6 even balls and chill at least 15 minutes. Roll out for pie or freeze for later. To freeze, lay the balls on a cookie sheet and flatten like a hamburger. When frozen store in a baggie up to 6 months.

Yield: 3 double-crust shells or 6 single-crust shells.

Apple Pie
Torta di Mele

There is something different about this apple pie. I can't tell you what it is, but any time I am invited to dinner, I know immediately by just looking at their apple pie if it is similar to ours. Once you bake it, you will know what I mean.

2 balls of Foolproof Pie Crust
3 tbsp. flour, divided
6-8 Granny Smith apples
⅓ cup granulated sugar
⅔ cup brown sugar
Juice 1 lemon
¼ lb. butter
2 tbsp. milk
1 tbsp. granulated sugar

Place ball of dough (see preceding recipe) on pastry cloth, dust with flour, and roll to fit pie pan (we use a 9½-inch Pyrex dish). Once rolled, fold in half, and lift into pie pan. Sprinkle with 1 tbsp. flour.

Peel apples. Cut into quarters, core, and slice each quarter into 5 to 6 pieces. Lay slices on dough. When half full, sprinkle half the sugars and lemon juice over apples. Dot with half the butter and a little flour. Continue until apples rise over the top. Add remaining sugars, lemon juice, butter, and flour.

Roll out second ball of dough. Fold in half and cut 6 short slits along folded end to allow steam to escape while cooking. Lift and lay over half of pie plate. Open fold to completely cover pie and press edges together with fingers. Trim excess dough from both top and bottom crusts. Once sealed, press edges with thumb to form ridges. Combine milk and a little sugar and sprinkle over top of pie to form a glaze while baking.

Heat the oven to 425 degrees. Bake pie for 15 minutes. Reduce heat to 350 degrees and bake an additional 45 minutes or until crust is golden.

Serves: 6-8.

Cream Pie
Torta di Crema

This was Nonno's favorite pie. Along with *panforte, torrone,* and *amaretti,* it graced every holiday table (and half the Sundays in between). After Nonno died we never served it again. My mother just could not make it.

crust:
1 ball foolproof pie crust
1 tbsp. flour

filling:
1 qt. and ½ cup cold milk
3 eggs
½ cup cornstarch
1 cup granulated sugar
1 tsp. salt
2 tbsp. butter
2 tsp. vanilla

meringue:
8 tbsp. granulated sugar, divided
1 tbsp. cornstarch
½ cup water
½ tsp. vanilla
3 egg whites
Very small pinch salt

Place dough ball (see preceding recipe) on pastry cloth sprinkled with flour and roll out pie crust to fit your pie pan (we use a 9½-inch Pyrex). If pie pan is 9½ inches roll dough to 12½ inches to allow it to go up the sides of the pie pan. Once rolled, fold in half, and lift into pie pan. Trim off any excess dough and press down around the top of the pie pan to form a ridge. Pierce the pie dough 5 or 6 times with the prongs of a fork. Bake in 350-degree oven until slightly brown.* Remove and set aside.

Place a 4-qt. saucepan over medium-high heat. Add milk. Separate the eggs, setting the whites aside. In a small mixing bowl add yolks, cornstarch, sugar, and salt and beat together slowly.

When milk on stove begins to scald (bubble around the edges) slowly add yolk mixture. Stirring constantly with a spoon, simmer for 10 to 15 minutes or until it thickens to a pudding consistency. Remove from burner and add butter and vanilla. Mix with a wooden spoon and pour into baked pie shell.

To make the meringue, combine 2 tbsp. sugar, cornstarch, and water in a small saucepan. Cook over medium-high heat, stirring constantly, until thick and glossy. Remove from stove, add the vanilla, and set aside to cool.

Place egg whites in a mixing bowl and add a few grains of salt. Beat at high speed for a few minutes or until peaks begin to form. Add remaining sugar 1 tbsp. at a time, alternating with cooled cornstarch mixture (also a spoonful at a time). Continue to beat until stiff.

Pile meringue high on pie and bake in 325-degree oven until browned to your taste.

Serves: 6-8.

*Pie shell may shrink while baking. We place a smaller, empty pie plate over the shell while baking.

Puddings
Budini

Cream Pudding
Budino di Crema

This wonderful cream pudding filled with sponge cake and maraschino cherries is another of Nonno's favorite desserts. It is probably a version of *Zuppa Inglese* (recipe follows) for the dish has a number of variations. We never called it that, but it is always a hit when we serve it to guests. I like to eat the pudding hot, fresh from the stove. It has a different taste when cooled.

4 egg yolks
9 tbsp. granulated sugar
4 tbsp. flour
4 tbsp. cornstarch
1 qt. cold milk
1 tsp. vanilla
1 oz. butter
12 oz. pound or sponge cake
10 oz. maraschino cherries and juice

Beat egg yolks in small mixing bowl. Add sugar and continue beating. Meanwhile mix flour, cornstarch, and milk together. Pass milk mixture through a strainer into yolks.

Place in medium-size saucepan and cook over medium-high heat stirring constantly until it boils (about 10 minutes). Lower heat and continue to simmer for 20 minutes or until it thickens. Stir constantly or it will stick. Remove from heat, add vanilla and butter. Stir.

Slice cake into 1-inch slices. Line bottom of deep casserole with half of cake. Sprinkle each piece with a little cherry juice. Spoon in enough pudding to generously cover. Top with half of cherries. Lay in remaining slices of cake. Add cherry juice. Spoon on remaining cream. Top with cherries and remaining juice.

Eat hot or cold. Store in refrigerator.

Serves: 8.

Note: This recipe and the one for cream pie (see above) are Nonna's recipes. The Pelini family made their cream as in the *Zuppa Inglese* recipe that follows. All recipes are interchangeable.

English Soup (Cream)
Zuppa Inglese

Originally called *zuppa del Duca*, the Duke's Soup, this rich dessert from Siena became *zuppa Inglese* because English residents in Tuscany enjoyed it so much.

Recently it has enjoyed a resurgence in Italy under the name *tiramisu*, "pick me up," a modern variant which includes *mascarpone* cheese and coffee. Actually one could add any flavoring to it and it would be good.

4 egg yolks
9 tbsp. granulated sugar
4 tbsp. flour
4 tbsp. cornstarch
1 qt. cold milk
1 tsp. vanilla or liqueur of your choice
1 oz. butter
6-8 *biscotti* or ladyfingers
Whisky or liqueur to taste

Beat egg yolks in small mixing bowl. Add sugar and continue beating. Meanwhile mix flour, cornstarch, and milk together. Pass milk mixture through a strainer into yolks.

Place in medium-size saucepan over medium-high heat and bring to a boil stirring constantly until the mixture comes to a boil (about 10 minutes). Lower the heat and continue to simmer for 20 minutes, or until it thickens. Stir constantly with a wooden spoon or it will stick. Remove from heat, add vanilla or liqueur and butter. Stir.

Place *biscotti* or ladyfingers on a large platter. Sprinkle cookies with whisky or liqueurs. Slowly spoon cream over all and let cool.

Serve hot or cold. Store in refrigerator.

Serves: 6.

Note: Some recipes for *Zuppa Inglese* are reminiscent of English Trifle—layers of cream, cake, fruit, and gelatin with whipped cream. We never made it that way.

Fresh Fruits, Nuts, and Cheeses
Frutta Fresca, Noci, e Formaggi

Fresh fruits, mixed nuts, and cheeses are a favorite way to end an Italian meal. Even when a rich dessert is served, this mixed medley follows. A glass bowl filled with an assortment of fruit, a wooden bowl with a variety of unshelled nuts, and a platter of assorted cheeses are placed on the table. The bread and the wine are already there. Today this is called a wine and cheese party.

2 apples
2 pears
Red and green grapes
1 wedge each of
  Parmesan, Gorgon-
  zola, Gorgonzola
  con mascarpone,
  Fontina
Assortment of Brazil
  nuts, walnuts, al-
  monds, hazelnuts
1 loaf Italian bread
1 bottle dry red wine
1 bottle dry white
  wine or *vin santo*

Arrange apples, pears, and grapes in a fruit bowl. Arrange cheeses on a cheese board, each with its own small knife. Pile nuts into a wooden bowl, complete with nutcracker and picks. Place bread on bread board with knife. Place all on table along with bottles of wine. You will talk for hours while you pick and eat.

Serves: The various quantities depend on the number of guests. Prepare the cheeses and nuts in equal proportions: pound for pound.

Note: This is good eating, especially when the tastes mingle in the mouth. As a child I would take one bite of an apple or pear, one bite of *Parmesan* cheese, and one bite of the bread, then chew.

Fresh Peaches with Red Wine
Pesca con Vino Rosso

When the peaches are ripe, the mouth waters in anticipation of this delicious concoction. Today, peaches tend to be hard, so we have a standing order at our local fruit store to buy the old, bruised, soft peaches.

1 very ripe peach
6 oz. dry red wine

Peel outer skin. Discard any dark or bruised parts. Cut peach in half. Remove stone. Cut into small wedges.

Place in a wine glass or deep crystal bowl. Add wine. Refrigerate for 1 to 2 hours or overnight. Serve cold.

Serves: 1.

Roasted Chestnuts
Castagne al Forno

Roasted chestnuts were a November favorite in our home, always accompanied by the first taste of the new red wine. When I was young I remember seeing street vendors selling roasted chestnuts.

1-2 lb. chestnuts

Cut a crosswise slit on the flat side of each chestnut to vent. Place chestnuts on a cookie sheet and bake in the oven at 350 degrees.

Open the oven occasionally and, with a long-handled wooden spoon, rotate the chestnuts. Bake for 30 minutes (see notes).

Remove chestnuts from oven. Place on a good-size clean cloth and fold the edges to cover the chestnuts. Press down on the cloth with your palm to crush the chestnuts. Allow to stand about 5 to 6 minutes. Remove. Skin and serve with dry red wine.

To microwave chestnuts prepare in the same manner. For 5 chestnuts zap for 60 seconds on high power. For 10 chestnuts, zap for 2 minutes. Remove, cover, and let set for 3 minutes. Proceed as above.

Serves: 5-6.

Notes: To test, remove a chestnut from the oven and place it in a clean white cloth. Cover, and with the palm of your hand press down on the chestnut. If it crushes easily, it is done.

In every dozen chestnuts there is at least one that has mildewed, rotted, or gone bad. A good chestnut is firm, chewy, and pale yellow.

Fish and Game
Pesce e Cacciagione

When I would curl up on my Nonno's lap and beg for stories about Italy as ardently as I begged for a puff on his pipe, his stories always included the fish in the sea. The closer our imaginary boat got to Italy's golden shores, the bigger the fish. To my young mind they were all goldfish, each as big as a whale. I still see them in my mind's eye.

With seas on three sides of the Italian peninsula, Italy has an abundance of fresh fish, but our village of *Quarata* was inland and had a limited supply. In America we did not live near the sea, nor did our family have avid sportsmen, so fresh fish, when we could find it, was always a treat. But salted cod is as essential to our Christmas table as bread. We serve it in a variety of ways, all the delicious dishes prepared for the same meal.

Game, too, eluded us. Game dishes are a specialty of Tuscany where the hills and mountains hold wild boar, hare, pheasant, quail, ducks and other game birds (once including peacocks). Wild boar still come down from the forests, where they feed on truffles, and invade my cousin Beppe's fields looking for water and a change in their diets. We never cooked wild boar in America, but I have eaten it in Tuscany and it is delicious. Game birds were hunted in the marshes around *Quarata*, especially in autumn. Duck recipes are found in the poultry section. Both wild boar and duck are signature dishes of the *Arezzo* region.

One of the most famous Florentine dishes of the Renaissance came from the kitchens of Catherine de Medici. It was rabbit prepared in a sweet and sour sauce flavored with rosemary and garlic to which candied lemon, lime, and orange peel had been added. Although we enjoy rabbit with rosemary and garlic, we never prepared Catherine's exotic dish, so it is not represented in the recipes in this book. But a dish equal to Catherine's rabbit is Pheasant with Black Olives. Whether prepared with pheasant or chicken, it is flavorful, delicious, and worthy of your best china and your most important guest.

Braised Blue Pike
Luccio Blu in Umido

Pike is a freshwater fish that thrives in colder climates; thus it is abundant in northern streams and lakes. It is a fleshy and tender fish and can be prepared in a variety of ways. This is our favorite. Each fall Pino Guiducci would go to Canada to fish and always bring us a cooler full of Blue Pike.

2 lb. blue pike
3-4 tbsp. flour
1 tsp. salt
2 tsp. pepper
2-3 cloves garlic
4-5 sprigs fresh sage
1 cup corn oil
1½ cups canned whole or crushed tomatoes (not pureed)
1 cup broth or water

Be sure the pike is dressed. Wash thoroughly in and out in running water. Pat dry with cloth. Place fish on a cutting board. Remove head and tip of tail and discard. Depending on the size, cut into 5 to 7 equal 3-inch pieces. First, cut the body into thirds and any large pieces in half. Set aside.

Clean cutting board and place flour in center. Add salt and pepper to flour, toss. Roll each piece of pike in flour until evenly coated. Peel and cut garlic into 3 or 4 pieces. Cut sage into small pieces. Do not use many stems.

Place medium-size iron skillet over medium-high heat and allow to heat. When hot, add oil. Heat to hot. Place floured fish into hot oil and sear. Turn once. Remove when golden brown and place on a paper towel to drain.

In the same oil (or if dirty from flour, discard, wipe skillet, reheat, and add new oil), sauté garlic. When garlic is brown, crush with fork until mashed. Add sage and simmer a few minutes. Add tomatoes and crush with a fork; simmer 10 minutes. Rinse tomato can with ½ cup broth or water and add to mixture. Salt and pepper to taste, if necessary. Mix well. Lower heat and simmer uncovered for 15 minutes more.

Remove from heat and run sauce through a sieve to remove pulp and sage. Return strained sauce to skillet, return heat to medium-high, simmer for 5 minutes; reduce heat, and simmer uncovered for 15 minutes or until sauce begins to lose bright red color. Add fish. Cover and simmer slowly for 30 minutes or until sauce is a brown-red and oil begins to separate and float on surface (skim if desired). Do not stir or turn. If sauce begins to dry, add remaining broth. Serve with fresh homemade bread.

Yield: 5-7 pieces.

Cod
Baccalà

Hard as nails, dried, salt-cured *baccalà* arrived in Italian food stores in America in late autumn, adding one more pungent aroma to an already saturated atmosphere. A week before Christmas the *baccalà* was set to soak in a pan of water to begin the process of removing the salt and softening the flesh. The water was drained daily and, if enough salt was not removed, the entire Christmas Eve feast was ruined.

Today *baccalà* is not as dry as in Nonna's day. It does not require as much soaking and can be bought without bones. To prepare the modern *baccalà*, soak in cold water for 8 hours, changing the water twice. Remove from cold water, rinse well in running water, and cut into serving pieces. A large fish yields 12 to 14 3-by-3-inch pieces.

Boiled or Broiled Cod with Chickpeas
Baccalà Lesso o Arrostito con Ceci

Always, always, the second course of the Christmas Eve meal, boiled or broiled cod is refreshing, a good choice for a light meal.

1 salted and soaked whole cod fish
2 qt. water
¼ tsp. pepper
1-2 tbsp. olive oil

Soak and prepare cod as directed in the preceding introduction.

To boil: Cut cod into 3-inch pieces. Put water in a 6-to-8-quart pot and bring to a boil. Add the cod fish and boil until tender, about 8 to 10 minutes. Drain.

Place in a deep casserole, pepper to taste, and sprinkle with a good olive oil. Do not add salt until you taste it.

To broil: Cut fish into 3-inch pieces. Place in broiler for 5 minutes, turn, and continue for 5 more minutes. Do the same over an open flame or on a grill. Arrange on a platter, and sprinkle with pepper and oil. Do not add salt until you taste it.

Serve boiled or broiled cod with chickpea salad (see index).

Serves: 5-8, depending on size of fish.

Note: As a low-cal alternative I mix the cod and chickpeas together and add salt, pepper, and wine vinegar. Occasionally I add slices of onion, pitted black olives, celery, and avocado. It is filling, healthy, and tasty.

Cod in Sauce with Onions
Baccalà in Umido con Cipolle

Like boiled cod, cod in onion sauce or with sage and garlic (recipe follows) is part of our Christmas Eve tradition. Every time we eat it, we also serve up the story of the last time Nonna cooked this meal. She was 78 years old. It was a Friday in the late fall, and we came home expecting the aroma of simmering *baccalà* and onions. Instead when we opened the door there was no smell at all. When we took the lid off the iron skillet the *baccalà* smelled strange and when we tasted it, it was awful and fell to pieces. We had no choice but to throw it away and as we poured it down the disposal and turned on the water, mounds of bubbles filled the sink. Nonna had fried the cod in liquid detergent instead of oil. I could see the pain in her eyes. She never cooked again.

1 salted and soaked whole cod fish
½ cup flour
1 tsp. pepper
1 cup corn oil
5-6 medium onions*
2 cups whole or crushed canned tomatoes (not pureed)
1 cup broth or water

Soak and prepare cod fish as directed in the introduction to this section. Wash, drain and pat dry. Mix flour with pepper and place on a board (do not add salt).

Place a large-size iron skillet on medium-high heat. Heat to hot and add oil. Press fish into flour. Turn and press again. Coat well. When oil is hot, place fish in skillet. Cook until a golden brown, turning once to brown both sides. Remove from skillet and place on paper towel to drain.

If oil is dirty from flour, discard, wipe the skillet, reheat, and add new oil.

Peel, wash, and slice onions. Add to oil and sauté for 10 minutes, or until transparent.

Add tomatoes and crush with a fork. Simmer 10 minutes. Rinse tomato can with ½ cup broth or water and add to mixture. Do not add salt. Mix well.

Lower heat and simmer uncovered for 15 to 20 minutes or until sauce begins to lose bright red color. Add fish. Cover and simmer slowly for 30 minutes or until sauce is a brown-red and oil begins to separate and float on surface (skim if desired). Do not stir or turn. If sauce begins to dry, add remaining broth.

Serves: 6-8, depending on size of fish.

Note: The amount of onions is a matter of taste: 1 to 2 onions add flavor, 3 to 5 make the onions, like potatoes, a component of the stew. We like lots of onions.

Cod in Sauce with Sage and Garlic
Baccalà in Umido con Salvia e Aglio

There is little difference in the preparation of cod with onions or cod with sage. The flavor, of course, is different. The choice is not an easy one and we always had to have a family council to decide which to prepare, keeping in mind that we would not taste the losing recipe for another year.

1 salted and soaked
 whole cod fish
½ cup flour
2 tsp. pepper
1 cup corn oil
3-4 cloves garlic
6-7 sprigs sage
2 cups whole or
 crushed canned
 tomatoes (not
 pureed)
1 cup broth or water

Soak and prepare cod fish as directed in the introduction to this. Wash, drain, and pat dry. Mix flour with pepper and place on a board. Do not add salt.

Place a large-size iron skillet on medium-high heat. Heat to hot and add oil. Press fish into flour. Turn and press again. Coat well. When oil is hot, add fish. Brown to a golden brown. Turn once and brown second side. Remove from skillet and place on a paper towel to drain.

If oil is dirty from flour, discard, wipe the skillet, reheat, and add new oil. Peel and cut garlic into medium-size pieces. Wash sage and cut into pieces. Do not use a lot of stems.

Add garlic to hot oil. When garlic is brown crush with fork until mashed. Add sage and simmer a few minutes. Add tomatoes and crush with a fork. Simmer 10 minutes. Rinse tomato can with ½ cup broth or water and add to mixture. Mix well. Lower heat and simmer uncovered for 15 minutes.

Remove from heat and run sauce through a sieve removing pulp and sage. Return sauce to skillet, return heat to medium-high, simmer for 5 minutes, reduce heat and simmer uncovered for 15 minutes or until sauce begins to lose bright red color. Add fish. Cover and simmer slowly for 30 minutes or until sauce is a brown-red and oil begins to separate and float on surface (skim if desired). Do not stir or turn. If sauce begins to dry, add remaining broth.

Serves: 6-8, depending on size of fish.

Cod with Sweet and Sour Sauce
Baccalà in Agro Dolce

This was not one of Nonna's favorites. It should have been. It was Tuscan and specific to our village. It was made by many of the fine Tuscan cooks in our neighborhood, including our friend, Sophia Poletini, whose daughter Lena Poletini Falbo gave us this recipe. And it is absolutely delicious.

¼ cup olive oil
1 cup thinly sliced medium yellow onions
2½ cups whole or crushed canned tomatoes (not pureed)
½ tsp. salt
½ tsp. pepper
2 tbsp. red wine vinegar
2 tbsp. sugar
2 tbsp. fresh mint or 2 tsp. dried
1 salted and soaked whole cod fish
½ cup flour
¼ tsp. pepper
½ cup corn oil

Place a medium-size iron skillet over medium-high heat. Heat to hot and add oil. Heat to hot. Peel, clean and slice onions. Add to oil and reduce heat. Sauté until soft and transparent (about 10 minutes), stirring regularly. Do not brown.

Add tomatoes, salt, pepper. Cook uncovered, stirring frequently until slightly thick, about 15 minutes, or until tomatoes begin to lose bright red color. Add vinegar, sugar, and mint (you can cut mint into small pieces if desired). Mix well and set aside.

Soak and prepare cod fish as directed in the introduction to this section. Wash, drain, and pat dry. Mix flour with pepper (do not add salt) and place on a board.

Place a large-size iron skillet on medium-high heat. Heat to hot and add oil. Press fish into flour. Turn and press again. Coat well. Fry until a golden brown, turning once to brown both sides. Remove from skillet and place on paper towel to drain.

Place *baccalà* in *agro dolce* sauce. Bring to a boil. Cover, reduce heat, and allow to simmer slowly for 20 to 30 minutes, or until the sauce is deep brown-red in color. Oil will float on surface when done (skim, if desired). Do not stir while simmering or *baccalà* will fall apart.

Serves: 6-8, depending on size of fish.

Notes: If sauce is too sour add a little more sugar, if too sweet, add more vinegar. If sauce becomes too thick, add a little broth and continue to simmer.

Other Fish
Altri Pesci

Fish Stew
Cacciucco o Zuppa di Pesce

The French call this dish *bouillabaisse,* but the origin is Italian. Folk legend maintains the fishermen of a small Tuscan village near *Livorno* were lost in rough seas and the poor women sent the children begging for food. The children brought back bits and pieces. Out of the medley this wonderful stew, called *cacciucco* in the village, but *zuppa di pesci* in the rest of Italy, was created. Another myth relates that the men in lighthouses had an abundance of fish but were forbidden to use oil needed to keep the lamps lit. They created the stew.

The choice of fish is really up to you, but in *Livorno,* where it is the signature dish, the belief is you should have five varieties of fish, one for each *c* in the dish's name.

1 lb. lobster tail
1 lb. cod, pike, sea-
    bass, or roughy
½ lb. shrimp
½ lb. squid
12 clams or sea dates
1 lb. scallops
2 tbsp. olive oil
1 cup sliced onions
1 cup chopped car-
    rots
2 cloves minced
    garlic
4 cups fresh tomatoes
8 oz. clam juice
2 tbsp. fresh parsley
¾ tsp. thyme
⅛ tsp. salt
⅛ tsp. pepper
½ cup broth (op-
    tional)

Wash and clean all seafood. Cut lobster into 3 to 4 pieces, shell and all. Cut fish of choice into 3-inch pieces. Clean and de-vein shrimp and squid. Wash clams and scallops.

Place extra-large iron skillet over medium-high heat. Allow to heat and when hot, add oil. Wash and slice onions and carrots, add to oil. Peel garlic, add to oil. When garlic is brown, crush with a fork into small pieces. Sauté until onions are transparent, about 10 minutes.

Add tomatoes, reduce heat, and simmer uncovered for 20 minutes, or until tomatoes begin to thicken and darken. Add clam juice, parsley, thyme, salt, and pepper. Bring to a boil, cover, lower heat and simmer for 15 to 20 minutes or until brown-red in color. Add lobster and fish. Simmer 5 minutes. Add shrimp, squid, clams, and scallops. Simmer 5 minutes or until clam shells begin to open. If sauce is too thick, add ½ cup broth and simmer for a few minutes. Serve in soup bowls with fresh Italian bread.

Serves: 6.

Note: You can add pasta to this fish stew by cooking it separately, laying down a bed of pasta on a plate, and covering with stew.

Grilled Fish
Pesce Arrostito

Sea bass, orange roughy, trout, halibut, and cod are good fish to grill. Fish is best when grilled whole rather than in fillets. The secret to grilling fish is to marinate the fish and oil the grill. Then the flesh does not stick.

1 whole, dressed fish
Salt and pepper, to taste
1 tbsp. lemon juice
1 clove crushed garlic
1 bay leaf
Dash olive oil
1 tbsp. corn oil
Lemon wedges

Wash and clean the fish. Salt and pepper the inside. Combine lemon juice, garlic, bay leaf, salt and pepper in a flat dish. Add fish and top with dash of olive oil. Allow to marinate for 20 minutes, turn, and marinate the second side for 20 minutes.

Place in broiler or on an oiled grill (to oil grill, place 1 tbsp. corn oil on a paper towel, rub over grill, place fish on oiled area).

Grill for 4 to 5 minutes on one side, turn, and grill 4 to 5 minutes on second side. Serve with lemon wedges.

Serves: 1-4, depending on size of fish.

Halibut Steak with Anchovy Sauce
Passera di Mare con Acciugata

4 slices inch-thick halibut steaks
Pepper
Acciugata sauce (see index)

Wash the fish. Place in broiler or on an oiled grill. Grill for 4 to 5 minutes on one side, turn, and grill 4 to 5 minutes on second side. Add pepper (no salt).

If you grill the fish, be sure to oil the grill to stop the fish from sticking. Place oil on a paper towel, rub over grill, place fish on oiled area.

Remove fish from broiler or grill, place on a serving tray, and cover with *Acciugata* sauce.

Serves: 4.

Note: *Acciugata* sauce is good on any fresh fish—grilled, broiled, boiled, or baked—but especially good on halibut.

Smoked Herring or Shad on the Open Fire
Arringa o Salacca Arrostite al Fuoco

Smoked herring (*arringa*) and shad (*salacca*) are seasonal foods found in Italian food stores during Lent all over America. Available in imported or domestic varieties, they once came crated in wooden boxes and the store would be saturated with the strong aroma, a smell Italians loved, but one that kept *stranieri* (foreigners) away. Both fish are salty so additional salt need not be added. Nonno often cooked his afternoon lunch in the furnace. He simply stoked up the coal fire, opened the furnace door, and with specially made skewers held the meat or fish over the open fire. Gino cooked his smoked fish in the brick ovens of the cement factory where he worked.

1 smoked herring or shad
3 tbsp. olive oil
1 tbsp. vinegar
Pepper to taste

Place whole fish in a wire rack over open coals for few minutes until hot (or broil in oven for 2 minutes on both sides). The fish has been smoked and therefore does not need to be cooked.

Remove from wire, peel off skin, split lengthwise, remove scales, trim fins and part of tail with scissors, and cut each side into thirds. Sprinkle with oil, vinegar, and pepper (no salt) to taste.

Serves: 1-2, depending on size of herring or shad.

Note: We always served smoked herring or shad with a side dish of boiled white beans (see index for bean salad).

Tuna Fish in Oil with Radishes
Tonno all'olio con Ravanelli

When Nonno picked the first radish from the spring garden out came the tuna and this tasty entree was prepared.

6 oz. Italian tuna
12-14 fresh garden radishes
Olive oil
Ground pepper
Vinegar

Drain tuna, break into chunks, and place in serving dish. Clean radishes and slice. Add to the tuna and mix well.

Top with olive oil, ground pepper, and vinegar to taste. Do not add salt.

Serves: 2-3.

Game
Cacciagione

We always treat game to eliminate the wild taste. After gutting and skinning, wash carefully in water and ½ tsp. baking soda. Let stand 30 minutes. Drain and place in salt water. Let stand 2½ hours. Drain; repeat salt bath overnight. Wash in clear water. This removes excess blood and eliminates the wild taste.

Pheasant
Fagiano

Pheasant was one of our favorite game birds, and because we did not have it often, we relished it whenever it came our way.

A freshly killed pheasant should be aged before cooking. To do this, hang it on a pole, gut it, and allow it to stand from 5 to 8 days. Do not remove the feathers. After it has aged, pluck the feathers, clean the bird, and soak as described above.

Pheasant with Black Olives and Sage
Fagiano con Olive Mature e Salvia

Early one Sunday morning the Pelini family arrived at our house unannounced with a picnic basket in hand. They had all the ingredients for this wonderful dish and the pots were soon simmering on the stove. We enjoyed it so much that, when we do not have pheasant, which is most of the time, we substitute chicken. Today I often buy only chicken thighs for this dish. I have the butcher chop each one in half (widthwise). *Keep the skin on and bone in.*

3 lb. pheasant (or 3 lb. chicken with skin and bone)
2-3 tbsp. butter
Salt and pepper
½ cup strips of *prosciutto* (or *pancetta*)
⅓ cup sage leaves
¼ cup broth or dry white wine
12 oz. small black pitted olives

De-game pheasant as described above. Cut in pieces. Place large-size dry iron skillet over medium-high heat. Do not add butter. Add pheasant. Cover. Simmer 5 minutes. Uncover and drain off any accumulated liquid. This rids the pheasant of gamy taste (if using chicken omit this step).

After removing all liquid add butter, salt, and pepper. Brown 15 minutes, turning at least once. Once brown, lower heat to medium and add prosciutto and sage. Simmer 10 minutes. Add wine or broth to keep moist. Simmer 10 minutes. Add black olives and a little of olive juice. Finish simmering on low burner for an additional 10 minutes or until done.

Serves: 4-6.

Note: Cook pheasant longer than chicken.

Quail
Quaglia

Nonno enjoyed song birds served this way. When he did, he ate alone, for none of us enjoyed or approved. In fact, any small bird is good following this recipe.

4 quail
1 tsp. salt
1 tsp. pepper
8 sage leaves
4 tsp. butter
2 (¼-inch-thick) slices *pancetta*
2 tbsp. corn oil

Wash quails inside and out, drain, and pat dry. Combine salt and pepper in a small bowl and mix well.

Rub inside cavity of each quail with a little salt and pepper mixture. Place 2 sage leaves in each cavity. Tie the legs of each quail together with a piece of string.

Rub salt and pepper mixture on the outside of each quail. Rub with unmelted butter and place half a strip of pancetta over the breast.

Heat oven to 400 degrees. Put oil in bottom of roasting pan. Place quails, breast side up, into the oil, moving each to coat bottom of bird.

Bake in oven for 15 minutes. Lower heat to 325 degrees and roast 45 minutes.

Serves: 4.

Note: You can add oven potatoes to the roasting quail. Peel and cut 3 large potatoes into 5 or 6 pieces, smaller ones in half (for crunchy potatoes cut into smaller pieces). Place the potatoes around the quail, making sure they are in the oil. Do not salt or pepper potatoes. Turn potatoes every 15 minutes, coating them with the oil in the pan.

Rabbit
Coniglio

A rabbit is a *lepre* when it is wild and a *coniglio* when it is domesticated. Either way, we prepare it in sauce and as a roast. It is one of the best Tuscan dishes.

Rabbit Sauce
Salsa di Coniglio

1 dressed rabbit
4 onions
2 cloves garlic
¼-inch-thick slice *pancetta*
1 small carrot
½ cup celery
3-4 sprigs fresh parsley
¼ cup corn oil
1 tbsp. pepper
1 tbsp. salt
1 lb. ground chuck
½ lb. pork sausage
4 oz. red table wine (optional)
28 oz. whole canned tomatoes (not pureed)
1 cup broth
12 oz. tomato paste
Salt
Pepper

De-game wild rabbit as described above. Cut into serving-size pieces. Place medium-size skillet over medium-high heat. Do not add oil. Add rabbit. Cover. Cook a few minutes. Uncover, drain. Simmer. Drain. Repeat until no liquid is formed. Set aside. If using domesticated rabbit omit this step.

Peel onions, wash, cut into quarter wedges. Peel garlic, chop. Cut *pancetta* in half. Peel carrot and celery, wash, cut into pieces. Wash parsley. Combine and grind in a meat grinder or food processor (the grinder is better because it releases the juices).

Place large-size iron skillet over medium-high heat. Heat to hot. Add oil. Heat to hot. Add rabbit. Brown on both sides. Remove. Add chopped ingredients, pepper, salt, and sauté until onions are transparent. The longer it cooks (at least 20 minutes), the better the sauce. When mixture begins to stick to skillet, add ground meat, shredding with fork into small pieces (you can add scraps of rabbit to this mixture). Simmer until meat is dark brown and turning crispy, stirring often so it does not stick to skillet. Add wine and continue to sauté.

While meat mixture is simmering, heat tomatoes in 6-qt. pot over low heat. Add paste.

Rinse both tomato and paste cans with ½ cup broth or water and add to meat mixture. Let simmer 10 minutes, remove meat mixture from skillet and add to simmering tomatoes. Raise heat to high. When it begins to bubble, reduce heat, cover, and simmer slowly.

Add rabbit to simmering sauce. Simmer very slowly for 3 to 4 hours. Stir often to avoid sticking. A good sauce will look dark, almost brown, not red, and oil will separate and float on top (skim if desired). Serve over wide pasta.

Serves: 10-12.

Rabbit in Tomato Sauce
Lepre in Salsa di Pomodoro

1 dressed wild rabbit
3 tbsp. corn oil
Salt and pepper
2-3 cloves garlic
Pinch allspice
5-6 sprigs rosemary
¼ cup red table wine
3-4 tbsp. whole or
  crushed canned
  tomatoes (not
  pureed)
1 cup broth

De-game wild rabbit as described above. Cut into serving-size pieces.

Place a dry iron skillet on medium-high heat. Do not add oil. Place rabbit into the dry skillet. Cover. Let simmer for a few minutes. Uncover and drain off any liquid that has accumulated. Simmer again. Drain again. Repeat until no more liquid is formed. This rids the rabbit of gamy taste. If using domesticated rabbit omit this step (see note).

Remove rabbit pieces from skillet. Heat skillet and add oil. Return rabbit to skillet. Add salt, pepper, garlic, allspice, and rosemary and allow to brown on all sides, turning once. Add wine and continue to brown for 5 minutes. Remove meat from the skillet.

Add tomatoes to the juices in the skillet, crushing with a fork into small pieces. Simmer 10 minutes. Rinse tomato can with ½ cup broth or water and add to mixture. Salt and pepper to taste, if necessary. Mix well. Reduce heat and simmer uncovered for 15 minutes or until sauce begins to lose bright red color.

Add rabbit. Cover and simmer slowly for 30 minutes or until sauce is a brown-red and oil begins to separate and float on surface (skim if desired). Do not stir or turn. If sauce begins to dry add remaining broth.

Serves: 4-6.

Note: If a domestic rabbit is used, once the rabbit has been cut, omit the dry skillet process. Instead, add a small amount of oil to the skillet, add the rabbit, and proceed as above.

Roast Rabbit with Rosemary or Fennel and Oven Potatoes
Lepre (Coniglio) al Forno con Rosmarino o Finocchio e Contorno di Patate

1 rabbit
Salt and pepper, to taste
3-4 slices *prosciutto*
4-5 cloves garlic
4-5 sausage links, optional
3-4 tsp. fennel seeds or 3 tsp. rosemary
Corn oil
4 large potatoes (red)

De-game wild rabbit as described above. Rinse well and pat dry with a clean cloth.

Salt and pepper the inside of the cavity. Set aside. Lay in the prosciutto end to end covering the entire bottom of the cavity. Top with crushed garlic and fennel and fill remaining space with sausage (optional). Close the opening and sew it securely shut with a trussing needle and thick cord or wire.

Heat the oven to 350 degrees. Generously cover the bottom of a large roasting pan with oil. Place rabbit on its side in the roaster. Slide rabbit in pan and coat bottom with oil so it does not stick.

Roast for 20 minutes. Turn rabbit over on second side. Baste from the oil in the pan and continue roasting.

Peel and cut large potatoes into 3 to 4

pieces, small ones in half (for crunchy potatoes cut into smaller pieces).

After the rabbit has been roasting for 30
minutes, add the potatoes. Do not salt or pepper potatoes. Turn all potatoes, coating them
with the oil in the pan.

Roast for an additional 1 to 1½ hours, basting the rabbit and turning the potatoes every
20 minutes. When almost done, salt and pepper the outside of the rabbit.

Serve with fresh garden salad and an additional vegetable.

Serves: 6-8.

Beef
Manzo

The beef used by many northern Italian chefs comes from the heavy *Chiana* cattle from the valley of the *Chiana* River, just south of *Arezzo*. The name is often associated with Florentine dishes, but the *Chiana* River empties into the *Arno* near our small village of *Quarata* and the beef is enjoyed by peasant and noble alike. The cattle are slaughtered at age 15 to 17 months when the meat is called *vitellone* (large veal), further enhancing its quality.

In the U.S. our immigrants did not live in an area that produced exceptionally fine beef, but Nonna always went to a neighborhood butcher to buy beef freshly cut and selected a specific type of beef for each dish. The right cut of beef is as important as the right brush is to a master artist, and years of experience have taught us which cut is the best for a particular dish.

One reason our meals are so delicious is that we never compromise on the quality of the meat. We never buy ground meat; we always use ground chuck. The shank, a tougher meat, is used mainly for soups and cubed stews that simmer a long time, tenderizing the meat. For roasts, we used eye of round or rump (both are boneless cuts) and prime rib, with bone in and fat on. For *umidi,* where the meat is not cubed but kept intact and simmered in sauce, we use the top of the round or block rump, both boneless cuts and both tough. These cuts are cooked for a long time, thus tenderizing them. You know the *umido* is done when the meat is tender.

Modern, fat-free meat is not very good for traditional recipes. You need fat for tenderness, moisture, and flavor. Try to get marbleized meat and some fat on the outside. If your roast is too lean, ask the butcher for some fat or gristle to place on top of the roast. *Do it!* When a cut has a bone, you must insist on bone-in. Cooking without the bone reduces the flavor considerably. *You need the bone.* Do without takeout for a week, but keep the bones and the fat to make good food.

As you can see from the variety of recipes in this chapter, beef is a major part of our diet. Ironically, it was never the main event at a holiday meal, but served as a second course, boiled or in a sauce. The succulent sauce recipes speak for themselves, but a word is in order for the equally tasty boiled meats. Often the by-product of a good soup, boiled meat is never discarded, but carefully prepared in a number of ways.

To cut meat, cut against the grain to keep the meat tender. If you cut with the grain, the meat will be stringy, fall to pieces, and be tough like some pulled pork. You pull it with the grain—that is why it is long and stringy. The string is the grain. If you cut it in slices against the grain, it would be just as delicious and tender, tender, tender.

Boiled Beef
Lesso

Whenever the soup pot is boiling, and that is once a week, one can be sure part of the meal of the day is a *bollito misto*, a mixed boil of beef or chicken.

1 lb. boiled beef from
    soup*
1 sweet onion
3-4 sprigs fresh
    parsley
1 tbsp. fresh basil
Salt and pepper
Olive oil
Wine vinegar

After removing the beef from the broth (see soups chapter), remove excess fat from meat and discard fat.* Cut meat into small pieces. Place on a platter. Slice onion and arrange around beef. Chop parsley and basil and sprinkle over top. Add salt and pepper. Top with olive oil and wine vinegar.

Serves: 2-3.

*"What is this?" you might ask. "Discard fat?" Yes, now that the fat has done its job and flavored the soup, you can discard what is left behind.

Boiled Beef with Potatoes
Lesso Rifatto

1 lb. boiled beef from soup (see soups chapter)
1 onion
1 tsp. parsley
½ tsp. basil
3 potatoes
2 tbsp. corn oil
Salt and pepper
1 ½ cups crushed tomatoes (not pureed)*
1 cup water or broth

Remove beef from broth, trim away fat from meat, and discard fat. Cut meat into inch pieces. Peel and slice onion into thin slices. Chop parsley and basil. Cut raw potatoes into inch pieces.

Place a large iron skillet over medium-high heat. Heat to hot. Add oil. Heat to hot. Add boiled meat and stir. Meat is already cooked so it will break into smaller pieces. Cook for 4 minutes. Add onions and sauté until transparent. Add parsley, basil, salt, and pepper. Allow to simmer a few minutes and add the tomatoes. Simmer for 15 minutes.

As sauce begins to dry, add a little broth or hot water. Add potatoes, cover, and let simmer for 20 to 25 minutes adding water if necessary. Turn potatoes carefully. Simmer until potatoes are cooked.

Serves: 3-4.

Notes: You can peel potatoes, add to simmering broth for last half-hour or until done, and use them for this dish. They will slightly alter the taste of the broth but enhance the potatoes. Alternately, you can use leftover roast beef. A variation is to dust the meat with flour before frying.

*If you cannot find crushed tomatoes without puree buy whole tomatoes in juice (not pureed) and either chop them in a food processor or meat grinder or crush them in the pot until no big pieces remain.

Boiled Meat Patties
Polpette

True Italian hamburgers that we always serve as a main course, *polpette* made in smaller portions are excellent served as appetizers or on a buffet table. We always served *polpette* with Italian potato salad (see index). Both are surplus from making soup.

2 small potatoes
Water or broth
1 tsp. fresh parsley
2 fresh leaves or ½ tsp. dry basil
1 clove garlic
1 lb. boiled beef from soup or left-over roast (see soups chapter)
2 eggs
1 tsp. salt
¼ tsp. pepper
½ cup freshly grated Parmesan cheese
4-5 tbsp. corn oil
1 cup flour

Peel and dice potatoes, place in a small pot, add water or broth to cover, and boil until soft. Drain. If you already boiled the potatoes in broth, disregard this step.

Chop parsley and basil. Peel garlic and chop into fine pieces or pass through a garlic press.

Remove meat from broth. Grind in grinder but do not turn to mush. Place meat in a medium-size bowl and add eggs. Mash potatoes and combine with meat. Add parsley, basil, garlic, salt, pepper, and Parmesan cheese and mix well. Divide into 8 or 10 portions and form into patties.

Place a medium-size iron skillet over medium-high heat. Heat to hot. Add oil.

Place flour on a board, roll each patty in flour, coating well, and place in hot oil. Brown on one side. Turn. Brown on other side. Remove from skillet and place on paper towel. Serve hot or cold, as is, or in a delicious sandwich.

Yield: 8-10 patties.

Notes: You can peel 3 potatoes and add them to the simmering broth for the last half-hour or until they are done. They will slightly alter the taste of the broth but enhance the taste of the potatoes (remember this dish was always prepared on soup day).

Variation: The above recipe is from the Pelinis. Nonna never used basil, always chopped the meat into pieces, and ground the meat and potatoes in a meat grinder or food processor. Then she would add eggs and continue as above.

Meatloaf Italian Style
Polpettone

meatloaf:
3 hard-cooked eggs
2 8-inch sausages
2 lb. ground chuck
1 cup breadcrumbs
½ tsp. fresh parsley
½ tsp. basil
3 eggs
⅔ cup freshly grated
   Romano cheese
1 tsp. salt
1 tsp. pepper
1 tsp. corn oil
2 fat slices *provolone*
   cheese (½ inch
   thick)

sauce:
1 tbsp. corn oil
1 clove garlic
2 cups crushed
   canned tomatoes
   (not pureed)
3 tbsp. tomato paste
¼ tsp. salt
¼ tsp. pepper
1 cup broth or water

Place a small pot over high heat. Add water and bring to a boil. Add eggs and boil for 4 minutes (be sure eggs are at room temperature or they will crack). Allow to cool in water, and shell.

Place a medium-size iron skillet over medium-high heat. Do not add oil. Add sausage links and fry 10 minutes, turning once. Drain on paper towel, cool, and skin sausage. Set aside.

Combine chuck, breadcrumbs, parsley, basil, eggs (unboiled), cheese, salt, and pepper. Mix. Oil pastry board. Turn meat onto board, keeping ½ cup aside. Roll with greased rolling pin until 10 by 14 inches in size. Place 3 boiled eggs in a row in center. Place a sausage on either side. Cover with *provolone*.

Fold sides up and over, placing extra meat on top. Once formed, patch with remaining meat. If not sealed properly the cheese will spill out. Slide onto an oiled cookie sheet and bake at 375 degrees for 1 hour and 10 minutes or until brown and firm.

Place medium-size iron skillet over medium-high heat. Heat to hot. Add oil. When oil is hot, add clove of garlic. Allow to brown, but do not burn. When brown crush with a fork. Add tomatoes, crushing with a fork. Simmer 8 to 10 minutes. Add tomato paste, salt, and pepper. Rinse both tomato and paste cans with ½ cup broth or sausage drippings and add. Simmer 30 minutes, or until sauce begins to thicken and deepen in color. If it dries, add remaining broth.

Check meatloaf. If cheese is spilling out, spoon onto top of loaf. Spoon ¼ of sauce (about ½ cup) over top of meatloaf. Re-set oven to 300 degrees and bake for an additional 25 to 30 minutes.

Remove meatloaf from oven and place on cutting board. Slice meatloaf into equal slices. Lay each slice on serving tray. Cover with sauce. Each slice should have section of egg, 2 sections sausage, and piece of melted cheese (see illustration).

Yield: 12-14 slices.

Note: Make extra sauce and serve *polpettone* with *spaghettini* and sauce.

Roasts
Arrosti

Roast beef is served in a variety of ways in our home, all well spiced and tasty. Some cuts do not have a bone, but those that do we *always roast with the bone in,* and always with fat on the outside. You need both for flavor. Try to find a marbleized cut: marbleizing tenderizes. Cut back on fast food for a week and keep the bone and the fat on these dishes.

Roasting Times for Beef

Roast	weight/lb.	temp.	rare	medium	well done
rib	2-3 rib	325	2 hr.	3 hr.	4 hr.
rib eye	4-6	325	1¾ hr.	2 hr.	2¼ hr.
boneless rump	4-6	325	2 hr.	2½ hr.	3 hr.
thermometer reading	140	160	170		

Pot Roast
Arrosto Morto

2-3 sprigs fresh rose-
 mary
4-5 large garlic cloves
¼-inch-thick slice
 pancetta
3 lb. rump roast
1½ tbsp. salt
1 tbsp. pepper
Corn oil
2-3 tbsp. broth (op-
 tional)
4 potatoes (red)
3-4 carrots

Wash rosemary and set aside. Peel garlic and cut each clove in halves or thirds. Cut *pancetta* into strips. Make sure roast is at room temperature. With a sharp paring knife cut 1-inch-deep slits in the top of the meat, approximately 1½ inches apart. Into each pocket place salt, pepper, a piece of garlic, a sprig of rosemary, and a piece of *pancetta* (in exact order). Salt and pepper entire outside of roast.

Place 4-qt. pot on high heat. Add oil. Heat. Place meat into pot. Brown well on all outer edges to sear in the juices. Add broth. Lower heat to medium. Cover the pot with a lid and allow to simmer for 30 minutes.

Wash and peel potatoes and cut in half or thirds. Wash and peel carrots and cut in 2-inch pieces. Add to pot roast and cook for 10 minutes on medium-high heat. Reduce heat to medium and cook an additional 1 to 1½ hours.

When done, remove meat and place on cutting board. Allow to set for 10 minutes. Slice against the grain to keep tender. Arrange on platter surrounded by vegetables and top with juice.

Serves: 6-8.

Roast Beef
Rosbif al Forno

3 lb. eye of round or
 rump roast
2 cloves garlic
¼-inch-thick slice
 pancetta
1½ tbsp. salt
1 tbsp. pepper

Place meat on pastry board and cut 3 or 4 half-inch slits in top. Peel garlic and cut in two. Cut *pancetta* into strips. Place salt and pepper, a piece of garlic, and a slice of *pancetta*, in each cut (in exact order). Salt and pepper entire roast.

Place roast in shallow pan. Insert meat thermometer in center of thickest part of the roast. Do not hit fat pocket.

Roast in 325-degree oven 28 to 30 minutes for each pound or until the thermometer indicates the roast is done to your taste. Remove from oven and allow to set 20 minutes before cutting. To cut slice against the grain to keep it tender.

Serves: 6-8.

Note: Roast needs no oil or water.

Standing Beef Roast
Le Costole Ritte al Forno

3-rib standing rib
roast, bone in
2 cloves garlic
1½ tbsp. salt
1 tbsp. course pepper

Place meat on pastry board and cut 2 deep slits about 2 inches apart in the fleshy side of the ribs. Peel garlic and place one piece of garlic, salt, and pepper in each cut. Salt and pepper the entire roast.

Place roast in shallow roasting pan with rib ends and fat side up. Insert a meat thermometer in the center of the thickest part of the roast. Be careful not to hit a fatty pocket or bone.

Roast in 325-degree oven 28 to 30 minutes for each pound or until the thermometer indicates the roast is done. Remove from oven and allow to set 20 minutes before cutting. To cut slice along the ribs and against the grain to keep it tender.

Serves: 8-10.

Note: Roast needs no oil or water.

Grilled Steak Florentine Style
Bistecca alla Fiorentina

Bistecca alla Fiorentina is a 1- to 2-inch-thick T-bone steak grilled over a wood fire and seasoned with salt, pepper, and olive oil. That is the simplicity of Tuscan cooking. Famous throughout the world, it is usually cooked *quasi cruda* (raw), or *al sangue* (rare), but if you do not tell anyone you can have it *cotta a puntino* (medium rare), or *ben cotta* (well done). To cook well done always toughens the meat—always!

For our recipe we have replaced the wood fire with a charcoal one, which diminishes the dish. A propane grill is a further insult and leaves the taste of the propane on the meat. It would help to add a few chips of cherry wood to the fire. They are available in gourmet shops.

1 8-12 oz. T-Bone or Porterhouse steak at least 1 inch thick
Salt, pepper
Olive oil

Prepare the grill in your usual manner. Add enough charcoal to produce strong heat. Allow charcoal to reduce to red hot embers. Be sure the grate is hot and the steak is at room temperature.

Rub a little oil on the grill. Place the steak on the hot grill and allow to cook according to your taste (see chart below). Turn. Salt and pepper cooked side. Allow to cook as per your taste. Remove from fire and sprinkle with olive oil. Serve immediately.

With the grill 6 inches away from the coals:
rare, 3 minutes both sides
medium rare, 5 minutes both sides
well done, 7 minutes both sides

Serves: 1-2.

Notes: Two sauces that are delicious with charcoal-grilled steak are *acciugata* (anchovies and caper sauce) and mushroom with garlic and butter (see index for recipes).

One time I went to my friend's house and her mother fried a steak and made this sauce. To the juices in the frying pan, add about ½ cup ketchup per steak. Stir until the ketchup absorbs all the juices. I know, I know, it's very strange and very modern, not immigrant at all. But it tastes good.

I like my steak Pittsburgh style: crispy on the outside and rare to medium rare in the center. It stays tender that way. To grill a steak Pittsburgh style, oil the grill and get it really hot. Place the steak on the grill and allow it to sear 3 minutes on each side. That should do it.

Stews
Umidi (Stufati)

The second course of the great Sunday feast is always an *umido*, a stew in deep red sauce. *Umido* means damp and the meat is usually accompanied by a specific vegetable, also in *umido*. The two dishes are even better reheated for a second meal. I would take the leftovers as a sandwich to work on Monday.

Beef Rounds with Stuffing
Braciole Arrotolate con Ripieno

Once this specialty was served as a second course on Sundays, but today we serve it as a meal in itself. It can be made into one large roll or 3 to 4 equal pieces to make individual rolls.

stuffing:
1 small onion
¼ cup celery leaves and tender ribs
1 small carrot
2 tbsp. fresh parsley
¼ cup corn oil
1 tbsp. pepper
2 tbsp. salt
Pinch thyme
⅓ cup grated bread-crumbs
¼ cup freshly grated Parmesan cheese
2 eggs
1 slice round steak (¾ inch thick)
2-3 thin slices *prosciutto*
Length of butcher cord or 5-6 small skewers

sauce:
¼ cup corn oil
1 ¼ cups whole or crushed tomatoes (not pureed)
3 oz. tomato paste
1 cup broth

Peel onion and cut into quarter wedges. Peel celery and carrot; cut into 1-inch pieces. Combine with parsley and grind in meat grinder or chop in a food processor into fine pieces (grinder is better because it grinds fine pieces and releases the juices).

Place medium-size iron skillet over medium-high heat. Heat to hot. Add oil. When oil is warm, add all chopped ingredients, pepper, salt, and a pinch of thyme, and sauté about 20 minutes until onions are transparent, stirring often. The longer this mixture simmers, the better the stuffing.

Remove from heat and place in a bowl. Add breadcrumbs and cheese and mix well. Beat eggs in a separate bowl, and then add to the mixture. Mix. Mixture must be moist enough to hold together. If dry, add water or broth.

Place steak flat on bread board with length running left to right. Lay prosciutto slices to cover steak. Spread mixture on top (see A). Beginning at the wide end nearest you, form the steak into a roll (see B). Secure with skewers or tie with butcher cord (see C). You may cut steak into several serving pieces, stuff, and roll each one separately.

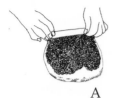

A

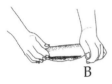

B

C

Sauce:

Place medium-size iron skillet on medium-high heat. Heat to hot. Add oil. Heat. Place beef roll into oil and brown well, turning gently. When well browned remove from skillet and set aside.

To juices in skillet add tomatoes, crushing into small pieces. Simmer 8 to 10 minutes. Add tomato paste. Rinse tomato and paste cans in water or broth and add to mixture. Simmer 20 to 25 minutes. Remove tomato mixture from heat and run through sieve, pushing pulp through with spoon. Throw excess pulp away. Return to skillet, return heat to medium-high, simmer for 5 minutes; reduce heat and simmer uncovered for 15 minutes or until sauce begins to lose bright red color. Add rolled beef. Cover; simmer slowly for 30 minutes or until sauce is a brown-red and oil begins to separate and float on surface (skim if desired). If sauce begins to dry, add broth.

D

To serve: Place beef on board. Let it sit for 10 to 15 minutes. Cut and remove string. Slice into ½-inch-thick rounds (see D). Place on a platter. Cover with sauce; serve with Italian bread.

Serves: 6-8.

Beef Rounds without Stuffing
Braciole Arrotolate Senza Ripieno

Rind of ⅓ lemon
⅓ cup fresh parsley
4 fresh basil leaves or
  1 tsp. dry basil
1 clove garlic
1 lb. thinly sliced
  round steak
¾ tsp. salt
⅛ tsp. pepper
¼ cup freshly grated
  Romano cheese
10 to 12 small skewers
2 tbsp. corn oil
8 oz. crushed canned
  tomatoes (not
  pureed)
¼ cup broth

Wash and chop lemon rind with parsley and basil into fine pieces. Peel garlic and mince. Combine.

Place steak flat on bread board. Cut into 8 to 10 pieces. Top each piece with mixture, then salt, pepper, and cheese. Roll; secure with skewer.

Place medium-size iron skillet on medium-high heat. Heat to hot. Add oil. Heat. Place rolls in oil; brown well, turning gently. When browned remove from skillet and set aside.

To the juices in the skillet add tomatoes, crushing into small pieces. Simmer 8 to 10 minutes. Rinse tomato can with broth or water and add to mixture. Simmer 20 minutes. Remove from heat and run through sieve, pushing pulp through with spoon. Throw excess pulp away.

Return to skillet, return heat to medium-high, simmer for 5 minutes; reduce heat and simmer uncovered for 15 minutes or until sauce begins to lose bright red color. Add rolled beef. Cover and simmer slowly for 30 minutes or until sauce is a brown-red and oil begins to separate and float on surface (skim if desired). If sauce begins to dry, add broth.

To serve: Remove skewers. Place on a platter. Cover with sauce and serve.

Serves: 6-8.

Beef Rump in Red Sauce with Celery
Manzo in Umido con Sedano Cotta Tre Volte

2-3 sprigs fresh rose-
mary
4-5 large garlic cloves
¼-inch-thick slice
pancetta
3 lb. beef rump
2 tsp. salt
1 tsp. pepper
2 tbsp. corn oil
1¼ cups whole or
crushed canned
tomatoes (not
pureed)
3 oz. tomato paste
1 cup broth

Wash rosemary. Set aside. Peel and cut each clove of garlic into 2 to 3 pieces. Set aside. Dice *pancetta* into strips. Make sure roast is at room temperature.

With a sharp paring knife cut 1-inch-deep slits in the top of the meat approximately 1½ inches apart. Into each pocket place salt, pepper, a piece of garlic, a sprig of rosemary, and a piece of *pancetta* (in exact order). Salt and pepper entire outside of roast.

Place 4-qt. pot on burner. Heat to hot. Add oil. Heat. Place meat into pot. Brown well on all outer edges to sear in juices. Lower the heat. Cover the pot with a lid and allow to simmer about 40 to 45 minutes. Turn occasionally. Remove meat from pot.

To the juices in the pot, add tomatoes and crush with a fork. Simmer 10 minutes. Add tomato paste. Rinse tomato and paste cans with ½ cup broth or water and add. Simmer 20 minutes. Salt and pepper to taste. Mix well.

Lower heat and simmer uncovered for 15 minutes or until sauce begins to lose bright red color. Add beef. Turn occasionally and simmer for an additional hour, or to taste (use a meat thermometer).

If the sauce begins to dry, add remaining broth. When done, remove meat and place on cutting board. Slice against the grain to keep it tender.

Arrange on platter and cover with 8 to 10 tbsp. of the tomato mixture. Serve with fried celery in thin sauce, *cotta tre volte* (see index).

Serves: 6-8.

Beef Rump in Red Sauce with Spinach
Manzo in Umido con Spinaci Cotta Tre Volte

Working in the mill carried responsibilities outside the mill gate, including entertaining the boss. Nonno's boss was a friend, never a duty, but the boss's boss was. The first time Nonno invited his family, Nonna prepared a usual Sunday feast: homemade pasta, an *umido*, a roast, and dessert. The guests only saw the pasta. When Nonna served this *umido*, everyone laughed. They did not expect more food and vowed they could not eat another bite. But as the *umido* was piled on their plates, they ate and laughed and became friends.

5 lb. fresh spinach
1 cup water
1 tbsp. salt
2-3 sprigs fresh rosemary
4-5 large garlic cloves
¼-inch-thick slice *pancetta*
3 lb. beef rump
2 tsp. salt
1 tsp. pepper
¼ cup corn oil
1 cup canned tomatoes, no puree
3 oz. tomato paste
½ cup broth
2-3 tbsp. butter
⅓ cup freshly grated Parmesan cheese

Wash spinach.

Place water in 6-quart pot. Boil, add salt, and add spinach; boil again, turn, cover, and remove from stove. Cool, drain, squeeze well to eliminate all water, chop, and set aside. Do not add too much water.

Wash and cut rosemary. Peel and cut garlic into 2 to 3 pieces. Cut *pancetta* into strips. With roast at room temperature, cut inch-deep slits in the top, 1½-inches apart. Into each pocket, place salt, pepper, garlic, rosemary, and piece of *pancetta* (in exact order). Salt and pepper outside.

Place 4-quart pot on burner. Heat to hot. Add oil. Add meat and sear all sides. Cover, lower heat, and roast 40 to 45 minutes. Remove roast from pot.

To juices in pot add tomatoes, crushing with fork into small pieces. Simmer 8 to 10 minutes. Add tomato paste. Rinse cans with ½ cup broth or water and add to mixture. Simmer 20 minutes or until tomatoes lose bright red color. Remove from heat and run through a sieve, pushing pulp through with a spoon. Throw away remaining pulp. Return to pot. Simmer 10 minutes. Add meat, and salt and pepper to taste. Simmer until tender, another 30 minutes to an hour. Turn occasionally. If sauce begins to dry, add more broth. When done, oil should rise to top. Remove meat, slice against the grain to keep tender, arrange on platter, and cover with 8 tablespoons of tomato mixture.

Melt butter in medium-size iron skillet. Squeeze spinach one more time (can blot with a paper towel). Add spinach, turning to coat. Spoon ¼ of tomato sauce over spinach and simmer, adding sauce to moisten. Let simmer for 10 to 15 minutes.

To serve: Place meat, spinach, and sauce in separate dishes. Then lay bed of spinach on dinner plate, and add 2 to 3 slices of meat and tomato sauce. Top with Parmesan cheese. Serve with Italian bread.

Serves: 8-10.

Note: Spinach will absorb sauce, so always serve it separately. When cold, it makes a good sandwich.

Beef Rump in Red Sauce with String Beans
Manzo in Umido con Fagiolini Cotta Tre Volte

3-4 lb. fresh green beans
2 cloves garlic
¼-inch-thick slice *pancetta*
1-2 tbsp. dry rosemary
3 lb. beef rump
2 tsp. salt
1 tsp. pepper
¼ cup corn oil
1 ¼ cups whole or crushed canned tomatoes, no puree
3 oz. tomato paste
¼ cup broth

Snap both ends off green beans; wash and break into 2-inch pieces. Wash and drain.

Peel each clove of garlic and cut in halves or thirds. Cut *pancetta* into strips.

Make sure roast is at room temperature and cut 1-inch-deep slits in top of meat. Into each pocket place salt, pepper, a piece of garlic, a sprig of rosemary, and a piece of *pancetta* (in exact order). Salt and pepper entire outside of roast.

Place medium-size iron skillet over medium-high heat. Heat to hot. Add oil. Add meat and brown well to sear in juices. Cover, lower heat, and allow to simmer 40 to 45 minutes. Remove meat.

To the juices in the skillet, add tomatoes, crushing with a fork into small pieces. Simmer 8 to 10 minutes. Add tomato paste. Rinse both tomato and paste can with broth or water and add to mixture. Simmer 20 minutes, or until tomatoes begin to lose their bright red color. Remove from heat and run through a sieve, pushing pulp through with a spoon or fork. Throw away any pulp remaining in the sieve.

Place tomato mixture in 6-quart pot. Simmer. Place meat in tomato mixture and simmer an additional 45 minutes Add salt and pepper to taste. Turn occasionally. If the sauce begins to dry, add a small amount of broth. Add green beans. Allow to simmer 15 to 20 minutes, or until beans are done to your taste.

When done, sauce should be a deep brown-red. Test, and add salt and pepper if necessary. Remove meat and place on cutting board. Slice against the grain to keep it tender. Place in serving dish and spoon on sauce to cover. Remove beans and sauce from pot and place is deep tureen. Serve with good bread.

Serves: 8-10.

Beef Organs
Frattaglie di Manzo

Nothing is wasted in an immigrant's kitchen. In Italy we were *contadini,* peasant farmers, on the land of the *padrone,* the owner. When the animals were slaughtered, the best cuts went to the owner. We learned to eat all the parts and made good dishes from them.

Calf's Liver and Onions
Fegato di Vitello con Cipolle

½ cup flour
1 tsp. salt
½ tsp. pepper
1½ lb. sliced calf's
   liver
8-9 tbsp. corn oil,
   divided
4-5 medium onions
1 tsp. salt
½ tsp. pepper
½ to ¾ cup broth

Place flour on pastry board. Add salt and pepper and toss. Place liver slices on flour and coat both sides.

Place large-size iron skillet over high heat. Heat to hot. Add half the oil to cover the bottom of the skillet. Heat to hot. Add liver and quickly sear until brown, about 2 minutes. Turn, and sear second side, about 2 minutes. When done, remove from skillet.

Remove skillet from burner. Drain oil and clean skillet with paper towel. Add remaining oil. Heat to hot. Add finely sliced onions, salt, and pepper.

Sauté onions over medium-high heat until transparent, about 10 minutes. Add broth, lower heat, and simmer for 5 minutes; add liver, cover, and simmer 20 minutes.

If the liquid begins to dry, add additional broth a little at a time.

Serves: 4-6.

Note: Onions today tend to be larger than those the immigrants used. The medium onion here is about 2-2.5 inches round. Although calf's liver is recommended, it is hard to find. Baby beef liver will also work for this recipe.

Tripe in Sauce
Trippa nel Sugo

Tripe is the stomach the cow uses to store its cud before chewing. It is not a meal enjoyed by everyone, but those who like it are fanatical about it. Tripe is very Tuscan, and in Florence it is sold by street vendors. It can be served a variety of ways, including simply boiled and garnished with olive oil. You must have a good meat sauce for this recipe.

Nonno and my father loved tripe. I never enjoyed it, but I loved to dip fresh Italian bread in the sauce once the tripe was made. The sauce is absolutely delicious.

6-8 lb. tripe
1 carrot
1 onion
1 rib celery
1 tsp. salt
1 tsp. pepper
2 quarts meat sauce*
⅓ lb. butter
½ cup freshly grated
   Parmesan cheese
Red hot pepper (op-
   tional)

Wash and clean tripe in running water. Place a large pot over medium-high heat, add water, and bring to a boil. Add carrot, onion, celery, salt, and pepper. Simmer for 10 to 15 minutes. Add tripe and simmer for 15 minutes. Drain.

Place in large bowl, cover with cold water (tripe can be stored in the refrigerator overnight), and let stand until ready to use.

Remove tripe from water, cut into strips ½-inch-wide and 3-to-4-inches long. Fill a large pot with a good meat sauce (see note). Add butter and heat. Add tripe, turn, coat, and simmer for 2 to 3 hours. Serve hot with grated cheese and red hot pepper.

Serves: 6-8.

Note: *We always made our traditional meat sauce for tripe. See index.

Lamb and Veal
Agnello e Vitello

Lamb is the heart and soul of the Easter feast, and each spring in preparation for Easter, Nonna and Nonno made an excursion to their friend's farm near the small coal patch called Star Junction, Pennsylvania, to select the baby lamb, the *abbacchio* or *agnello da latte*. As in all things Tuscan, there is strict criteria for the selection. The *abbacchio* must be between thirty and sixty days old and weigh fifteen to twenty pounds. Younger, it is too fatty; older, too tough. Southern families from *Abruzzo, Calabria,* Sicily, and other regions follow the same tradition, but, instead of an *abbacchio*, they prepare a *capretto,* which is a baby kid (goat).

Many people do not like to eat lamb, some perhaps because of the reminder of the gentle animal, others because their first taste of lamb was really not the young lambs of spring, but an older sheep or mutton. Mutton has a stronger taste and is unpleasant if cooked in the variety of ways described here. New Zealand lamb also is not recommended for these dishes, because it, too, has a strong taste.

Like lamb, veal plays an important part in our kitchen. Although it was never a tradition that carried a symbolic meaning, and therefore was seldom served on holidays, it is considered a specialty and is always served with our best china and linens. It is hard to find today, especially veal steak and veal shank. Veal is a young calf. It has a delicate pink meat and is very tender; therefore, veal must be carefully prepared. Roasts are best cooked well done, but the less you cook slices or medallions of veal, the more tender and delicate the taste.

All of the lamb and veal dishes in this chapter are elegant enough to serve your most important guests. I can't say this enough: Bones add flavor. Put them in soups, in stews, and most of all keep them on roasts. To me boneless is brainless. Keep the fat too! It does the same thing.

Stewed Lamb in Thin Sauce with Spinach
Agnelletto in Umido con Spinaci

The second course of the Easter meal, this succulent lamb stew is a favorite all year round. It is delicious as a leftover, alone, or in a sandwich. Have the butcher make big cubes. Lamb shrinks more than 50 percent.

5 lb. fresh spinach
1 cup water
1 tbsp. salt
2 lamb shanks or
   3 slices lamb
   shoulder
4-5 large cloves garlic
2 tbsp. corn oil
2-3 sprigs fresh rosemary
2 tsp. salt
1 tsp. pepper
1 cup whole or
   crushed canned
   tomatoes, no
   puree
3 oz. tomato paste
1 cup broth
2-3 tbsp. butter
½ cup freshly grated
   Parmesan cheese

Wash and clean spinach. Place water in a 6-quart pot. Bring to boil. Add spinach and salt. Stir, remove from heat, cover, and set aside to cool. Once cool, drain and squeeze out water. Before using, squeeze again. Chop fine with a knife. Set aside.

Have the butcher cut each lamb shank into 3 or 4 (2-3-inch) pieces. If pieces are too large, cut again. They should be 2-3 inches square (lamb shanks shrink considerably when cooked). Crush garlic by hitting it with a kitchen mallet or blunt object (do not peel).

Place a medium-size iron skillet over medium-high heat. Heat to hot. Add oil. Heat oil until warm, and add lamb, garlic, rosemary, salt, and pepper. Turn frequently. When browned (15 minutes), remove meat and set aside.

To same oil, add tomatoes, crushing with a fork. Allow to simmer 20 minutes, and add tomato paste that has been softened with ½ cup broth (may use water). Stir and simmer slowly for 30 to 40 minutes or until tomatoes lose bright red color.

Press tomato mixture through a sieve. Throw away pulp. Return sauce to skillet, and simmer 10 minutes. Add lamb. Simmer for 1 to 1½ hours. It is done when sauce is thick and oil rises to top (skim if desired). Taste, and add salt and pepper if necessary.

Place medium-size iron skillet over medium-high heat. Add butter and melt, but do not brown. Squeeze spinach one more time, then add butter and turn to coat well. Spoon ¼ of tomato sauce over the spinach and simmer for 15 minutes. You may have to add more sauce as the spinach simmers. If it begins to dry, add remaining broth.

To serve: Bring lamb, spinach, and sauce to table in separate containers. For individual servings, lay bed of spinach on dish, top with 2 to 3 pieces of meat, 2 tablespoons of tomato sauce, and 1 tablespoon Parmesan cheese. Do not place spinach and meat in same platter as spinach absorbs too much sauce. Serve with homemade Italian bread.

Serves: 4-6.

Leg of Lamb Roast with Rosemary and Oven Potatoes
Coscia di Agnellino con Rosmarino e Contorno di Patate

The final meat course of the Easter meal is always roast leg of lamb with oven potatoes. We never serve a sauce or gravy with any of our roasts; they are so moist and well seasoned they do not need additional flavoring.

5-6 large cloves garlic
2-3 sprigs fresh rosemary
¼-inch-thick slice *pancetta*
1 leg of baby lamb, bone in (5 lb.)
2 tsp. salt
1 ½ tsp. pepper
¼ cup corn oil
4-5 potatoes (red)
Juice of 2 lemons

Peel garlic and cut in halves or thirds, depending on size. Set aside. Wash rosemary and remove from stems. Cut *pancetta* into 8 or 9 strips. Set aside.

Make sure roast is at room temperature. With a sharp paring knife, cut 1-inch-deep slits on all sides of the leg of lamb approximately 1½ inches apart. Into each pocket place salt, pepper, a piece of garlic, a pinch of rosemary, and a strip of *pancetta* (in exact order). Salt and pepper entire outside of roast. Allow to sit 30 minutes before putting in oven.

Preheat the oven to 450 degrees. Cover bottom of roaster with oil. Place leg of lamb in roaster and put into oven. Sear the lamb in the hot oven for 10 minutes. Reduce the temperature to 350 degrees.

Peel and cut large potatoes into 3 or 4 pieces,

and cut small ones in half (for crunchy potatoes cut into smaller pieces). After the lamb
has been roasting an hour, add the potatoes.
Turn all potatoes, coating them with the oil in
the pan. Do not salt potatoes.

Roast an additional 1½ hours, basting
the roast and turning the potatoes every 20
minutes. Insert a meat thermometer halfway
through the roasting time, making sure to
avoid fat pockets or bones. Roasting time depends of the size of the leg of lamb, but usually averages 1 to 1½ hours.

Just before serving, pour lemon juice over
the lamb. Serve with fresh garden salad and
an additional vegetable.

Serves: 8-10.

Snack Idea: Cold lamb is an excellent snack.
Make a sandwich with mayonnaise and lettuce.

Veal
Vitello

Veal Roast with Oven Potatoes
Vitello al Forno e Contorno di Patate

It is hard to find any kind of veal anymore. When you do, it is very
expensive. This roast is also good using lamb, beef, pork, or chicken.

3-4 garlic cloves
¼-inch-thick slice
  pancetta
2-4 sprigs fresh rose-
  mary or 1 tbsp.
  dry
4 to 4½ lb. veal loin,
  bone in
2 ½ tsp. salt
1 ½ tsp. pepper
¼ cup corn oil
5-6 potatoes (red)

Peel each clove of garlic and cut in halves or
thirds, depending on size. Set aside. Cut *pancetta* into ½-inch pieces. Set aside. Wash rosemary and remove from stems. Set aside.

Make sure roast is at room temperature. With
a sharp knife, cut 1-inch slits in the top of the
veal loin approximately 1½ inches apart. Into
each pocket place salt, pepper, a sliver of garlic,
a pinch of rosemary, and *pancetta* (in exact order). Salt and pepper entire outside of loin.

Heat the oven to 350 degrees. Cover the bottom of a large roasting pan with oil. Place roast,

slit side up, in the roaster. Roast for an hour.

Peel and cut large potatoes into 3 or 4 pieces (for crunchy potatoes, cut into smaller pieces). After the veal has been roasting for an hour, add the potatoes. Turn all potatoes, coating them with the oil. Do not salt potatoes.

Roast for an additional hour or more, basting the veal and turning the potatoes every 20 minutes. Use a meat thermometer.

Serve with fresh garden salad, and an additional vegetable.

Serves: 8-10.

Note: We often ordered a veal roast with kidney attached because my father enjoyed the kidney so much. Remember, bone-in and fatty.

Snack Idea: Left-over veal roast makes an excellent sandwich served with mayonnaise and lettuce on good Italian bread.

Pocket Veal Roast with Stuffing
Vitello Ripieno

4 lb. veal breast with pocket, bone in
2 onions
¼-inch-thick slice *pancetta*
3 celery ribs
1 carrot
1 tsp. parsley
1 clove garlic
2 tbsp. corn oil
½ tsp. pepper
1 tsp. salt
3 cups bread crumbs or cubes
½ cup freshly grated Parmesan cheese
¼ lb. butter
3 eggs
½ tbsp. salt
¼ tsp. pepper
¼ tsp. dry thyme
¼ cup corn oil*

When buying veal breast, have the butcher cut a pocket by cutting the meat away from, but not completely off, the bone.

Peel onions, wash, and cut into quarter wedges. Cut *pancetta* into ½-inch pieces. Peel celery and carrot, wash, and cut into 1-inch pieces. Chop parsley. Peel garlic and cut in half. Combine all and grind in meat grinder or food processor (the grinder is better because it releases the juices).

Place a medium-size iron skillet over medium-high heat. Heat to hot. Add oil. When oil is hot, add chopped ingredients, pepper, and salt. Sauté, stirring often. The longer this mixture simmers, the better it tastes. It is done when onions are transparent and it begins to stick to the skillet, about 20 minutes.

In a large bowl combine bread crumbs and cheese. Melt butter, and pour over bread. Beat the eggs and add. Add onion mixture. Mix well. Do not add salt and pepper. Mixture must be moist enough to hold together. If dry, add water or broth.

Place veal pocket on a work space. Spread the pocket away from the bone and fill with stuffing. Skewer the opening of the pocket with sticks or cooking pins. Rub outside of roast with salt, pepper, and thyme.

Place oil (see note) in roasting pan. Add veal. Bake in 350-degree oven for 1½ to 2 hours. Serve with green salad.

Serves: 4-6.

To serve with oven potatoes: Peel and cut 4 or 5 potatoes (red) into 3 or 4 pieces (for crunchy potatoes, cut into smaller pieces). After veal has been roasting for an hour, add potatoes. Turn all potatoes, coating them with oil in pan. Do not salt potatoes.

Note: *This roast can be roasted without oil, but in that event you cannot make oven potatoes.

In Sauces
Nella Salsa

With veal as expensive as it is today, we often substitute chicken for some of the following recipes.

Veal Birds
Uccellini di Vitello

2 slices veal steak
¼ lb. *Fontina* cheese
1 cup bread crumbs
2 tbsp. freshly grated
   Parmesan cheese
2 tbsp. olive oil
1 egg
2 tbsp. celery leaves
2 tsp. fresh parsley
2 small onions, diced
2 tbsp. butter
¼ tsp. salt
⅛ tsp. pepper
½ lb. *prosciutto* or
   ham
10-12 cooking pins
1½ cups bread
   crumbs
2 tbsp. freshly grated
   Parmesan cheese
Dash salt
2 eggs
¾ cup corn oil
2 cans cream of
   mushroom soup*
1 cup broth

Both veal and *Fontina* cheese should be thinly sliced. Place veal on a pastry board and pound with a mallet or the heavy side of a knife until it is ¼-inch thick. Cut into 3-by-5-inch pieces.

In a small bowl, combine bread crumbs, grated cheese, olive oil, egg, celery leaves, and parsley (cut with scissors). Dice onions.

Place small iron skillet over medium-high heat. Heat to hot. Add butter, and melt. Add onions, salt, and pepper, and sauté until transparent (5 to 7 minutes). Remove from heat, add to bread crumb mixture, and mix well.

Cover piece of veal with slice of *prosciutto*. Add 1½ tablespoons of bread mixture and top with slice of cheese. Roll and fasten with a cooking pin. Repeat until all pieces are filled and rolled.

Mix second batch of bread crumbs, cheese, and dash of salt together; lay on flat dish. Beat eggs in a wide bowl. Place a medium-size iron skillet over medium-high heat. Heat to hot. Add oil. Heat to hot.

Roll birds in beaten egg and immediately into bread crumbs, pressing firmly. Place in hot oil and fry until golden brown, rolling to fry all sides (about 7 minutes). Remove from skillet one at a time and place on a paper towel to absorb extra oil. Continue until all are fried. Place in a baking dish.

Place a medium-size saucepan over medium-high heat. Add soup. Rinse cans with broth, and add to saucepan. Stir. Heat to simmer. Pour over birds. Bake in 350-degree oven for 1 to 1½ hours or until tender. Serve with mashed potatoes and a good green salad.

Serves: 6-8.

Note: *This recipe was originally made with no sauce. Over the years we began to use cream of mushroom soup. Nonna liked it, too!

Veal Jump in Your Mouth
Saltimbocca

4 slices veal steaks
Salt, to taste
Pepper, to taste
16 fresh sage leaves
  or 1 tbsp. dried
  sage
8-10 thin slices of *prosciutto* (or ham)
2 tbsp. butter, divided
1-2 tbsp. olive oil
1 cup dry white wine

Lay veal on pastry board and pound with kitchen mallet or heavy side of a knife until ¼-inch thick. Cut each slice into 2 pieces. Season with salt and pepper to taste.

Place 2 to 3 fresh sage leaves on each piece of veal. Cover with a slice of *prosciutto*.

Place a medium-size iron skillet over medium-high heat. Heat to hot. Melt 1 tablespoon butter and when melted, add oil. Be sure butter does not burn. When hot add veal, prosciutto-side-up, one piece at a time. Sauté quickly for 1 to 2 minutes until lightly browned. Do not turn. Remove and place in an oven-proof dish. Do not stack. Heat oven to 350 degrees and bake for 5 to 10 minutes.

To the juices of the skillet, add wine and bring to a boil over high heat. Scrape up juices from bottom of skillet until all are dissolved. Reduce to half. Whisk in the remaining butter, and season with salt and pepper to taste. Remove veal from oven. Pour sauce over all and serve at once.

Serves: 6-8.

Variations:
With cheese and nuts: Prepare veal as directed. When ready to assemble, place sage and *prosciutto* on veal. Top each serving with a slice of *Fontina* or mozzarella cheese and 1 tablespoon pine nuts or walnuts. Roll each piece of veal and secure with cooking pins or tie with butcher cord. Brown as directed, but turn to brown all sides, and bake in 350-degree oven for 20 minutes. Add the juice of 1 lemon to the wine sauce. Serve hot.

With mushrooms: Prepare veal as directed. To the juices in the skillet, add wine and bring to a boil over high heat. Scrape bottom of skillet until juices are dissolved. Reduce to half. Add 16 sliced mushrooms. Simmer for 5 minutes. Whisk in the remaining butter, and season with salt and pepper to taste. Remove veal from oven. Pour sauce over all and serve at once.

Veal Parmesan
Vitello alla Parmigiana

¾ cup corn oil, divided
2 cloves garlic
1½ cups whole or crushed canned tomatoes, no puree
4 oz. tomato paste
¾ cup broth
Salt, to taste
Pepper, to taste
1½ lb. veal steak*
1 cup bread crumbs
¾ cup freshly grated Parmesan cheese
2 eggs
½ tsp. salt
¼ tsp. pepper
4 (½-inch-thick) slices *mozzarella* cheese

Peel each clove of garlic and cut in halves or thirds depending on size.

Place medium-size iron skillet over medium-high heat. Heat to hot. Add ¼ cup oil. Heat to hot. Add garlic to skillet. When brown, mash into small pieces. Add tomatoes, crushing with a fork into small pieces. Simmer 15 to 20 minutes. Add tomato paste. Rinse both tomato and paste cans with broth or water and add to mixture. Simmer 25 to 30 minutes, or until tomatoes reduce and begin to lose their bright red color.

Remove from heat and run through a sieve, pushing pulp through sieve with a spoon or fork. Throw away any pulp remaining in the sieve. Taste, and add salt and pepper as desired.

While sauce is simmering, place veal (see note) on a pastry board. Pound with a kitchen mallet or the handle of a knife to tenderize. Cut each slice in half.

Mix bread crumbs and ½ cup freshly grated Parmesan cheese and place on a flat dish. Beat eggs in a shallow dish, and add salt and pepper.

Place a large-size iron skillet over medium-high heat. Heat to hot. Add remaining oil. Heat to hot. Dip lightly and quickly into egg, then press into bread crumbs coating both sides, and place in hot oil. Fry on one side, then the other (6 to 8 minutes total). Remove from skillet one at a time, and place on a paper towel to absorb extra oil. Continue until all is fried.

Place veal in a baking dish. Cover with tomato mixture and mozzarella. Place in 350-degree oven for 30 minutes. Remove from oven and sprinkle with remaining Parmesan cheese. Serve immediately.

Serves: 4.

Note: *Can substitute chicken for veal.

Classic Veal *Scaloppine*
Scaloppini di Vitello

7-8 mushrooms
1 lb. veal steak
Salt, to taste
Pepper, to taste
2 tbsp. flour
2 tbsp. butter
½ cup broth
⅓ cup white wine or
  *Marsala**

Take one mushroom at a time and cut off the tip of the stem and remove any blemishes on the crown. Slice lengthwise into ¼-inch-thick slices.

Lay veal steak on a pastry board and beat with a kitchen mallet (or the handle of a knife) to tenderize. Cut into 2-to-3-inch cubes. Salt and pepper to taste. Place flour on a board. Roll each *scaloppine* in flour.

Place a medium-size iron skillet over medium-high heat. Heat to hot. Add butter. When melted, add veal pieces and cook quickly, turning once. After 10 minutes add broth and wine. Simmer 5 minutes.

Add mushrooms to veal. Cover and simmer for 20 minutes. If mixture begins to dry, add a little more broth. Serve at once.

Serves: 4.

Variation: Add slices of green pepper when you add the mushrooms.

Note: *Marsala* is a Sicilian cooking wine found in supermarkets and liquor stores.

Veal *Scaloppine* with *Prosciutto*
Scaloppini di Vitello con Prosciutto

1 lb. veal *scaloppine* (or veal steak)
1 tbsp. corn oil
1 tbsp. butter
½ cup flour
½ tsp. salt
¼ tsp. pepper
¾ cup crushed canned tomatoes, no puree
3 tbsp. fresh parsley
¼ lb. thinly sliced *prosciutto*
¾-1 cup white wine
⅔ cup shredded *mozzarella* cheese

Be sure veal is thin and *scaloppine* cut into bite-size pieces. Place a medium-size iron skillet over medium-high heat. Heat to hot. Add oil and butter. Heat.

Place flour, salt, and pepper on pastry board. Dust each *scaloppine* in flour and add to oil. Sauté 5 minutes, turning occasionally. Remove, and set aside.

Place small saucepan over medium heat. Add tomatoes. Dice parsley and add. Allow to simmer for 10 minutes.

Place *scaloppine* in baking dish. Top with *prosciutto*. Add tomato mixture. Pour wine around meat. Bake in 350-degree oven for 45 minutes.

Remove from oven, top with *mozzarella* cheese, and return to oven until cheese is melted (about 5 minutes).

Serves: 4.

Veal in White Wine
Vitello con Vin Bianco

2 veal steaks
2 eggs
1 tbsp. flour
1 tbsp. milk
¾ tsp. salt
¼ tsp. pepper
¼ cup corn oil
¼ lb. butter
1 cup white wine, sauterne or Chablis
2 tbsp. chopped, fresh parsley
1 lemon

Veal should be thinly sliced, then cut into serving pieces. Beat eggs in a medium-size bowl. Add flour, milk, salt, and pepper. Beat into a batter.

Place a medium-size iron skillet over medium-high heat. Heat to hot. Add oil. Heat to hot. Dip veal pieces in batter and one at a time place in hot oil. Brown until golden, turn, and brown second side. Place in a shallow casserole dish.

In a second skillet, melt butter until hot, but not brown. Add wine and simmer on high heat for 2 to 3 minutes. Pour mixture over veal. Bake at 325 degrees for 45 minutes to an hour. If liquid is soupy, raise oven to 350 degrees and bake an additional 5 to 10 minutes, or until liquid dries a bit.

Remove from oven. Place on serving tray. Sprinkle with freshly chopped parsley and serve with lemon wedges.

Serves: 6.

Stews
Stufati

There are so many good stews in the Tuscan pantry. Many follow a similar cooking method. Yet, the cut of meat and the spice used turns each into its own flavorful dish. These veal dishes are no exception.

Veal Stew with Potatoes and Peppers
Stufato di Vitello con Patate e Peperoni

1½ lb. cubed veal
   shank, bone in
1 clove garlic
6 potatoes (red)
4 green peppers
¼ cup corn oil
¼ tsp. salt
Dash pepper
1 cup dry white wine
1 cup crushed canned
   tomatoes, no
    puree*
½ cup broth

Remove gristle from veal and, if not cubed, cut into 2-inch pieces. Peel garlic. Peel and dice potatoes into quarters or eighths (depending on size). Slice green peppers into strips.

Place a medium-size iron skillet over medium-high heat. Heat to hot. Add oil. When oil is hot, add the garlic; fry until brown, and remove from skillet.

Place cubed veal in the skillet, and salt and pepper to taste. Turn the meat often until all is lightly browned. Remove meat from skillet.

Add wine and tomatoes (see note) to oil in skillet. Crush tomatoes with a fork into small pieces. Rinse can with broth and add to skillet. Simmer 8 to 10 minutes or until they reduce slightly.

Remove from heat and run through a sieve, pushing pulp through with a spoon or fork. Throw remaining pulp away and return sauce to skillet. Simmer an additional 10 minutes, or until sauce begins to lose its bright red color.

Add meat and simmer slowly for 20 minutes.

Add potatoes and continue to simmer for 20 minutes. When meat is tender, add peppers, and simmer an additional 10 minutes or until tomato sauce is thick, dark in color, and oil rises to the top (skim if desired).

Turn into a serving dish and serve with good Italian bread.

Serves: 6.

Note: *You can eliminate the tomatoes from this dish if you desire.

Veal Stew with Peas
Stufato di Vitello con Piselli

One of my favorite dishes, veal stew with peas is excellent, excellent, excellent served with fresh Italian bread. It is even better the second day and I am always careful that there is enough left over for my lunch.

1½ lb. cubed veal
shank, bone in
¼ cup corn oil
¼ tsp. salt
Dash pepper
2 tsp. fresh thyme
leaves
3 cups peas*
½ cup broth (optional)

Veal cubes should be 2 inches square. Cut gristle from the cubed veal.

Place a large-size iron skillet over medium-high heat. Heat to hot. Add oil. When oil is hot, add veal cubes. Salt and pepper to taste. Add thyme and quickly sauté the veal until it is browned on all sides (about 7 minutes).

Pour the peas, liquid and all, into the skillet. Stir. Cover and simmer about 1½ hours, stirring every 15 minutes.

When veal is tender, the stew is done. If it begins to dry add ½ cup broth.

Serve with good Italian bread.

Serves: 4.

Note: *Over the years we found we prefer the softer canned peas to fresh peas for this dish. In fact, I often mash some of the peas while they are cooking to make a thicker sauce.

Pork
Maiale

Pork, offered as a sacrifice to the gods in ancient Rome, is eaten often in an Italian home. In our home we eat both fresh and cured pork, and some of the best and most exotic recipes in this book are found in this chapter. *Arista* is a dish fit for a king, and so tasty it is certain to bring accolades to the cook time and time again. Not to be outdone, pork chops on a spit and suckling pig in *porchetta* are the culinary art brought to perfection. You will find these pork dishes, often wedded to garlic, rosemary, sage, or fennel, are the centerpieces of good Tuscan eating—the reason why Italian cooking is rated the best in the world (I am a bit prejudice, but not wrong). Remember, keep the bone in and the fat on or your meat will be dry and less tasty.

In most Tuscan immigrant families, a meal of pork began with dressing the pig, a process called the *maialatura*. For one week every winter, the whole family was involved in the process. The *maialatura* could be done anytime from November to February. Many families saved the labor for mid-January as the Catholic calendar indicated, but we did not. As soon as the November wine was stored, the cellar was cleaned and the *maialatura* began.

In Italy, the *norcino*, pork butcher, would often come to the family to kill and bleed the pig. But the immigrants either had to do it themselves, or call on a friend for help. Not all people raised their own hogs, so a trip to the farm was in order. Buying a pig was a major event and one often selected the pig just after it was born, and it was raised expressly for the family, eating a diet dictated by the new owner. "You are what you eat," is true. A corn-fed pig tastes better than one fed slop or garbage.

Our Nonnos and Nonnas are gone and Nonno had no sons to carry on the traditions of making wine and cured pork. We relied heavily on Bob Pelini and Maria Albertini for the recipes for the special dishes of the *maialatura*. It was a struggle. All of us remember, but what we remember is not exactly the same. For example, we agree Gino and Nonno rubbed the leg of the ham with a garlic paste when making *prosciutto*, but we have different recollections as to when this process was done. Despite the obstacles, these recipes had to be included in this book because they are so important to our lives and represent the men's contribution to our heritage. It took a lot of searching to find all the answers.

Suckling Pig in *Porchetta*
Maialino da Latte in Porchetta

Tuscans say, *"Non è festa se non c'e la porchetta"* (It is not a festival if there isn't a *porchetta*), and honor that saying both in the home, where they make their own *porchetta*, and in public where they buy *porchetta* from vendors and eat it while strolling through the streets.

Suckling pig in *porchetta* was a specialty of my Nonno. When my mother was a young girl, Nonno was responsible for the barbecue at the October Saturday-night dances at the NIPA (Northern Italian Political Association) in our town. He would prepare the pig early in the day and take it to a local bakery where it was baked in the ovens for 6 to 10 hours and delivered to the club around 9 p.m.

Traditionally the pig used for *porchetta* was milk-fed. Our version of *porchetta* is Aretine (from *Arezzo*), filled with garlic and wild fennel, as opposed to garlic and rosemary in the rest of Tuscany. But there are as many variations in Italy as there are provinces, including stuffings of bread and fruit. If you do an Internet search on *porchetta*, you will find recipes that combine rosemary and fennel. Not in our home. I found one that added dill. An online shop was selling *porchetta* in 10-pound rolls, like salami, for $119. That *porchetta*, more a lunch meat, was seasoned with rosemary, laurel, sage, and juniper. Another recipe found on the Internet used paprika, *oregano*, Italian seasoning, and Italian dressing. One person called *porchetta*, "pulled pork." *No*, never, never, never! I have great respect for the variations in recipes, but some of these diminish this incredibly delicious dish.

I must admit, however, that we, too, altered the recipe a bit. *Porchetta*, as my Nonno made it, required a massive number of people to eat it. We were not always a crowd when our taste buds screamed for this fantastic dish. Through the years we devised a method of making *porchetta* without using a whole pig. That recipe is also presented following our more traditional version. We did not change the ingredients.

2-3 buds garlic
1 lb. *prosciutto* or *pancetta*
7 tbsp. fresh fennel seeds
⅛ cup peppercorns
⅛ cup salt
1 (20-lb.) suckling pig
3 lb. sausage (optional)
1 cup olive oil
1 potato
1 apple
Aluminum foil
Lemons for garnish
1 trussing needle and thin wire or heavy thread

Break garlic buds into individual cloves. Crush each with a mallet and set in a small dish (do not peel). Slice *prosciutto* or *pancetta* into thin slices and place in a dish. Crush fennel seeds and place in a dish. Grind pepper, mix with salt, and place in yet another dish.

Place dressed pig (see note) on a large pastry board. Be sure it has been cleaned inside and out. Turn pig on its back. Rub inside of pig with a damp cloth and then the salt and pepper mixture. Lay in the *prosciutto* end to end covering the entire bottom of the cavity. Top with crushed garlic and fennel and fill remaining space with sausage (optional). Close the opening and sew it securely shut with a trussing needle and thick cord or wire. Rub entire pig with oil.

Rub a large roasting pan with oil. Place the pig in the pan. Tuck the legs under the body. Insert whole potato in the snout. Wrap snout, ears, and tail with aluminum foil to avoid burning. Insert a meat thermometer (do not hit a bone) in the body near the ribs.

Bake at 350 degrees for at least 6 hours (could take considerable longer) or until meat thermometer reaches 170 degrees and skin is brown. Baste every half hour with drippings. When cooked, raise oven temperature to 450 degrees and roast 15 minutes to crisp the skin. The crisp skin is a delicacy and a portion should be included with each serving.

Remove pig from oven. Slide onto a large platter or board. Remove foil. Replace potato with apple. Garnish with lemons. Set for 15 minutes.

To cut: Remove a leg and cut chunks of serving-size meat and skin away from bone. These should be between 4-to 6-inches square. Then do remaining legs. Split the body, exposing the steamed sausage. Cut one half at a time, not in slices but in chunks, including skin.

Note: You can use half a pig and place stuffing under the carcass.

Serves: 30-35.

Pork Pocket in *Porchetta*
Maiale Ripieno in Porchetta

If you never intend to roast a suckling pig, you can still enjoy the wonderful taste of pig in *porchetta*.

3 lb. pork loin with pocket, bone in a must
½ tbsp. pepper
1 tsp. salt
3 large cloves garlic, crushed
2 thick slices *prosciutto*
½ tbsp. fennel seeds
3-4 sausage links (optional)
Corn oil as needed
3-4 kitchen skewers

When buying the loin, ask the butcher to keep at least an inch of fat on and cut a pocket close to the bone. It would be wonderful if you could find a loin with the rind on it, but that is highly unlikely unless you go to a farmer.

Prepare the loin following the instructions in the preceding recipe, but with the quantities in this recipe. Use half the salt and pepper to rub the inside and half to rub on the outside.

Lay the *prosciutto* in the pocket topped by garlic, fennel, and sausage (optional). Close pocket with skewers.

Rub bottom of roaster with a little oil, add roast, slide to oil bottom of roast, place in oven, and roast for 1½ to 2 hours or until thermometer says done. Remove from oven and slice along bone, like a pork chop.

Serves: 4-6.

Fresh Pork Belly in *Porchetta*
Pancetta Fresca in Porchetta

This recipe calls for fresh pork belly, not one that has been cured. And it should still have the rind on it. Pork Belly is usually used as a savory, added to roasts and *soffritto*. This is the only recipe we have where it is a meal in itself. There is lots and lots of fat in this dish—too much for most people.

2 lb. fresh pork belly with rind
3-4 cloves garlic
1 tsp. salt
1 tsp. freshly ground pepper
3 thick slices *prosciutto*
½ tsp. fresh fennel seeds

Lay the fresh pork belly *(pancetta)* on a pastry board, rind-side-down. Crush garlic cloves (do not peel) by hitting each one with a kitchen mallet or the handle of a large knife.

Salt and pepper the *pancetta* to taste. Scatter the crushed garlic over the *pancetta* and lay on slices of *prosciutto* to completely cover it. Next, scatter the fennel seeds.

Beginning at one end, roll the pork belly into a roll. Tightly secure the roll with butcher cord (the rind should be on the outside).

Place in a low baking pan. Do not add oil, because it has plenty of fat for basting.

Roast in a 325-degree oven for 1½ to 2 hours or until the rind becomes crisp.

Remove from oven and eat immediately. Rind is delicious hot, but none of this roast is very appetizing when cold.

Serves: 4-6.

Note: Despite the lack of oil, if there is enough juice you can add potatoes to this roast. Peel and cut 5 large potatoes (red) into 4 or 5 pieces (for crunchy potatoes, cut into smaller pieces). After pork has been roasting for an hour, add potatoes. Turn potatoes, coating them with the juice in the pan. Baste every 20 minutes. Do not salt potatoes.

Pork Chops with Sage on a Spit
Costolette / Salvia allo Spiedo

Pork chops with sage on a spit is a must for *Martedi Grasso,* Fat Tuesday, the last feast of carnival before the Lenten season. My aunt in *Quarata* prepares this wonderful dish over an open grate, using aromatic woods as fuel, and has a special machine called a *giarrosto,* to turn the spit. We are not as fortunate and do not have an open fireplace in our kitchen, so my mother bought a broiler with rotisserie, which we used exclusively for this dish. Vivian and Tom had a fireplace built in their kitchen and bought a machine in Italy to turn the spit.

The more you baste this dish the more succulent, moist, and tender the chops. Best pork chop dish ever!

8 (¾-inch-thick) pork loin chops, bone in
Salt and pepper, to taste
3-4 tbsp. olive oil
12 sprigs fresh sage

Place chops on a large platter. Sprinkle with salt and pepper to taste. Pour olive oil over chops, turning each until well-coated, but not dripping. Place a sprig of sage on each chop and let stand for 20 minutes.

Pick up a chop and hold it in the palm of your hand.

Fold the loin (fillet) side toward the bone (see A) to tuck in the flap. This is a short fold. Make sure the sage sprig is not tucked into this fold. Fold again bringing the flap side to the bone and enclosing a sprig of sage (see B).

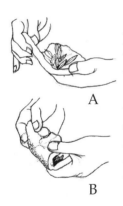

A

B

Place the skewer through the center of the chop and the sage within. Do this for each chop. Be sure to skewer both folds and alternate them on the skewer so that the first chop has the bone side up, the second chop the closed side up (see C), etc. This balances the chops and helps them stay firm on the skewer. Secure firmly.

C

Place skewer 6 to 7 inches from heat. Skewer must rotate. Take the final 4 sprigs of sage, and tie them together with a cord to use as a brush. Dip the sage brush into the remaining oil mixture on the platter and brush the chops every 10 to 15 minutes. Cooking time will depend on your grill and the distance between the skewer and the heat source. We cooked this dish for 3 to 3½ hours. If using an electric spit, lower the spit to 3 to 4 inches for the last 45 minutes.

Yield: 4 servings.

Note: A variation is to add chicken wings. Yes, we have been enjoying wings for centuries. Salt and pepper wings. Fold tip of wing under the back and fill the hole with a sprig of sage. Place on the spit, alternating with the pork chops.

Pork Roast with Oven Potatoes
Arista con Patate al Forno

The king of all pork dishes in Tuscany and in our home is *arista*, named in Florence at a meeting of the Ecumenical Council of the Catholic Church. The time was around 1440 and Constantinople was being threatened by the Ottoman Turks. The emperor of the Eastern Roman Empire came to Italy for help (the moment is immortalized in Benozzo Gozzoli's painting, *Journey of the Magi)*. Many of the meetings of this lengthy council were held in Florence, and at one feast this dish was prepared. When it was served, one of the visiting orthodox bishops exclaimed in Greek, *arista*, "the best." And it is. Do *not* use a boneless roast for this dish. If you keep the bones, then this is the best dish ever!

3 large cloves garlic
6-7 sprigs fresh rosemary
3 lb. center cut pork rib roast*, bone in and fat on
1 tbsp. salt
¾ tbsp. pepper
¼ cup corn oil
5 large potatoes (red)

Peel each clove of garlic and cut in halves or thirds, depending on size. Set aside. Wash rosemary and remove from stems. Set aside.

Make sure roast is at room temperature. With a sharp paring knife, cut 1-inch-deep slits in the top of the pork center cut, approximately 1½ inches apart. Into each pocket, place a rosemary, salt, pepper, and a piece of garlic (in exact order). Salt and pepper entire outside of roast.

Heat the oven to 325 degrees. Add enough oil to cover the bottom of a roasting pan. Place roast in roaster bone-side-down. Slide in pan to coat bottom with oil. Insert oven thermometer. Be sure not to touch a bone. Place in oven.

Peel and cut potatoes into 4 or 5 pieces (for crunchy potatoes, cut into smaller pieces). After the pork has been roasting for 45 minutes, add the potatoes. Turn all potatoes, coating them with the oil in the pan. Cook for an additional 1 to 1½ hours, or until thermometer says done to your taste. Baste the roast and turn the potatoes every 20 minutes. Do not salt potatoes. Let your thermometer be your guide, as ovens vary. I roast just shy of pork well done.

Remove from oven and set on a board. The roast will continue to cook as it sits. Do not cut for at least 15 minutes to allow the juices to flow back into the meat and tenderize it.

Serve with garden salad and a vegetable (fried savoy cabbage in garlic is an excellent choice, see index).

Serves: 6-8.

Note: *In order to slice the roast easily, ask the butcher to crack the bone in 2 or 3 places.

Snack Idea: Cold pork roast, cut thin, topped with mayo and lettuce and served on good Italian bread makes an excellent sandwich.

Stews
Umidi

Pork is an excellent meat for stewing. It gives us a unique flavor. Pork stews use a variety of vegetables. Although the manner of making the different stews is similar, like all the stews in this book, the combination of spices and vegetables changes the flavor completely.

Pork Chops with Cauliflower in Sauce
Costolette di Maiale con Cavolfiore nella Salsa

In recent years fried vegetables like cauliflower, *broccoli*, and green beans have been a big hit at festivals and other events. We've been making them for years and you will find an entire section devoted to the methods to use in preparing them properly in this book. Adding the fried vegetable to tomato and meat adds an extra dimension. That method is also explained in this book. When you combine both methods, it is called, *cotta tre volte*, "cooked three times" and that takes time. It is worth it, as this is an incredibly tasty dish.

1 cauliflower
1 cup flour
Salt and pepper, to taste
3 eggs
¾ cup corn oil, divided
4-5 loin pork chops, bone in
2-3 cloves garlic
2-3 tsp. fresh rosemary
2 cups whole or crushed canned tomatoes, no puree
½ cup broth or water

Place 4-quart pot on medium-high heat. Fill half-full with water, and add salt. Cut cauliflower in half. Add to boiling water, cover, and boil 3 minutes. Turn off burner (if overcooked, it will fall apart in final preparation). When cool, remove and drain.

Break into florets. Place flour on pastry board. Add dash salt and pepper, and stir. Gently roll each floret in flour, coating generously. Stack on flat dish. Beat eggs with a dash of salt. Set near stove.

Place medium-size iron skillet over medium-high heat. Heat to hot. Add ½ cup oil. When hot, shake floret to remove excess flour, and dip in beaten egg, coating generously. Drop into oil. Repeat until skillet is full. Fry until golden brown, turning as necessary to fry all sides. Remove, and place on paper towel to absorb oil. Continue until all are fried. Set aside.

Place large-size iron skillet over medium-high heat. Heat to hot. Add remaining oil. Salt and pepper pork chops. Place in skillet. Crush garlic with mallet or side of knife (do not peel), and place in skillet. Add rosemary. Sear chops quickly, about 2-3 minutes each side. Remove chops from skillet and set aside. They should have a brown color.

To juices in skillet, add tomatoes and crush with a fork. Simmer 10 minutes. Rinse tomato can with broth or water and add to mixture. Taste, and salt and pepper if necessary. Mix. Lower heat, and simmer uncovered 15 minutes.

Remove from heat and run sauce through a sieve, removing pulp. Return sauce to skillet, return heat to medium-high, and simmer for 5 minutes; reduce heat and simmer uncovered for 15 to 20 minutes or until sauce begins to darken. Add cauliflower. Cover and simmer slowly for 10 minutes. Add chops. Simmer an additional 20 minutes or until chops are tender, sauce is brown-red, and oil begins to separate and float on surface (skim if desired). Do not stir or turn. If sauce begins to dry, add additional broth.

Serves: 3-4.

Pork Chops with White Beans
Costolette di Maiale con Cannellini

This is the same process as the previous recipe only unbuttered, unfried cannellini beans are substituted for the cauliflower. I don't know which dish I prefer. If you want a spectacular bean dish without the sweetness of baked beans, this is it. Nonna never used canned beans, and, although they are softer, dried beans are better for this dish.

1½ lb. dried or 1 (2 lb. 8 oz.) can Great Northern White beans
2 tbsp. corn oil
6 thick pork loin chops, bone in
2 tsp. salt
2 tsp. pepper
2 tsp. dry rosemary
4 large cloves garlic
1½ cups whole or crushed canned tomatoes, no puree
3 oz. tomato paste
1 cup broth

If using dry beans (see note), place the beans in a 4-quart pot. Fill pot with water. Allow to soak overnight, drain, add fresh water, cover, and boil for 4 to 5 hours or until tender. If using canned beans (softer than dry), simply open the can and pour the contents into a 4-quart pot and heat. Rinse can with a little broth and add to pot.

Place a large-size iron skillet over high heat. Heat to hot. Add oil. Add pork chops, but do not stack. Sprinkle with salt, pepper, and rosemary and sear on both sides. Lower heat. Remove chops, and set aside.

Peel garlic and add to oil in skillet. When garlic begins to slightly brown, crush with fork until broken into small pieces. Do not burn garlic. To juices in skillet add tomatoes, crushing with a fork into small pieces. Simmer 8 to 10 minutes. Add tomato paste. Rinse both tomato and paste cans with ½ cup broth or water and add to mixture. Taste, and salt and pepper if necessary. Mix well. Lower heat and simmer uncovered for 30 minutes, or until tomatoes begin to lose bright red color.

Place boiled beans in a 4-quart saucepan or a deep Dutch oven over medium-high heat. Add 1 cup sauce and simmer (about 10 minutes). Add remaining sauce and the chops and allow to simmer about 15 minutes. Reduce heat, cover, and simmer for 1 to 1½ hours. If sauce begins to dry, add more soup stock or water. Serve with good Italian bread. Dish is done when chops are tender.

Serves: 4-6.

Note: This meal is even better the second day. You can also chop the meat into small pieces or use pork steak.

Pork Steak with Potatoes in Sauce
Braciole di Maiale con Patate e Salsa di Pomodoro

A different cut of pork and a different vegetable, and yet another variation of the same recipe: each with rosemary, each with tomatoes, each uniquely delicious.

¼ cup corn oil
2 cloves garlic
2-3 pork steaks, bone in
1 tsp. salt
1 tsp. pepper
1 tbsp. rosemary
1½ cups whole or crushed canned tomatoes, no puree
3 oz. tomato paste
½ cup broth
Salt and pepper, to taste
4-5 potatoes (red)
4 tbsp. corn oil

Place a large-size iron skillet over high heat. Heat to hot. Add oil. Peel garlic and add to oil. When beginning to brown, crush with a fork into small pieces. Do not burn. Cut pork steaks in half and add to skillet. Sprinkle with salt, pepper, and rosemary and sear on both sides. Lower heat. Remove steaks and set aside.

To the juices in the skillet add tomatoes, crushing with a fork into small pieces. Simmer 8 to 10 minutes. Add tomato paste. Rinse both tomato and paste cans with broth or water and add to mixture. Simmer 20 minutes, or until tomatoes reduce and begin to lose their bright red color.

Remove from heat and run through a sieve, pushing pulp through sieve with a spoon or fork. Throw remaining pulp away. Return sauce to skillet and continue to simmer. Taste, and add salt and pepper if necessary.

While tomatoes are simmering, peel and dice potatoes into 1¼-inch cubes. Place a smaller iron skillet over medium-high heat. Heat to hot. Add oil. Add potatoes to oil and cook until golden brown.

Add pork steaks and potatoes to tomato mixture. Simmer for 30 minutes or until tomatoes are dark brown-red and oil floats on top (skim if desired). Pork should be tender.

Serves: 4-6.

Note: For a lighter sauce, eliminate the tomato paste.

Sausage
Salsiccia

Most Americans have eaten sausage at least once in their lives, and my guess is the majority enjoy it. Almost every ethnic group has its own version of sausage: the Polish have *kielbasa*, the Germans have at least a dozen variations including knockwurst and bratwurst, the Spanish have *chorizo*, Jews *kishke*, and Chinese *Lap cheong*. In America we have regional sausages like Cajun *andouille*, Cincinnati *mettwurst*, and Pennsylvania Dutch *scrapple*. Today, modern kitchens make sausage from a variety of meats: pork (of course), pork blood, beef, wild boar, and even chicken.

In Italy the various regions offer a plethora of sausages too. One could do a book solely on the sausages of the regions of Italy. It is safe to say than in the south sausage tends, but not always, to have hot peppers in the mix and in the north (not always) sausage tends to be sweeter. *Salami* and *mortadella* are called *salume* in Italy and are not sausages. They are ground and stuffed into sacks, like sausage, but they are not sausage. The trick in making sausage is to keep it simple and use natural, fresh ingredients: no garlic powder or garlic salt, please. Use garlic.

Just as it was for most immigrants, sausage is a staple in our kitchen. We prefer it spiced with garlic and nutmeg. The Pelini family prefers it with garlic and fennel. Both Tuscan recipes are found in this chapter.

Aging is a factor in sausage. Fresh is the most well-known and the most popular way Americans eat sausage. But we also have a dry sausage, *salsiccia secca*. Once the sausage is made, it is hung in a cool, dry place. Nonno always hung it in his wine cellar. One line of sausage was set aside, and as we used the fresh links, it was not touched. As time passed, the untouched sausage began to cure. After it hardened it was sometimes cooked, but it was more often sliced like a *salami* and eaten raw.

There are dozens of recipes in this book that use sausage as an ingredient. Sausage is the flavor that makes the Stuffed Mushrooms appetizer so tasty. Sausage as a sandwich appears as Sausage in a Blanket and Sausage with Onion and Green Pepper Sandwich. Sausage works well with eggs and is found in the Sausage Omelet and the Easter Pie. Accompanying pasta, it is found in the Grand Lasagna with Sausage, Ricotta, and Béchamel and Polenta with Sausage. As a stuffing, sausage is used in the Meatloaf Italian Style, the Suckling Pig in Porchetta, the Pork Pocket in Porchetta, and Roast Capon with Fennel and Oven Potatoes (see index).

The recipes that offer sausage as a main ingredient in a stew are featured on the following pages. To fry a sausage, see following recipe.

Sausage
Salsiccia

1 sausage link

Place a small-size iron skillet over medium-high heat. Heat to hot. Add sausage and cover. Do not add oil. Allow to fry for 5 minutes. Turn. If sausage sticks (the more sausages you fry at one time the less likely they will stick), add a little water to the skillet. Cover, lower heat to medium, and continue to fry for 10 minutes.

Serves: 1.

Sausage and Potatoes in Sauce
Salsiccia con Patate in Umido

6 sausage links
3-4 large potatoes
(red)
4 tbsp. corn oil
2 cups whole or
crushed canned
tomatoes, no
puree
3 oz. tomato paste
1 cup broth
Dash of salt, pepper

Place a medium-size skillet over medium-high heat. Add sausage and brown (do not add oil as sausage will produce its own grease).

While sausages are frying, peel potatoes and cut into 1-inch cubes. Place a second medium-size iron skillet over medium-high heat. Heat to hot. Add oil. Heat to hot. Add potatoes and fry until browned.

Remove sausage from first skillet. To the juices in the skillet, add tomatoes crushing with a fork into small pieces. Simmer 8 to 10 minutes. Add tomato paste. Rinse both tomato and paste cans with broth or water and add to mixture. Simmer 20 minutes or until tomatoes reduce and begin to lose their bright red color.

Remove tomatoes from heat and run through a sieve, pushing pulp through sieve with a spoon or fork. Throw away any pulp remaining in the sieve.

Return tomato mixture to skillet. Taste and add salt and pepper if necessary. Simmer 10 minutes.

Place sausage and potatoes in tomato mixture and continue simmering for an additional 10 minutes or until potatoes are cooked and sauce is dark brown red. Oil should rise to the top (skim if desired). Turn occasionally. If the sauce begins to dry, add a small amount of broth. Serve with good Italian bread.

Serves: 3-4.

Note: This is a good recipe for dry sausage, too.

Sausage Roll with Lentils
Cotechino con Lenticchie

This is a northern Italian New Year's Day dish said to bring prosperity and good fortune all year long. We did not serve it for New Year (and never any other time of year) very often, because too many of us did not like this type of sausage. "Don't like it," is the reason many traditions change. If a family doesn't like a dish, tradition or not, it will slowly disappear from the family table.

1 *cotechino* sausage*
   (1 lb.)
1 lb. lentils
6 cups water
⅛ tsp. salt
4 cups broth
2 medium onions
1 celery rib
1 carrot
2 cloves garlic
¼-inch-thick slice
   pancetta
4 tbsp. corn oil
8 fresh sage leaves
½ tsp. salt
½ tsp. pepper
1 cup whole or
   crushed canned
   tomatoes, no
   puree
¼ cup freshly grated
   Parmesan cheese

If *cotechino* is dry and hard like a *salami*, soak it overnight. Remove from water and set aside. If wrapped in plastic seal, you do not need to soak.

Rinse lentils in running water. Place a medium-size pot over medium-high heat. Add fresh water, salt, and lentils. Boil for about 30 minutes or until tender to taste.

Place a large-size pot over medium-high heat. Add broth and *cotechino*. Boil. Cover and lower the heat. Simmer 45 minutes. Remove and cool. Broth need not cover *cotechino*, but turn it at least once.

Wash, peel, and chop onions, celery, and carrot. Set aside. Peel garlic and cut into 2 to 3 pieces. Dice *pancetta* into ½-inch pieces. Combine all and grind in a meat grinder or food processor (the grinder is better because it releases the juices).

Place medium-size skillet over medium-high heat. Heat to hot. Add oil. Add onions, celery, carrots, *pancetta*, and garlic. Stir, and sauté 5 minutes. Dice and add sage, salt, and pepper. Sauté until onions are transparent, about 15 to 20 minutes. The longer it simmers, the better it tastes.

Add tomatoes, crushing with fork into small pieces. Rinse tomato can with broth from *cotechino* and add. Simmer 40 minutes or until tomatoes reduce and lose bright red color. If sauce dries, add broth. Taste, and add salt and pepper if necessary.

Drain lentils, and combine with tomato sauce. Stir well. Simmer 15 minutes. Remove from stove, lay on large platter, and sprinkle with Parmesan cheese.

Remove bladder or plastic (may have broken while boiling) from *cotechino* (if it was wrapped in plastic) and slice; lay on top of lentils.

Serves: 3-4.

Variation: Add pasta. Use a short, heavy pasta like *diti*. Par cook for 5 minutes in water with a pinch of salt. Add to tomatoes with lentils last 15 minutes.

Note: *Cotechino* is available in Italian meat markets.

Sausage Roll with Savoy Cabbage
Cotechino con Verza

1 *cotechino* sausage*
4 cups broth
1 head Savoy cabbage
2 tsp. salt
2-3 tbsp. pan
  drippings or olive
  oil
2-3 cloves garlic
Salt and pepper

If *cotechino* is dry and hard like a *salami*, soak it overnight. Remove from water and set aside. If wrapped in plastic seal, you do not need to soak.

Place a large-size pot over medium-high heat. Add broth and *cotechino*. Broth need not cover *cotechino*, but turn it at least once. Bring to a boil, cover, and lower the heat. Simmer 45 minutes. Remove and cool.

In the meantime, wash the cabbage and cut in half. If extra large, cut again. Place in a large pot over medium-high heat. Fill halfway with water and add salt. Boil for 8 to 10 minutes until soft. Test with a fork. Remove and drain (may be placed in the refrigerator for up to 4 days).

When ready to fry, take 1 to 2 pieces of boiled Savoy. Squeeze out as much liquid as possible. On a pastry board, chop Savoy into small pieces.

Place a medium-size iron skillet over medium-high heat. Add oil or pan drippings from a good roast. Peel garlic, add to oil in skillet, brown, and crush with a fork until no large pieces remain.

Place Savoy in oil and salt and pepper to taste. Allow to brown about 15 minutes, turning often. If it begins to dry, add 2 to 3 tablespoons of broth from the *cotechino.*

When ready to serve, remove *cotechino* from the broth and cut into ½-inch-thick slices. Arrange the Savoy cabbage on a large serving tray and place the *cotechino* slices on top. Cover and allow to sit 5 minutes. Serve with good Italian bread.

Serves: 4-6.

Note: *Cotechino* is available in Italian meat markets.

Cured and Dressed Pork
Maiale Salato e Condito

The preparation of the meal was woman's work in the immigrant's kitchen, but the preparation of the food before the meal belonged to everyone in the family, especially the men. The garden, the wine cellar, and the curing of pork products were definitely the work of my Nonno. He brought his bounty to the kitchen where Nonna turned it into food fit for the gods. One of the most important steps in this process was dressing the pig, the *maialatura.* Once the pig was killed, it was never refrigerated. Boiling water was poured over the carcass and the skin was scraped to remove dirt and hair. Then the pig was hung by its hind legs, scrubbed, and gutted. The organs—liver, kidneys, lungs, heart, intestines, and caul—were set aside to be used in the various recipes which follow. Then the carcass was cut to make *prosciutto, salami*, sausage, roasts, chops, blood pudding, headcheese, lard, pork rinds, etc. Nothing was wasted.

Lard and Pork Rinds
Strutto di Maiale e Ciccioli

All the fat on the pig was rendered into lard, which was one of the most important products the pig gave the immigrants, because before refrigeration, lard was not only used for cooking but, more importantly, to preserve foods (That is why you can save pan drippings in a jar under the sink and take them out, scrap off the solidified oil, and scoop out the delicious drippings to use in Savoy cabbage and other dishes. That is how Nonna and my mother did it).

Lard has impurities, or pork rinds, and as it renders, they do not melt. They were stored and used in breads and pizzas, or eaten by themselves.

Lard

Remove all fat from pork with a sharp knife. Dice or grind fat into very small pieces and place in a large pot (preferably an iron kettle). Place pot over medium-high heat and cook the fat until it melts into a liquid. This could be an all-day affair, depending on the amount of fat. Once the fat is rendered into lard, strain, drain into a large crock, and allow to set.

Pork Rinds

Once lard has liquefied and solid impurities are visible and become golden brown, run through a sieve to catch impurities and place lard in a crock.

The small, hard pieces that remain are rinds. Place rinds in a cloth. Roll up and squeeze tightly to remove excess lard. Place cloth on a board, sprinkle rinds lightly with salt, and eat. To store, place rinds in crock and cover with liquid lard. Stir and store.

Headcheese
Soprassata (Coppa)

Some call this dish *coppa*, but we call it *soprassata*. In *Basilicata, Apulia,* and *Calabria*, all southern regions, a *soprassata* is more like a *salami*, filled with the raw meat of the pig, seasoned with special herbs and spices, and aged. That is how it is sold in Italian food stores in America, too. To add further complications, Neapolitans call their *capcolla*, a *salami*-type cold cut made from the shoulder or neck of the pig, by the name *copa*, and it is a different cut altogether. This is not the only time such confusion reigns over food.

Headcheese, our *soprassata*, is the boiled head of the freshly slaughtered pig: cooked, chopped, spiced, stuffed into a casing, and eaten as a cold cut. The only difference between *soprassata* and *cotechino* (see index) is the first is chopped and cooked and the second is ground and raw.

1 pig's head or 4 lb. pork butt and 1 lb. pork rind*
1½ tbsp. salt
¾ tbsp. pepper
1 tbsp. peppercorns
¼ tsp. nutmeg
Canvas or sturdy cloth or large pan

Clean head, sear off all hair by holding head over burner, remove eyes, and discard. Remove brains and set aside.

Place an 8-to-10-quart pot over medium-high heat. Fill half-full with water and bring to a rolling boil. Cut pig's head in half and add to boiling water (if using butt and rind, slice into large chunks). Cook until meat falls from bone (for head this takes several hours, for butt and rind about 1 hour). Skim off impurities from surface as needed.

Remove from water, drain, and place on large work space. Remove tender, cooked meat of tongue, cheeks, and jaw. Cut into 1-inch pieces, including fat and rind. Discard bones. Add salt, pepper, peppercorns, and nutmeg to meat. Mix 15 minutes and taste. Add additional seasonings if necessary.

Lay cloth on board (or sew 3 sides together). Fill cloth with mixture and fold over to form a cylinder (if using a sack, fill sack, and tie tightly at top). Wrap outside with sturdy cord

A

(see illustrations with Salami recipe). Squeeze hard to release excess fluids. Alternately, press mixture into large, deep (4-5 inch) pan (see A) and place a weight on top.

Place a heavy (5-lb.) weight on mixture and let set overnight, pressing occasionally. This will press out excess moisture and make firm. Grease will rise to top or sides and gel. It can be taken off. Hang wrapped *soprassata* in a cool place for a day or two.

Once meat has set, remove cloth and slice like lunch meat (it will have a marbled pattern, see B). Can be stored in a cool place, preferable a wine cellar.

B

Yield: 1 roll.

Note: *Pork rind or skin is found at most supermarkets.

Blood Pudding
Migliaccio

It sounds awful, but blood pudding is delicious and Italians enjoyed it long before Boccaccio made it famous in the *Decameron*. Called by a variety of names throughout Italy, and *sanguinaccio* as well as *migliaccio* in some parts of Tuscany, *migliaccio* is served in a variety of ways with a host of different ingredients including fennel, milk, onions, raisins, brains, chocolate, and pistachio nuts. It can also be made into a sausage called, of course, blood sausage. There are so many variations called by so many names that even I get confused. Ours is a simple, savory pudding with Parmesan cheese.

The secret in preparing blood pudding is that once the blood is drained from the pig's throat, a handful of salt must be added to keep it from clotting.

2¼ lb. fresh pig blood
3 tbsp. corn oil
¼-inch-thick slice
    pancetta
2 eggs, beaten
Salt and pepper, to
    taste
½ cup freshly grated
    Parmesan cheese

Run the blood through a sieve to remove any small clots.

Place a medium-size iron skillet over medium-high heat. Heat to hot. Add oil. Allow to heat. Dice *pancetta* and allow to render, mashing with a fork. Simmer 10 minutes.

In a medium-size bowl, beat eggs and add salt and pepper. Combine blood with beaten eggs and add cheese.

Pour into skillet, mixing with a fork until it begins to thicken and solidify.

Turn onto board (like an omelet). To serve, cut into wedges like a pie.

Serves: 4-8.

Brain Fritters
Frittelle di Cervello

When I was little and brains were on the menu, I tried to disappear. I hated them. I would sit there and stare at my plate until the meal was over. My mother insisted I had to eat at least a few bites. It was one stubborn Tuscan verses another. I am sure anyone reading this will remember this type of confrontation over a particular food. I hated brains then. I hate brains now. But, to be true to the Tuscan kitchen and my grandparents and parents, who liked this dish, here it is.

1 pig brain
Salt, to taste
2 cups rice
¼ cup flour
1 tbsp. lemon rind
1 tsp. lemon juice
½ cup sugar
½ cup corn oil

Remove brain from pig and wash. Place a medium-size pot over high heat. Add water, brain, and a pinch of salt. Bring to a boil and boil for 2 minutes. Remove and cool. When cool, remove membrane from around brain and discard. Mash brain like potatoes.

Place medium-size pot over high heat. Cook rice as directed. Drain. Combine brains, rice, flour, lemon rind and juice, and sugar. Mix well. Place a medium-size iron skillet over medium-high heat. Heat to hot. Add oil. Place heaping tablespoonfuls of mixture into skillet and fry golden. Serve at once.

Serves: 4-8.

Pork Liver Wrapped in Web
Fegatelli Avvolti con Rete di Maiale

One of the first meals Nonna prepared from the dressed pork was delicious tasting *fegatelli*. The entire pork liver was cubed and prepared. Leftovers were placed in a deep crock, covered with rendered lard, and stored for future use. This recipe, that uses laurel and fennel, is from *Quarata* and the province of *Arezzo*. Traditional *fegatelli* from other areas of Tuscany replaces fennel with sage. We do not use sage in this dish.

The web (caul) is the fatty, net-like membrane which covers the intestines of the pig. It is essential for this dish, because it bastes the liver and keeps it tender. While cooking, the web nearly disappears.

Traditionally, *fegatelli con rete di maiale* is fried or roasted over a wooden fire. The stems of fresh bay leaves are used as skewers, adding additional flavor. The recipe below is the fried version.

Don't knock it till you try it. This is a very special dish and it is absolutely delicious!

1 pork web (caul)*
1 whole pork liver
¼-inch-thick slice *pancetta*
½ tbsp. salt
½ tbsp. pepper
⅓ cup fennel seeds
15-20 bay leaves
¼ cup corn oil
5-8 wooden skewers

Soak the pork web in water for about 10 minutes, and then lay it on a clean cloth and spread it out. Top with a second cloth and gently roll the cloth into a roll. Let sit until needed. Cut *pancetta* into 5-8 pieces.

Wash the pork liver and pat dry with a clean cloth. Cut into 3-inch squares. Cut away any gristle. Allow to dry. Unwrap the web and cut into as many pieces as you have chunks of liver. Use scissors. Set aside.

In a flat dish, combine salt and pepper. Mix. Place fennel seeds on another plate. Roll the individual pieces of pork liver in the salt and pepper mixture, then in the fennel seeds. Wrap the liver in a piece of the web. Take a wooden stick and skewer one bay leaf, wrapped liver, *pancetta*, bay leaf, second wrapped liver, and a final bay leaf. Pick up next skewer, and continue until all the liver is skewered.

Place a medium-size iron skillet over medium-high heat. Heat to hot. Add oil. Heat

to hot. If you have any leftover *pancetta*, cut it into small cubes and add to the oil. It adds flavor and moisture. Add skewered liver and sear quickly on all sides. Lower the heat, cover, and cook 20 to 30 minutes.

Serve hot with good bread and endive salad (see index).

Serves: 4-6.

Note: *Caul, like blood and other specialty items from the pig, is only available from a farmer.

Pork Sausage
Salsiccia di Maiale

Sausage is easy to make, especially if one is satisfied with making patties instead of links. Links require a little more work for they need casings. A sausage casing is the thin intestine of the pig. Casings can be purchased from any supermarket and are usually packed in salt. Once the package of casings is opened it should be stored in the refrigerator and can be kept for more than a year as long as casings are covered with salt. Some markets are willing to sell a few casings at a time.

Don't be intimidated. This is easy. Give it a try.

4½ lb. ground pork butt
2 large cloves garlic
1 tbsp. salt
1 tbsp. ground pepper
2 tsp. nutmeg
3-4 lengths pork casings
Butcher cord

Sausage Patties

Ask your butcher to **fine** grind the pork butt. Place ground pork on a pastry board or in a large low pan. Peel garlic and press through a garlic press releasing the juices over the ground pork until very little pulp remains. Discard extra pulp. Sprinkle the meat with salt, pepper, and grated nutmeg.

Using your hands, mix the ground pork for at least 15 minutes to be sure that all the seasonings are evenly distributed. Allow to stand for 10 minutes and taste for seasonings (if you do not want to taste raw pork, fry a little and then taste).

Form into patties. You can freeze sausage patties for more than a month. Lay the individual patties on the pastry tray and put in freezer. Freeze for a few hours then place in freezer bag. Now you can remove one at a time without disturbing other patties.

Sausage Links

Ask your butcher to **course** grind the pork butt (if too fine it will be harder to stuff into the casings). If you prefer to grind your own meat, ask the butcher to remove the bone from the pork butt. Cut pork butt into 1-inch cubes and run the cubes through a meat chopper with a coarse blade. Then follow the recipe for sausage patties (above). When the pork has been mixed it is time to stuff the casings.

Select 4-5 casings and soak them in cold water for a few minutes. Squeeze, wrap in a clean cloth, pat dry, and set aside.

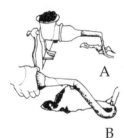

A

B

Select a casing, find an end and blow into it with your mouth. It will blow up like a balloon. If it does not inflate, discard it, for there is a hole somewhere in the casing.

Gently place the end of the casing over the funnel (see A) of a meat grinder and slide it until all the casing is on the funnel (if casing resists, run a little meat through the funnel and then push the casing on—the meat greases the inside of the casing). Tie the opposite end in a knot.

Stuffing the Sausage

Slowly stuff meat into grinder and run through. It will begin to enter the casing (see B). These links should be 1 ¼ inches in diameter. Make sure stuffing is not packed too tight or casing will break (it might not break right away, but it will when cooking). When you reach the end of the casing, remove it, place another casing on the funnel, and begin again. Continue until all meat is gone.

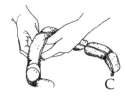

C

Making Links

Once all casings have been stuffed, tie sausage into 4-5-inch links (see C). Begin at end with cord. Measure (or judge) desired length, pinch sausage with your thumb and forefinger, wrap cord around dent forming a knot. Continue to the end.

Prick sausage with pin or needle 2-3 times in each link to release air that may be trapped in casings. Hang sausage over pole and allow to dry overnight. Place in cool cellar, refrigerator, or freezer.

If freezing, lay the links on the pastry tray so they do not touch each other and put in freezer. Freeze for a few hours then place in freezer bag. Now you can remove one at a time without disturbing others.

Yield: 25-30 (4-inch) links, or 25 patties.

Variations:

Breakfast Sausage *(Salsiccia per Prima Colazione)*. Eliminate garlic, add 2 tsp. cinnamon or 2 tsp. cloves.

Fennel Sausage *(Salsiccia con Finocchio)*. Boil 2 cloves garlic in ¼ cup dry red wine. Discard garlic. Add wine and 1 tbsp. fennel to mixture.

Hot Sausage *(Salsiccia Coppa)*. Keep garlic, add 2 tbsp. hot pepper.

Dried Sausage *(Salsiccia Secca, stagionata)*. As sausages age they take on different textures and Nonno would hang them in the cellar. Dried sausage wrinkles up and is very good sliced and eaten like *salami*, uncooked. Age at least 40 days.

Sausage Roll
Cotechino

Cotechino is a sausage made from leftover and second-grade pork meat. It looks like a *salami*, but is 3 inches in diameter and 8-9 inches long. When stuffed into a pig's foot, as they do in *Moderna*, it is called *zampone*, but when stuffed into a casing like a sausage, it is *cotechino*.

The filling begins with ground pork, but the other ingredients vary from district to district in Italy. For us, *cotechino* is the same as headcheese *(soprassata)*, except it is ground and raw whereas headcheese is diced and cooked. You cook the *cotechino* just before eating.

4 lb. pork butt, or 1 pig's head
1 lb. pork skin (rind)
1½ tbsp. salt
¾ tbsp. pepper
¼ tsp. nutmeg
3-4 casings*

Ask the butcher to fine grind the pork butt. If you prefer to grind your own meat, ask the butcher to remove the bone from the pork butt. Cut pork butt into 1-inch cubes, and run the cubes through a meat chopper with a fine blade. If using a pig's head follow instructions under Headcheese recipe (see index).

Select 3-4 casings and soak them in cold water for a few minutes. Squeeze, wrap in a clean cloth, pat dry, and set aside.

Combine pork, rind, salt, pepper, and nutmeg and mix for 15 minutes or until well blended. Let set for 10 minutes and taste (if you do not want to taste raw pork, fry it in a skillet).

Wash the casings one more time and dry with a clean cloth. Select one, find an end and blow into it with your mouth. It will blow up like a balloon (if not, discard). Tie one end in a knot. Slowly stuff the meat into the casing using your hands or a large spoon. Be gentle or the casing will break.

When casing is full, tie remaining end. Pierce casing in several places with a toothpick to allow trapped air to escape. Attach a string to one end and hang it in a cool place. Continue until all casings are stuffed.

Store in a cool place. Allow to age for 2-3 weeks. *Cotechino* is not aged like *salami* and should be eaten before 3 months.

Yield: 3-4 sausages.

Note: *You need a wider casing for *cotechino* than the casing used for sausage.

Salt Belly
Pancetta

Pancetta is the Italian answer to bacon. It is used so often in our cooking that no stew, stuffing, pasta sauce, or roast would be complete without the rich flavor *pancetta* provides.

Called by various names including pork belly and salt belly, *pancetta* is available in supermarkets. It is usually next to the bacon.

Making *pancetta* is like making *prosciutto*. The difference is the time it ages and the cut of meat.

1 side fresh bacon with rind
2 cups salt, divided
½ cup pepper
6-8 cloves garlic (optional)
Large wooden box

The cut of meat for *pancetta* is from the side of the hog, next to the ribs. When buying meat ask for an uncured piece of bacon with rind. If the meat has been refrigerated, it can still be cured, but do not make this recipe with frozen meat. Fresh meat is available from a slaughterhouse or a farmer.

Lay meat on a clean workspace. Combine 1 cup salt and pepper in a large bowl. Rub salt mixture generously over both sides of the meat. Be sure to coat well.

Place 1 cup salt in wooden box (box should be slightly larger than piece of meat). Be sure bottom of box is covered (use more salt if necessary).

Place pork in salt-lined box rind side down,

A

B

and cover with remaining salt and pepper. Age 10 days, massage the salt into the meat daily, and add more salt as needed (see *prosciutto* illustrations that follow).

After 10 days, remove from salt. Wash in warm water. Soak for half hour. Pat dry. Rub more pepper into meat.

Garlic is optional. To add garlic place *pancetta*, rind side down, on a flat surface. Make ½-inch slits in a diagonal pattern across the surface. Peel garlic and place half a clove in each slit (see A).

Begin at one end and roll the *pancetta* like a jellyroll (see B). Tie securely and hang in cool, dry place for 90 days.

If meat smells rancid or pungent it is spoiled and must be thrown away.

Yield: 1.

Prosciutto

One hundred men will have one hundred secrets for homemade *prosciutto*, but only five men will talk about them. All will agree that the pig must be ten to eleven months old and weight about four hundred pounds, and *prosciutto* must be made in winter, begun before February in a cool, dry place. In addition to the secrets, salting is the most important process in making *prosciutto*. If salted too little, the *prosciutto* will go bad. If salted too much, it will be cured, but inedible.

Likewise one hundred villages in Italy will have one hundred different ingredients in their *prosciutto* that makes it special and specific to them. In *Parma* in *Emilia-Romagna*, the incredible, unbelievable, inconceivable world-famous *prosciutto di Parma* is made from pigs that have been fed the curd of Parmesan cheese. No spices are added, only salt. The other famous *prosciutto*, *Prosciutto di San Daniele*, made in *Friuli*, uses sea salt.

In Tuscany they use more salt than elsewhere. There are also differences from province to province. As you will see below our *prosciutto* has garlic and red wine. In *Il Casentino*, a valley between *Arezzo* and Florence, our cousins coat the rind of their *prosciutto* with red pepper giving it a reddish look and a tangy taste. There is another Tuscany *prosciutto* but I do not think I have ever tasted it. It is cured with pepper, garlic, rosemary, and juniper.

1 hind leg of pig
5-10 lb. salt, more as needed
1-2 cups pepper
5-6 cloves garlic
1 cup dry red wine
Large wooden or plastic box

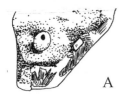

A

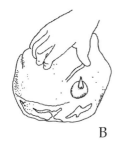

B

C

D

Be sure the leg is cleaned of dirt and hair and still has its skin. Be sure meat is dry before beginning the process.

Lay leg on a clean workspace. Clean and be sure two bones are visible: the round leg socket and a rectangular bone slightly below and to the side of the socket bone (see A). The round bone is the gauge that tells you when to stop salting the meat.

You must remove excess blood from the vein that runs the length of the leg between the two bones. Begin at the bottom and with your thumb press and move firmly to the top (see B). A little blood will come out. Pat dry. Do this at least twice a day for 2 days.

Now you are ready to salt. The rule is 1 day of salt bath for every pound of meat, or 7 days for every inch of thickness measured at the thickest part of the fresh leg. Begin by rubbing the entire leg with salt. Cover the bottom of the box with ½-inch layer of salt. Lay leg on top. Spread salt over leg to 1 inch thickness, adding more in the middle of the leg. Keep one end of the box elevated (see C) to allow the juice to settle away from the meat.

Allow to sit a few days. You will notice a little moisture in the bottom of the box. This must be drained daily.

After the second day the leg must be massaged each day (see D) to break the salt crust. Massage for about 5 minutes. Never turn the leg. Add additional salt as it is depleted.

This process will continue for at least a month. Our family maintains the meat must be left in the salt for 40 days, others say 25-30 days. The gauge is the socket bone (see E). In the center of the bone is a little bit of flesh. It will be pure white and malleable when the

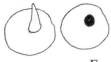

E

F

G

process begins. As the days pass it will begin to turn color, and when the meat is cured it will have formed a black spot in the center of the bone. When the center is black, the meat is cured.

Once the *prosciutto* is cured it must be cleaned. Soak it in warm water for 10-15 minutes to remove excess salt. Pat dry.

Rub the entire *prosciutto* generously with black pepper kneading it into fleshy parts.

The *prosciutto* must now be sealed to hold in the flavor. In our family we crush 2 heads of garlic and boil in wine. Mash it into a paste and rub into the cured *prosciutto*. Rub with the palm of the hand, pressing with great care for at least 30 minutes. Be sure pepper remains on the *prosciutto*.

Cut a slit in the skin near the end of the leg and run a piece of cord through the hole. Hang the *prosciutto* from the rafters in a cool, dry place for 6 months before cutting (see F).

When cutting *prosciutto* (see G) begin at round end and slice down. Remove an inch of rind (good as a flavoring in cooking). Cut each slice paper-thin.

If meat smells rancid or pungent it is spoiled and must be thrown away. In Italy they test the *prosciutto* with a long needle made of horse bone. They insert the needle into the fleshy part of the meat and withdraw it. The odor left on the needle attests to the success of the curing process.

Once cut the *prosciutto* can remain hanging in a cool place. Wrap it in a cotton cloth to keep it fresh. Never wrap in plastic or freeze any cured ham.

Salami

There are an endless variety of *salamis*, too. Almost every Italian village had their own method of making this excellent pork cold cut. In *Calabria* they are known for adding a lot of red hot peppers to their *salami*. A *salami coppata*, combining a *coppa* encased with ground pork and a number of spices including juniper comes from the *Veneto*. The people of *Verona* spice their *salami* with cinnamon and cloves. The *Milanese* add cracked peppercorns to their *salami*. This recipe is our standard, but true Tuscan *salami*. It is called *finocchino*, in the masculine *(-ino)* if the fat pieces are small, and *finocchiona*, in the feminine *(-iona)*, if the fat pieces are large. In either instance the *finocch* is because it has fennel *(finocchio)*. When Gino made this *salami* he did not use the fennel at all.

8 lb. pork butt
1½ tbsp. salt
1 tbsp. pepper
⅓ cup whole
   peppercorns
2 tbsp. fennel seeds
1 cup red wine
4-5 large cloves garlic
1 tbsp. corn oil
Casing
Cord

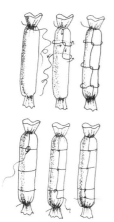

Pork butt must be unchilled. Ask your butcher to course grind the pork butt (if too fine it will be hard to stuff into casings). If you prefer to grind your own meat, ask the butcher to remove the bone from the pork butt. Cut pork butt into 1-inch cubes and run the cubes through a meat chopper with a course blade.

Place pork on large workspace. Combine salt, pepper, whole peppercorns, and fennel seeds with pork. Mix for 10 minutes and allow to set.

Place a medium-sized pan over medium-high heat. Add wine. Bring to a boil. Crush garlic cloves (do not peel) and add to wine. Simmer for half hour. Remove garlic from wine and pour wine over ground pork. Mix pork for at least 15 minutes. Let stand for a few hours to allow flavors to blend.

Place a medium-sized iron skillet over medium-high heat. Heat to hot. Add 1 tbsp. oil. Take a handful of pork mixture and add to skillet. Allow to fry until cooked. This is a tester. Taste the meat to see if it needs additional flavoring. Add as necessary.

Wash the casing and pat dry. Put the remaining pork in casings, one handful at a time pressing down to firm and eliminate air pockets. Tie the casing. Allow to set in casing overnight.

The next day tie the *salami* with cord (see illustration) by beginning at the top of the *salami* and circling it twice so the *salami* is in quarters. Tie very tightly. Now circle the *salami* with the cord every inch or so.

Hang *salami* in a cool dry place and pierce the casing with a needle in 5 or 6 places to let out any air. Allow to cure for 3 months.

Note: *Salami* casings are not the same as sausage casings; they are larger and thicker.

Omelets, Eggs, and Egg Tortes
Frittate, Uova, e Torte di Uova

Eggs appear in almost every course of an Italian meal from appetizers, soups, stuffings, and sauces to salads and desserts. Italians do not use eggs sparingly, but abundantly.

Our Tuscan omelet is not puffy and fluffy, but flat and filled with vegetables and cheeses. The choice of vegetables might be considered exotic to some palates, because in addition to the traditional peppers, onions, and mushrooms our omelets feature artichokes, asparagus and tomatoes. As usual, the dish is well-spiced and tasty. When I started cooking, I pushed the envelope even further. I have made omelets with tuna fish, fried ham, and even fried salami. Just add it to the frying vegetables.

Egg tortes are another Italian specialty our family has enjoyed for years. Popularly called quiches in America and offered in upbeat restaurants, the egg pie is stuffed with vegetables and meats and dressed with a pastry shell. Our versions are prepared not only for daily fare, but on special occasions and include Italian cured meats.

Americans have embraced many Italian dishes from pastas and pizzas to *scaloppine* and Parmesan, but the marriage of eggs to tomatoes has yet to be discovered by the majority of Americans. Three recipes are listed here, each one a favorite. Seldom served for breakfast, the tomato recipes are good for any daily meal. They will also delight guests served on a buffet. Our favorite is poached eggs in tomato sauce laced with garlic.

Eggs have not fared well in the modern day battle against high cholesterol; however, we are discovering that they may have been falsely accused. Again, enjoy these egg recipes and skip a fast food meal. For those of you who insist on using them, we have tried all the egg recipes in this chapter with low cholesterol egg substitutes, which are available on the market. Elizabeth did not concede, but, except for the poached egg recipe, the substitutes can be used. Another major change is to cut back on the oil. Where we used it abundantly before, now we use only 3 tablespoons of oil. The oil must cover the bottom of the pan. If you do not use enough oil, your eggs will stick to the pan, so use good judgement.

Basic Omelet
Frittata Classica

3-4 tbsp. corn oil
3 eggs
Salt and pepper

Place a medium-size iron skillet over medium-high heat. Heat to hot. Add oil to cover the bottom of the pan. Heat. Add ingredients as listed in following variations. Beat eggs in a bowl and add salt and pepper to taste. Pour over simmering ingredients. Cover and allow to cook for 2 to 3 minutes or until firm. Serve immediately.

Serves: 2-3.

Note: If I have it, I sometimes add a little cream. The key to a successful omelet, as well as a good fried egg, is enough grease to keep it afloat: it won't stick, it will turn easily, and it does not absorb the oil. The oil *must* cover the bottom of the pan.

Variations
Variazioni

Artichoke Omelet *(Frittata di Carciofi)*: 2 fresh artichokes, 1 tsp. lemon juice, 3-4 tbsp. corn oil, ¼ cup water, 3 eggs, salt, pepper. Wash artichokes. Clean by removing outer hard leaves (see artichokes in index for information on how to prepare them). Spread to expose center of artichoke. Remove pointed and hairy parts in center of artichoke. Cut away the tips of all hard leaves with kitchen shears. To loosen the leaves, hit each artichoke on a drain board three or four times. Wash by placing in fresh water, to which 1 tsp. of lemon juice has been added. Drain upside-down on drain board. Cut each artichoke in half lengthwise. From each half, cut 5 to 6 wedges Check each edge for prickly centers, and if any remain, remove them. Place a medium-size iron skillet over medium-high heat. Add oil. Place the artichoke pieces in the oil and add ¼ cup water. Allow to boil and lower the heat. Simmer until tender. Add eggs, salt, and pepper, and continue as for Basic Omelet.

Note: Baby artichokes do not have all the prickly innards and will do nicely for this recipe. They are hard to find at the market but should not be more than about 2.5 inches high not counting the stem.

Asparagus Omelet *(Frittata di Asparagi)*: 1 bunch fresh asparagus, 3-4 tbsp. corn oil, ¼ cup water, 3 eggs, salt, pepper. Wash asparagus. Discard the hard, white bottom and drain asparagus on a paper towel. Place a medium-size iron skillet over medium-high heat. Heat to hot. Add oil. Cut the asparagus into 2-inch pieces and place in oil. Add water. Allow to boil and lower the heat. Simmer for 5 minutes. When water is gone, add beaten eggs, salt, and pepper, and continue as for Basic Omelet.

Note: I now prefer asparagus a little crunchy, so I cut the water entirely and fry for only a minute. The amount of crunch depends on your taste, but simmering for a minute will add more crunch. The taste is better.

Cheese Omelet *(Frittata di Formaggio)*: 3 eggs, 3-4 tbsp. corn oil, 1½ cups shredded *Fontina* or cheddar cheese, salt, pepper. Prepare Basic Omelet and just before eggs are done add cheese, salt, and pepper. Cover and allow the cheese to melt. Serve immediately.

Green Pepper and Onion Omelet *(Frittata di Peperoni e Cipolle)*: 1 small green bell pepper, 1 small onion, 3-4 tbsp. corn oil, 3 eggs, salt, pepper. Wash pepper and onions. Clean and cut pepper in strips and onions in slices. Place a medium-size iron skillet over medium-high heat. Heat to hot. Add oil. Place peppers and onions in oil and fry until tender. Add eggs, salt, and pepper, and continue as for Basic Omelet.

Mushroom Omelet *(Frittata di Fungi)*: ¼ lb. fresh mushrooms, 2 tbsp. butter, 2 cloves garlic, salt, pepper, 3 eggs. Working one mushroom at a time, clean and cut off the very tip of the stem and remove any blemishes on the crown. Slice mushrooms. Place a medium-size iron skillet over medium-high heat. Heat to hot. Melt butter in skillet. Add garlic. When garlic is brown, mash into small pieces with fork. Add mushrooms, salt, and pepper to taste. Lower heat and sauté for 5 minutes. Add eggs and continue as for Basic Omelet.

Green Onion Omelet *(Frittata di Cipolle):* 6 fresh green onions (scallions) or 1 onion, 3-4 tbsp. corn oil, 3 eggs, salt, pepper. Wash onions. Clean and dice. Place a medium-size iron skillet over medium heat. Heat to hot. Add oil. Place onion pieces in oil and fry until transparent. Add eggs, salt and pepper and continue as for Basic Omelet.

Salami or Dried Sausage Omelet *(Frittata di Salame o Salsiccia Secca o Stagionata):* 3-4 thick slices of *salami* or 2 dry sausages (see index), 2-3 eggs, salt, pepper, 3-4 tbsp. butter. Cut meat into pieces, skin sausage, and cut in half lengthwise; you can also break it into pieces if you prefer. Place in a medium-size iron skillet over medium-high heat and sauté until browned. Do not add oil. Beat eggs until frothy, and add salt and pepper to eggs. Add butter to another skillet. Melt. Add meat. Add eggs and continue as for Basic Omelet.

Omelet with Tomatoes
Frittata con Pomodori

1 large very ripe tomato
Sprig fresh parsley
3-4 tbsp. corn oil
3 eggs
Salt and pepper
3 tbsp. freshly grated Parmesan cheese

Place a medium-size iron skillet over medium-high heat. Heat to hot. Dice tomato and parsley; add to warm skillet. Cook 10 minutes, or until juices evaporate.

While tomatoes are reducing, place a medium-size iron skillet over medium-high heat. Add oil. Heat to hot. Beat eggs, and add salt and pepper to taste. Add eggs to warm oil, cover, and allow to cook for 2 to 3 minutes or until firm. Turn if desired.

Remove omelet from skillet. Lay on platter (you can fold the omelet over and stuff it with cheese if you like). Pour tomatoes over omelet and sprinkle with cheese.

Serves: 2-3.

Omelets in Tomato Sauce
Frittate con Sugo di Pomodoro

3-4 tbsp. corn oil
6 eggs
2 tbsp. freshly grated Parmesan cheese
Salt and pepper, to taste
2 tbsp. butter
2 cloves garlic
1 cup whole or crushed canned tomatoes, no puree, or 2 very ripe fresh tomatoes

Place a small-size iron skillet over medium-high heat. Heat to hot. Add oil. Beat 1 egg in bowl, add pinch of cheese and salt and pepper to taste. Pour into oil. Cover, and cook for a few minutes. Remove, place on a board, begin at one end, and roll. Repeat for remaining eggs.

Place a medium-size iron skillet over medium-high heat. Heat to hot. Add butter; allow to melt. Peel and dice garlic. Add to butter and sauté until brown. Add tomatoes, crushing into small pieces with a fork. Simmer 15 to 20 minutes, or until tomatoes begin to solidify.

Remove from heat and run through a sieve, pushing pulp through sieve. Throw remaining pulp away. Return tomato mixture to skillet. Add salt and pepper if necessary, but it should be savory enough. Continue to simmer until tomatoes begin to lose their red color and turn brown-red, about 20 minutes. If tomatoes begin to dry, add ¼ to ½ cup broth.

Add omelets; simmer 5-10 minutes.

Serves: 3-4.

Note: As an alternative, stuff omelets with *salami*, sausage, or cheese before rolling.

Poached Eggs in Tomato Sauce
Uova Affogate in Sugo di Pomodoro

5-6 very ripe fresh tomatoes
3-4 tbsp. corn oil
2 cloves garlic
¼ tsp. salt
¼ tsp. pepper
6 eggs

Wash tomatoes and blanch in boiling water for a few minutes. Peel, quarter, and set aside.

Place a medium-size iron skillet over medium-high heat. Heat to hot. Add oil (or pan drippings) and heat. Peel and dice garlic. Add and sauté until brown, then crush with fork into small pieces. Do not burn. Add tomatoes, crushing into small pieces with a fork. Add salt and pepper. Simmer 10 to 15 minutes or until tomatoes begin to lose their liquid.

Break and add eggs one at a time. Salt and pepper to taste. Do not allow to touch. Occasionally spoon tomatoes over eggs. Simmer 5 to 10 minutes or until poached to taste. Serve at once with good Italian bread.

Serves: 3.

Note: I sometimes use this sauce over spaghetti with lots of Parmesan.

Egg Pies
Torte di Uova

Egg pies are a specialty at Easter. Some immigrant families made such big pies that they were steamed in buckets over the open hearth. Nonna never made them, but Sandrina did.

Usually baked, distributed, and eaten on Holy Saturday, these pies exist in almost every region of Italy. Usually the shell is filled with cheeses and meats, and the eggs are combined with the other ingredients and baked. In *Liguria,* the Easter pie is called *Torta Pasqualina* and consists of 33 layers—one for each year of Christ on earth—including pastry, spinach (and other vegetables), *ricotta* (and other cheeses), and of course, eggs. In *Calabria,* the pie is filled with ham, sausage, hard-boiled eggs, *mozzarella,* and *ricotta.* In Sicily, *macaroni* is added to the meats and cheeses. My mother's good friend Valia Dalfonso Ray, from *Abruzzo,* remembers her mother making a sweet pie *pizza repiena* filled with *ricotta,* ground beef, sausage, cheese, and eggs. Italian-Americans call these pies by dozens of dialect names including *pizz piena, pizza gain,* and *pizza rustica.*

Easter Pie
Torta di Pasqua

dough:
3 cups flour
¼ oz. dry yeast
2 tsp. granulated
    sugar
1 tsp. salt
2 tbsp. corn oil
1 cup warm water

filling:
6 oz. sausage
6 oz. ham
6 oz. basket cheese
12 eggs*
¼ tsp. salt
¼ tsp. pepper

Place flour in a bowl. Add yeast, sugar, and salt. Mix together. Make a well in the flour mixture. Add oil and water. Mix together until it forms a stiff dough. Knead until all flour is absorbed, about 15 to 20 minutes.

Cover dough and let rise for 1 hour. Punch down and let rise again for 30 minutes.

Place a medium-size pot over high heat. Add enough water to cover meats. Bring to a boil. Add sausage and ham. Boil for 15 minutes, drain, cool; remove skin from sausage and cut meats into bite-size pieces. Cube basket cheese.

Place eggs in a large bowl and beat. Add sausage, ham, cheese, salt, and pepper. Stir. Set aside.

Place dough on floured pastry board. Divide in half, setting one half under a bowl to rest. Using a rolling pin, roll dough until 12-to-13 inches in circumference (at least 4 inches wider that pie plate). Repeat with remaining dough.

Grease 2 deep-sided (9-inch) pie plates (see following note) with a little oil. Lift dough and place in one pie plate allowing to spill over the sides. Press down. Do the second dough in the same manner.

Divide egg mixture into two equal amounts and pour egg mixture into dough-lined pie plates. Lift remaining dough up over the eggs to form a large 2-to 3-inch-wide crust.

Place both pies in oven and bake at 350 degrees for 1 hour or until eggs are set and top is slightly brown.

Yield: 2 pies, each serving 6 to 8 persons.

Notes: Pie plates must be deep to keep eggs from spilling in oven. Placing the crust over the edges of the torte helps prevent spillage.

*If using extra large eggs, use only 10.

Savory *Prosciutto* and *Ricotta* Pie
Torta di Prosciutto e Ricotta Gustosa

This tangy and savory egg pie with cheese and meat is a meal in itself and stunning on a buffet.

crust:
1 cup flour
Pinch salt
2 tbsp. granulated
   sugar
3 oz. shortening
½ tsp. vanilla
3-4 large eggs

filling:
6 slices *prosciutto* or
   cured ham
6 slices *salami*
3-4 oz. *Fontina* cheese
½ cup freshly grated
   Parmesan cheese
1 ⅓ lbs. *ricotta*
1 egg

In a mixing bowl combine flour, salt, and sugar. Mix. Cut in shortening with a pastry cutter. Add vanilla and eggs (save the yolk of 1 egg in a separate bowl). Slowly combine ingredients. Knead until firm. Add additional flour as needed to keep from sticking.

Turn out onto pastry board. Using a rolling pin, roll out to 12-to-13 inches in circumference. Line the bottom of a 9-inch pie plate, allowing dough to spill over at least 4 inches.

Dice all meats and hard cheese into 1-inch pieces. Mix together in a large mixing bowl. Add Parmesan cheese, *ricotta* cheese, and egg. Mix again.

Fill the pie shell. Bring the edges of the pie crust up and over the filling, leaving a 2-to-3-inch hole in the middle of the pie.

Beat the remaining egg yolk and brush the top of the pie crust.

Bake in a 325-degree oven for 50 to 60 minutes, or until the top browns.

Yield: 1 (9-inch) pie.

Note: You can create your own filling for this *ricotta* pie, adding sausage or other meats.

Pasta
Pasta

Pasta is Italy's gift to the world and is at the heart of Italian cooking. Despite the popular misconception that Marco Polo brought pasta to Italy from China, Italians have been enjoying pasta since the Etruscan civilization of the fifth and fourth centuries B.C. It did not become the popular dish it is today until 150 years ago, and it was not wedded to tomatoes until they arrived from the Americas and the Neapolitans discovered the blending in the last century. Since then, the number of sauces and cuts of pasta has grown into what seems to be an endless variety (see *Shopping all'Italiana* for list).

Every region in Italy has unique pasta dishes, not all well-known in America: *macaroni alla guitarra*, made with a special machine laced with strings had its birth in *Abruzzo; cavatelli* from Naples (surprise); and, of course, *pappardelle* from the *Arezzo* province of Tuscany, are just a few of the hundreds of cuts of pasta accompanied by their own special sauces.

Traditionally, pasta was intended as a first course, but for many immigrants (and peasants in Italy) it often became the meal: an inexpensive way to feed a large family. Nonna had only one child and Nonno was lucky enough to work during the Depression, so in our family we were able to follow the tradition of pasta as a first course. We ate some type of pasta every day—either in soup or in sauce—and it was always homemade.

To help you make the different pasta specialties in various quantities we have created a variety of choices. There are three different basic pasta recipes in this chapter, two for pasta and one for crepes, each for a different quantity. The two pastas are interchangeable (the crepe is not). There is one meat stuffing and two cheese stuffings in various quantities. All pastas and stuffings can be cut in half or in fourths successfully. Quantity is an issue. When we make the dish, we get the yield listed. If you make your *cappelletti, ravioli,* or *cannelloni* smaller than we do, you will get more, and if you make them larger, you will get less.

Specialty sauces appear with the pasta dishes, but our basic pasta sauce and sauces that can be used in a number of ways are in the sauce chapter. In that chapter we have also created a chart for various quantities of sauce.

Homemade Pasta
Pasta della Casalinga

Pasta is at the heart of Italian cooking and the immigrant women, from all regions, took great pride in the delicacy of their noodles and the thinness of their cuts.

Pasta making was a day-long affair, especially if the pasta was to be stuffed for *ravioli* or *cappelletti*. The whole kitchen was turned into a pasta factory. When I think of Nonna, the moment I remember most is the image of her in the kitchen bending over an old, yellow crank pasta machine, her hair in a net, her apron covered with flour, and surrounded by a variety of cut pastas hanging to dry from a variety of coat hangers.

Nonna used this pasta recipe for everything from *ravioli* and *lasagna* to fine noodles for soup: only the quantity and cut varied. When she made pasta, she called it *pasta asciutta* when it was drained after cooking and topped with a sauce, and *pastina* when it was cooked in a broth.

Nonna never made less than double the following recipe—that is why she worked all day. Sandrina's recipe for homemade pasta is found later in the chapter.

4 eggs
⅛ cup water
1 tsp. salt
2 tbsp. butter
2 tbsp. olive oil
3 cups flour

Making the Sponge

In mixer: Break eggs and place in large mixing bowl. Add water, salt, butter, and olive oil. Beat with heavy dough-beater. Gradually add 2-to-2½ cups flour to mixture until all is firm. Remove from bowl and place on pastry board (*spianatoia*) that has been slightly coated with fresh flour. Knead.

Mix by hand: Sift flour onto a pastry board. Make a well in center of flour by scooping out a hole (see A). Crack each egg and place in small bowl or the center of the flour (see A). Add water, salt, butter, olive oil and beat

A

B

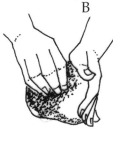

C

D

till fluffy with whisk or fork. If using a bowl, pour egg mixture into flour well. Slowly begin to pick up flour from inner ring of well, blending it into egg mixture (see B).

Continue to pick up flour until dough becomes firm and manageable. Use your hands. Knead until dough is firm and no longer sticky (could be 5 minutes, could be 20). Set aside. Clean lumps on board with dull side of knife; clean board. Dust board with flour.

Once dough is firm and board is cleaned and dusted, place dough on board and knead for 30 minutes (see C). While kneading, dough may become sticky. Keep adding small quantities of flour and continue kneading. Once no longer sticky, form into a ball. Sprinkle a small quantity of oil on a corner of the board. Place ball on top. Brush top of ball with oil to keep from getting crusty, cover with a bowl, and allow to rest 1 to 1½ hours.

Rolling Out the Dough

Rolling out dough is a very important step in the process of making pasta. If rolled dough is allowed to sit too long, it will dry out and be unmanageable, so work at a good pace. Send the family to the movies, put the answering machine on, and turn cell phones off.

To roll out with pasta machine: Cut prepared dough into 6 pieces. Dust hands with flour and work 1 piece at a time. Flatten into an oblong shape. Set pasta machine to highest (thickest, usually an 8) setting. Place short end of dough into rollers and roll 3 times (see D). Each time the dough will become longer and wider. Set machine to a thinner setting (6) and roll 2 to 3 times. Change position to number 4 setting and roll 2 to 3 times. By this time, the dough is thin and nearly a yard long (for

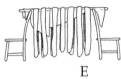

E

soup noodles roll one more time at the no. 2 setting). Remember, different machines may have different settings. We have lowered the setting three times and four for soup noodles. Place on drying rack (a clean broom handle covered with a cloth and stretched between 2 chairs will do—see E). Repeat process for each piece of dough.

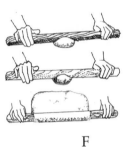

F

To roll out by hand: Good hand rolling depends on a good rolling pin (*matterello*). Cut dough into 3 pieces. Roll first piece with the *matterello* into a round shape, allowing dough to get larger and larger (see F) until the desired thickness is reached. For *tagliatelli*, the dough should be ¼-inch thick. Once dough is rolled out, lay it on a clean sheet to dry a little before cutting.

Cutting the Dough

It is important to cut the dough at the right time, especially for soup noodles. If allowed to dry too long, the dough becomes stiff and breaks apart as you cut. As far as we know there is no way to save the dough once this happens. There is no set time for drying because each batch of dough has its own life and humidity is also a factor, but the dough should have some elasticity in it.

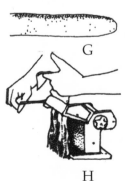

G

H

Cutting with the pasta machine: Today one does not have to bother with rolling out and cutting by hand: the pasta machine does it all.

All you have to do is prepare the dough for the machine, allow it to dry, cut 14-to-18-inch lengths (see G), select the proper cutter, and run the dough through the machine (see H) one time.

Cutting by hand: The pride of the cook was bound up in the way she cut her noodles.

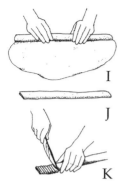

I

J

K

Sandrina was a master at cutting pasta. She worked so fast her knife would sing. Her noodles were thin and wonderful.

Dry the noodles as directed.

Then, fold the dough over on itself twice (see I, J) and perhaps again, until it is 3 inches wide. Begin at one end and cut to desired thickness: barely 1/16 of an inch for soup, 1/8 of an inch for *fettuccine* and *tagliatelli*, 1/4 of an inch for *linguini*, 1 inch or more for *pappardelle*, and 2 to 3 inches for *lasagna* (see K).

Drying the Pasta

L

Once pasta is cut, it must be dried again. Either lay it on a clean sheet, turning to dry all sides, or hang it over a pole or cardboard-lined coat hanger (see L). Pieces are dry when they break when pressed. After the noodles have dried, they can be stored in a plastic bag until ready to use. We put our soup noodles in a long wicker bread basket and cover basket and all with plastic.

Cooking

For sauce: If you are preparing 4 cups pasta, you will need 8 cups water. Fill a pan with water and boil. As water bubbles, add 2 tsp. salt. Bring to rolling boil. Add pasta and turn immediately to keep from sticking. Boil for 6 to 8 minutes for *al dente,* or 8 to 9 minutes for well done. Test by taste. Drain. Place on serving dish and cover with sauce. Sprinkle with freshly grated Parmesan cheese (some prefer to cover the pasta and let stand for 15 minutes before serving for the pasta to absorb the sauce. In this case store in warm oven).

For soup: Replace water with soup stock. Use 1 quart broth to 3 handfuls of homemade pasta. Boil soup, add pasta, and turn to keep from

sticking. Lower the heat and allow to soft boil
for 6 to 8 minutes or until done to taste.

Yields: A full pasta recipe will yield approximately 35 *cannelloni,* 70 *ravioli,* and 300 *cappelletti* or copious amounts of *fettuccine* and
smaller pasta cuts.

Stuffed Pastas
Paste Imbottite

Some form of stuffed pasta exists in most cultures. In Italy, the
varieties of stuffings are astounding--everything from the traditional meat or cheese found in this chapter to more exotic blends
of fish, spinach, and even squash and beets. They make a stuffing of marmalade and marzipan in *Bologna;* lobster and *scampi*
in Piedmont; capon, pigeon, pork, brains, and sausage in *Gub-
bio;* pumpkin in Ferrara; and *tortelli di zucca* and spiced cookies in
Cremona. Our stuffing, be it for *cappelletti, ravioli,* or *cannelloni* is
veal, chicken, spinach, egg, thyme, nutmeg, a few bread crumbs,
and grated Parmesan. Tuscan cuisine includes *nicchi,* also called
cappelli del prete (priest's hats), but we never made them. *Cappelletti* are featured on many northern tables. Of course, the shape
provides the name for all pastas. The suffixes denote the size: *letti*
or *lini* are small; *telli* are medium; *loni* or *lacci* are large.

As varied as the filling are the sauces that cover these pastas. They
vary from a little butter and herbs to a hearty deep-red meat sauce.

Meat Stuffing
Ripieno di Carne

You will not find a better meat stuffing. Never, never, never. When my mother would be sitting at the kitchen table before a holiday making the stuffed pasta, I would steal into the kitchen to dip my fingers in the bowl filled with stuffing. Boy, was it good!

4 oz. chopped Swiss chard or spinach

½ cup water
½ tsp. salt
10 oz. boneless veal
    (steak preferred)
10 oz. chicken breast
2 tbsp. butter
Pinch salt
Pinch pepper
Pinch thyme
¼ cup broth
1 medium onion
¼-inch-thick slice
    pancetta
1 small carrot
2 small celery ribs
    with leaves
1 tsp. fresh parsley
3 tbsp. corn oil
¼ cup freshly grated
    Romano cheese
⅓ cup freshly grated
    Parmesan cheese
¼ cup fine bread
    crumbs
1 grate nutmeg
2 eggs, beaten

Clean and wash Swiss chard (or spinach). Remove stalks and save. Place medium-size pot over medium-high heat and add water. Allow to boil, and add salt and leaves of chard. Cover and boil for 1 to 2 minutes, remove from stove, and steep until cool. Drain, squeeze dry, and set aside.

Cut veal and chicken breasts into 1-to-2-inch pieces. Discard fat, chicken skin, and bones. Place a large-size iron skillet over medium-high heat. Heat to hot. Add butter and melt, but do not brown. Add meat mixture, salt, pepper, and thyme. Cook until browned, 25 minutes, stirring often. Remove from skillet. Place a large bowl under a meat grinder. Run the meat mixture through the meat grinder, adding chard as you grind.

Add ¼ cup broth to the empty skillet, return to burner and stir with a fork to pick up all the good drippings in the skillet. Add the juice from the skillet to the mixture in the bowl and mix well.

While meat is browning, peel onion, wash, and cut into ¼ wedges. Dice *pancetta*. Peel carrot and celery. Wash, and cut into 2-inch pieces. Wash parsley. Combine and grind in a meat grinder or chop in a food processor (the grinder is better, because it releases the juices).

Place medium-size iron skillet over medium-high heat. Heat to hot. Add oil. When oil is hot, add chopped ingredients and sauté until onions are transparent (20 minutes), stirring often. The longer you cook this mixture the better the taste.

Combine cheeses, bread crumbs, and nutmeg in a bowl and mix. When onion mixture is well cooked, remove from skillet and add to the cheese mixture. Then add the onion-cheese mixture to the bowl with the meat mixture. Mix well. Add beaten eggs and mix again (see note).* If dry, add another egg. Set aside until ready for use. Can be stored in refrigerator overnight. Be sure to bring to room temperature before using.

Yields: This stuffing is enough for 70 *cannelloni*, 140 *ravioli*, or 600 *cappelletti*, depending on how big you make them. It can be divided in half, a fourth, or an eighth (and probably more) for smaller yields.

Note: *We add eggs and refrigerate stuffing, but with the current concern about contamination of poultry products, one can refrigerate the stuffing and bring it to room temperature and add eggs just before using.

Stuffed Canes
Cannelloni (Manicotti)

Of all stuffed pastas, *cannelloni* (canes) are the largest (*loni*) and easiest to prepare. *Ravioli* are small by comparison, and *cappelletti* (*etti*) are tiny. *Cannelloni* take big portions of stuffing and serve well for hearty appetites. Topped with béchamel sauce, they are even better. You can buy large *manicotti* in the pasta department of any supermarket, but we always preferred to make our own crepes.

½ stuffing recipe
½ pasta recipe
1 tbsp. corn oil
3½ cups sauce recipe
2 cups broth
2⅓ cups béchamel
  sauce

Prepare half recipe Meat Stuffing found earlier in chapter and set aside. Prepare half of the Homemade Pasta dough recipe found earlier in the chapter. Roll the dough to ⅟₁₆-inch thickness. Cut into 4 to 5-inch squares (see A).

Place a large pot over medium-high heat. Add water and oil and bring to a boil. Parboil the squares for 5 to 10 seconds.* Remove

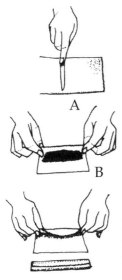

A

B

C

squares one at a time from boiling water and place in cold water. Place a square of pasta on a pastry board. Pat dry. Add 2 tbsp. stuffing at the very edge of the pasta (see B). Beginning at the edge with the stuffing, roll the pasta into a tubular shape (see C).

Prepare meat sauce recipe (see index). Heat 3½ cups of sauce to boiling. Add broth to thin sauce (see note).**

Place half the sauce in a long baking dish. Place the *cannelloni* on top of the sauce to form a row, or, if individual servings are preferred, place *cannelloni* in a small casserole (3 to 4 *cannelloni* per serving). Pour remaining sauce over *cannelloni*.

Prepare a double recipe of béchamel sauce (see index). Spoon the béchamel sauce carefully over the *cannelloni*, covering entirely.

Place in a 350-degree oven and bake for 45 minutes. Remove, cover with aluminum foil, and allow to stand for 10 to 15 minutes. Serve carefully.

Yield: 20-25 *cannelloni*, depending on size.

Notes: *If you plan to freeze *cannelloni*, do not par- boil. Place stuffed pasta on wax paper-lined cookie sheet, freeze, remove from freezer, place in plastic container, and refreeze. Now you can take out as many as you want.

**Cannelloni* absorb most of the sauce. If you like a lot of liquid, add more sauce and broth.

Mrs. Amico's Cheese Stuffed Canes
Manicotti al Formaggio della Signora Amico

Mrs. Amico, Bob Pelini's mother-in-law, is the master chef when it comes to fried *manicotti,* so we Tuscans bow to her Sicilian culinary expertise. She also creates another type of basic pasta in the recipe below. This recipe has become a tradition of the Pelini family in America.

sauce:
3 tbsp. olive oil
1 clove garlic
29 oz. canned toma-
    toes, no puree
6 oz. tomato paste
1 cup water
3 sprigs fresh parsley
1 fresh basil leaf
1 tsp. salt
1 tsp. pepper

crepes:
4 eggs
¼ cup corn oil
2 cups flour
½ tbsp. salt
2 cups cold water
1 tbsp. corn oil

stuffing:
2 lbs. *ricotta*
¾ cup freshly grated
    Parmesan cheese
4 tbsp. chopped
    parsley
2 eggs
½ tbsp. salt
¼ tbsp. pepper

Place a 6-quart pot over medium-high heat. Heat to warm and add olive oil. Peel garlic and add to hot oil. Brown garlic and remove from oil. Blend tomatoes into a puree. When garlic has been removed from oil, pour tomatoes quickly into the hot oil (there should be a *whoush* sound) and simmer for 45 minutes. Dissolve tomato paste in water and add to simmering tomatoes. Chop parsley and basil. Add parsley, basil, salt, and pepper to tomatoes. Simmer for an hour. If you want to add meatballs or sausage, do it at this time. Simmer for another hour. If too thick, add a little water. This sauce can be used on any pasta.

In a large bowl combine eggs, ¼ cup oil, flour, salt, and water. Beat to consistency of a thin pancake batter. Place a small, iron skillet over medium-high heat. Heat to hot. Grease slightly with remaining oil. Pour ¼ cup batter into skillet. Fry one side until dry; turn and fry second side (should not be browned). Continue until you have 20 pancakes.

Mix together *ricotta*, Parmesan, parsley, eggs, salt, and pepper. Place a crepe on a pastry board. Pat dry. Add 3 tablespoons stuffing at the very edge of the crepe. Beginning at the edge with the stuffing, roll the crepe into a tubular shape (see illustrations accompanying the Stuffed Canes recipe).

Prepare a large baking dish. Cover bottom of dish with sauce. Add the crepes (if individual servings are preferred, place into a small casserole, 3 to 4 *manicotti* per serving). Cover with sauce.

Bake in 350-degree oven for 30 to 45 minutes, or until bubbly.

Yield: 20.

Little Hats
Cappelletti (Tortellini)

In addition to the region, the shape determines the name of these stuffed pastas. *Cappelletti,* originating in Tuscany and *Emilia-Romagna,* means "little hats" and, true to the name, each looks like a hat. Similarly, *tortellini,* from *Bologna,* means "look like little bellybuttons" and by wrapping the stuffed dough around the finger, a bellybutton is made. Both can be filled with any stuffing.

In our home we make *cappelletti* in copious quantities, and prefer a meat filling. We always serve *cappelletti* in good broth with either freshly grated Parmesan or *Romano* cheese.

1 full stuffing recipe (either meat or cheese)
2 full pasta recipes

A

B

C

Prepare Meat Stuffing recipe or Cheese Stuffing recipe (see index). It is important to prepare your work space for comfort and convenience. Line a cookie sheet with wax paper. If you have made the stuffing ahead, take stuffing mixture from refrigerator and bring to room temperature.

When you are ready to make the *cappelletti* prepare two full recipes of Homemade Pasta (see index). Do not allow pasta to dry. Instead keep the dough covered and work with small quantities—roll one pasta line at a time, make the *cappelletti,* roll another pasta line, and continue until all is done.

Run dough through the pasta machine until you reach desired thickness and length, or roll with a rolling pin until 1/16-inch in thickness. Place long dough in front of you. Cut into 1½-inch squares, placing the excess in a pile that can be rerolled.

Fill square with a small pinch of stuffing (see A).

Bring one edge diagonally over the stuffing to opposite edge. Pinch down to seal on all sides (see B).

Take two edges of rectangle and bring behind the mound of stuffing and seal again, forming into a small hat (see C).

Place on wax-paper-lined cookie sheet. Continue until strip of dough is gone. Knead remnants. Repeat process, making squares and stuffing.

Take another piece of dough. Run through the pasta machine until desired thickness and length, or roll with a rolling pin until 1/16-inch in thickness. Proceed as with the first long dough.

When cookie sheet is filled, place in freezer. Prepare another cookie sheet with wax paper. Continue until finished.

When finished, remove one cookie sheet at a time from freezer, remove pasta from cookie sheet, and place *cappelletti* in plastic storage containers. Be sure all have frozen for at least 1 hour. *Cappelletti* are now individually frozen and will not stick together.

Yield: 600 *cappelletti*. For 300 use ½ the stuffing recipe and 1 pasta recipe. For 150, ¼ stuffing, ½ pasta, etc.

Note: It is best to prepare the *cappelletti* ahead of time, but if you wish to prepare and serve it immediately you must allow the freshly made *cappelletti* to age 10 minutes before putting them into broth, or they will fall apart.

To cook: Place 2 quarts of broth in a 4-quart pot. Heat over high heat until boiling.

When broth is at a boil, remove 60-70 *cappelletti* from freezer and slowly add to broth. Stir. Return broth to boil. Reduce heat. Cover and simmer for 15 minutes or until done to taste.

Serve with freshly grated *Romano* or Parmesan cheese.

Serves: Two quarts of broth serves 8 generously.

Ravioli

Ravioli is a Renaissance dish. It is now ubiquitous and some version of stuffed pasta appears in every region of Italy, albeit un-der different names, shapes, and with a variance in ingredients: from brains and fish, to cheese, cured meats, pumpkin, beets, and Meat Stuffing.

For us, *ravioli* are the same as *cappelletti*—only larger. In our home *ravioli* are always served with a sauce, while *cappelletti* are exclusively for broth—that was until the great pasta salad revolu-tion of the 80s. Now, it is anything goes, although we had trouble convincing my mother that *cappelletti* in salad is not a sacrilege.

Here are more types of *ravioli* from the various regions of Italy. In Parma they eat *tortelli di erbette di Parma, ravioli* with the grass-es of *Parma*, on Saint John's Day (June 24) to celebrate a victory in 1210. For Christmas there is a *ravioli* called *pansoti*, which are large triangles (sometimes squares) of egg dough stuffed with a very special herb stuffing of beet, borage, dandelion, wild chic-ory, and chervil called *preboggion* and made only in *Liguria*. The filling is blended with *precinsena*, a special curd cheese which is also uniquely Ligurian. All is combined with Parmesan, egg, and garlic, and topped with walnut sauce. *Ravieu de pescio* are also from *Liguria* and are stuffed with fish: sea bass, porgy, ricotta, bor-age, beets, and Parmesan cheese. They are usually dressed with a mussel or clam sauce. In *Alto Adige, ravioli* are called *ravioli di Val Pusteria.* The dough is made with rye flour and the stuffing is either spinach and *ricotta* or fried sauerkraut (a Balkan influence). The sauce is melted butter with sage and maybe garlic (also Bal-kan). In the Marches, the *ravioli* are *ricotta*-filled and covered with *sugo di sogliole*, a sauce of sole fish poached in wine and tomato sauce. In *Basilicata* the filling is *ricotta, prosciutto,* and parsley with a sauce of oil, chili pepper, garlic, and *pecorino.*

Ravioli with Meat Stuffing
Ravioli Ripieni di Carne

½ meat stuffing recipe, with double quan-tity of Swiss chard
1 full pasta recipe

It is important to prepare your work space for comfort and convenience. Stuffing the *ravioli* is a long process, so you may prefer to sit down. Line a cookie sheet with wax paper and place on the table or work space. Take stuffing mixture from refrigerator and set on table (see index for Meat Stuffing recipe).

When you are ready to make the *ravioli* prepare pasta as directed in the Homemade Pasta recipe (see index). Do not allow pasta mixture to dry. Instead keep the dough covered by a bowl and work with small quantities—roll one pasta line at a time, make the *ravioli*, roll another pasta line, and continue until all is done.

Run through the pasta machine until desired thickness (⅛-to-¼-inch) and length. Place long dough in front of you (see A). Cut into 2-½-inch squares, placing the excess in a pile that can be rerolled.

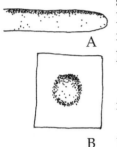

Fill one square with 1 tablespoon of stuffing (see B).

Bring one edge diagonally over the stuffing to opposite edge (see C).

Pinch down to seal on all sides (see D).

Turn slightly to alter shape (see E).

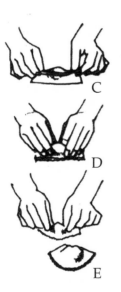

Place *ravioli* on wax-paper-lined cookie sheet. Continue until strip of dough is gone. Knead remnants. Make squares and stuff. Take another piece of dough. Run through the pasta machine until it reaches desired thickness (⅛-to-¼-inch) and length. Proceed as with the first long dough piece (there are forms available to make 10 ravioli at a time).

When cookie sheet is filled, place in freezer. Prepare another cookie sheet with wax paper. Continue until finished.

When finished, remove one cookie sheet at a time from freezer. Be sure last cookie sheet has been in the freezer for at least 1 hour. The *ravioli* are now individually frozen and will not stick together. Remove from cookie sheet and store in plastic container in freezer until ready to use.

Ravioli can be served in tomato sauce,

meat sauce, cream, butter, vegetable sauce, or in a salad.

Yield: 60-70.

To cook: Place 2 quarts of water in a 4-quart pot. Heat over high heat. Just as bubbles begin to appear at the bottom of pot, add a little salt. When at rolling boil, remove 25 ravioli from freezer and slowly add to boiling water. Stir. Return to boil. Reduce heat. Cover and simmer for 15 minutes or until done to taste.

Drain *ravioli* and keep in colander for 10 minutes until all water is drained. This is very important, because water can enter the *ravioli* and make even the thickest sauce runny.

Heat 3 to 4 cups meat sauce (see index). Place *ravioli* on a dish, top with sauce, and serve with freshly grated *Romano* or Parmesan cheese.

Serves: 4-6.

Ravioli with Cheese Stuffing
Ravioli Ripieni di Formaggio

This is the Pelini's favorite cheese *ravioli* recipe and it includes a different pasta dough from those previously included in this chapter and a new filling. The pasta recipe is the Pelini standard and is used to make everything from *ravioli* and *cannelloni* to pasta for soup. The type of cheese you use in the *ravioli* will affect the taste and make it unique. In *Molise*, some chefs use *Provolone* cheese, a smoky, cow's milk cheese. That alters the taste considerable.

filling:
1 lb. *ricotta*
1 egg
½ cup freshly grated *Romano* cheese
1 tsp. salt
½ tsp. pepper
2 tsp. fresh parsley
½ tsp. basil

In a large bowl combine *ricotta*, egg, cheese, salt, pepper, parsley, and basil. Mix well and allow to stand for 30 minutes or more to allow the ingredients to blend.

Prepare a large work space, preferably a pastry board. Place flour on board and make a well. Add eggs, salt, and oil to the well. Beat eggs and work flour into them until dough is firm (see illustrations accompanying Homemade Pasta recipe).

pasta:
2 to 2 ½ cups flour
3 eggs
1 tsp. salt
2 tbsp. corn oil

Knead dough for 10 to 20 minutes. Form into a ball and cover with a bowl. Let stand for 30 minutes.

Do not allow pasta mixture to dry. Instead keep the dough covered by a bowl. Roll one pasta line at a time, make the *ravioli*, roll another pasta line, and continue until all is done.

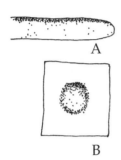

Run through the pasta machine until you reach desired thickness (⅛-to-¼-inch) and length. Place long dough in front of you (see A). Cut into 2 ½ inch squares, placing the excess in a pile that can be rerolled.

Fill one square with 1 tablespoon filling (see B).
Bring one edge diagonally over the stuffing to opposite edge (see C).
Pinch down to seal on all sides (see D).
Turn slightly to alter shape (see E).

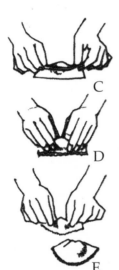

Place *ravioli* on wax-paper-lined cookie sheet. Continue until strip of dough is gone. Knead remnants. Make squares and stuff. Take another piece of dough. Run through the pasta machine until you reach desired thickness (⅛-to-¼-inch) and length. Proceed as with the first long dough (there are forms available to make 10 *ravioli* at a time).

When cookie sheet is filled, place in freezer. Prepare another cookie sheet with wax paper. Continue until finished.

When finished, remove one cookie sheet at a time from freezer. Be sure last cookie sheet has been in the freezer for at least 1 hour. The *ravioli* are now individually frozen and will not stick together. Remove from cookie sheet and store in plastic container in freezer until ready to use.

Ravioli can be served in tomato sauce, meat sauce, cream, butter, vegetable sauce, or in a salad.

Yield: 32-36.

To cook: Place 2 quarts of water in a 4-quart pot. Heat over high heat. Just as bubbles begin to appear at the bottom of pot, add a little salt. When at rolling boil, remove 25 ravioli from freezer and slowly add to boiling water. Stir. Return to boil. Reduce heat. Cover and simmer for 15 minutes or until done to taste.

Drain *ravioli* and keep in colander for 10 minutes until all water is drained. This is very important, because water can enter the *ravioli* and make even the thickest sauce runny.

Heat 3 to 4 cups meat sauce (see index). Place *ravioli* on dish. Spoon on sauce and let stand 10 minutes. Serve with freshly grated *Romano* or Parmesan cheese.

Serves: 6-8.

Fettuccine, Tagliatelle, **or** *Pappadelle*

When a ¼-inch wide and thick, this long, flat, pasta is called *fettuccine (Bologna).* When thinner, but still ¼-inch wide and with more eggs, it is called *tagliatelle* (Florence). When it is 1-inch wide, it is called *pappadelle,* the signature pasta of *Arezzo* and our village of *Quarata.* Regardless of the cut, this wide pasta is used for a variety of specialty dishes. You can buy *fettuccine* in any supermarket; *tagliatelle* are harder to find, but you can find them. I have never seen *pappadelle* on a grocer's shelf. You must make your own (use the Homemade Pasta recipe and cut into the correct width).

Fettuccine Alfredo

Created by a restaurant owner in Rome after our immigrants came to America, this dish was absorbed into our family.

2-3 quarts water
1 tbsp. salt
1 lb. *fettuccine*
2 tbsp. butter
¼ lb. butter
1 cup heavy cream
1 cup freshly grated
    Parmesan cheese
Freshly ground pepper

Place a 4-quart pot on the burner. Fill ¾-full with water. Bring to a boil. Just as bubbles begin to appear at the bottom of the pot, add salt. When at a rolling boil add *fettuccine.* Stir with a wooden spoon a few times. Water will stop boiling. Return to boil, reduce heat, and simmer for 10 minutes or until done to your taste. Drain. Return to pot, add 2 tablespoons butter, and toss.

Place a second 4-quart pot over medium-high heat. Melt remaining butter. Add cooked noodles. Mix well. Add half the cream and half the cheese. Mix again until cheese is melted. Add remaining cream and cheese. Mix. Place on serving dish. Top with freshly ground pepper. Serve.

Serves: 4-6.

Note: This sauce can be used with any pasta.

Fettuccine alla Carbonara

The name of this dish is not a tribute to bacon or cream, but to black pepper that should appear in abundance on the dish, like black coal dust. Thus it is sometimes called Coal Miner's Spaghetti. There are a number of theories as to its origin. The most likely is that during World War II, American quartermasters supplied the local markets with an abundance of bacon and eggs. The Romans, perhaps in a restaurant called *Carbonara*, created the dish. Like *Fettuccini Alfredo*, it snuck into our Tuscan kitchen and we kept it.

2-3 quarts water
1 tbsp. salt
1 lb. *fettuccine* (or
    spaghetti)
¼-inch-thick slice
    pancetta or bacon
½ cup heavy cream
2 eggs plus 2 egg
    yolks
½ cup freshly grated
    Parmesan cheese
4 tbsp. butter
Coarse black pepper

Place a 4-quart pot on the burner. Fill ¾ full with water. Just as bubbles begin to appear at the bottom of the pot, add salt. Allow to come to a rolling boil. Slowly add *fettuccine* and cook until tender or to taste (about 10 minutes). While *fettuccine* are cooking, prepare sauce.

In a medium-size skillet fry the bacon or *pancetta*. Do not add oil. When crisp remove from skillet and place on paper towel to drain. Throw away half the drippings. Add cream to remaining drippings and allow to simmer. Crumble bacon and add to cream. Beat eggs and extra yolks in a small bowl. Add cheese to eggs and beat again.

Drain *fettuccine* in a colander. Place in large bowl. Add butter and toss until well blended. Add cream and bacon and toss. Add egg mixture and toss again. The heat from the pasta will cook them. Now sprinkle with an abundance of black pepper, the coarser the better. Serve at once.

Note: *Carbonara* can be made with any pasta. If it is too dry, add a little milk or more cream.

Serves: 4-6.

Fettuccine with White Clam Sauce
Fettuccine con Vongole e Salsa Bianca

2-3 quarts water
1 tbsp. salt
1 lb. *fettuccine*
½ cup green onions
4 cloves garlic
24 oz. minced clams
4 tbsp. butter
4 tbsp. flour
1 ½ cups milk
4 tbsp. chopped fresh
    parsley
Dash salt
Freshly ground pepper

Place a 4-quart pot on the burner. Fill ¾-full with water. Bring to a boil. Just as bubbles begin to appear at the bottom of the pot, add salt. When at a rolling boil, add *fettuccine*. Cook until tender or to taste (about 10 minutes). While *fettuccine* is boiling prepare sauce.

Peel and dice onions and garlic; open and drain clams, and keep half the juice.

Place a medium-size iron skillet over medium-high heat. Heat to hot. Add butter and melt. Do not allow to brown. Add onions and garlic and sauté until onions are transparent (about 5 to 7 minutes). Stir in flour until all liquid is absorbed. Slowly add milk, stirring constantly to keep from forming lumps. Add clams with juice, parsley, salt, and freshly ground pepper.

Simmer on medium-high heat for 3 to 4 minutes until sauce thickens. Keep stirring. When done, remove from heat and allow to stand for 10 minutes for flavors to blend.

Drain *fettuccine*. Return to pot. Add sauce and stir until well blended. Turn into serving platter. Serve at once.

Serves: 4-6.

Notes: If sauce dries out, add a little broth or milk and stir. This sauce can be used with any pasta.

Dumplings
Gnocchi

All hail the mighty *gnocchi* that had its birth centuries ago when the Roman Army brought a semolina or cornmeal-type back from its wars in the Middle East. Throughout Italy, *gnocchi* is made in a variety of ways, either flat semolina rings Rome, chestnut flour *(Genoa)*, cornmeal *(Sardinia)*, bread crumbs *(Fruli)*, potatoes *(Verona)*, or *ricotta*. In *Verona*, where the potato variety was invented in the sixteenth century when the potato was imported into Italy, *gnocchi* are celebrated on the last Friday of carnival topped with *pastissada*, a sauce of horsemeat. They even have *Il Papa del Gnocco*, a Pope of *gnocchi*, to rule over the festivities.

Two varieties of *gnocchi* are presented here: potato and *ricotta*. Like most Italian pastas, there is a traditional sauce in each region where it is served, but any chef can create a new, exciting sauce because *gnocchi* lends itself to creams, vegetables, meats, and casseroles. We always serve *gnocchi* steeped in our traditional meat sauce (see index) and topped with plenty of freshly grated Parmesan cheese.

I have a real pet peeve about *gnocchi*. I cannot stand it when TV chefs pronounce it gnOOHH ki, with a long o. To me this is an affectation. I pronounce it gnaAAWki. Same thing when they pronounce *risotto*. It should be pronounced like *gnocchi* with an AAW, risAAWto, not risOOHHto.

Potato Dumplings
Gnocchi di Patate

3 cups riced potatoes (red)
2 egg yolks, beaten
1½ cups flour, divided
2 tbsp. freshly grated Parmesan cheese
½ tsp. salt
2 cups meat sauce
Freshly grated Parmesan cheese

Peel potatoes and boil until soft. Drain, and set aside to cool. When cool, pass through a ricer. Turn out into a large pan and add egg yolks, 1¼ cups flour, cheese, and salt. Mix slightly with hands.

Place remaining flour on large bread board. Turn out potatoes onto floured board. Knead lightly together until firm (about 5 minutes). The longer you knead, the tougher the dough. Divide dough into 3 to 4 pieces.

Roll each piece by hand into a long cylinder about 1-inch in circumference (see A). Keep floured so it does not stick to the board.

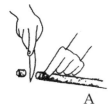

A

B

Begin at one end and cut small, 1-inch pieces until the dough is gone (see A). As each piece is cut, flick it with the thumb (see B) to slightly flatten. Place on cookie sheet that has been lined with wax paper. You can also use a fork to flick the dough. Do not stack the individual *gnocchi* or they will stick together. Repeat until all the dough is gone.

Cook (see note), and add sauce and cheese. Serve.

Serves: 2-3.

Note: Cooking instructions accompany the *Ricotta* Dumplings recipe.

Ricotta Dumplings
Gnocchi di Ricotta

We prefer the delicate texture of *ricotta* to potato in *gnocchi*; therefore, this is our favorite *gnocchi* recipe. But it is not traditional for our Italian village. My mother got this recipe from a friend in Monessen many years ago. I cannot find its origin.

1½ lbs. *ricotta*
3 egg yolks
3 tbsp. freshly grated
   Parmesan cheese
1 tsp. salt
3-4 cups flour
3 cups meat sauce
Freshly grated Par-
   mesan cheese

Turn *ricotta* onto floured pastry board. Combine egg yolks, cheese, and salt. Stir. Add flour and combine mixture with *ricotta*. Knead lightly together until firm (about 5 minutes). The longer you knead it, the tougher the *gnocchi*.

Divide dough into 3 to 4 pieces. Roll each piece by hand into a long cylinder about 1-inch in circumference (see illustrations accompanying Potato Dumplings recipe). Keep floured so it does not stick to the board.

Begin at one end and cut into 1-inch pieces until the dough cylinder is gone. As each piece is cut, flick it with the thumb to slightly flatten, and place piece on wax-paper-lined cookie sheet or other flat surface. You can also use a fork to flick the dough. Do not stack the individual *gnocchi* or they will stick together. Repeat until all the dough is gone.

Yields for potato and *ricotta gnocchi:*

½ recipe	full recipe	doubled recipe
servings: 2-3	4-5	8-10

To freeze potato or *ricotta gnocchi:*
After preparing the *gnocchi* as described above, put entire cookie sheet into freezer. Allow to freeze for an hour. Remove from freezer and place *gnocchi* in a storage container. If frozen in this manner, *gnocchi* freeze separately and not in one lump.

To cook potato or *ricotta gnocchi:*
To serve in meat sauce: Fill an 8-quart pot ¾ full of water and place over high heat. As bubbles begin to appear at the bottom of the pot, add 1 teaspoon salt. Bring to a rolling boil. Slowly add *gnocchi* a few at a time and turn immediately or they will stick. Boil until they all rise to the surface and float (5 to 7 minutes). Drain well. Rinse out the 8-quart pot. Put 3 cups of good meat sauce (see index). Add *gnocchi*. Stir well over very low heat for 2 to 3 minutes. Add more sauce if desired and ¾ cup freshly grated Parmesan or *Romano* cheese. Remove from heat. Cover with lid and allow to steep for 5 minutes. Serve hot.

Note: *Gnocchi* require less sauce than pastas.

Lasagna

Lasagna was born in ancient Rome when it was called *Laganum*. It was a favorite of Cicero who liked it with cheese, saffron, and cinnamon. Not to be outdone, Horace wrote about it in his satires. In modern times, blended with the tomato, it re-emerged in Naples and was made exclusively for carnival before Lent. Since then it has spread throughout Italy where each region has developed its own variation. Like all the other pasta dishes, the regions of Italy have placed their own stamp on *Lasagna*.

In the village of *Mola di Bari in Apulia* they eat *lasagna* with a white sauce of almonds, anchovies, toasted bread crumbs, and a red tomato sauce. In the region of *Basilicata* at the instep of the boot, they eat a *Legane con lenticchie e fagioli, lasagna* with lentils and beans. In *Cuneo* in the Piedmont they eat *Lasagne di San Giuseppe alla Cunese*, with a chopped meat sauce, béchamel, grated cheese, and a butter-topped crust. The *timpano* of *Abruzzo*, with layers and layers of different ingredients, is also a form of *lasagna*. Each of these dishes reflects the region: its history of conquest, its land, its soil, and its climate.

Lasagna is an important part of the Christmas day feast. *Genoa* serves *lasagna* with *pesto* for Christmas Day, quite simply because *pesto* is the specialty of the city. In *Calabria, sagne chine*, stuffed *lasagna*, is for the grandest occasions. It is layered with veal balls, sliced hard boiled eggs, sliced *scamorza, mozzarella*, and *pecorino* cheeses, and swims in tomato sauce. In spring, peas or artichokes are also added.

Lasagna in the Oven
Pasta al Forno

This is our Tuscan version, which our cousins in Italy call *Pasta al Forno*. They also use béchamel between layers, but we do not in our kitchen. It was never on our Christmas table, either in Italy or in Pennsylvania.

2 tbsp. salt
2 tbsp. corn oil
1 lb. *lasagna* noodles
1 lb. *mozzarella* cheese
½ cup freshly grated
  Romano cheese
½ cup freshly grated
  Parmesan cheese
1-½ quarts meat
  sauce
2 cups broth

Half fill a wide 8-quart pot with water and place on burner over high heat. When bubbles begin to appear at the bottom of the pot, add salt and oil. Place noodles one at a time into boiling water. Turn with long-handled spoon to keep from sticking and boil for 3 to 4 minutes. Do not cook noodles until done. Drain noodles, rinse in cold water, and leave in water while assembling *lasagna*.

Cut *mozzarella* into 1-inch squares. Grate cheeses. Make piles of each on a pastry board. Empty sauce into a large bowl (see index). Add broth and stir until blended (thick sauce must be diluted for *lasagna*).

Select a large, 9-by-9-by-2-½-inch pan. Place 2 soup ladles full of diluted sauce in bottom of pan,

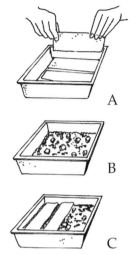

A

B

C

coating every corner. Place a layer of *lasagna* noodles one beside the other (see A) along bottom of pan. Do not overlap. Cover with enough sauce (see B) to coat well. Scatter 9 squares of *mozzarella* over noodles. Sprinkle 1 tablespoon each *Romano* and *Parmesan* cheese over the noodles.

Arrange next row of noodles in the pan running perpendicular to the first layer (see C) of noodles (forming a checkerboard). Add sauce, *mozzarella*, *Romano*, and *Parmesan*. Continue alternating until noodles are gone. Top with extra sauce and cheeses. Cover with aluminum foil.

Heat oven to 350 degrees and bake for 30 to 45 minutes. Remove from oven. Let sit 10 minutes and uncover. Cut the *lasagna* into 9 square pieces: three cuts lengthwise and three cuts widthwise. Serve with a steel spatula.

Serves: 6-9.

Grand *Lasagna* with Sausage, Ricotta, and Béchamel
Gran Lasagna con Salsiccia, Ricotta, e Besciamella

This recipe is close to the Neapolitan *lasagna*, but it was made in our Tuscan kitchen with variations.

béchamel sauce:
8 cups milk
16 tbsp. butter
12 tbsp. flour
¾ tsp. salt
8 tbsp. salt

lasagna:
8 tbsp. corn oil
4 lbs. *lasagna* noodles
12 (3-inch) sausage links
4 lbs. *mozzarella* cheese
2 cups freshly grated *Romano* cheese
2 cups freshly grated Parmesan cheese
3 lbs. *ricotta*
6 quarts meat sauce
2 quarts broth

Prepare béchamel sauce first. Place a small pot over medium-high heat and heat milk to near boiling. Do not boil or it will curdle. Place a medium-size pot over medium-high heat and melt butter. Do not allow to brown. When butter is melted, add all the flour to the butter, stirring constantly. If the flour discolors you have overcooked it.

Remove flour mixture from heat and slowly add the hot milk a tablespoon or two at a time, stirring constantly. When more than half the milk has been added you may add in larger portions. If thickening slows, return to heat. When all is mixed, add salt. Sauce should be the consistency of thick cream. Set aside until ready to use.

Place an 8-quart pot filled with water over

high heat. Add salt and oil. Add 1 pound of noodles one at a time. Turn to keep from sticking. Boil 3 minutes. Drain, rinse, and leave in water while assembling *lasagna.* Repeat as necessary.

Select 1 extra-large (18-by-13-by-4-inch) pan or 2 large pans. Place 4 soup ladles of sauce in bottom of pan, coating every corner. Lay in *lasagna* noodles, one beside the other, along the bottom of the pan. Do not overlap. Cover with enough sauce to coat well. Sprinkle 18 squares of *mozzarella* over the pasta. Do the same with the sausage and *ricotta,* laying them beside the other ingredients. Sprinkle 4 teaspoons each of *Romano* and Parmesan. Continue alternating noodles and dressings, ending with sauce and cheese.

Pour béchamel sauce over top layer, and spread with a spatula. Be sure it completely covers the noodles. Cover with aluminum foil to keep moist.

Heat the oven to 350 degrees and bake for 45 minutes. Remove from oven, but allow to sit 10 minutes before uncovering. You may wish to place it under the broiler for 5 minutes to brown the béchamel sauce. Before serving, cut the *lasagna* into 2 ½-x-2 ½-inch squares. Serve with spatula.

Serves: 25-30. To serve 40 to 50 people use 6 lbs. *lasagna* noodles, 3 lbs. *mozzarella,* 2 lbs. *Parmesan,* 1 lb. *Romano,* 2 ½ gallons meat sauce, 1 gallon broth.

Note: An alternative is to layer béchamel in the center of the *lasagna* as well as on the top. In that case, you need to double the béchamel recipe and cut two layers of noodles. You can also eliminate sausage and/or *ricotta* and not ruin the dish. To eliminate *mozzarella* will ruin the dish.

Cornmeal and Semolina Mush
Polenta e Farina

Polenta, made with maize, was a staple of the Roman legions as they went out to conquer the world. Corn came from the Americas and was introduced to Italy by Christopher Columbus in the 1400s. Buckwheat, which was used to make *polenta* in Tuscany, came from the Arabs in the Middle Ages. Ancient recipes call for *polenta* to be cooked over a wood fire in a *paiolo,* a copper pot with a round bottom, and stirred with a wooden spoon. When it was done, it would come away from the sides of the pot and be poured onto a wooden board and cut with a thread. The dish is prevalent in northern Italy, especially in *Fruili,* where corn is grown. The good folks there are often called *polentonni* because they eat so much *polenta.* It is also cold in *Fruili* and *polenta* is said to stick to the bones.

Polenta is a festival food throughout Italy. For carnival before Lent in southern Italy they eat a *polenta* called *migliaccio di polenta,* which includes blood sausage and cheese. Tossignano in *Emilia-Romagna* makes a *polentata* of 440 pounds, cooked in wood-fired copper cauldrons.

Although we did not have a fireplace and thus no wood fire or *paiolo,* Nonna used a wooden spoon, poured the *polenta* onto a wood board, and cut it with a thread. We never ate the *polenta* directly from the board. It was always placed on plates after cutting. Today the only portion of the ancient traditions we still maintain is the use of a wooden spoon.

Polenta is good for breakfast, for lunch, or for dinner. It is good freshly made or day old and fried. It can be dressed with any topping from beans, to greens, to cheeses and mushrooms, but it is especially flavorful with a rich tomato sauce, *baccalá,* or sausage. It is extra, extra special in the morning with nothing but butter—the way true *polenta aficionados* enjoy it.

Believe it or not, instant *polenta* works and can be substituted for these dishes. Simply follow the directions on the box. Don't tell the immigrants.

Basic *Polenta*
Polenta

Over the years we have used our good stock (broth) to replace the water in making *polenta.* It definitely adds flavor, but it spits if you fry the leftovers.

4 cups broth (water may be used)
2 cups yellow cornmeal
1½ cups cold water
1½ tsp. salt

Place broth in a 4-quart pot on high heat. Place cornmeal in a large bowl and pour the cold water and salt over meal. Stir well. When broth is at a hard boil, stir in cornmeal and keep stirring until well mixed or lumps will form.

When mixture comes to a boil again, turn burner to low. Stir often, but be sure meal continues to soft boil. Cover with a lid and allow the contents to slow boil for 25 to 30 minutes. Remove from heat.

Serves: 3-5 (6 cups).

Note: *Polenta* sticks to the pot. To clean pot, fill with water and soak until *polenta* lifts off easily.

Polenta with Tomato Sauce
Polenta col Sugo

Polenta, see Basic Polenta recipe
3 cups meat sauce, see index
¼ cup Parmesan cheese

Prepare *polenta* as directed in recipe. Pour onto a large platter. Cover with your favorite tomato sauce and freshly grated Parmesan cheese.

Serves: 3-5.

Polenta with Mushroom Sauce
Polenta con Funghi

6 cups cooked *polenta*
½ lb. fresh mush-
rooms
4 tbsp. butter
2 cloves garlic
Salt, pepper

Prepare *polenta* according to the **Basic Polenta** recipe (see index). Wash or brush dirt from mushrooms. Take one mushroom at a time and cut off the tip of the stem and remove any blemishes on the crown. Slice mushrooms.

Place a medium-size iron skillet over medium-high heat. Heat to hot. Melt butter in skillet. Peel and add garlic. When garlic is brown, mash with fork into small pieces. Add mushrooms, and salt and pepper to taste. Lower heat and sauté for 5 minutes. Pour *polenta* onto a large platter. Top with mushrooms and juice.

Serves: 3-5.

Variation: Try adding 1 *porcini* mushroom to the white mushrooms for added flavor.

Polenta with Sausage
Polenta con Salsiccia

6 cups cooked *polenta*
3 cups meat sauce*
6 sausages
½ cup freshly grated
Parmesan cheese

Prepare *polenta* according to the **Basic Polenta** recipe (see index). Either make the meat sauce found in this book or heat sauce that is already made.

Fry sausages in a medium-size skillet over medium-high heat. Do not add oil to the skillet.

When ready to serve, scoop out a cup of *polenta*, pour into dish, top with ½ cup meat sauce and cheese, and top again with sausage and pan drippings. Serve hot.

Serves: 4-6.

Notes: *See index for meat sauce.
A slice of good *Fontina* or *mozzarella* cheese placed over the *polenta* before the meat sauce is also good.

Polenta in the Morning
Polenta della Mattina

There is nothing, absolutely nothing, that can compare to *polenta* to warm your belly on a cold winter morning.

6 cups cooked *polenta*
6-8 tbsp. butter

Prepare *polenta* according to the **Basic *Polenta*** recipe (see index). Serve steaming hot in small custard cups. Add a pat of butter to each cup.

Yield: 6 cups.

Notes: You can add milk, cinnamon, sugar, or any other topping, but the best and most traditional topping is butter.

Left-over *polenta* can be stored to fry later (see following recipe). Just pour *polenta* into a deep dish to mold, and place in refrigerator.

Polenta Pie
Polenta Pasticciata

12 (¾-inch-thick) squares cold, cooked *polenta*
2 cups sauce
½ cup freshly grated Parmesan cheese
5-6 slices *mozzarella* cheese (optional)
Sausage (optional)

Prepare *polenta* according to the **Basic *Polenta*** recipe (see index). Once made, pour into a deep-sided dish and refrigerate overnight or until cold. Prepare a sauce of your choice (see index).

Remove *polenta* from dish and cut into a dozen 3-inch squares. Sprinkle a medium-size baking dish lightly with sauce.

Place the squares over the sauce to form a layer. Cover with half of sauce and freshly grated Parmesan cheese (you also may add slices of *mozzarella* cheese and chunks of cooked sausage). Cover bottom layer with remaining *polenta* squares. Top with remaining sauce and cheeses.

Bake in oven at 350 degrees for 35 to 45 minutes. Serve hot.

Serves: 4-5.

Note: You can toast *polenta* squares under the broiler before assembling this dish.

Fried *Polenta*
Crostini di Polenta

Polenta with butter is delicious, but fried *polenta* is better. Today it is served as an appetizer in exclusive restaurants, often topped with a pimento or other garnish. For us, it was, and still is, breakfast fare. But one can serve it with a good salad, as a snack, or on a buffet table. It is best to make this *polenta* with water and not broth because broth makes it spit in the oil as it is frying.

6 cups cooked *polenta*
1½ cups corn oil

Prepare *polenta* according to the **Basic Polenta** recipe but use water instead of stock (see index). Pour into a deep-sided dish and refrigerate overnight or until cold.

Remove from pan (it will come out in a firm mass). Slice into 3-by-3-by-½-inch thick squares.

Place medium-size iron skillet over high heat. Heat to hot. Add oil to generously cover bottom of skillet. Heat to hot. Lay sliced *polenta* in skillet. Fry until edges begin to brown (about 5 to 7 minutes). Turn. Fry other side (*polenta* is fragile, turn only once). Remove and drain on paper towel. Eat hot. If oil becomes too hot, lower heat, but *polenta* must fry in hot oil.

Yield: 25-30 squares.

Notes: *Polenta* can also be placed on a grill or in a broiler. In this case it is called *polenta ai ferri*. Allow one side to crisp, about 5 minutes, turn, and grill the second side. Nonna covered *polenta ai ferri* with sauce.

Sweet Semolina
Farina Dolce

Any recipe in the *polenta* and *farina* section of this cookbook can be made with *farina*, but this is the only recipe that originates with *farina*. Cornmeal is good prepared this way, too.

The recipe was given to us by our friend, Rene Moncini, whose family comes from *Torino* in the Piedmont where *farina dolce* is a specialty.

Farina dolce is sweet to the taste, but it is not served as a dessert. Instead it is prepared as a side dish to fried veal or chicken. It is also great as a snack, or on a buffet table.

When buying *farina* for this dish you may purchase semolina, cream of wheat, or *farina*. They are all available in supermarkets.

3 cups milk
¾ cup semolina
½ cup granulated
  sugar
1 egg yolk
¼ cup grated lemon
  rind
1 egg
1 tbsp. milk
1 cup bread crumbs
1 cup corn oil

Place a large pot over medium-high heat. Add milk and allow to boil. When milk begins to bubble, add semolina. Stir well and add sugar.

Allow to cook until thick (about 10 minutes). While semolina is simmering, separate an egg and beat the egg yolk. When semolina is thick, remove from stove and quickly stir in the beaten yolk, then the lemon rind.

Grease an 8-by-8-inch dish with a little oil and pour the cooked semolina into the dish. Cover with wax paper and refrigerate until cold (about 2 hours).

When cold, remove semolina from refrigerator and cut into 3-inch squares. The squares should be more than 1-inch thick.

Beat the remaining egg with the tablespoon of milk. Dip each square into egg, then into bread crumbs. Coat generously.

Place a medium-size iron skillet over medium-high heat. Heat to hot. Add oil. Heat to hot (must fry in hot oil). Drop squares of semolina in oil. Fry until golden, turn, and fry second side.

Remove from oil and allow to drain. Serve hot or cold.

Serves: 6-9.

Notes: If you use instant semolina all times change. You can sprinkle *farina dolce* with confectioners' sugar or syrup.

Spaghetti

Spaghetti, a round, long, thin pasta, was never served to guests in Nonna's house. It is only for the family and usually a weekday meal. The fact that its name has been elevated to mean just about any pasta serves us all right, for *spaghetti*, dressed up in a variety of ways, makes an excellent meal.

Spaghetti with Anchovy Sauce
Spaghetti con Acciugata

Tart and tangy, *spaghetti* with anchovies was often served when I was growing up. It is a good Lenten dish, but can be served any time.

1 tsp. salt
1 lb. *spaghetti*
⅓ cup olive oil
2 oz. flat fillets of
   anchovies

Place a 4-quart pot on the burner. Fill ¾-full with water. Bring to a boil. Just as bubbles begin to appear at the bottom of the pot, add salt. When at rolling boil, add *spaghetti* and cook until tender or to taste (about 10 minutes). While *spaghetti* is cooking, prepare the anchovy sauce.

Place olive oil in a small iron skillet. Place the skillet on medium-high heat. Do not overheat the oil. Add the anchovies, oil and all, and mash the fillets with a fork. Do not allow to cook.

When the *spaghetti* is cooked, remove from heat, drain in a colander, return to pot, add anchovy sauce, and mix well. Serve immediately.

Serves: 3-5.

Spaghetti with Butter and Cheese
Spaghetti con Burro e Formaggio

This simple *spaghetti* dish is the origin of *Fettuccine Alfredo*.

1 tsp. salt
1 lb. *spaghetti*
¼ lb. butter
½ cup freshly grated
   Parmesan cheese
Pepper, to taste

Place a 4-quart pot on the burner. Fill ¾-full with water. Bring to a boil. Just as bubbles begin to appear at the bottom of the pot, add salt. When water reaches a rolling boil, add *spaghetti*. Cook until tender or to taste (about 10 minutes). When the *spaghetti* is cooked, remove pot from heat, drain in a colander, return to pot, and add the butter and cheese. Mix well or until all the butter is melted. Add pepper. Serve immediately.

Serves: 3-5.

Spaghetti with Broccoli
Spaghetti con Broccoli

In Tuscany, there is a special pasta called *sedanini*, which looks like pieces of celery and is specially made for this type of dish. You cannot par cook the vegetable in this dish. It will not have the same taste, because it will not absorb the garlic and oil.

1 tsp. salt
½ lb. *spaghetti*
1-2 cups fresh *broccoli*
2 tbsp. salt
2-3 tbsp. corn oil
2-3 cloves garlic
½ tsp. salt
¼ tsp. pepper
⅛ lb. butter
¼ cup freshly grated
    Parmesan cheese

While *spaghetti* is cooking, prepare the *broccoli*. Wash and cut into pieces. Place in a large pot half-filled with water and salt. Boil for 8 to 10 minutes until soft. Test with a fork. The *broccoli* must be soft for this dish or it will not absorb the garlicky oil. Remove and place on drain board to drain (may be placed in the refrigerator up to four days).

When ready to fry, squeeze out as much liquid as possible from *broccoli*. On a pastry board, chop the *broccoli* into small pieces.

Place a medium-size iron skillet over medium-high heat. Heat to hot. Add oil. Peel garlic, add to oil in pan, brown, and crush with a fork until no large pieces remain.

Place the *broccoli* in the oil, and salt and pepper to taste. Allow to cook about 15 minutes, turning often and mashing with a fork to reduce bulk.

Place a 4-quart pot on the burner. Fill ¾-full with water. Bring to a boil. Just as bubbles begin to appear at the bottom of the pot, add salt. When water reaches a rolling boil, add *spaghetti*. Cook until tender or to taste (about 10 minutes).

When the *spaghetti* is cooked, remove it from heat, drain in a colander, replace in pot, add the butter, and mix well or until all the butter is melted. Add *broccoli*, oil and all, and freshly grated Parmesan cheese. Mix well. Serve immediately.

Serves: 3-5.

Notes: In place of the *broccoli*, you can use Savoy cabbage, cauliflower, spinach, or celery for this recipe. In every instance the vegetable must be well cooked to absorb the garlicky oil.

Spaghetti with Cinnamon
Spaghetti Bianchi con Cannella

This was one of my father's favorite meals. Very little of my father's family traditions are described in this book. My father, Alfred (Freddie) Vivian, was one of a herd of children born to Peter and Ida Cavalli Vivian of Monessen, Pennsylvania. I never knew my Nonno Pete or Nonna Ida—both died before I was born. But I have fond memories of my father's brothers and sisters, who are all dead now.

My father was an easygoing, loveable man whom, with great affection, we called, "Honey Boy." He, too, worked at Pittsburgh Steel. His family name, Vivian, was always shrouded in great mystery in our home and we never could get the story straight (we never really tried). Our cousins are called Viviani, but my father insisted that they changed their name and Vivian was the real name. He was wrong. The Viviani came from *Malchesni,* a small community around *Lago de Garda* in the *Veneto.* We have plenty of family there. I hope there is time in my life to find and treasure them.

1 tsp. salt
1 lb. *spaghetti*
¼ lb. butter
½ cup freshly grated Parmesan cheese
1 tbsp. cinnamon

Place a 4-quart pot on the burner. Fill ¾-full with water. Bring to a boil. Just as bubbles begin to appear at the bottom of the pot, add salt.

When water reaches a rolling boil, add *spaghetti.* Cook until tender or to taste (about 10 minutes).

When the *spaghetti* is cooked, remove from heat, drain in a colander, replace in pot, and add the butter, cheese, and cinnamon. Mix well or until all the butter is melted. Serve immediately.

Serves: 3-5.

Spaghetti **with Garlic and Oil**
Spaghetti Aglio e Olio

Like *spaghetti* and butter, this is a basic recipe served all across Italy. You can add just about anything to it: tuna (or any fish fried, boiled, or broiled), pre-boiled *broccoli* (or any green), pre-boiled Savoy cabbage (or any cabbage), pre-boiled cauliflower, raisins, olives, pine nuts, nuts (as in southern Italy—another Arab influence) *zucchini*, or even asparagus. The choices are endless.

spaghetti:
1 tsp. salt
1 lb. thin *spaghetti*

sauce:
½ cup olive oil
½ tsp. salt
3 medium cloves garlic
Freshly ground pepper
2 tbsp. fresh parsley
1 tbsp. olive oil
½ cup freshly grated Parmesan cheese

Place a 4-quart pot on the burner. Fill ¾-full with water. Bring to a boil. Just as bubbles begin to appear at the bottom of the pot, add salt. When water comes to a rolling boil, add *spaghetti* and stir a few times. Water will stop boiling. Return to boil, reduce heat, and simmer for 10 minutes or until done to your taste.

While *spaghetti* is simmering, make the sauce. Place a medium-sized iron skillet on low heat. Add ½ cup oil and salt. Peel garlic and add to olive oil, stirring frequently until brown. Once brown, crush with a fork until garlic breaks into small pieces.

Remove *spaghetti* from stove. Drain in a colander. Return to pot.

Pour olive oil mixture over *spaghetti*. Toss well and add pepper, parsley (chopped into small pieces), 1 tablespoon olive oil, and freshly grated cheese. Toss again and serve at once (oil falls to bottom of pot if allowed to stand).

Serves: 3-5.

Poultry
Pollame

When I was young Nonna had a chicken coop in the back yard, and I was forever feeding the chickens. Then one year she bought twenty live chickens and enlisted my sister-in-law Peggy and me to help her dress them. Cleaning chickens is not a pleasant job, and, as we sat under the grape arbor and chicken after chicken was brought up from the cellar where they had been killed and defeathered, we got so sick of the smell, the texture of the skin, and the minute plucking of remaining quills, that we did not eat chicken for a year. It was our loss, for it was the last time that Nonna made *galantina.* Where roast chicken was a favorite and a staple, *galantina* was one of the most unique dishes Nonna made. *Porchetta* was Nonno's specialty, *galantina* was Nonna's.

Italian chickens are corn-fed and by consensus the best chickens in Italy are from Tuscany. The Tuscan recipes are simple, easy to prepare, and heavily reliant on spices and herbs. When selecting a chicken for the following recipes, any old chicken will not do. First it must be grade A. Then it must be the proper age. A frying chicken is a young, tender chicken *(pollo)* two to three months old that weighs 2 to 3.5 pounds. It is to be used for frying, just as a roaster, higher in fat and ranging from 2.5 to 5 pounds, is used for roasting. A stewing chicken *(gallina),* more flavorful but tougher because it is older (ten to eighteen months) when harvested, should be used for soups, stews, and sauces. A good weight for a stewing chicken is 3 to 6 pounds.

Today's supermarket poultry is not the poultry of Nonna's day. Trying to tell the difference between various types is not easy. For those who use chicken pieces, the market has dozens of selections. We no longer have to fight over who gets the drumstick, but we certainly need to be concerned about hormones in chicken feed and the inhumane practices in raising chickens. We now try to buy free range chickens as often as we can. That is a chicken that is permitted to roam and have a decent life.

Capon held noble status in our home. A capon is a neutered rooster, castrated before it is eight weeks old, fed a fatty diet, and harvested before it is ten months old at 4 to 6 pounds. They were easily available in old neighborhood grocery stores. Today, they are hard to find. We ate capon on every holiday until we became Americanized and ate turkey on Thanksgiving and crown rib at Christmas.

We seldom served duck, but it was definitely served on the first Sunday in October, which was the *Festa di Quarata*, the festival of our village in Italy.

To serve a whole fowl—be it chicken, capon, or duck—one often cuts it into pieces. Here is how. Place the bird on its back on a cutting board. Using kitchen shears, cut off each leg, drumstick only. Next, cut off the thighs. Cut the wings. Lay the remaining carcass on its side and beginning at the bottom of the bird cut straight up either side of the carcass so that you have a breast and a back. If it is a roast or you intend to fry the bird, the breast should be cut straight up the middle and each piece cut into at least three pieces. To grill, keep the breast intact or cut it in half. Do the same for the back. There are many small bones in the back piece, but the meat between the bones is delicious. The adage is true, "The closer the bone, the sweeter the meat."

Capon
Cappone

Capon, more tender than chicken, was a specialty in Nonna's home, as it was in all of Tuscany. The tender meat of the capon is far superior to chicken and the taste is richer. Capon was the meal of tradition and choice for Christmas and other holidays.

Boiled Capon with Anchovy Sauce
Cappone Lesso con Acciugata

This tasty recipe is usually made from a capon that has been used to make soup. The meat on the carcass is never discarded and is absolutely delicious served up with *acciugata*, a sauce of anchovies and capers.

1 boiled capon
*Acciugata**

Remove capon from soup and allow to drain. Using kitchen shears, cut into serving pieces (legs, thighs, breast, wings, and back).

Arrange pieces of capon on a platter and cover with *acciugata* (see index).

If you want to boil capon specifically for this dish, fill a large pot with water, add an onion, carrot, stock of celery, salt, pepper, and capon. Boil until capon is tender (better to make the soup Capon Broth, because essentially that is what you are doing).

Serves: 4-6.

Notes: *See index for *acciugata*.

This dish can also be prepared with chicken.

Roast Capon with Fennel and Oven Potatoes
Cappone in Porchetta e Contorno di Patate

Roast capon was the main course of our Christmas dinner until we became Americanized and prepared crown ribs of beef. Although it is delicious seasoned in *porchetta* or with *oregano* or rosemary, our standard was capon with sage (see the **Roast Chicken with Sage and Oven Potatoes** recipe). This *porchetta* recipe was reserved for special occasions.

5-6 lb. roasting capon
Salt and pepper
3-4 cloves garlic
3-4 slices *prosciutto*
3 tsp. fresh fennel
   seeds
3-4 sausage links
   (optional)
¼ cup corn oil
5-6 potatoes (red)
Salt and pepper, to
   taste

Wash and clean the capon and pat dry with a clean cloth. Salt and pepper the inside of the cavity. Set aside.

Crush garlic with a kitchen mallet or handle of a knife (do not peel).

Lay *prosciutto* in cavity of capon. Top with crushed garlic, fennel, and then sausage (optional).

Heat the oven to 350 degrees. Generously cover the bottom of a large roasting pan with oil. Place capon, breast side up, into the roaster. Slide capon in roaster to coat back and wings with oil. Roast for 20 minutes. Turn capon breast side down. Continue roasting.

Peel and cut large potatoes into 3 to 4 pieces, and cut small ones in half (for crunchy potatoes, cut into smaller pieces). After the capon has been roasting for an hour, add the potatoes. Turn all potatoes, coating them with the oil in the pan. Roast for an additional hour, basting the capon and turning the potatoes every 20 minutes. When almost done, salt and pepper the outside of the capon (do not salt the potatoes). Use a thermometer to check if capon is done, because ovens vary.

Serve with fresh garden salad and an additional vegetable.

Serves: 4-6.

Variations: Capon can be roasted with sage, *oregano,* or rosemary. Use only one of these spices and eliminate the sausage and *prosciutto.* See chicken recipes that follow.

Chicken
Pollo

Chicken every Sunday is a treat when prepared in the variety of ways we serve it. The difficult choice is which herb or spice to use, because all are excellent.

Roast Chicken with Sage and Oven Potatoes
Pollo Arrosto con Salvia e Contorno di Patate

Without any question, roast chicken with sage and oven potatoes was the centerpiece for 60 percent of the Sunday dinners served in Nonna's house. Once you make it, you will understand why.

3½ to 4½ lb. roasting chicken
Salt and pepper
2 tbsp. butter
8-10 sprigs fresh sage
¼ cup corn oil
5-6 potatoes (red)

Wash and clean chicken inside and out. Dry with clean cloth. Cut away edges of wing tips and ends of legs. Salt and pepper chicken inside and out. Lift the skin off breast (do not break) and place a sliver of butter on each side of breastbone. Place a sprig of sage under skin beside butter. Place a generous sprig of sage under each wing. Fold tip under top of the wing to hold sage in place. Place several sprigs of sage in the cavity.

Heat oven to 350 degrees. Generously cover bottom of a large roasting pan with oil. Place chicken, breast-side-up, into the roaster. Slide chicken in pan to coat back and wings with oil. Roast for 20 minutes. Turn chicken breast-side-down. Continue roasting.

Peel and cut large potatoes into 3 to 4 pieces, or cut smaller ones in half (for crunchy potatoes, cut into smaller pieces). After chicken has been roasting for 45 minutes, add potatoes. Turn potatoes, coating with oil in pan. Do not salt. Roast for an additional 1½ to 2 hours, basting the chicken and turning the potatoes every 20 minutes. Use a meat thermometer to check if chicken is done, because ovens vary.

Serve with fresh garden salad and an additional vegetable (try any of the Fried Vegetables with Garlic and Oil).

Serves: 4-6 servings.

Notes: Chicken can be spiced with *oregano* (replace sage) or fennel (see preceding recipe) and stuffed (see following recipe). You can also make any of these flavorful recipes with chicken parts. Be sure each part has enough of the spice and follow the recipe as directed.

Stuffed Chicken with *Oregano*
Pollo Ripieno all'Origano

In Nonna's kitchen this chicken was always spiced with sage. I introduced *oregano*, usually a southern Italian herb, when I tasted *oregano*-spiced chicken at a traditional restaurant called *Andrea's* in Cairo, Egypt, where I lived for some years.

chicken:
3½ to 4½ lb. roasting chicken
Salt and pepper
4-5 leaves fresh *oregano**
2 tbsp. butter

stuffing:
1 small onion
¼-inch-thick slice *pancetta*
1 celery rib
1 carrot
1 tsp. fresh parsley
½ clove garlic
2 tbsp. corn oil
1 tsp. salt
1 tsp. pepper
4 cups bread cubes
4 tbsp. freshly grated Parmesan cheese
1 tbsp. butter
3 eggs
½ cup broth (optional)
¼ cup corn oil
5-6 medium potatoes (red)

Wash chicken. Dry. Cut off wing tips. Salt and pepper inside and out. Place 2 *oregano* leaves inside cavity. Lift skin off breast and place sliver of butter and ½ *oregano* leaf each side of breastbone.

Stuffing: Peel onion, wash, and cut into quarter wedges. Cut *pancetta* into ½-inch pieces. Peel celery and carrot, wash, and cut into 1-inch pieces. Chop parsley. Peel garlic and cut in half. Combine and grind in meat grinder or food processor (the grinder is better because it releases the juices). This is the *sofritto*.

Place medium-size iron skillet over medium-high heat. Heat to hot. Add oil. When hot, add chopped ingredients, salt, and pepper. Sauté until onions are transparent, stirring often. The longer this mixture simmers, the better it tastes. It is done when it begins to reduce in size and sticks to the skillet, about 20 minutes.

In a large bowl combine bread cubes and cheese. Melt butter and pour over bread. Beat eggs and add. Add onion mixture. Mix well. It must be moist enough to hold together. If dry, add broth or water.

Fill body cavity with stuffing. Pull skin over opening and secure with wooden skewer.

Place leaf of *oregano* under each wing. Fold tip under top of wing. Heat oven to 350 degrees. Cover bottom of a roasting pan with oil. Place chicken, breast-side-up, into roaster. Slide chicken in pan to coat back and wings. Roast for 30 minutes. Turn chicken breast-side-down.

Peel and cut large potatoes into 3 to 4 pieces, smaller ones in half (for crunchy potatoes cut smaller). After chicken has been roasting another 30 minutes, add potatoes. Turn, coating with oil in pan. Cook an additional hour, basting both chicken and potatoes every 20 minutes. Turn potatoes occasionally, but do not salt. Serve with garden salad and additional vegetable. Use a meat thermometer to check if chicken is done, as ovens vary.

Serves: 4-6 servings.

Notes: *You can sprinkle dry *oregano*. Or you can use sage in place of *oregano,* just as you can use *oregano* in the preceding recipe to replace the sage.

Chicken Galantine
Galantina di Gallina

Galantina was my Nonna's culinary masterpiece and she was often called upon to produce it for weddings when she made it either from capon or chicken. She learned the art from Amabile Sodi, her lifetime friend, who lived in the same town in Italy *(Castelluccio)* and came to live in the same town in America. I am sure this is not the only recipe they shared.

The art of *galantina* is to remove all bones through the neck without breaking the skin. The carcass becomes the casing for a stuffing of various meats. Nonna could make it without a mishap, and when she died in 1984 the art died with her. We cut the bird down the back and then remove the bones.

Galantina can be made with capon, chicken, duck, turkey, and even fish. Some say the origin is French, created after the French Revolution, but my Tuscan soul is not ready to accept that.

4 lb. stewing chicken
2 onions
3-4 celery ribs
1 small carrot
1 tsp. salt
1 tsp. pepper

Trussing needle and
   cord
Large cheesecloth
8-10 cups chicken
   broth (see index)

Although you should have a live stewing chicken to make *galantina*, while testing this recipe we used a chicken that had been frozen.

If you use a live chicken, it must be killed, defeathered, and gutted without dipping it in boiling water. If you do not have the stomach for the task, perhaps you can find a live chicken at a farm and the farmer will kill, defeather, and gut it for you. Be sure it is not placed in boiling water or the skin will not be pliable and it will be difficult to remove the bones. Removing the big feathers is the easy part; you must be sure that the small quills are also gone.

Once the chicken has been prepared, wash it inside and out. Cut off the neck, wing tips, and feet. Work quickly because as the chicken sets, the skin becomes tough.

Deboning by splitting the chicken

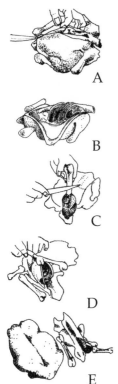

A

B

C

D

E

Cut chicken in half down the back (see A).

Once chicken is split, lay on a cutting board. Begin carving the meat away from the backbone (see B).

Once backbone is exposed, move to the legs. Remove the bones from the legs by cutting each leg at the joint (see C). Sever the tendon, scrape the meat from the bone, and free the bone. Twist the bone lose from the thigh and remove it. Remove thigh bones in the same manner. Next, move to the wings. Follow the same procedure as with the legs.

Turn the carcass over and begin removing the meat from the breast, scraping as close to the bone as possible (see D).

Once the bird is free from the bones, lay it flat on a clean work space (see E).

stuffing:
1 onion
1 celery rib
1 tbsp. carrots
½ tsp. fresh parsley
1 medium clove
   garlic
¼-inch-thick slice
   pancetta
3 tbsp. oil
½ tsp. salt
½ tsp. pepper
1 large piece Italian
   bread, decrusted
⅓ cup broth
10 oz. veal steak
3 egg yolks
½ tsp. salt
½ tsp. pepper
1 grate nutmeg
2 thick slices *prosciutto*
3 thick slices salted
   beef tongue

Truss ends of legs and wings with heavy string, tying securely. Using needle and thread, sew neck and tail openings shut. The bird is ready to stuff.

Put 8 quarts of water in a 12-quart pot and place over medium-high heat. Wash and peel onions, celery, and carrot. Place all chicken bones (including neck and head) in pot. Boil and skim. Add whole onion, celery, carrot, salt and pepper and bring to a boil. Lower heat, cover, and simmer for 1½ hours.

Preparing the stuffing

Peel onion, wash, and cut into quarter wedges. Peel celery and carrots, wash, and cut into 1-inch pieces. Chop parsley. Peel garlic and cut in half. Cut *pancetta* into ½-inch pieces. Combine and grind in meat grinder or food processor (the grinder is better because it releases the juices).

Place medium-size iron skillet over medium-high heat. Heat to hot. Add oil. Heat. Add chopped ingredients, salt, and pepper. Sauté until onions are transparent, stirring often. Sauté 20 minutes. The longer this mixture simmers, the better it tastes.

Cube decrusted bread. In a small bowl, combine bread cubes and broth. Allow to moisten and set aside.

Cut veal into small pieces and chop in a meat chopper, the finer the better. Place in a large bowl. Add moistened bread to veal. In a separate bowl beat yolks adding salt, pepper, and a single grate of fresh nutmeg. Add to veal mixture. Combine veal and onion mixtures. Blend well. Set aside.

Dice *prosciutto* and tongue into small pieces and set aside.

Stuffing the bird

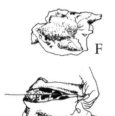

F

Place stuffing in cavity of chicken. Top with slices of *prosciutto* and tongue (see F).

Bring the two edges of the skin together and, using a trussing needle, sew up all openings (see G).

G

Once openings are secure (see H), wrap the chicken in a clean, thin cloth like a cheesecloth, and tie it securely (see I).

Remove all solid items from broth. Strain broth through sieve and return to pot. Bring to a boil.

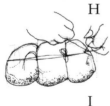

H

Place the stuffed and wrapped chicken in the boiling broth. Once the broth begins to boil again, lower the burner and simmer for 1½ to 2 hours. Remove from burner and allow to cool for an additional hour.

I

Slicing the *galantina*

Remove chicken from broth. Unwrap cloth and allow to cool for at least an hour.

Remove the threads. Slice like a ham (see J). Place on a large platter and serve. It is better to refrigerate the chicken overnight and then slice it the next day.

Yield: 25-30 slices.

Note: *Galantina* is usually served as an appetizer, at table, before the first course of the meal. So, the slice can be thin like *salami* or thick like a pork chop.

Deboning through the neck

Nonna deboned her chicken through the neck. We are not skilled enough to do this, but if you want to give it a try, here's how:

Lay cleaned chicken on cutting board. Using a sharp, pointed knife, enter carcass through neck. Remove neck bone by cutting as close to bone as possible. With fingers, feel for one wing bone. Follow to joint. Make a slit at joint and work bone loose with fingers, pulling bone out from slit. Do this for both wings.

As you finish a section, turn flesh and skin back onto carcass so that flesh will be inside out. Be sure to cut as close to bone as possible to leave as much meat as possible on bird.

Now move to breast and back. For breast, backbone, and legs, follow the instructions above. Once carcass has been removed, turn chicken right side out again, and follow the stuffing and cooking instructions above.

Chicken on a Spit
Pollo allo Spiedo

My Nonno and Nonna enjoyed going on picnics when my mother was still a girl. They were usually held on the farm of a friend and chicken on a spit was always part of the menu. This recipe is for a good-size picnic, but you can do a single chicken, a leg, or breast on a charcoal grill or in the oven. Ok, ok, propane too, if you must!

20 (3-lb.) spring chickens
Salt and pepper
1 lb. butter
120 sprigs sage
3 tbsp. salt
3 tbsp. pepper
1 cup olive oil

Wash and clean the chickens inside and out. Dry with clean cloth. Cut away the edges of the wing tips. Salt and pepper each chicken inside and out.

Lift the skin off the breast (do not break the skin) and place a sliver of butter on each side of the breastbone beneath the skin of each chicken. Place a sprig of sage under the skin beside the butter and a generous sprig of sage under each wing.

Fold the tip under the top of the wing, holding the sage in place. Place several sprigs of sage in the cavity and between the legs and the breast. Fold the legs into the skin left around the rectum.

Skewer the first bird onto the spit by piercing the bird below the wings, breast-side-up and facing you. Reverse the second bird so the back is facing you. Place it on the skewer upside-down, with the wings touching the legs of the first bird. Alternate this way to assure even weight distribution. If chickens are not well balanced, the spit will not turn. Place spit on fire.

In a large, deep bowl, combine salt, pepper, and olive oil. Mix well. Tie 8 or 9 sprigs of sage together and tie them to a long stick.

Once the chickens are on the spit, they must rotate constantly and the flesh must be basted. Dip the sage brush into the oil mixture and brush the chickens every 10 to 15 minutes. As

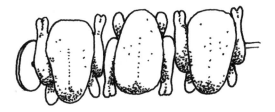

the chickens cook and the wood depletes, add more wood closer to the birds, bringing the heat nearer. Let birds grill over an open fire for 3 to 3½ hours, or until golden brown. The last part of the chickens to be cooked is the sides, because they touch each other and get less heat.

Duck
Anitra

The marshes around *Arezzo* are famous for their wildlife, especially their ducks, so it is not surprising that duck is the signature dish of the area. Duck was served on the most important day of our village, the *Festa di Quarata*, the yearly festival.

Duck in Tomato Sauce with Celery
Anitra in Umido con Sedano

4-5 lb. duck
¼ cup corn oil
Salt and pepper
3-4 cloves garlic, crushed
14 oz. whole or crushed canned tomatoes, no puree
3 oz. tomato paste
1 cup broth
Celery in duck sauce*

Cut duck into serving pieces: 2 legs, 2 thighs, 2 wings, 4 pieces of breast, and 2 backs. Wash and dry.

Place medium-size iron skillet over medium-high heat. Heat to hot. Add oil. Heat. Place duck in oil. Add salt, pepper, and crushed garlic. To crush garlic, hit it with a kitchen mallet or handle of a knife. Do not peel. Brown well to sear in juices. Lower burner. Remove duck from skillet.

Add tomatoes to juices in skillet and crush with a fork. Simmer 10 minutes. Add tomato paste. Rinse cans with ½ cup broth and add to mixture. Mix well. Lower heat and simmer uncovered for 15 minutes. Taste, and add salt and pepper if necessary.

Remove from heat and run sauce through a sieve, removing pulp. Place 1 cup of sauce in a bowl and set aside to make the celery dish below. Return remainder to skillet, return heat to medium-high, simmer for 5 minutes, reduce heat, and simmer uncovered for 15 minutes or until sauce begins to lose bright red color.

Add duck. Cover and simmer slowly for 30 minutes or until sauce is a brown-red and oil begins to separate and float on surface (skim if desired). Do not stir or turn. If sauce dries, add remaining broth.

Remove from skillet. Place on serving tray. Cover slightly with sauce. Place remaining sauce in gravy boat. Serve with Italian bread.

Serves: 6-8.

Fried Celery in Thin Sauce *(Sedano Fritto in Umido):* Follow **Fried Vegetables in Thin Sauce** recipe (see index), but substitute duck sauce for thin sauce. Once you have covered celery with sauce, simmer for 20 minutes. Remove from heat. Place in platter, sprinkle with freshly grated Parmesan cheese, and serve immediately.

Roast Duck with Fennel
Anitra in Porchetta

Cooking duck or chicken in *porchetta* was always a highlight of the year. The succulent aroma of fennel filled the house and made the mouth water.

Roast duck with fennel was the centerpiece of the homecoming festivities in *Quarata*. On the first Sunday in October, families or children who had moved away from the town came home to festooned streets, a bike race, and concession stands loaded with good Tuscan food. Duck was roasted all day and in the evening a sit-down dinner was served in the *piazza* (main square).

4-5 lb. duck
Salt and pepper
3-4 slices *prosciutto*
3-4 cloves garlic
2 tsp. fresh fennel
    seeds
3-4 sausage links
    (optional)
Salt, to taste
2 tsp. pepper

Wash and clean duck and pat dry with a clean cloth. Set aside.

Place cleaned duck on a large pastry board. Rub the inside of the duck with a damp cloth and salt and pepper the inside of the cavity.

Lay *prosciutto* end to end, covering the bottom of the cavity. Crush garlic by hitting it with a kitchen mallet or handle of a knife (do not remove skins). Sprinkle garlic over *prosciutto* and fennel seeds over garlic. Add the sausage (optional), stuffing the entire cavity. Secure the opening with cooking pins.

Heat oven to 350 degrees. Place roasting rack in a large roasting pan (duck makes a lot of drippings).

Place duck on rack and put into oven. Do not add oil.

Roast for at least 2½ hours. Use a meat thermometer to check if duck is done, as ovens vary.

When almost done, salt and pepper the outside of the duck and allow to finish cooking.

Serve with a fresh green salad.

Serves: 6-8.

Rice
Riso

When we were sick, Nonna brewed rice. As I got older I often wondered, "Why rice?" But I have discovered that it is an Italian tradition that reaches back to the Romans, who thought rice had curative properties. The saying goes, *Il riso fa buon sangue,* "rice makes the blood good." So, Nonna knew what she was doing.

Rice is a seed. It is an ancient food and a staple for most of the world. It is a wonderful food with no allergic reaction and, more important, it is gluten free. The healthiest rice is what we call brown rice, which is rice that has not been hulled. The outer layer of the seed is retained, and so are all the healthy properties found therein. White rice is hulled. The outer layer is removed.

Prepared both savory and sweet and served at the beginning, middle, or end of a meal, rice, like pasta, is a staple in Italy. The recipes in this chapter, although few in number, reflect rice's versatility. The most famous rice dish in Italy is *risotto,* a blend that elevates rice to a main course. It can be prepared in a number of ways and almost every region has its own variation: rice with Parmesan cheese and white wine, rice with mushrooms, or rice with tomato sauce.

Almost without exception, *risotto* is not rice topped with liquid, but rice cooked in liquid, be it broth or sauce. The difference is evident from the first taste: the rice is not coated, but the flavor has penetrated into each grain, making it flavorful down to its heart. By the way, the word, as we pronounce it and as our relatives in Italy pronounce it is with an "A" as in *awesome.* Risotto is RisAAWWto, not RisOOto as the current American magazine cooks pronounce it. They have created an affectation that drives me crazy.

Rice seems to have been cultivated in Asia not centuries but millennia ago. From there, it spread to the Middle East and the conquering Arabs brought in to Spain in the tenth century and then Sicily a few centuries later. By the fifteenth century, rice had spread throughout Europe. It did not arrive in northern Italy from Sicily, but from Spain, via Milan where modern rice fields are still cultivated. Both regions have fantastic rice dishes. My favorite from Sicily is *arancini*, saffron-colored rice balls filled with savory meats and sweets. *Arancini* were once eaten exclusively for St. Lucy's Day, but it is now served everywhere and for all occasions. Among the most famous *risotto* recipes is *Risotto alla Milanese*, a creamy version of *risotto* that also contains saffron. Another famous northern rice dish is *risi e pisi*, a rice and peas dish that is almost soup-like from Venice. Not to be outdone, the Piedmont serves rice with truffles. Of the sweet recipes for rice, we must return to the Sicilians with a wonderful rice pudding (like the *arancini*, it is very Arab) with chestnuts. My favorite of all favorites, and the most exotic, is the delicious rice fritter from *Arezzo* traditionally served on St. Joseph's Day. It is without equal in taste and texture.

In the United States, the best rice you can buy for Italian dishes is the imported *arborio* rice found in most Italian food stores and gourmet shops. A good, long-grained rice will also do, but under no circumstances should one use instant or minute rice for Italian dishes.

Rice Fritters
Frittelle di San Giuseppe

On St. Joseph's Day, March 19, Nonna prepared rice fritters. Throughout Italy, it is traditional to prepare a special sweet for St. Joseph's Day, a national holiday. The type of sweet varies from district to district. *Frittelle*, or *zeppole*, another name for the same thing, are common to regions as far afield as Sicily, Naples, and Tuscany, while the filled *bigne* or *confetti* are prominent in *Sardinia* and other southern provinces. There is also *sfinci* and *cassateddi*, which are filled *ricotta* turnovers. On St. Joseph's Day in all regions, the huge frying pans come out and the town squares are rich with the aromas of frying sweets.

Rice fritters are delicate and must be made carefully or they will fall apart. Arborio rice, with its heavy starch content, helps to hold them together, but I like long grain rice better (for all the rice dishes). This is not a *risotto*, but a sweet, served at the end of the meal.

3 cups milk
1 cup water
1 cup rice
2 tsp. salt
Rind of ½ lemon
½ cup granulated sugar
2 tbsp. butter
½ tsp. vanilla
1 tbsp. whisky or rum
4 eggs, separated
1 cup corn oil
¾ cup confectioners' sugar

Place a medium-size pot over medium-high heat. Add milk and water. When liquids reach a boil, add rice and salt. Stir until it reboils. Cut the lemon rind into ¼-inch wedges and add to boiling rice. Do not stir cooking rice.

When rice is cooked, remove from the burner and drain any excess liquid. Add sugar, butter, and vanilla to the warm rice and stir. Set aside to cool for 3 to 4 hours.

After rice reaches room temperature, add whisky or rum and egg yolks. The batter must be firm (see note). If runny, ½ tablespoon of flour may be added to hold the mixture together, but try not to add this because the true texture will change (too much flour and the fritters will be hard). Beat egg whites separately.

Place large iron skillet on medium-high heat. Generously cover bottom of skillet with oil. Heat oil to hot. While oil is heating, fold egg whites into rice mixture. When oil is hot, drop rice mixture by spoonfuls into the oil.

Fry until golden brown, turn, and finish frying other side. Turn only once. Drain on paper towel. Sprinkle with confectioners' sugar and serve immediately.

Yield: 24-26.

Note: Batter may be stored in refrigerator for a day, but do not add egg whites until ready to fry.

Rice with Angel-hair Pasta and/or Pine Nuts
Risotto con Capelli D'Angelo e Pinoli

This dish is my creation, combining Italian and Arab cooking. Please note that some pine nuts imported from China leave a bitter taste in your mouth. Worse, it comes back every day for a week or more every time you eat.

5 tbsp. butter, divided
1 cup angel-hair or
    pine nuts
1 clove garlic
1 cup rice
1½ cups broth
¼ tsp. salt
Freshly ground
    pepper
½ cup freshly grated
    Parmesan cheese

Place a small-size iron skillet over medium-high heat. Add 1 tablespoon butter and melt. Add angel-hair and/or pine nuts (I prefer both). Allow to brown in the butter, stirring often (about 5 minutes). Do not burn. Set aside.

Melt 2 tablespoons butter in 2-quart saucepan. Peel and dice garlic and add to butter. Sauté until brown. Do not brown butter. Once garlic is browned, crush with fork until it dissolves into pieces.

Add rice and stir for a minute, until butter is absorbed. Add broth and salt. Bring to a boil. Cover, and reduce heat. Simmer 10 minutes (do not stir cooking rice). Remove from heat. Stir in remaining butter (optional), browned angel-hair and/or pine nuts (see note). Cover and allow to steam until liquid is absorbed. Add freshly ground pepper and freshly grated *Parmesan* cheese. Stir and turn onto platter. Serve.

Serves: 3-4.

Note: If you want crunchy angel-hair, add to rice later with pepper and cheese.

Risotto

Our *risotto* is nothing like *Risotto alla Milanese.* There is no saffron—none at all. We make our *risotto* with meat sauce.

2 cups meat sauce (see index)
2 cups broth
1 cup rice
Salt and pepper, to taste
½ cup freshly grated Parmesan cheese

Place a large-size iron skillet over medium-high heat. Add meat sauce and broth and bring to a boil. Add rice, stir, bring to a boil, and lower the heat. Cover and let simmer. Do not stir cooking rice. If sauce begins to dry, stir and add more broth, a little at a time, until rice is cooked. Add salt and pepper. Simmer until sauce is absorbed and rice is tender.

Add freshly grated Parmesan cheese, mix, let stand for 5 minutes, and serve.

Serves: 3-5.

Rice Pudding
Budino di Riso

2 quarts milk
1 cup rice
⅔ cup granulated sugar
3 eggs
½ tsp. salt
1 tsp. vanilla
Cinnamon, to taste

Place a medium-size pot over medium-high heat. Heat milk to boiling. Add rice and stir. Continue stirring until all milk is absorbed (45 to 60 minutes). You must stir the rice and milk so the pudding will be creamy.

Combine sugar, eggs, salt, and vanilla in a large bowl. Beat. Add ½ cup cooked rice to the sugar mixture. Mix well. Pour this mixture into remaining rice and blend.

Pour into individual serving dishes. Cool and sprinkle with cinnamon. Refrigerate until ready to serve.

Serves: 8-10.

Rice Torte
Torta di Riso

Rice torte was a special Easter dessert in the Pelini home. It was never served any other time.

filling:
2 cups water
Pinch salt
1 cup rice
2 tbsp. butter
1¼ cups granulated
    sugar
4 eggs
1 cup milk
Juice of 2 lemons

crust:
2 cups flour
½ cup granulated
    sugar
2 tsp. baking powder
¼ tsp. salt
1 egg
½ cup shortening
Water as needed

Place a medium-size saucepan over medium-high heat. Add water and salt. Bring to a boil. Add rice and bring to a boil; reduce heat, cover, and allow to simmer until tender (about 15 minutes).

When rice is tender, add butter and sugar. Mix well. Cover and let cool. While rice is cooling, prepare crust.

In a medium-size mixing bowl combine flour, sugar, baking powder, and salt. Mix with a fork until well blended.

In a large bowl, beat the egg, combine with shortening, and add flour mixture. Combine all, mixing until well blended. Set aside.

Place half the dough on a pastry cloth or board. Dust with flour. Using a rolling pin, roll out dough to fit 9-inch pie pan and 4 inches beyond. Once rolled, fold in half, and lift into pie pan, allowing excess dough to spill over sides of pan. Repeat for second pie.

In a small bowl, beat eggs. Add milk. Pour into rice mixture, stirring well. Finally, add lemon juice and mix again.

Pour rice mixture into pastry shells, dividing evenly between the two. Fold excess dough over top of pie leaving a 3-to-4-inch hole in the center of the pie, or trim excess dough, cut it into designs, and place on top of pie.

Heat oven to 325 degrees. Place pies in oven and bake for 1 hour.

Yield: 2 (9-inch) pies.

Note: The dough contains baking powder, so it must be made last.

Salads, Snacks, and Sandwiches
Insalate, Spuntini, e Panini Imbottiti

In true Tuscan fashion, every salad green in Nonna's kitchen had its mate. Lettuce was married to green onions, endive and escarole to celery, and tomato to cucumber and green peppers. Nonna never combined tomatoes with lettuce. And the dressing was always a simple one: mainly olive oil and wine vinegar, salt and pepper, but sometimes only olive oil and pepper.

We never used extra virgin olive oil, so we do not recommend it for the dishes below. It changed the taste considerable.

Nonna never ate romaine lettuce; it was considered too tough. And iceberg was a last resort. Instead, the young leaf lettuce picked fresh from the garden while the leaves were still a delicate green, graced our table. Bean salad was a standard, and so was potato salad with olive oil and wine vinegar. Even dried bread was made into a salad.

Snacks in our kitchen were wholesome. Any "leftover" could be turned into a delicious snack, and because our table was bountiful, there was always food to be eaten another day. If one peeked into a Tuscan-American lunch pail on Monday morning, it would probably include a succulent, cold roast sandwich. One of the best was cold pork roast loaded with garlic and rosemary and garnished with mayonnaise and lettuce. Good lunch box sandwiches included cold spinach and lamb stew, Italian meatloaf, and, of course, *salami* and *prosciutto*. Nonna never went to the store to buy a pound of luncheon meat. Sometimes the lunch was not a sandwich at all, but fried veal or chicken, cold omelet, *schiacciata*, cod with chickpeas, pheasant with olives, or any part of the *gran fritto misto*, all with good homemade bread on the side.

My niece always says, "We're going to have a long life. Look at Nonna." I remind her that Nonna ate better than we do: no fast foods or packaged meats; no preservatives; no hormones in cattle, pigs, or chickens; no hot dogs; and definitely no potato chips, corn chips, cheese balls, etc. Nonna's favorite treat was fruit and the rind of Parmesan cheese.

There are dozens and dozens of low-cal recipes in this chapter.

Salads
Insalate

With a garden nearby, it is not surprising that the Tuscan kitchen is filled with wonderful, healthy, tasty salads. They are low in calorie and filled with good nutrients.

Anchovies with Onions and Parsley
Acciuge con Cipolle e Prezzemolo

So refreshing and delicious, this simple salad is not only a delight to the palate, but it is also good for you.

1 tbsp. + 1 tsp. wine vinegar
2 cups water
6-8 whole anchovies or 12-16 anchovy fillets
4 fresh scallions
20 sprigs fresh parsley
3 tbsp. olive oil
¼ tsp. pepper

If using salted anchovies, combine 1 tbsp. wine vinegar and water. Wash anchovies in wine vinegar water. Remove, and rinse in clear water. Cut off fins and tails. Split and remove scales (if using fillets, simply drain oil).

Lay in a serving dish. Slice onion and chop parsley. Top anchovies with onions and parsley. Season with olive oil, 1 tsp. wine vinegar, and pepper. Serve with fresh Italian bread. Do not add salt.

Serves: 3-4

Bean Salad
Insalata di Cannellini

This is a healthy, filling salad. Between the bean soups in the soup section and the bean salads here, it is easy to understand why Tuscans were called *Toscani mangiafagioli,* Tuscan beaneaters.

In most markets when you are looking for dried beans, you must buy the Great Northern White Beans. Canned and jarred beans go by both names: white northern and *cannellini.* In researching this book I found it was common in Tuscany for *cannellini* to be put into a flask and served that way. We never did that.

1 lb. Great Northern white beans*
Pinch salt
Water
Olive oil
Wine vinegar
Salt and pepper, to taste

If using dried beans, soak the beans overnight before boiling. Then place beans in a large pot, and add salt and enough water to fill pot ¾-full. Boil beans until tender, about 2 to 3 hours, adding additional water if necessary. Drain.

Allow to cool, and place in salad bowl. Blend with oil, wine vinegar, salt and pepper to taste. Serve with smoked herring (see index).

Serves: 3-4.

Notes: *You may substitute canned beans for this dish, but in that case drain and rinse the beans. Canned beans are softer.

Dried Bread with Parsley and Onion Salad
Panzanella

Nonna baked every week and when the bread got old and hard, in a truly Tuscan manner, she added it to soups, salads, and stews. Today we age bread especially for these dishes. *Panzanella* is refreshing on a hot day.

5 pieces stale (hard) Italian bread
½ cup fresh parsley
1 medium onion
1 tsp. salt
½ tsp. black pepper
3-4 tbsp. olive oil
2 tsp. wine vinegar

Soak bread in a little water for 2 to 3 minutes (sometimes I omit this step). Cut parsley with scissors, discarding tough stems. Wash and peel onion and slice as desired.

Once bread is softened, squeeze out excess moisture until it is just slightly damp. This is important, because the bread must absorb just the right amount of oil and wine vinegar.

Break bread into pieces. Add parsley, onion, salt, pepper, oil, and wine vinegar to taste. Toss mixture, allow to stand 15 minutes, and serve.

Serves: 3-5.

Variations: Although we never varied this dish, you may add any fresh vegetable: green beans, tomatoes, and even black olives. The choices are endless.

Chickpea Salad
Ceci Conditi

1 cup dried
    chickpeas*
Pinch salt
1 tbsp. olive oil
1 tbsp. wine vinegar
    (optional)
½ tsp. salt
½ tsp. ground black
    pepper

If using dried chickpeas, soak them overnight before boiling. Place chickpeas in a large pot, and add salt and enough water to fill pot ¾ full. Cover and boil chickpeas until tender, about 2 to 3 hours, adding more water if necessary. Drain.

Place in salad bowl and blend with oil, wine vinegar, salt, and pepper to taste.

Serves: 4-6.

Notes: *You may substitute canned chickpeas for this dish (1 cup dried beans is equal to 1⅔ cups cooked beans). Canned beans are softer.

Here is a nifty salad I created in recent years: chickpeas, chunky tuna in water, walnuts, chopped onions, chopped celery, chopped tomato, and dried cranberries mixed together and garnished with salt, pepper, and wine vinegar (Italian-style) or fresh lime juice (Arab-style).

Dandelion Greens and Hard-Boiled Egg Salad
Insalata di Denti-di-leone e Uova Sode

Some people think the dandelion is a weed, but I remember picking dandelion (teeth of the lion) greens with my Dad, expressly for this salad. He loved this salad.

3-4 dandelion greens
3 eggs, hard-cooked
Olive oil
Wine vinegar
Salt and pepper, to taste

Clean and wash dandelion greens. Break into pieces and place in a salad bowl. Chop eggs into pieces (size is a matter of taste). Add oil, wine vinegar, salt, and pepper to taste. Mix gently and serve.

Serves: 2-3.

Endive with Celery Salad
Insalata di Indivia e Sedano

Endive, with its prickly leaves, is a member of the chicory family. Endive and celery salad was part of the *Martedi Grasso* (Holy Thursday) meal in our home (see index for other endive recipe). Once again, we see the Tuscan idea of combining one or two ingredients into something special. Simplicity at its best!

1 head endive
3-4 celery ribs
Olive oil
Wine vinegar
Salt, to taste

Cut away outer leaves of endive. Wash inner leaves and allow to drain. Chop into bite-size pieces and place in bowl. Take tender inside ribs of celery and chop into ¼-inch slices. Mix with endive. Toss with olive oil, wine vinegar, and salt to taste. There is no pepper in this salad.

Serves: 2-3.

Escarole with Celery Salad
Insalata di Scarola con Sedano

Escarole can be bitter so use only the tender inner leaves for salad (see index for additional escarole recipe), and save the rest to cook down for stews, soups, and other specialties.

1 head escarole
4-5 celery ribs
Olive oil
Wine vinegar
Salt and pepper, to
    taste

Wash escarole carefully and break into bite-size pieces. Cut celery into small pieces. Place in medium-size bowl. Mix well. Season with oil, wine vinegar, salt, and pepper.

Serves: 3-4.

Boiled Potatoes with Parsley Salad
Patate Lesse con Prezzemolo

The refreshing flavor of this Italian potato salad will make it one of your favorites, as it is ours. Nonna often served boiled potatoes with parsley salad on soup day, adding the potatoes to the broth to boil in the last half hour (see index for other potato recipes).

2-3 large potatoes
    (red)
Water
Salt
3-4 sprigs fresh
    parsley
Salt and pepper, to
    taste
Olive oil
Wine vinegar

Peel and wash potatoes. Place in a medium-size pot that has been filled with water and a pinch of salt, and boil over medium-high heat (some prefer to add the peeled, whole potatoes to simmering broth for the last half hour or so, but they change the flavor of the broth).

Remove potatoes. Drain and allow to cool slightly. Slice or dice potatoes to taste. Place in a large bowl. Cut parsley into small pieces with scissors. Add parsley to potatoes. Toss.

Add salt, pepper, oil, and wine vinegar to taste. Serve hot or cold.

Serves: 4-6.

Variations: The Pelini family added 1 clove garlic, cut into 3 or 4 pieces (which I like), and 1 tsp. chopped fresh basil (which changes the taste considerably) to this salad. If you add garlic the longer the salad steeps in the juices, the stronger the garlic flavor. Actually, like *panzanella*, any fresh vegetable can be added: tomatoes, cucumber, peppers, green beans, and even black olives. Any way you try it, it is a delight and a favorite alternative to other salads. With good Italian bread, it is a meal in itself.

Snacks and Sandwiches
Spuntini e Panini Imbottiti

In Italy a snack is known by a variety of names. A *spuntino* is a little taste any time of day, while a *merenda* is a snack in the middle of the afternoon. I didn't know that until we started working on this book. We never used these terms at all.

Anchovy and Butter Sandwich
Panini di Acciughe e Burro

1 anchovy or 3
anchovy fillets
1 tbsp. wine vinegar
2 cups water
1 pat butter
1 slice Italian bread
1 sprig fresh parsley

If using salted anchovies, wash anchovy in wine vinegar and water. Rinse in clear water. Cut off fins and tails. Split and remove scales (if using fillets, simply drain oil). Spread butter on bread. Top with anchovies and leaves of parsley (large leaves are best).

Serves: 1.

Note: Makes an excellent and colorful appetizer.

Anchovies with Capers and Parsley Sandwich
Tramezzino di Acciughe con Capperi e Prezzemolo

Nonna belonged to the Italian ladies auxiliary of the Northern Italian Political Association, the NIPA, and once or twice a year it was her turn to make pasta and snacks to sell on Sunday at the club house. This sandwich was a favorite. In 1938, it sold for $2.

2 cups water
1 tbsp. vinegar
5-10 anchovies in salt or 15-20 anchovy fillets
30 sprigs fresh parsley
2 cloves garlic
3 tbsp. capers
6-7 tbsp. olive oil
5-6 Italian hard rolls, split

Combine water and wine vinegar. Wash anchovies in wine vinegar-water mixture. Remove, and rinse in clear water. Cut off fins and tails. Split and remove scales (if using fillets, skip this step and simply drain oil).

Wash parsley and cut into bits with kitchen shears. Peel and dice garlic. Wash capers, squeeze dry, and chop into coarse pieces. Combine parsley, capers, and garlic.

Line bottom of small casserole with parsley mix. Top with row of anchovies. Add 2 tablespoons oil. Continue layers. Refrigerate 2 hours or overnight. When ready to use, bring to room temperature, place 3 anchovies and 1 tablespoon of parsley mixture on a hard roll.

Serves: 4.

Note: Once made, cut rolls in ½-inch slices and arrange on tray for a tasty and pretty appetizer.

Cold Pork Roast Sandwich with Marinated Olives
Panini di Arista Fredda con Olive Marinate

marinade:
1 cup green olives
with pimentos
½ cup black olives
3 tbsp. pimentos
5 anchovy fillets
2 cloves garlic
4 tbsp. fresh parsley
½ tsp. oregano
1 tsp. lemon juice
⅛ cup olive oil
1 tsp. pepper

Place olives, pimentos, anchovies, garlic, and parsley in a bowl. Mix well and turn onto a pastry board. Chop into small pieces with a good knife or grind in meat grinder. Return to bowl. Add oregano, lemon juice, olive oil, and pepper. Mix well. Allow to set for at least 2 hours. Can be stored in refrigerator for weeks.

Cut 2 slices of good Italian bread (or use a hard roll). Lay on slices cold pork roast and top with 2 to 3 tablespoons olive marinade.

pork sandwich:
2 slices Italian bread
or hard Italian roll
3-4 very thin slices
cold pork roast
with rosemary

Serves: The olive mixture yields ½ cup. The remainder is enough for 1 extra sandwich.

Note: The marinade is good as an appetizer, on a buffet table, or in a hoagie or submarine sandwich. The pork sandwich was originally made without the marinade and served on Italian bread with mayonnaise.

Hot Italian Hoagie
Panini Caldi

Although we always ate our Italian cold cuts with bread, I invented this tasty sandwich. The key is to fry the meats and melt the cheese. I did this before the fast food places did.

16 slices Italian *salami*
12 slices Italian
cappicola
12 slices baked ham
8 slices pepper cheese
4 6-inch Italian rolls
8 large lettuce leaves
8 slices fresh
beefsteak tomato
30-40 pimento
olives (or olive
marinade, see
previous recipe)

Place a large-size iron skillet on medium-high heat. Layer *salami,* one slice at a time, to cover bottom. Try not to overlay. Cook, turning once. Pile on side of skillet and lay in *cappicola.* Let cook, turn once, and pile in another side. Repeat for baked ham.

Place 4 cooked *salami* slices in the shape of the roll. Cover with *cappicola,* then ham. Repeat until you have four piles of meat in the skillet. Top each pile with 2 slices pepper cheese. Cover and cook until cheese melts.

Slice each roll lengthwise. Lay meat on

bottom side of roll. Top with lettuce, tomato, and any other condiment. Slice 7 to 10 olives in half and lay on top (or use the olive marinade in the previous cold pork sandwich recipe). Cover with top of roll and enjoy.

Serves: 4.

Meat Sauce Sandwich
Panini con Salsa

This sandwich is usually made while meat sauce is being prepared (see index).

1 loaf good Italian
    bread
½ cup meat sauce
    (see index)

Cut the heel off a loaf of good Italian bread. Scoop out center of heel to make a hole and fill it with hot meat sauce. You eat it by nibbling around the edges. Nothing better.

Serves: 1.

Sausage with Onions and Green Peppers Sandwich
Panini con Salsiccia, Cipolle e Peperoni

Another one of my concoctions.

6 sausage links
1 large onion
1 large green pepper
¼ cup whole or
    crushed canned
    tomatoes, no
    puree
1 oz. tomato paste
¼ cup broth (or
    water)
Salt and pepper to
    taste
6 Italian rolls

Place sausage links in medium-size skillet and sear over medium-high heat (do not add oil). When browned, remove and set aside. Cut and peel onion and pepper. Wash and cut into long, ¼-inch-wide strips.

Add onions and peppers to juices in skillet. Cover and cook until onions are transparent. Add tomatoes, crushing with a fork into small pieces. Simmer 10 minutes. Add tomato paste. Rinse both tomato and paste cans with broth or water and add. Add salt and pepper to taste. Simmer 10 minutes, or until tomatoes begin to lose bright red color. Turn occasionally. If sauce begins to dry, add a little broth, but thick sauce is best.

Return sausage to skillet. Simmer 10 minutes. Sauce should be dark and oil should float on surface (skim if desired).

Slice rolls, place a sausage, several onions and peppers, and sauce on roll. Serve at once.

Serves: 6.

Prosciutto with Homemade Bread
Prosciutto con Pane di Casa

1 slice *prosciutto*
1 slice good Italian
    bread

Slice bread to desired thickness. Lay a slice of freshly cut prosciutto on top of the bread and eat. No garnish. No mayo. No tomato. Nothing. The simple taste of the thinly sliced, cured ham and the fresh bread is all you need. Serve with wine.

Serves: 1.

Note: When you buy your *prosciutto,* ask the store to cut it thin, but *do not chip.* In the attempt to get thin slices, some cut too thin and chipped *prosciutto* is not viable: it sticks to the paper; it cannot be rolled; you are paying high price for more paper than meat, etc.

Sauces
Salse

There are dozens of pasta sauces. *Ragù,* a sauce with meat, is known in America as *alla Bolognese* because *Bologna* is noted for its meat sauce. The true *ragù alla Bolognese* is a tomato and meat sauce with cream and so important to *Bologna* that the recipe was codified and placed with the Chamber of Commerce. This is not our traditional meat sauce.

The word *sugo* means any sauce that is derived from the juice of meat, and it may or may not have chunks of meat in it. That is what we call our traditional pasta sauce with meat: *sugo.* When we have a tomato sauce without meat, we called it *sugo finto* (thin or fake sauce), *sugo matto* (crazy sauce), or simply *umido* (stew).

There is one more name for sauce that I encountered recently. Back in 1996 when I was flush with the success of the first edition of this book and learning more and more about the differences in Italian-Americans, I came across the use of the word "gravy" for the typical Italian-American pasta sauce. I was floored. I had never heard of it. Neither had any Italian-American I asked in southwestern Pennsylvania. Neapolitan-Americans had no idea. Tuscan-Americans shook their heads in disbelief. Sicilian-Americans were aghast. To me, gravy required flour, and there is no flour in our pasta sauce. After years of discussion on various Internet lists and discussion boards, I have come to no conclusion as to the origin. There are theories, but no conclusions. The term 'gravy' must be added to the Pantheon of Italian-American cooking terms.

Speaking of names, the names of specialized sauces are also intriguing: *arrabbiata* (angry sauce) contains red-hot peppers, and so does *puttanesca* (sauce of the harlot). There are also rules: cheese is seldom combined with mushrooms and should never be used on fish; meatballs are never served with meat sauce; each cut of pasta has its own unique sauce; and each region, like *Bologna,* is known for a special combination of sauce and pasta. In *Arezzo* and out village of *Quarata* it is duck sauce with *pappardelle.*

But Italian sauces are not for pasta alone and are not all made with tomatoes. Tangy *acciugata* (anchovy sauce), the king of sauces in our home, is used on everything from spaghetti, boiled eggs, and boiled meats to fish and grilled T-bone steak. Béchamel, a true Italian sauce, is served as a topping in our home, but it is often used in other regions as a sauce for baked pasta.

Finally, there is *soffritto* and *battuto*, a combination of onion, celery, carrot, parsley, *pancetta,* and sometimes garlic. They are not sauces themselves, but they are used in making sauces and soups. When fried in oil, the mixture is chopped and called *soffritto;* without oil, as in broth, the various cuts are kept large and are called *battuto.* The most widely used mixture in our cooking, it is the base of sauces, stuffings, and soups. It produces the aroma that tells the senses something Italian is on the stove. Without *soffritto* and *battuto*, there would be no such thing as an Italian kitchen. It is worth repeating that if you master *soffritto* and *battuto*, the thin tomato sauce *(sugo finto)* used for pizza toppings, the meat sauce, the sauces for the various stews (including meat, fish, and vegetables), and a good soup stock, you have mastered the art of traditional Tuscan cooking.

Some specialty sauces are not found in this chapter, but in the pasta chapter because they are made exclusively for a particular cut of pasta.

Cream Sauce
Salsa alla Crema

3 tbsp. butter
⅔ cup heavy cream
⅔ cup freshly grated
    Parmesan cheese

Place medium-size pot over medium-high heat. Add butter and melt. Do not brown. Add cream. Mix well and add cheese.

Remove from heat and blend into cooked pasta.

Serves: 3-4.

Variation: Add 2 ounces drained and crushed anchovies and juice of 1 lemon to cream.

Anchovy and Caper Sauce
Acciugata

The first meal I ate in *Quarata* was in 1967 in the great hall of our ancestral home. I had just met my Uncle Gino's family that afternoon, and as I sat at the dinner table dish after dish arrived: soup with homemade pasta, *umido,* and finally grilled steak with this tangy, delicious sauce.

I was amazed. Every dish could have been prepared by my Nonna's hands. Our bond was so strong that even living thousands of miles apart, we were the same. On every holiday and for every celebration, our tables were heavy with foods that were called by the same names, prepared by the same methods, presented in the same order, and eaten with the same enthusiasm. By the time the *acciugata* arrived at the table, I had tears in my eyes. My sense of family expanded that day. It no longer encompassed western Pennsylvania, but expanded to Tuscany, a place I had only heard about in family stories.

A similar sauce is *salsa verde,* a sauce known in Germany, Spain, Mexico, and Italy. It begins as anchovies and capers, but includes parsley, garlic, mustard, and wine vinegar. Another sauce is *bagnet verde* from Piedmont with parsley, oil, anchovies, bread crumbs, garlic, and lemon.

⅓ cup olive oil
2 oz. flat fillets of anchovies
3¼ oz. capers
Juice of 1 lemon

Place a small, iron skillet over medium-high heat. Add olive oil. Do not overheat or the sauce will be ruined. Pour in the flat fillets of anchovies, oil and all, and quickly mash the fillets with a fork until they form a paste. Remove from heat (do not allow oil to bubble—the dish will be ruined).

Rinse capers under the faucet. Squeeze. Repeat 2 to 3 times. Add to anchovies. Add lemon juice. Stir. Place in a bowl and serve (we always served this sauce in a small crystal bowl with a matching crystal ladle).

For spaghetti: Omit the capers and lemon juice. Pour over ½ pound cooked spaghetti, toss, and serve.

For boiled eggs: Boil eggs. Cut eggs in half, lengthwise. Top with *acciugata*.

For steak, boiled or baked fish, boiled chicken, boiled capon, and boiled turkey: Boil or broil, and top individual servings with *acciugata*.

Serves: 4-5.

Béchamel Sauce
Salsa Besciamella

Traditionally, we only used béchamel sauce for *cannelloni* and *lasagna*, but it can be combined with a variety of dishes. Béchamel is an authentic Italian sauce, not borrowed from the French, but probably borrowed by them.

2 cups milk
4 tbsp. butter
3 tbsp. flour
¼ tsp. salt

Place milk in a small pot over medium-high heat and heat to near boiling. Do not boil or it will curdle. Place a medium-size pot over medium-high heat and while milk is heating, melt butter. Do not allow to brown.

When butter is melted, add all the flour, stirring constantly. If the flour discolors, you have overcooked it.

Remove flour mixture from heat and slowly add the hot milk a tablespoon or two at a time, stirring constantly.

When more than half the milk has been added, return to burner and add larger portions. Stir constantly and do not allow to stick. Continue stirring until consistency of heavy cream (5 to 8 minutes).

If sauce begins to bubble, remove from heat. If it thins when larger portions of milk are added, stir until thick before adding more milk. When all is mixed, add a dash of salt.

Yield: 1⅔ cups.

Note: For *cannelloni* double this recipe; for grand *lasagna* quadruple this recipe (see index).

Crazy Sauce
Sugo Matto

Crazy sauce is a meatless red sauce often served on Friday and during Lent in the Pelini home. It is especially good with fresh garden tomatoes and can be used with a variety of pastas. It cooks up quickly and is a good alternative to our traditional meat sauce that takes hours to prepare.

8-10 fresh tomatoes or 29 oz. crushed canned tomatoes, no puree
4 tbsp. fresh parsley
2 fresh basil leaves or ¼ tsp. dried basil
1 onion
½ clove garlic
⅛ cup corn oil
Salt and pepper, to taste

Blanch tomatoes by placing them in boiling water for a few minutes. Remove. Peel and discard as many seeds as possible. Chop tomatoes into small pieces. Chop parsley and basil. Peel and clean onion and garlic; chop fine.

Place a medium-size pot over medium-high heat. Heat to hot. Add tomatoes and cook for 15 to 20 minutes or until they have been reduced to pulp and all water has evaporated. When they begin to lose their bright red color, remove from pot and set aside.

Place medium-size pot over medium-high heat. Heat to hot. Add oil. Heat. Add onions and garlic and sauté until lightly browned. Add parsley, basil, tomatoes, salt, and pepper. Reduce heat and allow to simmer uncovered for 1 hour. Sauce should be brown-red with oil on surface (skim if desired).

To serve: Prepare pasta in usual manner. Once drained, add sauce. Mix well and turn onto platter. Garnish with cheese and serve.

Serves: 4.

Meatballs and Sauce
Polpette nel Salsa

In the village of *Quarata* when the pasta sauce is made with meat, meatballs are not made as an accompaniment. But taste does not always follow gastronomic rules, and when we had meatballs, which was seldom and usually at my insistence, we prepared the same sauce that we always used (see following recipe) and added meatballs to the mix.

We traditionally fried our meatballs before putting them in the sauce to simmer. Then a friend told me with great pride that she never did and they did not fall apart in the sauce. So, I tried it and liked it.

1 small onion
¼-inch-thick slice
    pancetta
2-3 celery ribs with
    leaves
1 carrot
3-4 sprigs fresh
    parsley
1 small clove garlic
    (optional)
½ cup corn oil,
    divided
1 tbsp. pepper
1 tsp. salt
¾ cup bread crumbs
    or diced, hard
    Italian bread
Milk to moisten
¼ cup freshly grated
    Parmesan cheese
3-4 beaten eggs
1 lb. ground chuck
¼ lb. ground pork

Prepare your favorite tomato sauce (either *sugo di carne* or *sugo matto;* see index). While sauce is simmering, prepare meatballs.

Peel onion, and wash and cut into quarter wedges. Cut *pancetta* into ½-inch pieces. Peel celery and carrot, wash, and cut into 1-inch pieces. Chop parsley. Peel garlic and cut in half. Combine all and grind in meat grinder or food processor (the grinder is better because it releases the juices).

Place a medium-size iron skillet over medium-high heat. Heat to hot. Add ¼ cup oil. When oil is hot add chopped ingredients, pepper, and salt. Sauté until onions are transparent, stirring often. The longer this mixture simmers, the better it tastes. It is done when it has reduced in size by almost half, has changed color, and it begins to stick to the skillet, about 20 to 25 minutes.

Place bread crumbs in a large bowl, dampen with enough milk to moisten (do not soak), and add onion mixture, grated cheese, and eggs. Combine beef and pork, mixing well, and add to bread mixture. Mix well. If dry add more milk (or broth). Mixture must be moist. If the mixture is tough, your meatballs will be tough.

Pick up a heaping tablespoon of mixture. Roll between hands to shape into 2-inch balls.

If the ball feels hard or is too hard to hold together, the mixture needs more moisture. If the ball feels too soft and the meatball will not hold together, it needs more breadcrumbs or meat.

Place a medium-size iron skillet over medium-high heat. Heat to hot. Add remaining oil (or more if necessary). When oil is hot, add meatballs and fry until golden brown. Remove from oil and drain on paper towel. I now eliminate this step. (It cuts calories too!)

Add meatballs to simmering sauce and continue to simmer for an additional hour. Be sure they are *completely covered* by the sauce. If covered, they will be very tender.

Yield: 15 meatballs, depending on size.

Meat Sauce
Sugo di Carne

Most cookbooks and restaurants call this type of sauce a *ragù* or *alla Bolognese,* but, although *Bologna* is noted for its meat sauce, this recipe is Tuscan and is as good as it gets. It is our standard sauce for pasta including *polenta, gnocchi, rigatoni, cannelloni, ravioli,* and just plain *spaghetti.* Nonna's kitchen was never without *sugo di carne.* Each Sunday, a large pot was set to brew and by the next Sunday it was all gone and she started all over again. It was her hallmark.

As I say in my essay *The Sauce of all Sauces, the Holy of Holies,* "Sauce is not a matter of fact. Sauce is explosive. It cannot be taken lightly. The Italian-Americans living in the United States would collectively croak if anyone tampered with their traditional sauce. Most of them might not know the names of their grandfathers and grandmothers in Italy, but they know how to make their grandparents' sauce. They might not know the name of the village, or even the province they came from, but they know the secrets of the sauce. Sauce is their connection. It is their roots. It is their one single, solitary, individual link to who they are. This is what being Italian is all about. Even the men go into the kitchen to make sauce. . . . Don't mess with the sauce!"

The saying goes: *Il sugo non è santo, ma dove casca fa miracoli,* "The sauce is not holy, but where it falls it makes miracles." It is not wrong.

Tuscan *sugo di carne* begins with the by-now familiar *soffritto* which serves as an ingredient for a large percentage of the recipes in this book. I always make extra *soffritto* and freeze it, because I am always in need. Just as in Milan, there are variations to the Tuscan pasta sauce. In the town of Lucca, cloves and nutmeg are added to *sugo di carne.*

2½ lb. onions
2 cloves garlic
¼-inch-thick slice
    pancetta
3 small carrots
5-8 celery ribs
3-4 sprigs fresh
    parsley
½ cup corn oil
1 tbsp. pepper
1 tbsp. salt
3½ lb. ground chuck
¾ lb. pork sausage
8 oz. red table wine
    (optional)
18 oz. tomato paste
84 oz. whole or
    crushed canned
    tomatoes, no
    puree
½ cup broth

Peel onions, wash, and cut into quarter wedges. Peel garlic and chop into thirds. Cut *pancetta* into ½-inch pieces. Peel carrots and celery, wash, and cut into 2-inch pieces. Wash parsley. Combine all and grind in a meat grinder or food processor into fine pieces (the grinder is better because it releases the juices).

Place a large-size iron skillet over medium-high heat. Heat to hot. Add oil. When oil is hot, add all chopped ingredients, pepper, and salt; sauté until onions are transparent, stirring often, about 30 minutes. The longer you cook this mixture, the better your sauce will be. It is done when it is dark, has reduced considerably in size, and begins to stick to the skillet.

When mixture is well cooked, add ground chuck and sausage a little at a time, shredding the meat with a fork to form small pieces. Allow to brown until meat is dark brown (about 30 minutes), stirring often so it does not stick. Add one glass of red table wine and continue to sauté. Simmer for 10 minutes on medium-high heat.

When meat is done, add tomato paste to meat mixture, blending well, and let simmer for an additional 15 minutes.

When you add the tomato paste to the meat, place crushed tomatoes in puree in a 6-quart pot over low heat and allow to warm. Rinse both tomato and paste cans with broth or water and add to simmering tomatoes (use only a quarter can of water).

Remove meat mixture from skillet and add to the simmering tomatoes in 6-quart pot. Put heat on medium-high. When boiling, reduce the heat; allow to simmer slowly for 3 to 4 hours. Stir often to avoid sticking. A good sauce will look dark, almost brown, and not red. It is done when oil rises to the top. Skim off excess oil.

Yield: 5 quarts.

Variations: A diced dry sausage is sometimes added to the meat. A pork rib is sometimes added to the simmering sauce. On Friday my mother would eliminate the *pancetta*, and substitute mushrooms or tuna for meat. She cut the mushrooms in half.

Note: Sauce may be stored in the refrigerator for several weeks or in a freezer for several months. It is best to store it in small containers for individual servings. If stored in freezer, it tends to take on water. Reheat, bring to a boil, and simmer for 20 minutes.

Snack Idea: While the sauce is simmering in the final hour, cut the heel off a good Italian bread, scoop out the dough inside, and fill the cavity with sauce.

Yields: The recipe as written makes 5 quarts of sauce. Below is a chart to increase or decrease the quantity. Unlike pasta and stuffing recipes, to reduce this sauce do not cut ingredients in half or fourths. For the best results, follow the quantities that follow.

	For 2 quarts:	**For 2½ gallons:**
onions	4 medium	4 lb.
garlic	2 cloves	6 cloves
pancetta	½-inch-thick slice	½ lb.
carrots	1 large	6 large
celery	4 ribs	2 whole
fresh parsley	2-3 sprigs	½ cup
corn oil	½ cup	1 pint
pepper	½ tbsp.	¼ cup
salt	1 tbsp.	⅓ cup
ground chuck	1 lb.	6 lb.
sausage	½ lb.	1 lb.
wine	4 oz.	16 oz.
tomato paste	10 oz.	40 oz.
tomatoes	32 oz.	1 gallon
broth	1 cup	1 qt

Sexy or Harlot's Sauce
Puttanesca

Named for the hot peppers that give it a kick, this is a delicious sauce with or without the hot taste. The amount of peppers you add is a matter of choice. We tend to keep it mild.

2 tbsp. olive oil
2 cloves garlic
2 slices *prosciutto*
1 fresh hot pepper or
 ¼ tsp. hot pepper
 flakes
10 mushrooms
 (optional)
2 sprigs fresh
 rosemary
½ tsp. salt
3½ cups crushed
 canned tomatoes,
 no puree
Freshly grated
 Parmesan cheese

Place a 2-qt saucepan over medium-high heat. Heat to hot. Add oil. Heat to hot. Peel and add garlic and brown. When brown, crush with a fork into small pieces. Do not burn garlic.

Dice *prosciutto*, hot pepper, and mushrooms into small pieces. The size is a matter of taste.

Add rosemary, *prosciutto*, hot pepper, salt, and mushrooms to hot oil and garlic. Reduce heat and simmer for 5 minutes. Add tomatoes all at once (they should make a swishing sound when they hit the hot oil).

Raise heat to high. Cover pot, bring to a boil, reduce heat, and simmer for 30 minutes, stirring once in a while.

Yield: 3½ cups.

Note: Serve with ¾ pound of long, thin pasta such as *spaghetti* or *spaghettini*. Top with freshly grated Parmesan cheese.

Soups
Minestre

Pasta may be the heart of the southern Italian meal, but soup is the northern Italian's soul. Despite the fact that my mother worked a full time job, a good soup began our evening meal and on all holidays, from Easter to Christmas, it is soup, not pasta, that is served (actually, at Christmas we have both). Throughout my youth, once a week the big kettle was hauled out and filled with vegetables and meat to make the stock—a tradition we maintained for nearly one hundred years. Since my mother died a few years ago, I make it less often because I live alone. My nephew, Michael, has taken over the task for holidays.

We make five basic stocks in our kitchen: beef, capon, chicken, chicken and beef, and a mixed holiday stock with a medley of meats. Eventually the chicken and beef broth with an ox tail thrown in for added taste became our favorite. We never eat soup on the day it is made in order to let it set and gel, so we can skim away the fat.

Out of that clear liquid come meals of boiled meat, broth for stews, bean soups, minestrone, and bowl after bowl of clear liquid gold in which a small *pastina* (soup pasta) is cooked. Brought to the table piping hot, soup is always accompanied by freshly grated Parmesan or *Romano* cheese.

If soup has a thin broth *(brodo)* it is a *minestra*, if thick, a *zuppa*, and if made with vegetables, it is a *minestrone*. Bean soups are *zuppa*. They are a Tuscan specialty and are wonderful winter fare. They are thick, hearty, and flavorful and sure to become a favorite in your home, as they are in ours. No Italian cookbook is complete without a good vegetable soup, a *minestrone*, and we have our Tuscan version. *Minestrone* is a summer favorite when fresh vegetables enhance the flavor. We always serve it heaping with freshly grated cheese.

Soups for special occasions include *cappelletti*, a homemade stuffed pasta; wedding soup, rich in greens; *passatelli*, homemade pasta passed through a machine; and *pasta grattata*, grated homemade pasta dropped into boiling broth. They are an elegant addition to a meal.

Most Tuscan soups are light and low in calories—one more example that the Mediterranean diet is good for us. Soup is yet another example of how important bones are in cooking. You must keep all the bones related to the various pieces of meat or poultry in order to have a good soup.

Stock Broths
Brodo Consumato

The secrets to a good stock are fresh ingredients, ample time, and straining the vegetables into the stock after they are cooked. The longer you cook broth, the better it is, and the stock that exits the refrigerator as a jelly is a prize.

The combined vegetables in the basic broths are called *batutto*: parsley, onions, celery, carrots, and whole tomato. The whole tomato can come from a can, but the other vegetables must be fresh. For excellent broth, use both bones and meat. The bones are essential, because they add the deep flavor. A good soup bone is the knee joint of the cow. Once the pot is on the stove and all the ingredients are simmering away, a lid is put on the pot to stop the liquid from dispersing into jets of steam, and additional water is never added. Finally, when the stored broth comes out of the refrigerator, the fat that has risen to the top is discarded.

For delicate broths, small pastas (*pastina*) are used: peppercorns called *acini di pepe;* tubular *ditallini,* miniature cousin to larger *diti* (used in heavier soups and with sauces); little dots of pasta called *manfrugil;* rice-shaped bullets of *orzo;* small squares of *quadrucci;* and *tripolini,* small eggbows. For holidays *cappelletti,* tiny stuffed hats, sisters of the larger *ravioli,* are a must.

Pastina is never, never, never cooked in the entire quantity of broth and stored away. It gets mushy. Rather, a fresh batch is brewed at each meal using the stock in the refrigerator, making just enough for the folks at hand.

The time needed to cook *pastina* in broth is determined by the amount of heat. The lower the heat the longer it takes: medium low, 8 to 10 minutes; very low, 15 to 20 minutes. The amount of *pastina* for soup is a matter of taste: 1 quart of broth to ½ cup *pastina* is our rule.

Beef Broth
Brodo di Manzo

1½ lb. beef shank
1 whole beef knee
   bone*
3-4 onions
3-4 carrots
3-4 celery ribs and
   leaves
3-4 sprigs fresh
   parsley
1 tbsp. salt
½ tbsp. pepper
2-3 very ripe
   tomatoes or
   canned whole
   tomatoes, no
   puree

Fill a 6-to-8-quart pot ¾-full with cold water and set on a burner at high heat. Add beef shank and knee bone. Bring to a boil. When boiling, skim off impurities that come to the top of the broth. Keep skimming until clear. The more you skim, the clearer your broth will be. Some people actually throw this water away, add new water, and begin again. Once the liquid is boiling, lower the heat to medium, but be sure the liquid continues to simmer.

Clean and cut onions into quarters. Pare and cut carrots into thirds. Clean and cut celery into thirds. Wash parsley. Once you have stopped skimming impurities from water, add all to pot. Add salt, pepper, and ripe tomatoes. Make sure the pot continues to simmer.

Cover with a lid to avoid loss of liquid. Lower heat so that broth simmers slowly. Simmer for 4 hours or until the meat falls away from the bones. Allow to cool.

When the broth cools to room temperature, remove all solid items from broth. Strain broth through a sieve. Place all vegetables in the sieve a little at a time and place the sieve over the pot of strained broth. Crush the vegetables through the sieve into the broth until only a small amount of pulp remains. To aid the process, scoop out a cup of broth and pour over vegetable pulp and continue to crush. When pulp is almost gone or looks dry, discard.

Jar the broth in individual serving containers. Refrigerate until ready to use. Broth may be stored in the refrigerator for up to a week, or frozen for a month or more.

When ready to use, remove broth from refrigerator and immediately lift the fat, which has settled on the top, and discard. If broth has turned into a gel, you will have excellent soup.

Yield: 4-6 quarts.

To serve: Place 1 quart broth in a 2-quart pot. If you are using only a portion of a jar of broth, be sure to shake the jar well before removing the stock, because heavy vegetable particles settle to the bottom. Bring to a boil. Add ½ cup *pastina* of choice, reduce heat to low, cover, and simmer for 15 to 20 minutes or until *pastina* is cooked to taste. Serve at once with freshly grated Parmesan cheese.

Serves: 3-4.

Notes: One more reminder to never add water to boiling broth while cooking. This will dilute the broth and destroy the flavor.

After the broth is made, cut up beef and make into any of the boiled dishes in the Meat: Beef section of this book.

*Beef knee bones are available in the meat department at your local market.

Capon Broth
Brodo di Cappone

As mentioned previously, capon is a neutered rooster.

5-6 lb. stewing capon, with bones
3-4 onions
3-4 carrots
3-4 celery ribs and leaves
3-4 sprigs fresh parsley
1½ tbsp. salt
½ tbsp. pepper
2-3 very ripe tomatoes or canned whole tomatoes, no puree

Fill a 10-to-12-quart pot ¾-full of water and set on a burner at high heat. Add capon. Bring to a boil. While boiling, skim off impurities that come to the top of the broth. Keep skimming until clear. The more you skim, the clearer your broth will be. Some people actually throw this water away, add new water, and start again. Turn heat down, simmer.

Clean and cut onions into quarters. Pare and cut carrots into thirds. Clean and cut celery into thirds. Wash parsley. After skimming is finished, add all to pot. Add salt and pepper and ripe tomatoes. Make sure the pot continues to boil. Cover with lid to avoid loss of liquid. Lower heat so that broth simmers slowly. Simmer for 4 hours or until the meat falls away from the bones. Allow to cool.

When the broth cools to room temperature, remove all solid items from broth. Strain broth through a sieve. Place all vegetables in the sieve a little at a time and place the sieve over the pot of strained broth. Crush the vegetables through the sieve into the broth until only a small amount of pulp remains. To aid the process, scoop out a cup of broth and pour over vegetable pulp and continue to crush. When pulp is almost gone or looks dry, discard.

Jar the broth in individual serving containers. Refrigerate until ready to use. Broth may be stored in the refrigerator for up to a week or frozen for a month or more. When ready to use, remove from refrigerator and immediately lift fat, which has settled on the top of the container, and discard. If broth has turned into a gel, you will have excellent soup.

Yield: 5-7 quarts.

To serve: Place 1 quart broth in 2-quart pot. If using only a portion, shake jar well before removing stock, because vegetable particles settle to bottom. Bring to a boil. Add ½ cup *pastina* of choice, bring to a boil, cover, reduce heat, and simmer for 15 to 20 minutes. Serve at once with freshly grated Parmesan cheese.

Serves: 3-4.

Notes: One more reminder to never add water to boiling broth while cooking. Water dilutes broth and destroys flavor. Cut capon and serve with *acciugata*, (see index).

Chicken Broth
Brodo di Gallina

5-6 lb. stewing
   chicken, with bone
3-4 onions
3-4 carrots
3-4 celery ribs and
   leaves
3-4 sprigs fresh
   parsley
1 ½ tsp. salt
½ tbsp. pepper
2-3 very ripe
   tomatoes or
   canned whole
   tomatoes, no
   puree

Fill 10-quart pot ¾-full with cold water and set on a burner at high heat. Add chicken. Bring to a boil. While boiling, skim off impurities that come to the top of the broth. Keep skimming until clear. The more you skim, the clearer your broth will be. Some people actually throw this water away, add new water, and start again. Turn heat down, and simmer.

Clean and cut onions into quarters. Pare and cut carrots into thirds. Clean and cut celery into thirds. Wash parsley. After skimming is finished, add all to pot. Add salt and pepper and ripe tomatoes. Make sure the pot continues to boil. Cover with lid to avoid loss of liquid. Lower heat so that broth simmers slowly. Simmer for 4 hours, or until the meat falls away from the bones. Allow to cool.

When the broth cools to room temperature, remove all solid items from broth. Strain broth through a sieve. Place all vegetables in the sieve, a little at a time, and place the sieve over the pot of strained broth. Crush the vegetables through the sieve into the broth until only a small amount of pulp remains. To aid the process, scoop out a cup of broth and pour over vegetable pulp and continue to crush. When pulp is almost gone or looks dry, discard.

Jar broth in individual serving containers. Refrigerate until ready to use. Broth may be stored in refrigerator for up to a week, or frozen for a month or more. When ready to use, remove from refrigerator and immediately lift the fat, which has settled on the top of the container, and discard. If broth has turned into a gel, you will have excellent soup.

Yield: 4-6 quarts.

To serve: Place 1 quart broth in a 2-quart pot. If you are using only a portion, shake jar well before removing soup, because vegetable particles settle to the bottom. Bring to a boil. Add ½ cup *pastina* of choice, bring to boil, cover, reduce heat, and simmer for 15 to 20 minutes or until *pastina* are done. Serve at once with freshly grated Parmesan cheese.

Serves: 3-4.

Notes: Cut up chicken and serve with *acciugata* (see index).

Holiday Broth
Brodo per la Festa

1½ lb. beef shank
1 whole beef knee bone*
½ soup chicken, with bones
3-4 pieces ox tail, with bones
2 turkey wings, with bones
8-10 onions
6-8 carrots
8-10 celery ribs and leaves
3-4 sprigs fresh parsley
1½ tbsp. salt
2 tsp. pepper
4 very ripe fresh tomatoes or 8 oz. whole canned tomatoes, no puree

Fill 20-quart pot with 15 quarts cold water and set on burner at high heat. Add beef shank, knee bone, chicken, ox tail, and turkey wings. Bring to boil. While boiling, skim off impurities that come to top of broth. The more you skim, the clearer your broth will be. Some people throw this water away and add new water. Lower heat to medium, but be sure pot continues to boil.

Clean and cut onions into quarters. Pare and cut carrots into thirds. Clean and cut celery into thirds. Wash parsley. After skimming, add all to pot. Add salt, pepper, and ripe tomatoes. Make sure pot continues to boil. Cover with lid to avoid loss of liquid. Lower heat so that broth simmers slowly. Simmer for 4 to 4½ hours or until meat falls from bones. Cool.

When the broth cools to room temperature remove all solid items from broth. Strain broth through a sieve. Place all vegetables in the sieve, a little at a time, and place the sieve over the pot of strained broth. Crush the vegetables through the sieve into the broth until only a small amount of pulp remains.

To aid the process, scoop out a cup of broth and pour over vegetable pulp and continue to crush. When pulp is almost gone or looks dry, discard.

Jar broth in individual serving containers. Refrigerate. May be stored in refrigerator for a week or frozen for a month or more. When ready to use, remove from refrigerator and immediately lift the fat, which has settled on top, and discard. If broth has turned into a gel, you will have excellent soup.

Yield: 2½ to 3 gallons.

To serve: Place 1 quart of broth in a 2-quart pot. If using only a portion of a jar, shake well before removing soup. Bring to a boil. Add ½ cup *pastina* (matter of taste), bring to boil, cover, reduce heat, and simmer for 15 to 20 minutes or until *pastina* are done. Serve at once with freshly grated Parmesan cheese.

Serves: 3-4.

Notes: One more reminder to never add water to boiling broth. It dilutes broth and destroys flavor. A good meal is the boiled ox tail. It must be hot, and if it is not falling off the bone, it will be tough (and the soup did not simmer long enough).

*Beef knee bones and ox tails are available at local markets.

Soups from Broth
Minestre dal Brodo

Once the basic stocks from earlier in this chapter are made, they can be used as a base for a variety of good tasting soups.

Cappelletti in Broth
Cappelletti in Brodo

Every holiday meal in our home begins with a good stock filled to overflowing with homemade *cappelletti* and topped with freshly grated Parmesan or *Romano* cheese. It is our favorite.

2 quarts holiday
 broth
80 *cappelletti*
½ cup freshly
 grated *Romano* or
 Parmesan cheese

Place a 4-quart pot over medium-high heat. Heat to boiling. Do not remove *cappelletti* from freezer until broth is at the boil; then slowly add *cappelletti* (see index) to boiling broth. Stir with a wooden spoon a few times. Broth will stop boiling. Return to boil, reduce heat, cover, and simmer for 15 minutes or until done to your taste.

Place in large tureen and bring to the table while still hot. Serve with freshly grated *Romano* or Parmesan cheese.

Serves: 4-8.

Note: At some point my mother added croutons to our holiday table to accommodate our expanding family. To make croutons, cut slices of good Italian bread into 1½-inch squares and allow to dry. Crack eggs and mix well with a little salt and pepper. Dip croutons a few at a time into the eggs and then into a pan of hot oil. Brown croutons on both sides, and set on paper towels to drain. Replenish eggs as needed. Salt fried croutons to taste. Sprinkle with grated cheese. Place in a big bowl on table. Each person will take a few and add them to his or her plate of *cappelletti*. Enjoy. (As the croutons were frying, which was the last thing the cook did so they would not be soggy—which you must do for all fried food—everyone snuck up and stole at least one crouton, more than likely two or three. So, make enough!)

Italian Lemon Soup
Minestra al Limone

1 quart broth
½ cup *pastina*
  (optional)
4 eggs, separated
Pinch salt
Juice of 2 lemons

Place a 3-quart pot on high heat. Add broth, bring to a boil, and, if using *pastina*, add. Cover, reduce heat, and allow to simmer about 10 to 15 minutes or until *pastina* is done. Remove from stove.

Separate the eggs and beat the egg whites until stiff. Add yolks and pinch of salt to whites and beat well. Slowly add 2 cups broth to the egg mixture and continue to beat. When the eggs and broth are well mixed, pour into remaining broth and *pastina*. Heat, but do not boil (it will poach the eggs). When ready to serve, squeeze lemon juice into the broth.

Serves: 4.

Wedding Soup
Minestra Maritata /Minestra di Scarola

Escarole soup, as the name reads in Italian, is a traditional soup in the south of Italy. Some say it comes from Naples. Others maintain it has a Roman origin. Either way, it was not meant to be served at weddings; rather, *maritata* means the wedding of certain ingredients to make a delicious soup. It was a favorite in Arnold Pelini's wife Rose's family and became a part of our kitchen tradition when she joined the Pelini family (It was served at their wedding).

1 large head escarole
3 cups water
2 tbsp. fresh parsley
¼ cup freshly grated
    Romano cheese
1 cup freshly grated
    Parmesan cheese
¼ lb. ground beef
⅛ lb. ground veal
⅛ lb. ground pork
¼ tsp. salt
⅛ tsp. pepper
¼ tsp. oregano
¼ tsp. basil
1 egg
¼ cup bread crumbs
4 quarts chicken,
    beef, or holiday
    broth

Wash escarole under cold, running water. Be sure to open the leaves to get out any hidden grit.

Place a large-size pot over medium-high heat. Add water and escarole and boil for 10 minutes or until done. Drain and allow to cool. When cool, chop into small pieces and set aside.

While escarole is cooling, chop parsley into fine pieces and grate cheeses.

In a large mixing bowl, combine beef, veal, pork, parsley, cheeses, salt, pepper, oregano, basil, egg, and bread crumbs. Mix well and shape into ¼-to-½-inch balls.

Place broth in 6-quart pot over medium-high heat and bring to a rolling boil. Add meatballs, cover, and simmer for 5 minutes. Add escarole, lower heat, and simmer an additional 10 minutes. Serve with additional freshly grated Parmesan cheese.

Serves: 10-12.

Notes: If you want to add a small *pastina,* add ½ cup 2 to 3 minutes after adding meatballs (see index).

The success of this soup is a good stock. Do *not* use broth from a can. Make one of the good stocks at the beginning of this chapter.

Dropped and Passed Soups
Minestre Cadute e Passate

Three types of soup are created by dropping homemade pastas into boiling broth: *stracciatella*, originally a Latium dish meaning "torn to rags," where the mixture is like a batter and is slowly drizzled into the boiling soup to form ribbons of various shapes and sizes; *passatelli*, originally from *Romagna*, where the ingredients are passed through a thick sieve of the same name and look like small sausages; and *pasta grattata*, where the fresh pasta is grated into the stock using the wide side of the cheese grater. All are special. Each has a different taste and texture.

Italian Egg Drop Soup
Stracciatella

Stracciatella, "torn into rags," is a favorite soup for babies. It is easy to make once the basic stock is made. Chinese egg drop soup is similar, but their stock is different.

2 eggs
Salt
2 tsp. flour
5 tbsp. Parmesan
    cheese
1 quart chicken, beef,
    or holiday broth

Beat eggs in a small bowl. Add salt, stir in flour, add cheese, and beat until it becomes a smooth batter.

Place a medium-size pot over medium-high heat. Add chicken or beef stock and bring to a boil. When soup is at rapid boil, take a spoonful of batter and drizzle it into the broth a little at a time.

Stir for 2 to 3 minutes. Batter should cook into long strings. Serve hot with additional freshly grated Parmesan cheese.

Serves: 4.

Notes: You can add *pastina* to this dish if you wish. Prepare broth, add ½ cup (matter of taste) *pastina*, bring to boil, cover, reduce heat, and when done to taste, add batter.

Passed Soup Tuscan Style
Passatelli alla Toscana

Passatelli is a form of Italian cooking where a stuffing is prepared and then passed through a thick sieve called a *passatelli* directly into simmering broth. The base is a mixture of eggs, bread crumbs, and Parmesan cheese. A variety of ingredients are added depending on the region, because it is popular in *Toscana, Marche,* and *Romagna.*

The *passatelli* iron was not easy to find in America, even in Italian stores, and if you wanted one you had look through Italian food catalogs until you found one. Today, you still have to look hard, but you can find them on the Internet under "Iron for Passatelli." Although it is similar to a potato masher, we have never been able to successfully use the masher to replace the *passatelli* iron. You need bigger holes.

3 eggs
6 tbsp. freshly grated Parmesan cheese
6 tbsp. dry bread crumbs
¾ tsp. grated lemon rind
½ tsp. salt
1½ tsp. corn oil
1½ quarts broth, chicken, beef, or holiday

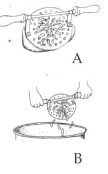

A

B

Break eggs into a medium-size bowl. Beat well. Add cheese, bread crumbs, lemon rind, salt, and oil. Blend (should be the consistency of dry, mashed potatoes). Knead.

Form mixture into a flat pancake, wrap in wax paper, and cool in the refrigerator for at least 4 hours, but preferably overnight.

When ready to use, place broth in a medium-size pot over medium-high heat. Bring to a boil. When broth is boiling, remove pancake from refrigerator. Unwrap and place on a pastry board.

Hold the *passatelli* iron in both hands and rock it over the pancake, pressing firmly. Pieces of the pasta will pass through the holes like very small sausages (see A).

Lift the iron and place it over the boiling soup. Scrap pasta into the soup (see B). Continue to rock the iron over the pancake and drop the pasta into the soup until all is used. You may have to reshape the pancake toward the end.

Work quickly, because when the pasta rises to the surface of the boiling broth, it is cooked. Serve with additional freshly grated Parmesan cheese.

Serves: 4-5.

Grated Pasta Soup
Pasta Grattata

The nineteenth century Italian cookbook writer Pellegrino Artusi called this pasta *malfattini*. Hailing from *Emilia-Romagna*, his book, *La scienza in cucina e l'arte di mangiare bene (The Science of Cooking and the Art of Eating Well)* sits at the heart of northern Italian fare.

Yet, another name for this noodle is *grattugiata*, which means simply, grated. What it is, is an excellent, weighty, pasta soup with a wonderful flavor, made often and with gusto in Nonna's kitchen. We lost the skill, but the Pelini family did not, and this is their recipe. However, we are happy to report that *pasta grattata* has become a regular addition to our kitchen once again.

2 eggs
⅔ cup freshly grated
    Romano cheese
¼ tsp. salt
1 to ½-2 cups flour
1 quart broth,
    chicken, beef, or
    holiday

Break eggs into a medium-size bowl. Beat well. Add cheese and salt. Mix well.

Slowly begin to add flour. When dough is manageable and not too sticky, turn onto floured board. Knead, adding flour, until it will not absorb any more flour (about 20 minutes).

Shape into a pancake. Wrap in wax paper. Refrigerate overnight, or for at least 4 hours. When ready to use, place broth in a medium-size pot over medium-high heat. Bring to a boil. When broth is boiling, remove pasta from refrigerator, unwrap, and place on a pastry board.

Using a regular cheese grater, grate on the thick (slow) side. Grate all the pasta.

Scrape pasta into the soup. Work quickly, because when the pasta rises to the surface of the boiling broth, it is cooked (about 5 minutes).

Serve with additional freshly grated Parmesan cheese.

Serves: 3-4.

Bean Soups
Zuppa di Fagioli

The bean is good for you. It is filled with protein, yes, protein. That is how the peasants survived the harsh centuries of serfdom. They ate a lot of beans. Beans are still inexpensive at the market, especially the dried bean.

Tuscans were not called *Toscani mangiafagioli* (bean eaters) for nothing. The wonderful, thick, bean soups of Tuscany are hearty, flavorful treats that can grace both an elegant table and a humble cottage and be at ease. Nonna often made *minestra di fagioli*, without the *pancetta* on Friday or during Lent, as the first (and sometimes only) course to a meatless meal.

Great Northern White Bean Soup
Zuppa di Cannellini

There are two main bean soup recipes presented here. The first is Elizabeth's adaptation of the original recipe brought to America by Sandrina and Nonna. The second is the original Tuscan recipe.

2 (2-lb., 8-oz.) cans Great Northern White Beans
4-6 cups broth (can use water)
2-3 fresh tomatoes or ⅓ cup whole or crushed canned tomatoes, no puree
3 large onions
¼-inch-thick slice *pancetta*
2 carrots
4-5 celery ribs and leaves
Sprig fresh parsley
¼ cup corn oil
1 tbsp. pepper
2 tbsp. salt

Place beans into 4-quart pot over medium-high heat. Rinse cans with a little broth and add to pot. Add remaining broth (for thick, thick soup use 4 cups, thinner soup 6 cups). Bring to a boil. Lower heat, cover, and simmer. After 10 minutes, add tomatoes. Allow to simmer 30 minutes.

Peel onions, wash, and cut into quarter wedges. Cut *pancetta* into pieces. Peel carrots and celery, wash, and cut into 2-inch pieces. Wash and chop parsley. Combine all and grind in meat grinder or food processor into fine pieces (grinder is better because it releases the juices).

Place a large-size iron skillet over medium-high heat. Heat to hot. Add oil. When oil is warm, add all chopped ingredients, pepper, and salt, and sauté until onions are transparent (about 20 minutes), stirring often. Add to bean mixture. Let simmer for 10 minutes. Remove from stove and pour into a blender a little at a time. Liquefy. Return to pot, return to stove, cover, simmer for additional 1½ to 2 hours or until thick and tasty. Be sure to stir often or it will stick.

Serve with freshly grated Parmesan cheese or a wedge of lemon, but not both.

Yield: 4-5 quarts.

Original Tuscan Bean Soup

1 lb. Great Northern White Beans (dried)
8 cups water
1 tsp. salt
Dash pepper
2 tbsp. corn oil
2 cloves garlic
½ tsp. dry rosemary or 2 sprig fresh
½ cup crushed canned tomatoes, no puree

Soak beans overnight in enough water to cover. Drain. Combine beans with water, salt, and pepper. Bring to a boil, cover, reduce heat, and simmer 2½ to 3 hours.

Place medium-sized skillet over medium-high heat. Add oil. Heat. Peel garlic and add. Sauté until golden. Remove and add rosemary and tomatoes. Simmer 5 minutes. Liquefy beans in a blender and add to 4-quart pot. Strain and liquefy tomatoes and add to beans. Add 3 to 4 cups water. Simmer over low heat for 1½ to 2 hours. Stir often.

Yield: 2½ to 3 quarts.

Pasta and Beans (Pasta Fagioli): Although pasta is not needed for this hearty soup, if you wish to use pasta, use heavy *ditallini*, elbows, or cut-up *spaghetti*. Never add pasta to entire stock unless you intend to serve all of it. After liquefying, return soup to burner, bring to a boil, add 2 cups pasta (quantity is matter of taste). Lower heat, cover, and simmer for 15 minutes or until pasta is cooked to taste.

Bean Soup with Ham Bone (*Zuppa di Fagioli con Osso del Prosciutto*): Use ½ a ham or *prosciutto* bone or 1 ham hock, 2 cups diced ham. Place a large pot over medium-high heat. Add bone and barely cover with water. Bring to a boil. Discard water and repeat process. Drain and set aside until soup is ready.

Prepare soup as in first recipe, but eliminate salt. After liquefying, return to stove, bring to a boil, add bone and meat, cover, and simmer for an additional 1½ to 2 hours. Serve with grated Parmesan cheese.

Bean Soup with Stale Bread and Green Onions *(Pappa ai Fagioli):* In Italy, this soup is known by a number of names including *ribollita, zuppa frantoiana* (soup in the style of the olive presser), and *pappa ai fagioli.* In Tuscany it is a specialty of the olive harvest. As oil is in its first pressing, the soup is in the pot. Good Tuscan bread is drizzled with olive oil and placed in the bottom of a deep bowl, and then topped by soup. To make, use 4 cups bean broth, 4 slices hard Italian bread, 5 to 6 scallions. Make bean soup from first recipe. Lay slice of bread in bottom of soup dish. Pour hot soup over bread. Steep 10 minutes. Serve with green onions.

Lentil Soup *(Zuppa di Lenticchie):* This same basic recipe is used to make lentil soup, just substitute lentils for beans. Garnish each serving with dash of cumin and squeeze of lemon juice.

Chickpea Soup with Egg Noodles
Zuppa di Ceci con Pasta

As children, my brother and I called chickpea soup Santa Claus soup because we only had it on Christmas Eve. If you want it Tuscan, then you must have it with rosemary. It makes the entire flavor.

48 oz. canned chickpeas*
1½ cups broth (or water)
¼ cup fresh rosemary sprigs
2 large cloves garlic
2 tbsp. fresh parsley
½ cup celery ribs and leaves
1 small carrot
Salt and pepper, to taste
¼ cup corn oil
¼ cup whole or crushed fresh or canned tomatoes, no puree
2½ cups wide pasta (optional)
Parmesan cheese or lemon wedge

Place a 4-quart pot over medium-high heat. Add chickpeas (including liquid), reserving 1 cup, and 1½ cups broth or water. Bring to a boil. Add rosemary, cover, lower heat, and simmer slowly for 30 minutes. While simmering chop garlic, parsley, celery, and carrot in a meat grinder or food processor (the grinder is better because it releases the juices). There are no onions in this soup.

Place a medium-size iron skillet over medium-high heat. Heat to hot. Add oil. Add garlic mixture, salt, and pepper to oil. Sauté 20 minutes. The longer you cook it, the better the soup will taste. Simmer until vegetables are dark and begin to stick to the skillet (about 20 minutes). Add tomatoes, and mash into small pieces. Simmer slowly an additional 10 minutes.

Add vegetable mixture to simmering chickpeas. Continue to simmer for an additional 30 minutes. Remove from stove and puree in blender at high speed. Return to pot and simmer slowly for about 1 to 1 ½ hours. Stir often or it will stick.

About 15 minutes before serving, add the remaining whole chickpeas. Some people prefer to eat *ceci* soup without pasta. If so, serve and garnish with *Parmesan* cheese or wedge of lemon.

To combine with pasta, add 1 cup wide pasta per quart of soup, cook 15 minutes or to taste, and serve with freshly grated *Parmesan* cheese or wedge of lemon, but not both.

Yield: 2 to 2½ quarts.

Notes: This is a thick soup and gets thicker as it sits. To thin, add additional broth. Can be stored in refrigerator for up to a week or in freezer for a couple of months. Do not add pasta to broth to be stored.

*To use dried chickpeas, soak 1 cup dried overnight then boil until tender (up to 4 hours), and add at least 1 cup of this liquid to the broth. Canned chickpeas are softer.

Vegetable Soups
Minestrone

Thick bean soup is not the only vegetable soup we prepare. Fresh vegetables of all kinds make good soups and we enjoy them year round. There are enough healthy soups in this chapter to keep even the most calorie concerned person happy.

Garden Soup
Minestrone dell'Orto

Fresh garden vegetables are the best to use in this soup. In the past, all the ingredients were taken from Nonno's garden. Today, we do not have a large garden and make the soup from farmer's markets or stores who sell organic vegetables.

1 onion
1 celery rib
¼ cabbage
2 carrots
2 fresh tomatoes
2 potatoes (red)
1 zucchini
2 tbsp. fresh parsley
1 tbsp. fresh basil*
2 tbsp. corn oil
½ lb. Swiss chard
1 tsp. salt
1 tsp. pepper
½ cup rice

Wash and peel all vegetables; chop all vegetables into bite-size pieces.

Place a 10-to-12-quart pot over medium-high heat. Add oil and when warm, add chopped onions. Sauté onions until transparent, then add remaining vegetables and herbs, saving the Swiss chard for last. Add enough Swiss chard to fill the pot to the top (chard will reduce dramatically).

Cook until all vegetables are soft, stirring often. Once soft, add enough water to cover vegetables, add salt and pepper, and cook 2 to 3 hours.

Remove vegetables from broth with a sieve. Puree vegetables in a blender or food processor. Return puree to broth in the pot.

Add rice, bring to a boil, cover with a lid, reduce heat, and simmer until rice is done.

Yield: 3-4 quarts soup.

Note: *If you do not have fresh basil, eliminate it from this soup.

Classic Vegetable Soup
Minestrone

2 cans (2 lb. 8 oz.) Great Northern White Beans
2 quarts water
3 cups broth (water)
2-3 medium-size fresh tomatoes or ⅓ cup canned, no puree
3 large onions
¼-inch-thick slice of *pancetta*
2 carrots
4-5 celery ribs with leaves
Sprig fresh parsley
¼ cup corn oil
1 tbsp. pepper
1 tbsp. salt
3 medium potatoes (red)
½ lb. fresh green beans
½ small head cabbage
10 oz. fresh spinach
2 *zucchini*
4-6 oz. whole or crushed, fresh or canned tomatoes, no puree

Place beans into a 4-quart pot. Rinse can with a little broth and add remnants to pot. Add remaining broth. Place pot over medium-high heat and bring to a boil. Lower heat, cover, and allow to simmer. Peel tomatoes and after 10 minutes, add to pot. Allow to simmer for 1 hour.

While beans are simmering, peel onions, wash, and cut into quarter wedges. Cut *pancetta* into pieces. Peel carrots and celery, wash, and cut into 2-inch pieces. Wash and chop parsley. Combine all and grind in a meat grinder or food processor into fine pieces (the grinder is better because it releases juices).

Place a large-size iron skillet over medium-high heat. Heat to hot. Add oil. When oil is warm, add all chopped ingredients, pepper, and salt and sauté until onions are transparent, about 20 minutes, stirring often. The longer you cook this mixture, the better your soup will taste. Add to soup. Let simmer for 10 minutes. Remove soup from stove and pour into a blender. Liquefy. Return to stove, bring to a boil, cover, reduce heat, and simmer.

Peel and dice potatoes, cut green beans into pieces, chop cabbage and spinach, and dice *zucchini*. Add all to pot and allow to simmer for 30 minutes. Crush second batch of tomatoes and run through a blender. Add to soup, cover with a lid, and simmer for an additional 1½ hours.

Serve with freshly grated Parmesan cheese.

Yield: 3 quarts.

Notes: If you wish to add pasta, use a heavy noodle and add for the last 15 minutes. We never added pasta to the entire pot. We took out the soup we needed for a single serving and added the pasta to that, cooking it in the soup for the required time. If you wish to add meat, add ¼ pound beef shank or 2 chicken legs with beans at the beginning of the process. When cooked, remove meat, break into pieces, discard fat, skin, and bones, and add pieces back to the soup.

Other Soups
Altre Zuppe

Baccalà Soup
Minestra di Baccalà

Baccalà soup was a specialty of Mrs. Sansone, the mother of Vivian's husband Tom. His family is from *Abruzzo*.

10-12 oz. dry *baccalà* (cod)
Water
1 onion
4 potatoes (red)
¼ cup corn oil
4 fresh tomatoes or 16 oz. whole or crushed canned tomatoes, no puree
¼ tsp. pepper
3 cups broth

Buy a dry strip of *baccalà* from an Italian store. Soak in cold water for 2 days, changing the water each day. Remove, and rinse well in running water. Peel and dice onion and potatoes.

Place *baccalà* in large-size pot. Add water to cover and boil for 10 minutes, or until water is clear. Drain and cool. Do not cut up; it will break up itself.

Place a large-size iron skillet over medium-high heat. Heat to hot. Add oil. Heat to hot. Add onions and sauté until transparent (7 to 10 minutes). Do not brown. Add tomatoes and pepper and bring to a boil; reduce heat to medium-low, cover, and simmer for 10 minutes. Add broth. Simmer 20 minutes.

Add *baccalà* and continue to simmer for an additional 10 minutes. Add potatoes and simmer an additional 30 minutes. Let stand one hour before eating. Cod is salty, so add salt only if necessary.

Serves: 6-8.

Potato Soup
Minestra di Patate

2 potatoes (red)
1 onion
1 tbsp. corn oil
¼ tsp. salt
Dash pepper
3 oz. tomato paste
4 cups water
½ cup *spaghetti*

Wash, pare, and cube potatoes. Peel onion and chop into fine pieces. Place a medium-size pot over medium-high heat. Heat to hot. Add oil. Heat to hot. Add onion and sauté until soft. Add potatoes, salt, and pepper. Toss and allow to cook 5 minutes. Add tomato paste and water. Bring to boil, cover, reduce heat, and simmer for 1 hour. If soup has reduced too much add more water.

Break *spaghetti* into small pieces and add to soup. Cook 10 minutes or until tender. Serve.

Serves: 4.

Cream of Tomato Soup
Minestra di Pomodoro Cremoso

2 onions
2 tbsp. corn oil
6-8 fresh tomatoes
2 tbsp. tomato paste
1 ½ tsp. salt
¾ tsp. pepper
1 ½ cups water
2 cups milk

Peel and chop onions. Place a medium-size iron skillet over medium-high heat. Heat to hot. Add oil. Heat. Add onions and sauté until transparent (about 7 or 8 minutes). Do not allow to brown.

Place tomatoes in a pot and cover with boiling water. Allow to blanch for 2 to 3 minutes and then drain and remove the skins. Chop tomatoes into pieces and add to onions. Reduce heat, cover, and simmer for 10 to 15 minutes.

Add tomato paste, salt, and pepper. Simmer 5 minutes. Add water. Simmer another 10 minutes.

Remove from skillet and puree in blender. Add milk (if too thick add more milk). Serve at once.

Serves: 4.

Tomato and Bread Soup
Pappa al Pomodoro

In this delicious Florentine soup we fry the bread before soaking it in the soup, so it need not be "hard as a rock." In fact, the texture of the bread and the soup is outstanding.

12 firm tomatoes
3 cloves garlic
½ cup corn oil
5 sprigs fresh sage
1 tsp. salt
½ tsp. pepper
6 slices stale bread
¼ tsp. salt
¼ tsp. pepper
2 quarts broth
8-10 tbsp. *Romano* cheese
Parsley, to garnish

Wash and peel tomatoes, and dice into fine pieces. Peel garlic. Set aside.

Place a large-size iron skillet over medium-high heat. Heat to hot. Add oil. When oil is hot add peeled garlic, chopped sage, salt, and pepper. When garlic begins to brown, crush with a fork.

Add bread to skillet, and brown both sides. Be sure it absorbs some garlic and sage. Remove bread from skillet. Place tomatoes in the same skillet. Allow to come to a boil. Add broth and additional salt and pepper, cover, and simmer for 40 minutes.

To serve: Place 1 slice browned bread in soup bowl. Cover with soup. Let set 5 minutes. It will become mushy (and delicious). Add cheese and garnish with sprig of parsley. Serve.

Serves: 4-6.

Vegetables
Le Verdure

Fresh, garden-grown vegetables created a bonanza of delightful eating from early spring to late autumn as day after day Nonno brought the freshly picked tomatoes, onions, lettuce, peppers, and *zucchini* to the table. "Eat your vegetables!" never had to be said, because our vegetables were tasty, spicy, and carefully selected to blend with the rest of the meal.

Among the first foods cultivated by early man, vegetables were introduced as an integral part of the daily meal by the Florentines in the Middle Ages. One vegetable that is poorly represented in this book, but should not be, is the cardoon *(cardi)*, a plant that looks somewhat like a celery. Cardoons were definitely a part of our cooking in Italy and were fried, stewed, and, when young, eaten raw; but, they were not readily available in the United States and disappeared from our culinary list.

By far, the largest number of recipes in this chapter belong to the *zucchini*, a vegetable whose Italian name has been incorporated into the English language. The *zucchini* is the most versatile of Italian vegetables. Its flower is delicately fried and its fruit is boiled, broiled, fried, stuffed, stewed, grilled, or eaten raw.

We use the carrot as an ingredient in recipes, but never serve it as a dish by itself. Spinach, kale, and Swiss chard are used mainly as stuffings and fillers in our kitchen, and are represented by few independent recipes, but cooked celery and escarole hold a noble place in Tuscan cooking and are represented in the recipes that follow.

Of the various ways of preparing vegetables, frying is our specialty. It is so important to our diet that the art and its recipes are given a separate chapter, which includes fried vegetables, meats, and fish.

If you try these vegetable dishes with canned vegetables you will diminish the taste by more than 50 percent.

Fried Vegetables in Thin Sauce
Verdure Fritti in Umido or Cotta Tre Volte

A very special vegetable dish that begins with most of the fried vegetables presented in the chapter of the *gran fritto misto,* but joins them with a tomato sauce, is *cotta tre volte* (cooked three times), which takes perfection beyond reality. It can be used for green beans, cabbage, cauliflower, celery, fennel, or Swiss chard and is an excellent accompaniment to meat in thin sauce or a roast. Celery or fennel is always served with duck, cauliflower with pork, and green beans and cabbage with beef. Swiss chard is never eaten fried in batter alone, but always fried and made in thin sauce. This is perhaps one of the most complicated methods of cooking in the Tuscan kitchen. Somewhere—from a cousin in Italy, from a discussion at a book signing, from someone, somewhere—I got the name *cotta tre volte* for this dish. Now I cannot find the connection again. However, that is exactly what it is: cooked three times. Believe me when I tell you that as soon as you put a bite in your mouth, you will agree that the taste is worth the effort.

Pick one:
1 lb. green beans
½ cabbage
½ head cauliflower
½ celery
1 Florentine fennel
1 Swiss chard

Fried Green Beans *(Fagiolini Fritti):* 1 lb. fresh green beans. Snap off about ¼-inch from each end of the bean and discard. If you like the beans long, leave as is, or snap into 2 or 3 pieces. Place in a large pot and wash with running water. Place a medium-size saucepan over medium-high heat. Add water and a pinch of salt. Add green beans and boil for about 10 minutes or to taste. Drain and allow to cool. Fry according to **Gran Fritto Misto** recipes on pages, then finish with the following Thin Sauce recipe (see index).

Fried Cabbage *(Cappuccio Fritto)* or Fried Savoy *(Verza Fritta):* Use 1 head cabbage. Wash cabbage and cut in half. Slice each half into ½-inch slices and cut each slice into smaller serving pieces. Place a medium-size iron skillet over medium-high heat. Add enough water to fill the skillet. Add a pinch of salt and bring to a boil. Gently place each piece of cabbage in boiling water and cook until tender. Cabbage tends to fall apart, so boil a few at a time. Remove carefully and set on paper towel to drain. Do not stack. Fry according to *Gran Fritto Misto* recipe, and then finish according to following Thin Sauce recipe (see index).

Fried Cauliflower *(Cavolfiore Fritto):* Wash the cauliflower and cut in half. If extra large, cut again. Place in a large pot half-filled with water and a pinch of salt. Boil for 8 to 10 minutes until soft. Test with a fork. Remove and place on drain board to drain (may be placed in the refrigerator for up to 4 days). Fry according to *Gran Fritto Misto* recipe and then finish according to following Thin Sauce recipe (see index).

Fried Celery *(Sedano Fritto),* **Fried Florentine Fennel** *(Finocchio Fritto),* **or Fried Swiss Chard** *(Bietola Fritta):* Use 2 to 3 ribs fresh celery, fennel, or Swiss chard (pick one; do not mix). Clean and wash ribs. Peel off tough strings by grabbing loose strings at bottom of rib, holding between thumb and a paring knife, and pulling. Cut rib into 4-inch pieces. Place small pot over medium-high heat. Add ribs. Add water until 1-inch above ribs. Bring to a boil. Add 1 teaspoon salt and boil until tender, about 5 to 10 minutes depending on the size of the vegetable. Drain and cool. May be stored in refrigerator for up to 3 days. Fry according to *Gran Fritto Misto* recipe on, and then finish according to following Thin Sauce recipe (see index).

Thin Sauce

Fried vegetables
2 tbsp. olive oil or
    pan drippings*
1 clove garlic
1¼ cups whole or
    crushed canned
    tomatoes, no
    puree
3 oz. tomato paste
½ cup broth
Salt, to taste
Pepper, to taste
5-6 pats butter
4 tbsp. freshly grated
    Parmesan cheese

Parboil vegetable of choice and fry according to the *Gran Fritto Misto* recipes (see index). Once fried, remove vegetables from skillet and set aside. Wipe skillet, and add oil or pan drippings. Heat to hot. Peel garlic, dice into thirds, and add. Brown garlic, crushing with a fork into small pieces. Add tomatoes to juices in skillet, crushing with a fork into small pieces. Cover and simmer 8 to 10 minutes. Add tomato paste. Rinse both tomato and paste cans with ½ cup broth or water and add to mixture. Simmer 20 to 25 minutes, or until tomatoes lose their bright red color. Taste, and add salt and pepper if necessary.

Remove from heat and run through a sieve, pushing pulp through sieve with a spoon or fork. Throw remaining pulp away.

Place fried vegetables in skillet, and dot with butter and freshly grated Parmesan cheese. Return sauce to skillet, covering vegetables well. Do not turn or stir. Simmer slowly for 15 minutes, or until sauce is brown-red and oil begins to separate and rise to the surface (skim if desired). Remove from heat.

Place in platter, sprinkle with more freshly grated Parmesan cheese, and serve immediately.

Serves: 4, as a side dish.

Notes: Time for tomatoes to simmer varies with type of tomato.

*Pan drippings from any of the roasts in this book make an excellent substitute for oil.

Fried Vegetables with Garlic and Oil
Verdure Fritte con Aglio e Olio

One more delicious way to fry vegetables is in garlic and oil. Vegetables that are superb prepared in this manner are *broccoli*, cabbage, Savoy cabbage, and cauliflower.

These are excellent side dishes for roasts. In fact, the best way to prepare them is to use the savory pan drippings from the roast in place of oil. When I am on one of my many diets, I spray the skillet with vegetable spray. Although never as good as oil or pan drippings, it is still delicious as a treat on an otherwise bland diet.

Pick one:
½ bunch *broccoli*
½ head cabbage
½ head Savoy
    cabbage
½ head cauliflower
1 tsp. salt

Broccoli: Wash *broccoli* and break into small bunches. Cut off extra leaves and discard; then, peel the tough part from the stem and discard.

Place in a large pot half-filled with water and dash of salt. Bring to a rapid boil. Add *broccoli*, cover, turn off burner, and steep for 5 to 6 minutes. Although I usually like my *broccoli* par cooked, this dish tastes better when the *broccoli* can mash easily, so I cook it for 15 minutes, or until it mashes with a fork.

Remove and place on drain board to drain (may be placed in refrigerator for up to 4 days). Continue as described in the following section.

Cabbage *(Cappuccio)* or Savoy Cabbage *(Verza)*: Savoy is a delicious winter cabbage found in any supermarket. To prepare either cabbage, wash and cut in half. If extra large, cut again.

Place in a large pot half-filled with water and a dash of salt. Boil for 8 to 10 minutes until soft. Test with a fork.

Remove and place on drain board to drain (may be placed in the refrigerator for up to 4 days). Continue as described in the following section.

Cauliflower *(Cavolfiore)*: Wash the cauliflower and cut in half. If extra large, cut again.

Place in a large pot half-filled with water and a dash of salt. Boil for 8 to 10 minutes until soft. Test with a fork.

Remove and place on drain board to drain (may be placed in the refrigerator for up to 4 days). When ready to fry, take 1 to 2 pieces of boiled cauliflower and chop into small pieces. Continue as described in the following section.

2 tbsp. olive oil or
pan drippings
from roast
3-4 cloves garlic
½ tsp. salt
¼ tsp. pepper

To fry in garlic and oil:

Do not combine vegetables. Select one. Parboil as directed in preceding sections. When ready to fry, take a bunch of boiled vegetables and squeeze out as much liquid as possible.

On a pastry board, chop the vegetable into small pieces—the smaller the better.

Place a medium-size iron skillet over medium-high heat. Add oil or pan drippings from a good roast.

Peel garlic, add to oil in skillet, brown, and crush with a fork until no large pieces remain.

Place the chopped vegetable in the oil, and salt and pepper to taste (test by taste before adding salt because pan drippings may already be salty).

Allow to sauté about 15 minutes, turning often, and mashing with a fork. Serve as a side dish.

Yield: 4, as a side dish.

Fresh Artichokes
Carciofi Freschi

The artichoke, a member of the thistle family, is a descendent of the cardoon. Known in ancient Rome, it was introduced to the world from the sun-drenched hills of Sicily and continued to spread until it became the centerpiece of the Renaissance table. Today it is grown in fields called *carciofaie* all along the Italian coast. In the spring, dozens of artichoke festivals are held throughout Italy, where the artichoke continues to be revered as a king among vegetables. When in season, it is always a part of the *fritto misto* and you will find no better recipe for fried artichokes than the one listed in that chapter. This book also includes a recipe for artichoke omelet (see index).

Except in the fried version, where the entire leaf is eaten, the edible part of the artichoke is the heart at the bottom of the fruit between the stem and choke and the fleshy part at the bottom of each leaf. To eat, pick off a leaf, put the end in your mouth, and pull the leaf through your teeth leaving the fleshy part in your mouth.

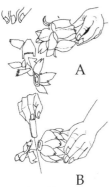

A

B

C

D

To Clean an Artichoke:

Wash all artichokes well in cold water.

Clean by removing hard outer leaves (see A).

Cut off stem (see B). *Optional.* After watching Mario Batali, I no longer cut off the stem when I fry artichokes. I cut off the very bottom which can be dirty.

Cut tips off leaves (see C).

Spread to expose center of artichoke (see D).

Remove pointed and hairy parts in center of artichoke (choke).

If you buy baby artichokes, they do not have the pointed and hairy parts. I find them only good for frying. To loosen the leaves, hit the side of each artichoke on a drain board three or four times.

Wash by placing artichoke in fresh water to which a pinch of salt and a teaspoon of lemon juice has been added.

Drain upside-down on drain board.

Artichoke flesh discolors if not used quickly.

Stuffed Artichokes
Carciofi Ritti Ripieni

My mouth waters every time I think of this delicious dish. It is a meal in itself and a great luncheon idea. We enjoy serving it on Friday, after a hearty dish of bean soup, but it is also elegant enough to grace our Easter meal. You cannot use baby artichokes for this dish.

3 artichokes
1 small onion
¼-inch-thick slice
    pancetta
½ celery rib
½ small carrot
1 tsp. fresh parsley
1 clove garlic
3 tbsp. corn oil
½ tsp. pepper
½ tsp. salt
1 cup bread crumbs
4 tbsp. freshly grated
    Parmesan cheese
Olive oil or water

Wash and prepare artichokes as described in previous section. Cut off stem.

Peel onion, and wash and cut into quarter wedges. Cut *pancetta* into ½-inch pieces. Peel celery and carrot, wash, and cut into 1-inch pieces. Chop parsley. Peel garlic and cut in half. Combine all and grind in meat grinder or food processor (the grinder is better because it releases the juices).

Place a medium-size iron skillet over medium-high heat. Heat to hot. Add oil. When oil is hot, add chopped ingredients, pepper, and salt. Sauté until onions are transparent, stirring often. The longer this mixture simmers, the better it tastes. It is done when it turns dark and diminishes to half its original size, about 20-25 minutes.

In a large bowl, mix bread crumbs and grated cheese. Add onion mixture. Mix well. Mixture must be moist enough to hold together. If dry, add water or broth.

Dry each artichoke. Sprinkle inside with a little oil. Spread outer leaves and stuff the center (see A) of the artichoke.

Spread second layers of leaves one at a time and stuff with mixture (see B), then stuff the third layer. Continue until all artichokes are stuffed.

Place artichokes upright (see C) in steamer or deep saucepan. Cover the bottom of the pan with water and sprinkle a little oil over each artichoke.

Cover and steam cook for 1½ to 2 hours.

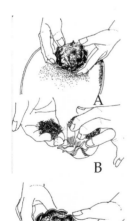

A

B

C

Check water level every 15 minutes, and, if necessary, add more water.

Serves: 3-6.

Fresh Asparagus
Asparagi Freschi

The asparagus is an ancient vegetable and member of the lily family. It also has diuretic and laxative properties. In other words, it is good for you. When buying asparagus, look for a rich, green color and closed tips.

To cook fresh asparagus trim bottom of stalks and leave fresh tips (about 8 inches long). Place a deep, narrow pot (a glass coffeepot will do nicely) over medium-high heat and add 2 cups water and ½ tsp. salt. Add asparagus so that the delicate tips are above the water line and the stalks of asparagus are upright. Cover and cook about 12 minutes. We always cooked our asparagus until soft. Now I prefer it a bit crispy. The taste and the texture are different; I like it better. If you want to try it crispy, cut the time to 3 minutes, or to taste. Asparagus is excellent dressed with oil, wine vinegar, salt, and pepper, but also delicious fried (see index).

To roast: Alternately, place sprigs of asparagus on aluminum foil, brush with grated or chopped garlic, drizzle with olive oil, and bake for 5 minutes.

To grill: Spray the grill with a bit of oil so the asparagus will not stick. Drop asparagus on the grill close together. Brush with grated or chopped garlic, drizzle with olive oil, and grill for a few minutes. Turn, and grill an additional 2 to 3 minutes.

Asparagus with Anchovy Sauce
Asparagi con Acciugata

1 lb. asparagus
1 bay leaf
4 hard-cooked eggs
*Acciugata**
Lettuce to line platter

Boil the asparagus as described in previous recipe, but add a bay leaf to the water. Drain and chill.

Boil eggs to taste. Drain, peel, and cut in half lengthwise.

Place a lettuce leaf on a salad plate. Top with asparagus and eggs. Cover with *acciugata*.

Serves: 4.

Note: See index for *Acciugata*. If you are going to roast or grill the asparagus, eliminate the garlic.

Fresh Green Beans
Fagiolini Freschi

I cannot count the number of times I saw Nonna sitting under the grape arbor in her back yard snapping the ends off freshly picked green beans. Every time I do it myself, I think of her.

Green beans, another gift to the New World from Italy, are a part of the *fritto misto* and are excellent in thin sauce. There is also a wonderful green bean appetizer recipe(see index). Perhaps the very best way to serve fresh green beans is to pick them from the garden, clean them, boil them to taste, sprinkle with salt, and drizzle with olive oil. That is all.

To clean green beans:

Snap ¼-inch off each end of the bean and discard. If you like beans long, leave as is, or snap into 2 or 3 pieces. Place in large pot and wash with running water. Place a medium-size saucepan over medium-high heat. Add enough water to cover the beans and a pinch of salt. Add beans, and boil 5 to 10 minutes or to taste. Drain and allow to cool.

Green Bean Salad
Insalata di Fagiolini Freschi

½ lb. fresh green beans
Pinch salt
1 clove garlic
Salt and pepper, to taste
3-4 tbsp. olive oil
1-2 tsp. wine vinegar

Prepare beans as described in previous section. While beans are boiling, peel garlic and crush with the broad side of a heavy knife. When beans are cool, place in a salad bowl, and add salt, pepper, and peeled, crushed garlic. Toss. Add oil and toss again. Add wine vinegar and give the beans a final toss. Serve.

Note: The longer the beans steep in the dressing, the sharper the garlic taste.

Serves: 3-4.

Green Beans in Tomato Sauce
Fagiolini al Pomodoro

1 lb. fresh green beans
2 large, very ripe, fresh tomatoes
1 clove garlic
¼ cup corn oil
¼ tsp. salt
Dash pepper

Clean beans. Wash and drain. Place medium-size pot over medium-high heat. Fill with water. Bring to a boil, blanch tomatoes, remove, and skin. Cut into small cubes. Peel garlic.

Place medium-size iron skillet over medium-high heat. Heat to hot. Add oil. Add peeled garlic and allow to brown, but do not burn. Crush with a fork into small pieces. Add beans to oil. Allow to blister for few minutes. Add tomatoes, salt, and pepper, and stir.

Cover and simmer for 50 to 55 minutes, until beans are tender and tomatoes lose bright red color.

Serves: 3-4.

Fresh *Broccoli*
Broccoli Freschi

Broccoli, rich in vitamins A and C, was developed from the cabbage in, of course, Italy. It was known in ancient Rome and was introduced to America by the Italian immigrants of the twentieth century.

When selecting *broccoli*, avoid bunches whose buds have turned yellow, because that is a sign that they are not fresh. To prepare, wash the *broccoli* and break into small florets. Cut all extra leaves and discard, then peel the tough part from the stem and discard.

Place in a large pot half-filled with water and 1 teaspoon salt. Bring to a boil. When at rapid boil, turn off burner, cover, and allow to steep for 10 minutes. Remove and place on drain board to drain (may be stored in the refrigerator for up to 4 days). *Broccoli* is a part of the *fritto misto*. It is also excellent drizzled with butter or sautéed in garlic and oil (see index).

Note: Boil time is up to you. Crunchy *broccoli* will require less boil; mushy *broccoli* needs more time.

Broccoli with Mushrooms
Broccoli con Funghi

10 oz. *broccoli*
½ lb. fresh
   mushrooms
2 large cloves garlic
2 tbsp. corn oil
Pinch salt
Pinch pepper
¼ cup freshly grated
   Parmesan cheese

Prepare *broccoli* as described in previous section. Remove florets from large, thick stems of *broccoli*.

Clean and slice the mushrooms and set aside. Peel garlic and slice into small pieces.

Place a medium-size iron skillet over medium-high heat. Heat to hot. Add oil, and when hot, add garlic. Sauté 1 to 2 minutes until garlic is brown (do not burn), then crush garlic with a fork into small pieces.

Add *broccoli* stems and sauté 2 to 3 minutes, stirring constantly. Add florets and sauté 2 to 3 minutes, stirring constantly. Finally add the sliced mushrooms. Continue to stir. Season with salt and pepper to taste.

After 3 minutes, remove from stove. Arrange in a serving dish and sprinkle with freshly grated Parmesan cheese. Serve at once.

Serves: 3-4.

Eggplant
Melanzane

Eggplant comes in a variety of shapes and sizes. The most common is deep-purple and bulbous, but eggplant can be white and tubular or green and long like a *zucchini*. We always use the purple variety. In addition to the recipes presented here, you can stuff eggplant according to the recipes for stuffed *zucchini* that follow.

Preparing the eggplant:
Cut top and bottom stems from eggplant, remove outer skin, and slice into ¼-inch slices. Place in large pot, and add water and pinch of salt. Allow the eggplant to soak. As the water turns brown, drain and add more water and more salt. Do this 3 or 4 times to blanch out the bitterness. Drain and pat dry.

Fried Eggplant
Melanzane Fritte

1 eggplant
½ cup corn oil
Salt, to taste

Prepare eggplant as described in previous section. Place medium-size iron skillet over medium-high heat. Heat to hot. Add oil (eggplant requires a lot of oil).

When hot, drop eggplant into oil (oil must be hot or the eggplant flesh will absorb all the oil). Repeat until skillet is full. Do not stack. Salt and allow to fry until golden brown; turn, and fry second side.

Remove from skillet and place on a paper towel to absorb extra oil. Serve hot.

Serves: 6-7, as a side dish.

Baked Eggplant with Tomatoes
Melanzane con Pomodoro al Forno

1 medium eggplant
½ cup fresh parsley
1 clove garlic
½ tsp. salt
¼ tsp. pepper
1 cup crushed,
    canned tomatoes,
    no puree, or 2 ripe
    tomatoes
1 tsp. corn oil

Wash. Remove top of eggplant. Dry and cut lengthwise into halves. Score each half several times and place in a broiler for 2 to 3 minutes or until the tops start to brown.

Wash and finely chop parsley. Peel and chop garlic. Place eggplant in casserole, cover with parsley, garlic, salt, and pepper. Spoon tomatoes over eggplant (for fresh tomatoes, cut each into two horizontal pieces, and place juice side down on eggplant).

Drizzle with oil. Bake at 350 degrees for 1 ¼ hours. Do not add liquid.

Serves: 2.

Eggplant Parmesan
Melanzane alla Parmigiana

1 fried eggplant
2 cloves garlic
1¼ cups whole or
    crushed canned
    tomatoes, no
    puree
3 oz. tomato paste
½ cup broth
Salt and pepper
4 oz. *mozzarella*
    cheese
½ cup freshly grated
    Parmesan cheese
5-6 pats butter

Prepare eggplant and fry as described in **Fried Eggplant** recipe (see index). Remove from skillet and set aside. Peel garlic. Add to oil in skillet. Brown and crush with a fork into small pieces. Add tomatoes to the juices in the skillet, crushing with a fork into small pieces. Lower heat, cover, and simmer 8 to 10 minutes.

Add tomato paste. Rinse both tomato and paste cans with broth or water and add to mixture. Simmer 20 minutes, or until tomatoes begin to lose bright red color. Taste; add salt and pepper if necessary.

Cut *mozzarella* into 1-inch squares. Grate Parmesan cheese. Make piles of each on a pastry board.

Place a layer of fried eggplant along the bottom of a square (8-by-8-by-2-inch) baking dish. Do not overlap. Place 9 squares of *mozzarella* in a checkerboard pattern. Sprinkle 1 teaspoon of Parmesan over the *mozzarella*.

Arrange a row of eggplant on top of the first. Add *mozzarella* and Parmesan. Continue alternating eggplant and toppings until all eggplant is layered in dish.

Finally pour tomato sauce over eggplant, then top generously with remaining *mozzarella* and Parmesan.

Heat the oven to 350 degrees and bake for 30 to 45 minutes. Remove from oven, cover with foil, and allow to stand 10 minutes.

Before serving, cut eggplant into 9 square pieces: 3 cuts lengthwise and 3 cuts widthwise. Serve with a steel spatula.

Serves: 9.

Notes: Eggplant Parmesan is an alternative to *lasagna* and accompanied by a fresh garden salad makes a delicious meal. It is also a good dish for a buffet.

You can top this dish with béchamel sauce (see index).

Fresh Endive
Indivia Fresca

Nonno planted endive and escarole in August and picked it in October. Just before picking, it was tied tight to blanch the inside leaves. After blanching, it was picked and stored for good eating all winter. The outer leaves were cooked and stored, to be used in wedding soup or as a cooked side dish. Once we got a freezer, we would freeze the outer leaves. The inner leaves were used in salad (see index). It is amazing what one can do with endive.

Endive Parmesan
Indivia alla Parmigiana

1 lb. endive
Pinch salt
2 cloves garlic
3 tbsp. corn oil
1¼ cups whole or crushed canned tomatoes, no puree
3 oz. tomato paste
1 cup broth
Salt and pepper, to taste
1 cup bread crumbs
½ cup freshly grated Parmesan cheese

Wash endive carefully and remove long, tough, outer leaves. Place a large-size pot over medium-high heat. Fill half-full with water and a pinch of salt. Add endive. Boil until tender, about 10 minutes. Drain, allow to come to room temperature, and squeeze out additional moisture.

Peel garlic. Place a medium-size iron skillet over medium-high heat. Heat to hot. Add oil. When oil is hot, add garlic and allow to brown. When brown, crush with a fork into small pieces.

Add tomatoes to the juices in the skillet, crushing the tomatoes with a fork into small pieces. Simmer 8 to 10 minutes.

Add tomato paste. Rinse both tomato and paste can with small amount of broth or water and add to mixture. Reduce heat, cover, and simmer 20 minutes, or until tomatoes begin to lose their bright red color. Taste, and add salt and pepper if necessary.

Remove from heat and run tomatoes through a sieve, pushing pulp through sieve with a spoon or fork. Throw remaining pulp away.

Place a layer of cooked endive in a 9-by-9-inch casserole dish. Pour ⅓ of tomato mixture over endive. Sprinkle with ⅓ of bread crumbs and freshly grated Parmesan cheese. Repeat for remainder of endive and top with sauce, bread crumbs, and cheese. Bake in 350-degree oven for 45 minutes.

Serving: 6.

Fresh Escarole
Scarola Fresca

Escarole looks like a cross between bibb lettuce and endive. It is good in salads, soups, and stuffings.

Stuffed Escarole
Scarola Ripiena

This unusual recipe comes from Norma Iervoline, one of our testers. It is delicious. The Pelini family has been enjoying it for years (see index for escarole salad recipe).

1 head escarole
1 clove garlic
6 anchovy fillets
¼ cup pine nuts
5-6 oz. pitted black
    olives
½ cup bread crumbs
¼ cup freshly grated
    Parmesan cheese
2 tbsp. olive oil

Wash escarole under running water, opening the leaves to clean the inside (do not break leaves). Turn upside-down and drain on paper towel. Allow to dry.

Peel and chop garlic into fine pieces. Chop anchovies and pine nuts into small pieces. Drain black olives and chop into small pieces.

Combine garlic, anchovies, and pine nuts in a small bowl. Add bread crumbs and grated cheese, then add oil and chopped olives (do not add salt as anchovies are salty enough). Mix well.

Place escarole on a pastry board. Spread mixture on each leaf, then gather leaves together and tie them at top with a string. If not secure, wrap string loosely around body.

Place a medium-size high pot (a glass coffee pot is good) over medium-high heat. Add 2 inches of water. Place escarole in pot so that it stands up. Bring water to a boil, cover with a lid, and allow to steam for 30 minutes, or until tender (you can also place escarole in a steamer).

Remove escarole from pot, lay on pastry board, allow to cool for 30 minutes, and cut into slices.

Yield: 7-8 slices.

Fresh Mushrooms
Funghi Freschi

On any given Sunday if we were in the car on our way to someplace along a country road, Nonna would cry from the back seat, "Stop, Freddy, I want to go look for mushrooms." So, out of the car we would go. My Dad would ask the farmer if we could walk in his field, and Nonna and I would crawl through the barbed wire fence and go traipsing through the mud pies looking for mushrooms. We always came back with a few for our pot.

As I was growing up, I always felt the mushroom, especially fried, was our secret and was a bit resentful when fried mushrooms began to appear on menus in restaurants and cocktail bars. I felt vindicated when they never tasted as good as ours.

The mushroom is a fungus without roots, stems, leaves, seeds, or reproductive cells. There are more than 44,000 varieties of wild mushrooms in the world and only a little more than thirty are poisonous. But thirty is enough of a reason for one to be very careful when going mushroom hunting. Today, as a result of pollution and deforestation, the wild mushroom is in trouble and not as abundant as it once was. In fact, in central Europe, many species are now extinct.

Unless we found exotic mushrooms in the fields, we bought button mushrooms grown in the caves of Pennsylvania for our recipes. We did not have the choices available today. When buying button mushrooms, look for unbruised caps with under sides that are dense and not opened. These are the freshest. The shelf life of a mushroom is short, so buy in small quantities. Some cookbooks and TV chefs recommend brushing mushrooms with a brush to take off any dirt instead of washing them. But we always washed them. Fried mushrooms are the centerpiece for the *gran fritto misto*. There is also an excellent stuffed mushroom recipe included in this book (see index).

Mushrooms in Garlic and Butter
Funghi con Aglio e Burro

½ lb. mushrooms
2 tbsp. butter
2 cloves garlic
Salt and pepper, to taste

Take one mushroom at a time and cut off the very tip of the stem and remove any blemishes on the crown. Slice each mushroom lengthwise into 4 or 5 pieces.

Place a medium-size iron skillet over medium-high heat. Heat to hot. Melt butter in skillet. Add garlic. When garlic is beginning to brown, crush with a fork into small pieces. Do not allow garlic to burn, because the taste will be bitter. Add mushrooms, salt, and pepper to taste. Lower heat and sauté for 5 minutes.

Serves: 3-4.

Fresh Green Pepper
Peperoni Freschi

Many people find green peppers hard to digest, but if you rub the pepper with a little oil and place it over coals, under a broiler, or on the stovetop burner for a few minutes, you can peel off the outer skin with a paring knife. Then the indigestible part is gone. This book includes additional recipes for green peppers in an omelet and green pepper with sausage sandwich (see index). Nonna didn't like green peppers. She always said, 'Even the cows don't eat them," so we didn't have them very often. "I don't like," is one of the reasons that traditions die.

Stuffed Peppers
Peperoni Ripieni

Peppers in all varieties—red, yellow, green, even jalapeno—are found in markets nationwide. The best peppers to use for this recipe are the small, long green peppers called Italian *Elle* or *cubanelle* (narrow) found in most supermarkets. This recipe is also good for stuffed, elongated white eggplant, small *zucchini*, and small tomatoes.

10-12 small peppers
1 clove garlic
½ tsp. fresh parsley
½ tsp. fresh basil
3 slices Italian bread
½ cup milk
1 egg
1 lb. ground round
½ tsp. salt
¼ tsp. pepper
⅓ cup freshly grated
   Romano cheese
Corn oil

Wash peppers, remove tops, and scrape out seeds and white inner ribs. Set aside.

Peel and chop garlic. Chop parsley and basil. Break bread into small pieces, and moisten with milk (it should absorb all the milk).

In a large bowl combine garlic, egg, meat, parsley, basil, salt, pepper, and grated cheese. Mix well. Finally add bread. Mix well.

Stuff each pepper. Rub a little oil between your hands and rub the outside of the pepper with oil.

Place on an oiled cookie sheet and bake at 400 degrees for 25 minutes, turning every 5 to 6 minutes. Peppers should be brown. Reduce oven temperature to 350 degrees and bake for an additional 45 minutes.

Serves: 6-8.

Note: This is a good item for a buffet table or to serve as an appetizer.

Potatoes
Patate

Potatoes are delicious no matter which way you serve them: roasted, fried, mashed, stewed, boiled, or baked. We prefer red potatoes: slightly more expensive, but sweeter. For *gnocchi* the Idaho is probably better because it has more starch, but we used red. For boiled potatoes, see the potato salad recipe; for stewed potatoes, see potatoes with pork steak or sausage; for roasted potatoes, see any roast in this book (see index).

Double Baked Potato
Patate Doppie al Forno

4 potatoes (red)
8 pats butter
4 tbsp. butter
½ cup milk
1 tsp. salt
Paprika
4 tsp. freshly grated
  Parmesan cheese
4 pieces aluminum
  foil

Wash each potato and pat dry. Place each on aluminum foil. Add pat of butter and seal foil around each potato. (Can eliminate the butter and foil and zap in microwave—just don't tell my mother). Bake in 350-degree oven for 30 to 45 minutes depending on size of potato.

When potato is done, remove from oven and unwrap. Cut off top of each potato. Scoop out inside trying not to break the skin. Place all pulp in a bowl and add butter, milk, and a pinch of salt. Whip potatoes and spoon back into skins. Lay potatoes on baking dish. Sprinkle with paprika and Parmesan cheese. Return to oven, and set oven on broil. Broil on high for 5 to 6 minutes or until crusty. Serve at once.

Serves: 4.

Fried Potatoes, Onions, and Peppers with Rosemary
Patate Fritte con Peperoni, Cipolle e Rosmarino

This is a good dish for breakfast, brunch, or a buffet. You can throw a few sausages in it for a main course.

3 large potatoes (red)
2 large onions
2 large green or red
    bell peppers
¼ cup corn oil
1 tbsp. rosemary
½ tsp. salt
Dash pepper

Clean, peel, and dice potatoes, onions, and peppers into ¾-inch pieces, the smaller the better. Place a large-size iron skillet over medium-high heat. Heat to hot. Add oil.

When oil is hot, add potatoes. Fry for 10 minutes. Keep on high heat until potatoes begin to turn brown, then add onions, peppers, rosemary, salt, and pepper. Reduce heat and cover with a lid. Allow to steam until vegetables are done to your taste.

Yield: 4-6.

Variation: Add diced *salami* or sausage.

Mashed Potatoes Italian Style
Pureà di Patate all'Italiana

4 potatoes (red)
¼ tsp. salt
¾ cup milk
5 pats butter
4 tbsp. freshly grated
    Parmesan cheese
4 tbsp. pine nuts

Wash potatoes, peel, and dice into 1-inch pieces. Place a medium-size pot on medium-high heat. Add water, potatoes, and salt. Bring to the boil, reduce heat, and simmer until potatoes are done.

Remove from stove and drain. Place potatoes in a mixing bowl. Add milk and butter and blend until all lumps are gone.

Remove potatoes from mixer and add cheese and pine nuts. Blend together and serve.

Note: Do not buy pine nuts imported from China. They will leave a bitter taste in your mouth every time you eat, for at least a week.

Serves: 4.

Roast Potatoes
Patate al Forno

Our favorite potatoes. This recipe appears with all the roasts in this book, including pork, veal, lamb, and beef. Potatoes made this way are delicious and so much a part of our cooking that we have repeated the recipe here. If you have never tasted potatoes this way, you have not eaten potatoes.

4 large potatoes (red)
¼ cup corn oil or pan drippings
¼ tsp. sage or fennel or rosemary (pick one)
Salt
Pepper

Wash and peel potatoes. Cut into 4 or 5 pieces (for crunchy potatoes, cut into smaller pieces).

If roasting potatoes with a roast, after the roast has been roasting for about an hour, add potatoes. Turn, coating them with the oil in the pan. Cook for an additional 1 to 1½ hours, basting and turning every 20 minutes.

If preparing the potatoes without a roast, place peeled and cut potatoes in a roasting pan, add pan drippings from a good roast, and roast as above.

If you do not have pan drippings, add oil, your favorite spice (fennel, sage, or rosemary), salt, and pepper; roast as directed above.

Serves: 4.

Note: It is the pan drippings and spices that make these potatoes so good. The better the roast, the more satisfying the potatoes. Keep the bone in and the fat on the roast.

Garden Tomatoes
Pomodori dall'Orto

Tomatoes arrived in Italy in the sixteenth century, long after the Italians had been enjoying pasta. They came from South America and the Italians called them *pomi d'oro*, golden apples. But the story of their migration does not end there. When the Italian immigrants brought them to the United States in the 1800s, they were soundly rejected by the average American. It was not until the 1860s that the tomato became an acceptable food in the United States.

Nonno always planted tomatoes. Each spring we went to a special hot-house to buy the plants. Once the plants were a foot high, poles were placed beside each one, and the vine tied so the plant would grow straight and tall.

The first tomatoes were ready by mid-July. Oh, how proud Nonno would be when he brought the first one to the table. Then all the delicious, fresh recipes would come out and day after day we enjoyed these truly "golden apples."

While writing this book I planted my first tomato patch (I could hear Nonno, long dead, laughing each evening as I watered and tended the plants). Although we had only eight plants, we got dozens and dozens of tomatoes. It was with great satisfaction that I picked them each evening. As the weather began to turn cold in the fall, green tomatoes were still on the vine. We picked them, wrapped each one in newspaper, and put them in a dry, cool place in the cellar. From week to week they would ripen and we had tomatoes well into the winter.

The very best way to eat a tomato is to chill it, cut it, dash it with a little salt, and drizzle it with oil.

Tomato, Green Pepper, and Cucumber Salad
Insalata di Pomodori, Peperoni, e Cetrioli

vegetables:
2-3 garden fresh tomatoes
1 large green pepper
1 large cucumber

dressing:
Olive oil
Wine vinegar
Salt, pepper

Wash the tomatoes, remove the green stems, cut in half, and cut each half into 4 or 5 wedges. Wash the green pepper, cut in half, and remove all seeds and pods; cut lengthwise into wedges. Peel the cucumber, cut lengthwise, and slice crosswise into pieces. Place all in a large, deep dish and add dressing to taste (we always enjoyed oil, wine vinegar, salt, and pepper, but lemon can be substituted for the wine vinegar).

Serves: 4-5.

Note: For people who find peppers hard to digest, a helpful hint is to peel the outer skin off the pepper. Rub it with oil and place it under a broiler for a few minutes. Then peel the skin off the pepper with a paring knife. The indigestible part is gone.

Garden Tomatoes and Basil
Pomodori al Basilico

This dish is called *Insalata Caprese* in the *Campania* where it originated and where the vegetables are blessed by volcanic soil, which makes them taste extra special. The tomatoes must be fresh from the garden.

1 firm garden tomato
1 tsp. fresh basil
2 tbsp. olive oil
½ tsp. salt
¼ tsp. pepper
1 tbsp. wine vinegar
(optional)

Wash the tomato, remove the green stem, cut in half, and cut each half into 4 to 5 wedges. Place in a bowl. Add the basil first, spreading it over all the tomatoes. Toss and let sit for 5 minutes. Add oil, salt, and pepper to taste. Wine vinegar is optional.

Serves: 2.

Fresh Tomatoes on Italian Bread
Struffa Struffa

Generations of our children have enjoyed this delicious, wonderful open-faced sandwich. They all love it and the family lore that accompanies the making. It will become one of your favorites, too. In *Liguria* it is known as *Pan e Pumata*. They use a whole loaf of good Italian bread and add garlic and basil. We simply call it *Struffa, Struffa*: Rub, Rub.

1 garden tomato,
   very ripe
2 slices fresh Italian
   bread
Salt, pepper
Olive oil

Slice the tomato in half. It must be very ripe for this dish. Rub half of tomato on bread, leaving a pinkish color and a few seeds. Add salt, pepper, and a little oil. Use second half of tomato for second slice of bread. Serve immediately.

Yield: 2 portions.

Stuffed Tomatoes
Pomodori Ripieni

10 ripe firm tomatoes
¼ cup fresh parsley
4 fresh leaves basil
1 clove chopped garlic
1½ cups fresh bread crumbs
Salt and pepper, to taste
½ cup freshly grated Parmesan cheese
Corn oil

Wash tomatoes and remove stems. Slice in half and remove seeds leaving interior pulp. Chop parsley and basil. Peel garlic and chop fine.

In a large bowl, combine parsley, basil, garlic, bread crumbs, salt and pepper, and grated cheese. Stuff tomato halves. Place tomatoes on oiled baking dish and bake at 350 degrees for 30 minutes or until tomatoes are tender.

Yield: 20 tomato halves.

Fresh *Zucchini*
Zucchini Freschi

Zucchini, native to Italy, is a staple of Italian-American gardens and is served in so many different ways that it is hard to believe all the dishes come from the same vegetable. It should never be allowed to grow too large or too long, but should be served young and tender at about 7 inches long and 1½ inches in diameter. The *zucchini* and its flower are a special part of the *gran fritto misto* (see index).

Zucchini, Onion, and Tomato Stew
Zucchini, Cipolle, e Pomodoro Stufati

This is good! It is even better with crusty bread. My brother and I loved it. My mother, not too much. I liked to squash it onto good bread, dripping with the juices.

2 medium *zucchini*
2 medium onions
4-5 very ripe tomatoes
2 tbsp. corn oil
¼ tsp. salt
¼ tsp. pepper
2 tbsp. tomato paste

Peel and wash *zucchini* and cut into 1 ½-inch cubes. Peel and wash onions, cut in half, and then cut into ⅛-inch wedges. Blanch tomatoes, remove skin, and cut into pieces.

Place a medium-size skillet over medium-high heat. Heat to hot. Add oil. Heat to hot. Add onion. Simmer for 10 minutes, or until onions are transparent. Add *zucchini*, salt, and pepper. Simmer for 10 minutes and add tomatoes. Crush tomatoes with a fork. Add paste, and stir; simmer.

Cover, lower the heat, and allow to simmer for at least an hour, until tomatoes lose their bright red color. Stir often. Serve with fresh Italian bread.

Serves: 6-8, as a side dish.

Boiled *Zucchini*
Zucchini Lessi

Whenever the soup is simmering on the stove and there are fresh *zucchini* in the garden, this refreshing, low-cal dish is conjured up. It is simple. It is tasty. It is healthy.

2 medium *zucchini*
Salt and pepper, to taste
Olive oil
Wine vinegar

Wash *zucchini* and remove stems. Place in simmering soup and boil for 1 hour. Remove and place in colander; let drain for 10 to 15 minutes. Split lengthwise, and let stand 10 minutes. Drain off any liquid. Dress with salt, pepper, oil, and wine vinegar to taste.

Serves: 4.

Zucchini with Cheese
Zucchini alla Parmigiana

2 *zucchini*
4 tbsp. butter
⅛ tsp. salt
⅛ tsp. pepper
3 tbsp. fresh parsley
1 tsp. basil
½ cup freshly grated Parmesan cheese

Wash *zucchini*, peel, and slice into thin slices. Place a medium-size iron skillet over medium-high heat. Add butter and melt. Add *zucchini*, cover, reduce heat, and sauté until brown, about 20 minutes. Add salt and pepper, parsley, and basil. Simmer 5 minutes.

Remove from skillet and place on serving tray. Sprinkle generously with Parmesan cheese. Stir and serve.

Serves: 2 (this is not a mistake, *zucchini* reduce).

Zucchini in White Wine
Zucchini con Salsa di Vin Bianco

2 *zucchini*
1 small onion
4 tbsp. butter
½ cup white wine
¾ tsp. salt
⅛ tsp. pepper
2 tbsp. fresh parsley
1 large leaf fresh basil

Place a medium-size pot over medium-high heat and parboil *zucchini,* skins and all (about 5 to 7 minutes depending on size).

Remove from water, drain, and let cool. Wash and peel onion and chop into fine pieces.

Place a medium-size iron skillet over medium-high heat. Add butter and melt. Add onions and sauté until onions are transparent. Add wine, salt, pepper, parsley, and basil.

Slice parboiled *zucchini* into ¼-inch slices. Add to skillet and cook for 15 to 20 minutes or until tender.

Serves: 4.

Zucchini with Bread Stuffing
Zucchini Ripieni di Pane

In addition to *zucchini,* this recipe can be made with eggplant, tomatoes, or peppers.

2 onions
1 clove garlic
¼-inch-thick slice
    pancetta
1 small carrot
2-3 celery ribs
2-3 sprigs parsley
2 tbsp. corn oil
1 tsp. pepper
2 tsp. salt
2 medium *zucchini*
2 cups bread crumbs
¼ cup freshly grated
    Parmesan cheese
2 eggs
⅛ cup corn oil

Peel onions, wash, and cut into quarter wedges. Peel garlic and chop into pieces. Cut *pancetta* into small pieces. Peel carrot and celery, wash, and cut into 1-inch pieces. Chop parsley. Combine all and grind in a meat grinder or a food processor into fine pieces (the grinder is better because it releases the juices).

Place a medium-size iron skillet over medium-high heat. Heat to hot. Add 2 tbsp. oil. When oil is warm add all chopped ingredients, pepper, and salt. Reduce heat, cover, and sauté until onions are transparent, stirring often.

Cut *zucchini* in half lengthwise. Scoop out the center, leaving about 1 inch of pulp. Chop scooped out pulp into small pieces and add to the already cooking onion mixture. Cover and simmer about 20 minutes, stirring often. The longer you cook this mixture, the better your stuffing will taste. It is done when the vegetables are dark and it begins to stick to the skillet.

When cooked, remove from skillet and combine with bread crumbs and grated cheese. Beat the eggs and pour over the mixture. Mix well. If dry, add a little broth or water.

Fill both halves of the *zucchini* with the mixture. Grease baking dish with a little oil and place *zucchini* halves side by side in the dish.

Bake in 350-degree oven for 1 hour.

Serves: 4-5.

Zucchini with Meat Stuffing
Zucchini con Ripieno di Carne

2 onions
¼-inch-thick slice
    pancetta
2-3 celery ribs
1 small carrot
2-3 sprigs parsley
2 large *zucchini*
¼ cup corn oil
1 tbsp. pepper
1 tbsp. salt
½ lb. ground beef
1 cup bread crumbs
¼ cup freshly grated
    Parmesan cheese
2 eggs, beaten
¼ cup corn oil
2 cloves garlic
1¼ cups whole or
    crushed canned
    tomatoes, no puree
3 oz. tomato paste
½ cup broth

Peel onions, wash, and cut into quarter wedges. Cut *pancetta* into small pieces. Peel celery and carrot, wash, and cut into 1-inch pieces. Chop parsley. Combine all and grind in meat grinder or food processor into fine pieces (the grinder is better because it grinds into fine pieces and releases the juices).

Cut *zucchini* in half lengthwise. Scoop out the center, leaving about 1 inch of pulp. Chop scooped out pulp into small pieces and add to onion mixture.

Place a medium-size iron skillet over medium-high heat. Add ¼ cup oil. When oil is hot, add all chopped ingredients, pepper, and salt. Cover, lower heat, and sauté, stirring often, until onions are transparent, about 20 minutes. The longer you cook this mixture the better the stuffing will taste. Remove from skillet and set aside.

When cooked remove skillet from heat and add ground meat, bread crumbs, grated cheese, and beaten eggs. Mix well. Fill the *zucchini* halves with the mixture and place them in a greased baking dish.

Place a medium-size iron skillet over medium-high heat. Heat to hot. Add ¼ cup oil. Heat. Peel garlic and add to oil. Allow to brown and crush with a fork into small pieces. Add tomatoes, crushing with a fork into small pieces. Bring to a boil, reduce heat, cover, and simmer 8 to 10 minutes. Add tomato paste. Rinse both tomato and paste cans with ½ cup broth (or water) and add to mixture. Cover and simmer 20 minutes, or until tomatoes begin to lose bright red color.

Remove from heat and run through a sieve, pushing pulp through sieve with a spoon or fork. Throw away remaining pulp. Taste, and add salt and pepper if necessary.

Pour tomatoes (see note) over stuffed *zucchini*. Bake in 350-degree oven for 1 hour.

Serves: 4-5.

Note: You can substitute 2 cans tomato soup for the tomato mixture, but don't tell Elizabeth.

Grand Mixed Fry
Gran Fritto Misto

If there is a more delicious dish in the world, I do not know it. Serving up a great mound of fried meats, fish, and vegetables sprinkled with fresh lemon and eaten with a fresh green salad with olive oil and wine vinegar was an event of paramount importance in Nonna's house. The word would go forth, "We are having *fritto misto* on Sunday," and the anticipation was almost unbearable. If someone in the family had made plans, they were changed, or the friends were invited to join us in this eating orgy. We served *fritto misto* as often as possible: as the holiday meal for Holy Saturday, as a favorite request for birthdays, and on summer picnics. When a particular vegetable came in season it was, "We are having artichokes with the *fritto misto*," and it was a solemn moment, almost a time to tremble with delight, but certainly a time for a big smile.

Fritto misto is prepared throughout Italy. It is so popular that *friggitorie* exist throughout the country, selling nothing but fried foods. Today fried vegetables have been discovered by American restaurants and are offered doused in liquid cheese. Nonna would consider that a sin. *Fritto misto* is prepared in three different ways, depending on the type of food. It is either dipped in batter, dredged in flour, or pressed into bread crumbs. The meats include veal, lamb, and chicken. The fish include cod, halibut, smelts, shrimp, oysters, and squid. The vegetables are the most exotic items on the Italian menu: artichokes, asparagus, green beans, cauliflower, celery, eggplant, Florentine fennel, mushrooms, *zucchini* (pumpkin) flowers, and *zucchini*. God help the cook who does not know which meat must be pressed in crumbs, which vegetable is dipped, or which fish is dredged. This is a secret as important as the cut of pasta or the quality of bread.

Frying Food
Cibi Fritti

The best way to fry food is with an iron skillet, a *padella di fritto*. We have a variety of sizes—one for every possible use. Unfortunately, by today's standards, you need plenty of oil when frying. The skillet should be filled ¼-to-½-inch full with good vegetable oil (we use corn oil). We never use olive oil to fry our food.

Place the skillet on medium-high heat and heat until hot. Add oil to cover the bottom. Heat to hot but not to smoking. Food that is fried in cold or warm oil will absorb the oil and be greasy. A good way to test the oil is to drop a small piece of meat or vegetable into the oil. If it begins to bubble with small bubbles around the food, it is ready. If it bubbles too vigorously, it is too hot.

Never stack food in the frying pan. Be sure each piece has ample space around it. Lay the food into the hot oil and allow to brown on one side. *Turn only once.* If food sticks to the bottom of the skillet, the oil is not hot enough or there is not enough oil. Let it be, for when it is cooked it will free itself.

If you are frying a large quantity of food, the oil will become depleted and begin to foam. It will have to be replenished. Remove the last piece of cooked food, drain existing oil, wipe the skillet with a paper towel, return it to heat, and add new oil. Heat and continue frying.

Always place fried food on a paper towel after removing from the frying skillet. This allows excess oil to drain. Nonna would always place a saucer upside-down in the center of the serving tray. That would help to drain the fried food.

You must fry the food and *serve it immediately.* Do not allow it to sit. Do not put it in a warming tray. I remember Nonna and my mother at the stove frying as we were eating: from the skillet to the table. There is nothing low-cal here. Eat light for a few days or give up a couple of fast food meals, but don't give up this wonderful experience.

Batter
Pastella

The amount of batter needed for various vegetables depends on the size of the vegetables, just as the amount of oil depends on the size of the skillet. If additional batter is required, do not add to existing batter, but begin fresh.

2 eggs
1 tbsp. olive oil
2 tsp. water
Salt to taste
3 tbsp. flour

Beat eggs in a medium bowl. Add oil, water, and salt. Mix well. Slowly add flour. Mix until it forms a smooth, thin paste. Prepare the batter ahead so that it can rest.

Place a large-size iron skillet on medium-high heat. Heat to hot. Add oil to generously cover bottom of the skillet. Heat to hot. Dip food into the batter, and coat well. If batter is too runny and does not adhere to food, add more flour to batter.

Place in hot oil. Brown one side, turn, and brown other. *Turn only once on each side* (Some vegetables have multiple sides, so turn to each side, but only once). Drain on paper towel. Eat immediately.

If you need more batter, do not add to the prepared batter, but start anew.

Dredged in Flour
Infarinati

When you use flour, roll the food in the flour first, then in the egg.

Be sure all sides are covered with the flour. Tap gently to remove excess flour or it will fall into the oil and burn. In recent years, we have placed the flour in a paper bag. When ready put light pieces of meat, fish, or vegetable to be floured in the bag and shake vigorously. It will coat evenly. Heavy pieces must still be dredged one by one.

1 cup flour
2 eggs
1½ tsp. salt
¾ tsp. pepper
Corn oil

Place flour on board or in flat dish. Gently roll each piece in flour, coating generously. Place on another flat dish, and do not stack. Beat eggs, salt, and pepper in a flat bowl. Set near stove.

Place medium-size iron skillet over medium-high heat. Heat to hot. Add oil. When oil is hot, dip floured food in the beaten egg, coating generously. Drop immediately into hot oil. Repeat until skillet is full. Do not stack.

Allow to fry until golden brown, turn, and allow the other side to brown. *Turn only once.* Remove from skillet one at a time and place on a paper towel to absorb extra oil. Continue until all is fried. Serve hot with a wedge of lemon.

If brown flour accumulates in the oil, you used too much flour and fried too hot. Be sure to tap off excess flour from food before dipping in egg.

Pressed in Bread Crumbs
Cibi in Pan Gratt ato

When you use bread crumbs, dip the food in the egg, then in the crumbs.

1 cup bread crumbs
¼ cup freshly grated Parmesan cheese
2 eggs
1 tsp. salt
½ tsp. pepper
Corn oil

Never use bought or seasoned bread crumbs. Save stale Italian bread until hard. Grate on a cheese grater. If you absolutely must buy them, buy unseasoned bread crumbs. When ready to use, add grated cheese to crumbs and mix well.

Beat eggs in flat dish, and add salt and pepper. Dip food into beaten egg, turn, and coat well.

Place a medium-size iron skillet over medium-high heat. Heat to hot. Add oil. Heat to hot.

Press egg-dipped food onto bread crumbs, turn, and press again. Drop immediately into hot oil. Do not stack.

Fry until golden brown, turn, and fry second side. *Turn only once.* Remove from skillet and place on a paper towel to absorb extra oil. Continue until all is fried. Serve hot with a wedge of lemon.

Fried Meat Medley
Fritto Misto di Carne

Fried meat is the linchpin of the mixed fry. And the best meats are chicken and veal. Always a favorite whether served in the *fritto misto* or alone, our unadorned chicken recipe stands far above all the heavily spiced fast-food varieties. Ambrosia, food of the gods, is the best way to describe our excellent, excellent, fried veal. Bushels of both were cooked and taken on picnics and the only thing that came back were the crumbs. They are easy to prepare and delicious to eat. Simplicity is the secret—no garlic, no spice—simple and uncomplicated Tuscan food.

Batter Dipped
Pastella

Fried Brains *(Cervello Fritto):* Use batter prepared as described in the Frying Food section with 1¼ pounds beef, lamb, or calf's brains, corn oil, wedge of lemon.

Prepare batter. Wash brains. Pour a small amount of boiling water over brains and remove covering membrane. Cut into serving pieces.

Place medium-size iron skillet over medium-high heat. Heat to hot. Add oil to cover bottom of skillet. Heat to hot. Drop a piece of brain into batter. Turn to coat well. If batter is too thick, add additional water and mix. If too thin, add more flour. Place in hot oil. Repeat. Fry until golden brown, *turning once.* Serve at once with wedge of lemon.

Serves: 4-6.

Note: Brains fry quickly, so do not overcook. Very good if served piping hot with fried mushrooms or fried artichokes.

Dredged in Flour
Infarinati

Fried Chicken *(Pollo Fritto):* Use the dredged in flour recipe found in the Frying Food section with 1 chicken fryer cut into pieces and 1 large lemon cut into wedges.

Cut breast in half and cut each half into thirds, bone in. Cut leg into thigh and drum stick. Separate wings from back and cut back into two or three pieces. Wash all pieces of chicken, remove extra (not all) skin and fat, and drain. Dredge chicken as described in recipe in Frying Food section. Most chicken pieces are too heavy to put in a paper bag to coat.

Place a large-size iron skillet over medium-high heat. Heat to hot. Coat bottom generously with oil. When oil is hot, dip a piece of the floured chicken into the egg, coating generously. Drop into hot oil. Repeat until skillet is full. Allow to fry until golden brown, turn, and brown next side. *Turn only once on each side.* (Chicken has multiple sides, so turn to each side, but only once.) Remove from skillet one at a time and place on a paper towel to absorb extra oil. Continue until all is fried. Serve hot with lemon wedges.

Serves: 6-8.

Fried Baby Lamb Chops or Ribs *(Costolette di Abbacchio Fritte):* Use 8-10 baby lamb chops or ribs, 3-4 eggs, 1 cup flour, salt, pepper, corn oil, 1 large lemon cut into wedges. Prepare the chops or ribs by cutting away any extra (not all) fat and gristle. Keep the bones attached. Dredge in flour as described in Frying Food section (see index). Most lamb chops are too heavy to place in paper bag to dredge.

Place a medium-size iron skillet over medium-high heat. Heat to hot. Add oil. When oil is hot, dip a floured lamb chop into the beaten egg, coating generously. Drop immediately into hot oil. Repeat until skillet is full. Do not stack. Allow to fry until golden brown. When the chops are golden brown, turn, and allow the other side to brown. *Turn only once.* Remove from skillet one at a time and place on a paper towel to absorb extra oil. Continue until all chops are fried. Serve hot with lemon wedges.

Serves: 5-8.

Fried Baby Lamb's Head *(Testina di Agnellino Fritto):* Use 1 baby lamb's head, water, 2 eggs, salt, pepper, ⅓ cup flour, corn oil, 1 large lemon cut into wedges.

Clean lamb's head by removing excess skin. Cut off ears. Remove eyes and brains. Place a large-size pot over medium-high heat. Add enough water to cover. Then add a pinch of salt. Boil lamb's head for 10 to 15 minutes. Remove from water and allow to cool. When cool, remove all meat from the bones. Discard bones.

Cut meat into serving pieces. Dredge meat in flour as described in recipe in Frying Food section.

Place a medium-size iron skillet over medium-high heat. Heat to hot. Add oil. Dip floured meat into egg a piece at a time and drop into the hot oil. Fry at a high temperature and brown on all sides. Remove and set to drain on a paper towel. Serve hot with lemon wedges.

Serves: 4-6.

Pressed in Bread Crumbs
Cibi in Pan Grattato

Breaded Veal Steak *(Vitello Impannato):* Use 2 slices veal steak, 4 eggs, 2 cups unflavored bread crumbs, 4 tbsp. freshly grated Parmesan cheese, 1 tsp. salt, ½ tsp. pepper, corn oil, 1 large lemon cut into wedges.

Prepare the veal cutlet by cutting away extra fat and gristle. Lay on a board and pound with kitchen mallet (or the rib end of a large knife) to tenderize. Beat egg with pinch of salt. Combine bread crumbs and cheese. Cut each steak into 4 or 5 pieces. Dip in beaten egg and press into bread crumbs as described in third recipe in the Frying Food section.

Place large-size iron skillet over medium-high heat. Heat to hot. Add oil. When oil is hot, add cutlets. Repeat until skillet is full. Do not stack. Allow to fry until golden brown. When cutlets are golden brown, turn and allow other side to brown. *Turn only once.* Remove from skillet one at a time and place on a paper towel to absorb extra oil. Continue until all the veal is fried. Serve hot (immediately) with wedges of lemon.

Serves: 4-6.

Fried Fish Medley
Fritto Misto di Pesce

Just as there is a mixed fry of meats or vegetables, the Italian table has a mixed fry of fish. The batter and dredging methods are the same. We never used bread crumbs for fish.

Dredged in Flour
Infarinati

Fried Cod, Halibut, Oysters, Shrimp, or Smelts *(Baccalà, Passera di Mare, Ostriche, Gamberetti, or Eperlano Fritti):* This is the final course of the Christmas Eve meal in many Italian regions. Use 1 lb. fish, 1 cup flour, 3 beaten eggs, salt (for dried cod prepare as directed in Cod recipe in fish chapter, omitting salt. See index), pepper, corn oil, wedge of lemon.

Clean fish. Wash carefully and place on a paper towel to drain. Dredge with flour as described in second recipe in the Frying Food section. Tap to remove excess flour. Shrimp, squid, and oysters can be dredged in a brown paper bag.

Place a medium-size iron skillet over medium-high heat. Heat to hot. Add oil. When oil is hot, dip floured fish in the beaten egg, coating generously. Drop immediately into hot oil. Repeat until skillet is full. Do not stack. Allow to fry until golden brown. When golden brown, turn, and allow the other side to brown. *Turn only once on each side.* (Some fish have multiple sides, so turn to each side, but only once.) Remove from skillet one at a time and place on a paper towel to absorb extra oil. Continue until all the fish are fried. Serve hot with a wedge of lemon, a good salad, and Italian bread.

Serves: 4-6.

Fried Squid *(Calamari Fritti):* Use 1 lb. squid, 2 eggs, 1 cup flour, salt, pepper, corn oil, lemon wedges. If the squid is fresh, you must clean it very well to remove all the inedible parts, especially the sack that holds the ink. Fresh is best, but frozen will also work.

The skin is coated with a tough outer film that can be removed by rubbing it gently with your hands. Cut off the head, and then remove tentacles from head. They are good eating. Cut into pieces and set aside. Remove insides through the opening left by the head. Clean the body, but do not slit. Be sure to remove the inner lining carefully. Wash the inside in cold water, then cut it into rings similar to onion rings.

Place flour with a dash of salt and pepper on a large work space and stir. Alternately, put flour in a brown paper bag. Gently roll each piece of squid in the flour, coating generously. If using a bag, put squid in bag and shake. The pieces will be evenly coated. Beat eggs with a dash of salt. Set all near stove.

Place a large-size iron skillet over medium-high heat. Heat to hot. When hot, add oil. When oil is hot, dip a piece of the floured squid in the beaten egg, coating generously. Drop immediately into hot oil. When the pieces are golden brown, turn, and brown second side. *Turn only once on each side.* Remove and drain. Serve hot with fresh lemon wedges and a good, green salad.

Serves: 4-6.

Mixed Vegetable Medley
Misto di Verdure Fritte

Batter-dipped and dredged vegetables fried to a golden brown form a major part of the *fritto misto,* a meal fit for a king in its variety and quantity.

Batter-Dipped Vegetables
Verdure con Pastella

There are two ways to prepare the vegetables for the *fritto misto:* dipped in a batter or dredged in flour and covered in beaten egg.

Fried *Zucchini* Flowers (*Fiori di Zucca Fritti*): Use 12 pumpkin or *zucchini* flowers, 2 eggs, 1 tbsp. olive oil, 2 tsp. water, salt, 3 tbsp. flour, corn oil. Delicate and tasty, fried pumpkin or *zucchini* flowers are an exotic treat served for only a few weeks every year. You cannot find these flowers in groceries; they must be picked fresh from the garden in early morning and cooked for dinner that day. The flowers bloom before the fruit. Flowers with bubbles near the stem will produce *zucchini* or pumpkins and are never picked. Although we call the flowers pumpkin flowers in Italian, we seldom prepared pumpkin flowers, but used *zucchini* flowers instead.

Prepare batter as described in Frying Food section. While batter is resting, carefully clean the fragile blossoms. Remove the yellow stamens as gently as possible so as not to tear the blossoms. Remove the green leaves near the stem. Clip the stem. Gently wash the blossoms, shake, and lay on a paper towel to dry. When ready to fry, dip flowers into batter one at a time, coating generously, and place in hot oil. If batter is too thin, add flour. *Turn only once on each side.* Eat immediately.

Yield: 12 fried flowers.

Fried *Zucchini (Zucchini Fritti):* Use 1 large *zucchini,* 2 eggs, 1 tbsp. olive oil, 2 tsp. water, salt, 3 tbsp. flour, corn oil. Wash and peel skin from *zucchini* and slice into thin slices like a cucumber (we never cut *zucchini* into strips). Prepare batter as described in Frying Food section. Dip the *zucchini* into the batter, coating well, and place in the hot oil. If batter is too thin, add more flour. Brown on one side, turn, and finish browning on the other. *Turn only once on each side.* Drain on paper towel. Eat immediately.

Serves: 3-4.

Dredged Vegetables
Verdure Infarinati

To cook dredged vegetables, place flour with a dash of salt and pepper on a large work space and stir. Gently roll each piece of vegetable in the flour, coating generously. Most vegetables can be dredged in a brown paper bag (put flour in bag, add handful of vegetables, shake vigorously, remove, and tap each piece to remove excess flour). Beat eggs and a dash of salt. Set all near stove.

Place a large-size iron skillet over medium-high heat. Heat to hot. When hot, add oil. When oil is hot, dip a piece of the floured vegetable in the beaten egg, coating generously. Drop immediately into hot oil. When the pieces are golden brown, turn, and brown second side. *Turn only once on each side.* (Some vegetables have multiple sides, so turn to each side, but only once.) Remove and drain. Serve hot with fresh lemon wedges and a good green salad.

Fried Artichokes *(Carciofi Fritti):* Use 2 fresh artichokes, 1 cup flour, 2 eggs, salt, pepper, corn oil, wedge of lemon. Clean artichokes as described in Fresh Artichokes recipe in vegetable chapter. Cut each in half lengthwise. From each half, cut 5 to 6 wedges. Check each wedge for prickly centers and if any remain, remove them. Roll in flour, dip in beaten egg, and fry. *Turn only once on each side.* Baby artichokes are best for this dish. They do not have the prickly center in them. When you cut them, try to keep the stems on. Often, cutting them in half or fourths is enough. They are delicious too.

Serves: 4-6.

Fried Green Beans *(Fagiolini Fritti):* Use 1 lb. fresh green beans, 1 cup flour, 2 eggs, salt, pepper, corn oil, wedge of lemon. Snap off about ¼-inch from each end of the bean and discard. If you like the beans long, leave as is, or snap into 2 or 3 pieces. Place in a large pot and wash with running water. Place a medium-size saucepan over medium-high heat. Add water and a pinch of salt. Add green beans and boil for about 10 minutes or to taste. Drain and allow to cool. Gather 5 to 6 beans into a bunch and dip the bundle in flour, and then the beaten egg, coating generously. Place in hot oil. Continue as described in preceding recipes.

Serves: 4-6.

Fried Cabbage *(Cappuccio Fritto):* Use 1 head cabbage, 1 cup flour, 2 eggs, salt, pepper, corn oil, wedge of lemon. Wash the cabbage and cut in half. Slice each half into ½-inch slices, then cut each slice into smaller serving pieces. Place a medium-size iron skillet over medium-high heat. Add enough water to fill the skillet. Bring to a boil. Gently place each piece of cabbage in boiling water and cook until tender. Cabbage tends to fall apart, so do a few at a time. Remove carefully and set on paper towel to drain. Do not stack. Dredge each piece of cabbage in flour and continue as described in preceding recipes.

Serves: 4-6.

Fried Cauliflower *(Cavolfiore Fritto):* Use 1 cauliflower, 1 cup flour, 2 eggs, salt, pepper, corn oil, wedge of lemon. Wash cauliflower and cut in half. If extra large, cut again. Place in large pot half-filled with water and dash of salt. Parboil 5 minutes until soft. Test with a fork. Remove and place on drain board to drain. Allow to cool (or it will break up). Break off florets and gently roll each piece in the flour, coating generously. Continue as described in preceding recipes. Can use paper bag for dredging.

Fried Celery *(Sedano Fritto):* Use 2-3 ribs fresh celery, 1 cup flour, 2 eggs, salt, pepper, corn oil, wedge of lemon. Clean and wash celery ribs. Peel off tough strings by grabbing loose strings at bottom of rib, holding them between thumb and a paring knife, and pulling. Cut into 4-inch pieces. Place small pot on stove over medium-high heat. Add celery. Add water until an inch above celery. Bring to a boil. Add salt and boil until tender, about 5 to 10 minutes depending on the size of the pieces. Drain and cool. Gather 3-4 boiled pieces together. Squeeze together to form a group. Roll in flour and continue as described in preceding section.

Serves: 4-6.

Fried Eggplant *(Melanzane Fritte):* Use 1 eggplant, 1 cup flour, 2 eggs, salt, pepper, corn oil, wedge of lemon. Cut top and bottom stems from eggplant, remove outer skin, and slice into ¼-inch slices. Place in large pot, and add water and pinch of salt. Allow the eggplant to soak. As the water turns brown, drain, and add more water and more salt. Do this 3 or 4 times to blanch out the bitterness. Drain and pat dry. Dredge in flour and continue as described in previous recipes.

Serves: 4-6.

Fried Florentine Fennel *(Finocchio Fritto):* Fennel, used by Prometheus to shield the source of fire, looks like celery, but has a bulbous bottom and tastes like anise. In season in the fall, we serve it raw with *pinzimonio,* or fried in the *gran fritto misto.* Use 1 fennel, 1 cup flour, 2 eggs, salt, pepper, corn oil, wedge of lemon. Wash fennel. Cut away ribs and save for another time. Use only the bulbous bottom. Slice into wedges like artichoke in the preceding Fried Artichoke recipe. Continue as described in other recipes in this section.

Serves: 4-6.

Fried Mushrooms *(Funghi Fritti):* Use 8 oz. fresh mushrooms, 2 eggs, 3 tbsp. flour, salt, pepper, corn oil, wedge of lemon. Take one mushroom at a time, cut off the tip of the stem, and remove blemishes on crown (you may wish to peel the top layer off crown). Mushrooms should be button-size for frying and if they are too large, cut into halves or quarters. Allow to drain. Beat eggs in a deep bowl. Place flour in a brown paper bag. Salt and pepper slightly. Shake well. Place all mushrooms in bag and shake very well until all are coated. Dip each mushroom in egg individually. Fry as described in previous recipes in this section.

Serves: 4-6.

Pressed in Bread Crumbs
Cibi in Pan Grattato

Fried Asparagus *(Asparagi Fritti):* Use 1 lb. fresh asparagus, 1 cup bread crumbs, 2 eggs, 4 tbsp. water, salt, pepper, corn oil, wedge of lemon. Place water in a large skillet. Bring to a boil with 1 tsp. salt. Add washed asparagus, cover, and let cook until tender, about 12-18 minutes, depending on size. Drain. If you like crunchy asparagus, eliminate this step. Roll asparagus in crumbs, pressing firming on both sides (crumbs will not cover entirely). Place a medium-size iron skillet over medium-high heat. Heat to hot. Add oil. Beat eggs with water, salt, and pepper to form a wash. Dip asparagus in egg, roll in crumbs again, and drop immediately into hot oil. Brown on all sides. *Turn only once on each side.*

Serves: 4-6.

Be sure to turn fried foods only once! The more your turn them, the more time it will take and the bigger chance the coating will fall apart. Serve all fried foods immediately.

Bibliography

Ainsworth, Catherine Harris. *Italian-American Folktales*. Buffalo: Clyde, 1977.

Anderton, Isabella. *Tuscan Folk-Lore and Sketches*. London: Fairbairns, 1905.

Battle of Lepanto and Other Tales, The. New York: The Catholic Publication Society, n.d.

Barolini, Helen. *Festa, Recipes and Recollections of Italian Holidays*. New York: Harcourt Brace Jovanovich, 1988.

Boni, Ada. *Italian Regional Cooking*. New York: Bonanza Books, 1965.

Boschi, Eleonora. Letter to author, September, 1996.

Bugialli, Giuliano. *Giuliano Bugialli's Classic Techniques of Italian Cooking*. New York: Simon and Schuster, 1982.

——. *Guiliano Bugialli's Foods of Tuscany*. New York: Stewart, Tabori, Chang, 1992.

De Medici, Lorenza. *De Medici Kitchen*. San Francisco: Collins, 1992.

——. *Florentine: A Tuscan Feast*. New York: Random House, 1993.

——. *Heritage of Italian Cooking*. New York: Random House, 1990.

——. *Tuscany, the Beautiful Cookbook*. San Francisco: Collins, 1992.

Del Conte, Anna. *Gastronomy of Italy*. New York: Prentice-Hall Press, 1987.

Falassi, Alessandro. *Folklore by the Fireside, Text and Context of the Tuscan Veglia*. Austin: University of Texas Press, 1980.

Fenlon, Iain. "Lepanto and the Arts of Celebration." *History Today*, 45 (September 1995): 24-30.

Field, Carol. *Celebrating Italy*. New York: William Morrow and Company, 1990.

——. *The Italian Baker*. New York: Harper and Row, 1985.

Gardner, Bob. "Italian Influence Strongly Felt in Valley." *Valley Independent*, 7 August 1987.

Gianni, Guido. *La Cucina Aretina*. F. Muzzio Editore. 1990.

Gombrich, E. H. "Celebrations in Venice of the Holy League and of the Victory of Lepanto," in *Studies in Renaissance and Baroque Art Presented to Anthony Blunt on his 60th Birthday*, edited by Jeanne Coutauld. London: Phaidon, 1967.

Hazen, Marcella. *The Classic Italian Cookbook*. New York: Ballantine, 1973.

———. *Essentials of Classic Italian Cooking*. New York: Knopf, 1992.

Hess, Andrew. "The Battle of Lepanto and Its Place in Mediterranean History Past and Present," *Past and Present* 17 (1957): 53-73.

Leader, Scott. *Tuscan Studies and Sketches*. London: Unwin, 1888.

Hooker, Katherine. *Byways in Southern Tuscany*. New York: Charles Scribner's Sons, 1918.

Malpezzi, Frances M. and William M. Clements. *Italian-American Folklore*. Little Rock: August House, 1992.

Mannucci, Umberto. *Bisenzio tradizioni e cucina*. Prato: Edizioni Libreria del Palazzo, 1973.

Pallini, Angelo. *Vita del North Italian Political Association*. Self-published poem. c. 1940.

Righi Parenti, Giovanni. *La cucina degli etruschi*. Milano: Sugar editore and C, 1972.

Pezzini, Wilma. *The Tuscan Cookbook*. New York: Atheneum, 1978.

Romer, Elizabeth. *The Tuscan Year: Life and Food in an Italian Valley*. New York: Atheneum, 1985.

Root, Waverley. *The Food of Italy*. New York: Atheneum, 1971.

Sansone, Thomas. Interviews with author, 1988-1996.

Sansone, Vivian Pelini. Interviews with author, 1988-1996.

Speroni, Charles. "The Observance of Saint Joseph's Day Among the Sicilians of Southern California." *Southern Folklore Quarterly* 4 (1940): 135-39.

———. "California Fishermen's Festivals." *Western Folklore*, 77-91.

Strafforello, Gustavo. *La Patria Geografia Dell'Italia: Provincie di Arezzo, Grosseto, Siena*. Torino: Unione Tipografico Editrice, 1981.

Tafi, Angelo. *Immagine di Arezzo*. Arezzo: Litostampa Sant'Agnese, 1978.

———. *Immagine di Arezzo: Guida storico-artistica*. Calosci: Cortona, 1985.

Tak, Herman. "Longing for Local Identity: Intervillage Relations in an Italian Mountain Area." *Anthropological Quarterly*, 63 (April 1990): 90-100.

Turner, Kay and Suzanne Seriff. "Giving an Altar. The Ideology of Reproduction in a St Joseph's Day Feast." *Journal of American Folklore,* 100 (1987): 446-460.

Turner, Kay. "The Virgin of Sorrows Procession: A Brooklyn Inversion." *Folklore Papers,* University Folklore Association. Austin, Texas: University of Texas. 1980, 9, 1-25.

Urick, Mildred. "The San Rocco Festival at Aliquippa, Pennsylvania: A Transplanted Tradition." *Pennsylvania Folklife* 19, 1 (Autumn 1969): 14-22.

Vivian, Cassandra. "Angelo Pallini: L'Ultimo Trovatore." Presented at Italian Americans in W. Pa History Conference of the Historical Society of Western Pennsylvania, April 28-29, 2000.

———. "Bloomfield: Alive and Well in the Heart of Pittsburgh." *Journal of Italian Food and Wine* (Winter 1994).

———. "Cassandra, Can You Tell Me . . ." Feature column for the *Journal of Italian Food and Wine.* 1993-1996.

———. "Festa di Quarata: A Binding Tradition." From A Tavola: Food, Tradition, and Community Among Italian Americans, a conference of the American Italian Historical Society. 1998.

———. *Immigrant's Kitchen: Italian.* Monessen, PA: TREE, 1993.

———. "An Italian American Christmas in Western Pennsylvania Part I: Christmas Eve." *Western Pennsylvania History* (December 1999): 154-68.

———. "An Italian American Christmas in Western Pennsylvania Part II: Christmas Day." *Western Pennsylvania History* (2000).

———. "The Italian Immigrant Kitchen: A Journey into Identity" in the article "Food, Recipes, Cookbooks and Italian-American Life" in the journal *Italian Americana,* 16, no. 2 (1998).

———. "The Italian Immigrant Kitchen: A Journey into Identity." in *American Women Italian Style* by Carol Albright Bonomo and Christine Palamidessi. New York: Fordham University Press, 2010.

———. *Monessen: A Typical Steel Country Town.* Making of America Series. Charleston: Arcadia Publishing. 2002.

Vivian, Cassandra. "Monessen's Italians." *Il Primo Magazine.* (Winter 2002).

———. *The Overseer's Family: A Memoir of the Tuscan Countryside.* PublishAmerica, 2006.

———. "The Sauce of all Sauces: The Holy of Holies" *Il Primo Magazine.* June 2001.

Vivian, Elizabeth Parigi. Interviews with author. 1985-1996.

English Recipe Index

Italian Recipe Index